Abbas Assi is a researcher at the Center for Arab Unity Studies in Beirut. He holds a PhD in International Relations from the University of Leeds, where he taught International Politics.

DEMOCRACY IN LEBANON

Political Parties and the Struggle for Power
Since Syrian Withdrawal

ABBAS ASSI

I.B. TAURIS

LONDON · NEW YORK

Published in 2016 by
I.B.Tauris & Co. Ltd
London • New York
www.ibtauris.com

Library of Modern Middle East Studies 166

ISBN: 978 1 78453 093 8
eISBN: 978 1 78672 004 7
ePDF: 978 1 78673 004 6

A full CIP record for this book is available from the British Library
A full CIP record is available from the Library of Congress

Library of Congress Catalog Card Number: available

Typeset in Garamond Three by OKS Prepress Services, Chennai, India

This book is dedicated to my father, Fawaz Assi

CONTENTS

LIST OF TABLES

CHRONOLOGY

1920   France entrusted with League of Nations Mandate for Lebanon and Syria. Creation of the state of Lebanon.

1943   President Bechara al-Khoury and PM Riad al-Solh concludes the 'National Pact'. End of French mandate.

1975   Lebanese civil war breaks out.

1989   Michel Aoun attacks the LFP and declares 'war of liberation' against Syria (March).

        Formation of Arab Tripartite Committee (May).

        Lebanese MPs ratify Ta'if Agreement (October).

        Elias Hrawi elected as president (November).

1990   Iraq invades Kuwait (August).

        US-led international alliance attacks Iraq (August).

        Michel Aoun forced into exile (October).

1991   End of Second Gulf War (February).

1992   Lebanon's first elections after the civil war with Christian boycott.

1996   Lebanon's second parliamentary elections after the civil war.

1998   Emile Lahoud succeeds Hrawi as president.

2000   Israel ends its occupation of southern Lebanon (May).

        Lebanon's third parliamentary elections after the civil war.

2004   UNSC issues Resolution 1559 (2 September).

        Parliament extends Lahoud's presidential term for three years (3 September).

        Rafic Hariri's cabinet resigns (October).

        PM Omar Karami nominated as PM-designate (October).

2005   Assassination of former PM Rafic Hariri (February).

Omar Karami's cabinet resigns (February).

Syria withdraws its military forces (April).

Lebanon's first parliamentary elections after the Syrian withdrawal (May–June).

2006   Ratification of the FPM–Hizbullah memorandum agreement (February).

First meeting of the National Dialogue Committee (March).

The Israel–Hizbullah war erupts (12 July – 14 August).

Lebanese government approves the establishment of an international tribunal.

Shiite ministers resign from the government (November).

The March 8 Coalition organizes a sit-in in Beirut (December).

2007   Lebanese army attacks Fatah al-Islam group (May–September).

Presidential term of Emile Lahoud ends without a successor (November).

2008   Violence erupts between March 8 and March 14 coalitions (May).

Lebanese political parties sign Doha Agreement (May).

Michel Sleiman elected as president (May).

2009   Lebanon's second parliamentary elections after the Syrian withdrawal (June).

PM Saad Hariri forms the new government (November).

2011   Saad Hariri's cabinet resigns (January).

Egyptian Revolution topples Mubarak's regime (February).

Syrian conflict erupts (March).

PM Najib Mikati forms the new government (June).

The STL accuses four members from Hizbullah of Hariri's assassination.

2013   Najib Mikati's cabinet resigns (March).

Hizbullah intervenes militarily in Syria (April).

The Lebanese Parliament extends its term for 18 months (June).

2014   The Lebanese Parliament extends once again its term until 2017 (November).

ACKNOWLEDGEMENTS

Warmest appreciation and gratitude must go to my family and in particular my father. I'm also grateful to the scholars at the University of Leeds, Dr Stuart McAnulla and Dr Hendrik Kraetzschmar, for their encouragement and advice. Their wise and meticulous comments were crucial for the completion of this research. Many others have helped me in countless ways. To all of them I express my gratitude.

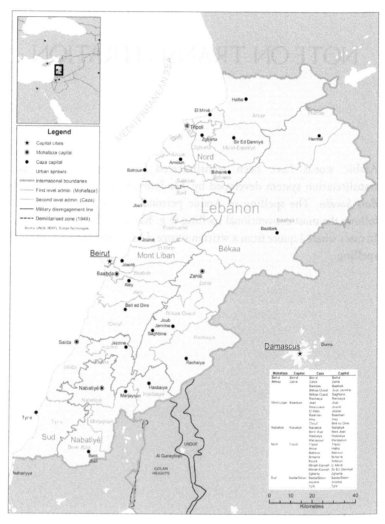

Map 1   Administrative Divisions of Lebanon. Based on OCHA Map

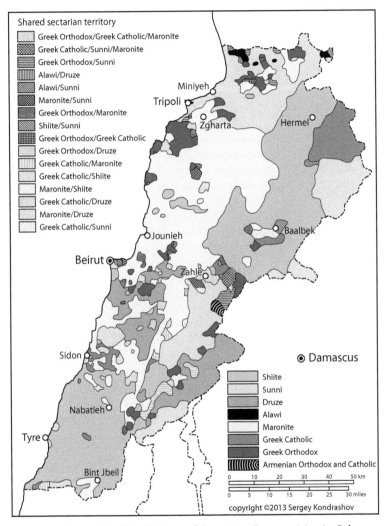

Shared sectarian territory

- Greek Orthodox/Greek Catholic/Maronite
- Greek Catholic/Sunni/Maronite
- Greek Orthodox/Sunni
- Alawi/Druze
- Alawi/Sunni
- Maronite/Sunni
- Greek Orthodox/Maronite
- Shiite/Sunni
- Greek Orthodox/Greek Catholic
- Greek Orthodox/Druze
- Greek Catholic/Maronite
- Greek Catholic/Shiite
- Maronite/Shiite
- Greek Catholic/Druze
- Maronite/Druze
- Greek Catholic/Sunni

Miniyeh
Tripoli
Zgharta
Hermel
Baalbek
Jounieh
Beirut
Zahle
Sidon
⊙ Damascus
Nabatieh
Tyre
Bint Jbeil

- Shiite
- Sunni
- Druze
- Alawi
- Maronite
- Greek Catholic
- Greek Orthodox
- Armenian Orthodox and Catholic

0 10 20 30 40 50 km
0 5 10 15 20 25 30 miles

copyright ©2013 Sergey Kondrashov

Map 2 Geographic Distribution of Sectarian Communities in Lebanon.
Source: Ministry of Municipalities in Lebanon

INTRODUCTION

The year 2005 marked the end of the Syrian military presence in Lebanon. The Syrian military forces, present from 1976 until 2005, withdrew after the assassination of the former prime minister (PM), Rafic Hariri (1992–8, 2000–4), on 14 February 2005 and after the subsequent mass demonstrations against Syrian interference in Lebanese domestic politics, also known as the 'Cedar Revolution'. The Syrian military forces entered the country in 1976 during the Lebanese civil war (1975–89). After the ratification of the Ta'if Agreement that ended the civil war in 1989 and until 2005, Damascus carried wide-ranging and significant influence on Lebanese politics, particularly on the formulation of the country's electoral laws, the appointment of various military and security positions, the election of presidents, and on the country's foreign policy. The Syrian military forces also marginalized and exiled political figures who opposed their presence in the country, for instance, the former head of the Lebanese army General Michel Aoun.[1]

The Syrian military withdrawal from Lebanon in 2005 was widely seen as a moment of great opportunity, providing the country with a chance to mould its own destiny without foreign tutelage for the first time in many decades. Many journalists who were following Middle Eastern politics raised hopes about the prospects of democracy in Lebanon and its implications for other Arab states. For instance, Ed O'Loughlin (2005) considered the first elections after the Syrian withdrawal as '[f]ree – or at least freer – of Syrian influence', therefore stating that 'the parliament will reflect more closely the views of the so-called "Cedar Revolution"'. These elections would be 'another uncertain step towards becoming the first free Arab democracy' (O'Loughlin, 2005). Similarly, the Lebanese journalist Rym Ghazal (2005) stated that '[t]he assassination of former Prime Minister Rafiq Hariri is now being hailed as a turning point for Lebanon, leading to unity among the different religious sects'. Ghayth Armanazi (2005: 29) also reflected the optimism that dominated the political scene after the eruption of the anti-Syrian protests, stating that 'listening to some of the triumphalism proclaimed almost incessantly from Washington, and which found ready echoes in Paris and London, the outbreak of the "Cedar Revolution" was an eye-catching, media-seductive example of the march of the forces of democracy'.

These hopes were raised because the Syrian withdrawal provided more 'political freedoms'. The prohibited political parties and those leaders who had been exiled or imprisoned during the Syrian era were able to return to the country and play a significant role in Lebanese political life, including such figures as the exiled General Michel Aoun and the imprisoned Samir Geagea (1994–2005).[2] In addition, the waning of Syrian influence on Lebanese domestic politics opened up an opportunity for the country's political parties to initiate key democratic reforms as mandated in the Ta'if Agreement of 1989.[3] In particular, the elimination of confessionalism, which is widely considered the main impediment to the democratization process by the Lebanese people and political class, had been blocked by the Syrian authorities and their domestic allies. The Lebanese political parties were now also free to formulate a new electoral law that would ensure fair and equal representation of all Lebanese social factions, unlike the electoral laws that were formulated during the Syrian era which were devised to suit the interests of Damascus' domestic allies.

However, these hopes did not materialize. The political and factional conflicts between Lebanon's sectarian parties, which erupted after 2005, have since then led to deep sectarian fragmentation, punctuated by episodes of sectarian violence, and encouraged foreign intervention in Lebanon's domestic affairs by Saudi Arabia, Syria, the US and France, all seeking to manipulate the political parties so as to further their own interests. The significance of these conflicts and divisions is reflected in the refusal of sectarian groups to reform the political system by eliminating confessionalism because of the lack of trust between them. As Ghayth Armanazi (2005: 29) argues:

[T]he ensuing Lebanese election [i.e. 2005 elections] campaign and the results of the vote were a great disappointment to those who dreamed of a new Lebanon [. . .] What was vaunted as a 'people's revolution' in some quarters has in fact delivered those people into the arms of the very same feudal war-lords and family patriarchs that, through most of Lebanon's modern history, have been at the heart of a dysfunctional political system: a system that periodically spawned waves of violent conflict and full-blown war.

After the Syrian withdrawal, the Lebanese political parties became more intransigent and stubborn in regard to reaching agreements on important issues, such as formulating a new electoral law. This book will argue that Lebanon's consociational model, effectively in place since the founding of the country in 1920, has helped increase rather than decrease the stubbornness and intransigence of the elite in the post-2005 era to reach compromises and push forward genuine democratic reforms. It will focus in particular on the intersection of three main factors that have shaped the behaviour of the Lebanese political parties since 2005, all of which have had significant implications for the democratization process. These are: (1) intra-sectarian conflicts; (2) inter-sectarian conflicts; and (3) external factors, which include the influence of foreign alliances and regional and international events. Exploring and analysing these factors is important because they can enhance our understanding of how the Lebanese parties 'spark' inter- and intra-sectarian conflicts, instil a sense of fear among their followers, react to regional and international developments, build inter-sectarian and foreign alliances, and make concessions, which are usually at the expense of political stability and democratic reforms.

Current Debates

While there is a vast array of literature that covers the Lebanese democracy and its failures (AbuKhalil, 1993; Alagha, 2005; Baydoun, 2012; Cammett, 2014; el-Khazen, 2003a, 2003b; Fakhoury-Mühlbacher, 2007, 2009; Hudson, 1988; Jabbra & Jabbra, 2001; Kerr, 2006, 2007; Norton, 2007a, 2007b; Rigby, 2000; Salamey & Tabar, 2012; Suleiman, 1967b; Zahar, 2012a), the literature that examines the behaviour of the Lebanese political parties and its implications for the democratization process is limited. Many of the existing studies about Lebanese parties either focus on their characteristics and development in general, or focus specifically on Hizbullah. What is missing from all the aforementioned studies is an exploration of how the intersection of inter- and intra-sectarian conflicts with external factors has shaped the behaviour of Lebanese political parties since 2005 and its implications for the prospects of genuine democratic reforms. This book aims to address this lacuna in the literature. Furthermore, there is as yet no book-length analysis dedicated to examining the intersection of these three factors and their implications for the behaviour of Lebanese political parties and consequently the democratization process, especially among those studies published in the post-2005 period. It differs from the existing scholarship, as it provides a detailed analysis of the factors that shape the behaviour of Lebanon's political parties in post-2005 period and their impact on the democratization process.

In addition, the book will explore the implications of the Syrian conflict for the behaviour of Lebanon's political parties regarding the formulation of a new electoral law and the postponement of the 2013 parliamentary elections. The existing studies pay little attention to how the repercussions of the Syrian conflict impacted upon the domestic inter- and intra-sectarian conflicts, and consequently on the behaviour of Lebanese political parties regarding the country's electoral rules and the postponement of the 2013 parliamentary elections (Hokayem, 2012; ICG, 2012, 2013; Khashan, 2013; Salem, 2012). There is a focus on the electoral law because it constitutes the most hotly debated democratic reform in Lebanese politics and society, with this debate gaining currency every four years prior to scheduled parliamentary elections.

This book argues that the main obstacle to democracy in Lebanon is in the current consociational form of governance. It will focus in particular on the influence of the consociational form of governance on the behaviour of the Lebanese political parties. The main research hypothesis of this book argues that Lebanon's consociational form of governance helps provoke political and sectarian conflicts within and between the sectarian communities that intersect with external factors (foreign alliances and/or external events), which then increase the intransigence and inflexibility of the Lebanese political parties with regard to initiating democratic reforms.

The analysis will cover the period that followed the Syrian withdrawal in 2005 until 2014. The book will argue that the Syrian withdrawal 'encouraged' the Lebanese parties to extensively employ sectarian language to mobilize the popular support of their religious groups. Unlike the Syrian era, when an alliance with Damascus was often a guarantee of political survival, during this period Lebanese political parties reverted to sectarian language to mobilize popular support and guarantee their victory in parliamentary elections as the main representatives of their communal groups. This can enable them to ask for the quota allocated for their sects in the consociational system, such as cabinet posts. Therefore, the more a political party is able to address the interests of its sect, the more it is able to mobilize popular support. This behaviour has created sectarian outbidding and conflicts between the representatives of each sect and the representatives of the various religious groups. What has fuelled further these domestic conflicts is their intersection with external factors. The unstable regional environment in the Middle East had encouraged the political parties to seek support from foreign actors, such as Saudi Arabia, Syria and Iran, that endeavoured to increase their regional influence, so as to bolster their domestic positions against their opponents. The willingness of the domestic parties to compete with their domestic opponents intersected with the interests of external players to weaken the domestic allies of their foreign opponents. The eruption of these political and sectarian conflicts took place at the expense of the initiation of democratic reforms. The Lebanese political parties, who are supposed to initiate the democratic reforms as stated in the Ta'if Agreement, did not push forward any of these reforms, such as the electoral law and the elimination of confessionalism. These conflicts had significant implications for political stability and widened the rift between the political parties, which rendered the initiation of democratic reforms almost impossible.

Consequently, this book questions the ability of the consociational form of governance to ensure political stability and democracy in a state located in a turbulent region, especially after the withdrawal of an occupation power. Firstly, it will be argued that the 'marginalization' and 'repression' of a certain ethnic group by the occupation force will provoke the 'repressed' ethnic group to ask for a larger share in the political system after the withdrawal. This is because of the lack of trust that the 'repressed' group feels towards other ethnic communities due to its marginalization during the occupation period. Secondly, the political parties will seek to employ extensively ethnic language to mobilize popular support to secure their victory in parliamentary elections after the withdrawal of the foreign power to be able to obtain the quota allocated for their ethnicities in the consociational system. This will help them replace their alliance with the occupation force which used to secure their share in the political system. Unlike majoritarian rule, the consociational model 'stimulates' the political parties to employ ethnic language to mobilize popular support and secure their victory in parliamentary elections, since it is based on an ethnic distribution of state positions. The political party employs ethnic language with the aim of portraying itself as the unique protector of the ethnicity interests in the political system. This will most likely spark inter- and intra-ethnic conflicts which will make the initiation of democratic reforms almost impossible. Furthermore, the consociational model is not often able to shield the country from foreign intervention as is evident in the Lebanese case where the country is located in a turbulent region, which will further fuel political and sectarian conflicts.

The book is based on 24 semi-structured interviews conducted by the author over three months in 2012 (April–June) and during November and December in 2014 in Lebanon. The research respondents selected for interview were local politicians, journalists, academics and media figures of all shades of opinion (March 8 and March 14 coalitions). The author sought to interview figures from the major sectarian parties (like the Future Movement and Kataeb) to ensure that their different views are reflected in the book and to prevent biased analysis. The focusing on different respondents was driven by the realization that in the Lebanese context interviewing politicians only is not always informative. Politicians are often very cautious in providing their opinions and usually simply reiterate the opinions that they provide to the public and media outlets. However, those interviews conducted with journalists, media figures and academics were more informative in so far as they provided in-depth analyses of the political and sectarian conflicts currently plaguing Lebanon, especially as these respondents were not usually organized in a certain party and were thus less cautious in providing their opinions. All Arabic sources (books, newspaper articles and political statements and speeches) used in this book are translated by the author.

Ethnic Identity and Ethnic Conflict

Before moving to the actual topic at hand, a number of key terms and concepts used throughout this book requires definition and discussion. These concern the concepts of ethnic identity, ethnic conflicts, democracy and democratization.

Ethnic identity is a concept that is widely interpreted and discussed by scholars. Anthony Smith (1985: 128), for instance, defines an ethnic community as a 'named collectivity sharing a common myth of origins and descent, a common history, one or more elements of distinctive culture, a common territorial association and a sense of group solidarity'. Donald Horowitz's definition in turn focuses primarily on kinship as the main determinant of the ethnic group. He (1985: 52) states that '[e]thnicity is based on a myth of collective ancestry, which usually carries with it traits believed to be innate. Some notion of ascription, however diluted, and affinity deriving from it are inseparable from the concept of ethnicity.' However, Gilley provides a wider definition. He (2004: 1158) defines ethnicity 'as that part of a person's identity which is drawn from one or more "markers" like race, religion, shared history, region, social symbols or language. It is distinct from that part of a person's identity that comes from, say, personal moral doctrine, economic status, civic affiliations or personal history.' Gilley's definition is more applicable to the Lebanese case, since Horowitz's and Smith's definitions exclude religious communities and focus mainly on the role of kinship to define the ethnic community.

The development of ethnic identity and ethnic conflicts has been widely researched by scholars in the field. Ethnic conflict refers to a conflict which erupts between at least two ethnic communities in which each side considers its objectives in initiating the conflict justified. Karl Cordell and Stephan Wolff offer a more precise definition. They (2009: 4–5) state that the concept of ethnic conflict refers to 'a situation in which two or more actors pursue incompatible, yet from their individual perspectives entirely just goals [...] in which the goals of at least one conflict party are defined in (exclusively) ethnic terms, and in which the primary fault line of confrontation is one of ethnic distinctions.' Donald Green and Rachel Seher (2003: 511) provide a similar definition, stating that an ethnic conflict:

an instance of political instability.' Ian Lustick provides a similar definition. He (1979: 325) defines political stability as 'the continued operation of specific patterns of political behavior, apart from the illegal use of violence, accompanied by a general expectation among the attentive public that such patterns are likely to remain intact in the foreseeable future.'

In Lebanon, abstention from resorting to violence is not sufficient to ensure political stability. The nature of the Lebanese power-sharing agreement entails that any non-violent conflict between the holders of power puts the agreement at risk. In cases where a political conflict erupts between the leaders of the sectarian groups,[5] their ability to share the state positions or form the government will be weakened. This usually results in paralysis of the state institutions, a resort to sectarian language and accusations of treachery. Michael Hudson (1985: 8) argues that '[d]emocratic institutions [in Lebanon] have been a requisite for political stability, not a result of it.' The democratic institutions which Hudson refers to are based on power-sharing agreements between the sectarian communities over the distribution of state positions. This is because the Lebanese sectarian communities 'are mutually suspicious, and they do not trust the formal institutions to be powerful or impartial enough to protect their local interests' (Hudson, 1985: 9). Therefore, 'in Lebanon pluralism plus democratic practices (the mechanism for the balance of power) make public security possible' (Hudson, 1985: 9). This book will argue that political stability must exist before the initiation of democratic reforms, as political and sectarian conflicts make the initiation of democratic reforms almost impossible. It will be argued that the inability of Lebanon's consociational model to ensure political stability and the success of the power-sharing agreement helped impede the democratization process.

The Ta'if Agreement reached at the end of the Lebanese civil war in 1989 clearly spelled out the steps that should be implemented to successfully complete the democratization process and reach a fully-fledged democracy. It stated that the Lebanese Parliament should form a National Body for the Elimination of Confessionalism, with the aim of developing the steps that are necessary to eliminate confessionalism, and should form the senate (to include representatives of the sectarian groups). It also stated that parliament should formulate a new electoral law based on large districts (*Muḥāfaza*) as electoral districts, the election of parliament on a non-sectarian basis, and the expansion of administrative decentralization at the level of the smaller administrative units (district and smaller units) through the election of local councils. However, so far none of these measures have been implemented. According to the Ta'if Agreement, the Lebanese political system is still in a transitional period.[6]

This book will refer to the reforms stated in the Ta'if Agreement in order to assess the democratization process in Lebanon. This agreement, which enjoys the support of the majority of the Lebanese sectarian communities, stated the main steps that are considered essential to transition Lebanon from the current confessional system to a non-confessional one. The book will argue that the ability of Lebanon's consociational model to help spark inter- and intra-sectarian conflicts that intersect with external factors has exacerbated political and sectarian conflicts and impeded the initiation and implementation of democratic reforms.

Outline of the Book

The first chapter will define and discuss the consociational theory and its critique. It will argue that the consociational model and theory suffer from weaknesses. It will also argue that the consociational model rests on background conditions which might not always exist and that this puts the stability of the state at risk. Chapter 2 will then focus on the empirical level. The weaknesses of the consociational model that are discussed in the previous chapter will be addressed in this chapter in order to explore the failures of this form of governance in the Lebanese case.

Chapter 3 will shift the focus to discuss and analyse the democratization process in the pre- and post-2005 periods (1990–present). By comparing these two periods (i.e. the pre- and post-2005 periods), the chapter will conclude that Syria's withdrawal was essential for the success of the democratization process, although it was not sufficient. Chapter 4 will then explore in detail the implications of inter- and intra-sectarian conflicts for the behaviour of the Lebanese parties after 2005. By exploring the intersection of these two factors, the chapter will conclude that they negatively influenced the behaviour of Lebanese political parties and consequently have a detrimental effect on political stability and the democratization process.

While Chapter 4 explores domestic conflicts, Chapter 5 will shift its focus to examine the role of external variables and their influence on the behaviour of the Lebanese political parties and on democratic reforms. The chapter will conclude that the external factors fuelled the inter- and intra-sectarian conflicts that are explored in the previous chapter, which put political stability at risk and increased the intransigence of the political parties in relation to the initiation of democratic reforms. Chapter 6 will provide a case study to show how the intersection of the three factors explored in the previous two chapters influences the behaviour of the political parties regarding the democratic reforms. It will explore and analyse how the inter- and intra-sectarian conflicts intersected with the implications of the Syrian conflict to influence the behaviour of Lebanese political parties regarding the formulation of a new electoral law and the postponement of the 2013 parliamentary elections.

The conclusion will discuss the insights that may be derived from the examination of the behaviour of Lebanon's political parties and the challenges and possibilities for a successful consolidation of the Lebanese fragile democracy. It will also elucidate the main lessons which can be drawn from the case of Lebanon regarding the consociational model and its principal weaknesses.

CHAPTER 1

CONSOCIATION

The consociational form of governance is widely considered as the most suitable political system for societies that are divided along ethnic lines (Lijphart, 1969; McGarry & O'Leary, 2006). The nature of ethnic divisions in a multi-ethnic state can make the formation of a stable government almost impossible. Therefore, the consociational model proposes mechanisms for forming and managing a stable government, such as segmental autonomy and proportional representation of ethnic groups. However, this model has failed in several states, such as Lebanon. Instead of promoting stability and democracy, the consociational model has played a significant role in sparking conflicts between ethnic communities.

This chapter will argue that the consociational model and theory contain several weaknesses. It aims to contribute to the answers to the following questions: how does the consociational model lead to political instability? How does it help entrench ethnic identity? Why is it sometimes unable to ensure political stability without foreign support? How does this form of governance lead to inter-ethnic conflicts? And finally, how does this form of governance generate adverse effects on the behaviour of political parties and the democratization process?

Firstly, the chapter will provide a discussion of the consociational form of governance, its background conditions, and the four components. Secondly, it will provide a critique of the background conditions, spelled out by scholars, such as Lijphart (1996) and Lehmbruch (1975). Thirdly, it will criticize its democratic quality and its ability to ensure stability in plural societies. Fourthly, it will examine the consociational state's ability to inhibit foreign intervention, and how foreign intervention is often essential for the stability of this form of governance. Finally, the chapter will explore the negative implications of the consociational model on the nature and behaviour of political parties.

The Consociational Form of Governance

Consociational Theory

There is a widespread assumption in the political science literature that the formation of stable democratic systems in divided societies is almost impossible (Lipset, 1960; Mill, 1991). Deep ethnic segmentation plagues these societies and prevents the formation of a shared sense of national identity. 'Plural societies are characterized by mutually reinforcing cleavages' which prevent the development of a shared sense of national identity (Lijphart, 1977b: 117). John Stuart Mill (1991: 310) contends that '[f]ree institutions are next to impossible in a country made up of different nationalities. Among a people without fellow-feeling, especially if they read and speak different languages, the united public opinion, necessary to the working of representative government, cannot exist'. Seymour Lipset shares Mill's point that shared national identity is necessary for the formation of a stable democratic system. He (1960: 88–9) argues that 'the chances for stable democracy are enhanced to the extent that groups and individuals have a number of crosscutting, politically relevant affiliations'. What might complicate more the formation of democratic systems in deeply divided societies is their existence in turbulent and unstable regions which could make them vulnerable to foreign intervention, especially if the ethnic communities are distributed across several states. Brenda Seaver (2000: 248) asserts that '[t]he challenge of building democratic regimes in deeply divided societies becomes even more complicated in regions where groups with shared identities transcend state boundaries. The transnational nature of many communal groups has the potential of transforming domestic policy issues into regional crises involving several states.'

However, the challenges to the formation of a stable democratic system in deeply divided societies are not insurmountable. Arend Lijphart (1977a: 1) claims that although the formation of a stable democratic system in plural societies is *'difficult'*, it is not *'impossible'*. He suggests the adoption of the consociational form of governance for plural societies as the only alternative for regulating the conflicts that might emerge in these societies. Consociationalism is a 'government by elite cartel designed to turn a democracy with a fragmented political culture into a stable democracy' (Lijphart, 1969: 216).[1] Lijphart (1969), one of the prominent scholars who developed this concept, considers that the consociational form of governance will lead to political stability in multi-ethnic states. The existence of diverse ethnic communities within the same state might lead them to enter into conflicts over, for instance, the distribution of state positions and revenues. Therefore, this form of governance has the ability to neutralize 'the destabilising effects of subcultural segmentation [...] at the elite level by embracing non-majoritarian mechanisms for conflict resolution' (Andeweg, 2000: 509). According to Lijphart (1989: 39), 'cooperative and coalescent elite behaviour can turn a potentially unstable political system into a stable one'. This form of governance ensures that the decision-making process is taken with the agreement of all political parties and elites that represent the ethnic communities in the political system.

The importance of the consociational theory and model, according to Lijphart, rests on two main points. Firstly, this theory can be used for empirical analysis to explain stability in divided societies (Lijphart, 1977a: 1). Seaver (2000: 251) considers that Lijphart's theory 'is able to explain the stability of democracy in the smaller European countries better than other theories that predicted democratic failure in societies lacking overlapping memberships, cross-cutting cleavages, and a considerable degree of homogeneity or cultural-ideological consensus'. It can serve as an explanation of the political stability in the states that have plural societies, such as Belgium, and the Netherlands. Secondly, the consociational model can be suggested as a form of governance for deeply divided societies which can help build stable democratic systems (Lijphart, 1977a: 1–2). Consociationalism is able to mitigate 'the centrifugal tendencies inherent in a plural society [...] by the cooperative attitudes and behaviour of the leaders of the different segments of the population' (Lijphart, 1977a: 1).

The Four Components of the Consociational Model

Lijphart (1977a: 25) identifies four main components that define the consociational form of governance: grand coalition, high degree of autonomy for each ethnic group to run its own internal affairs, proportionality as the principle standard of political representation, and the mutual veto of ethnic communities. The aim of these four components is to weaken the negative implications of the majoritarian rule in societies divided along ethnic lines. He (1977a: 37) considers that these four components are 'closely related to each other, and they all entail deviations from pure majority rule'.

The first component is the grand coalition which is considered, according to Lijphart, the most important component of the consociational model. He (1977a: 25) defines the grand coalition as 'a "grand" council or committee with important advisory functions, or a grand coalition of a president and other top officeholders in a presidential system'. An executive power-sharing 'is government by a grand coalition of the political leaders of all significant segments of the plural society' (Lijphart, 1977a: 25). Lijphart (1977a: 28–9) argues that common consensus between citizens is more democratic than majority rule in divided societies. The rationale behind Lijphart's support of the formation of a grand coalition is that in societies divided along ethnic lines the decisions taken by the government might be comprehended by a certain ethnic group as targeting it, especially in a case when it is not in the governing coalition (Lijphart, 1977a: 28). Therefore, he suggests the formation of a grand coalition that includes representatives of all ethnic groups in the political system.

What complements the grand coalition principle, according to Lijphart, is the second consociational component, that of segmental autonomy. Due to the existence of segmental cleavages which can be of a religious, ideological, linguistic, cultural, racial or ethnic nature, the segmental autonomy component can accommodate these cleavages by providing a high degree of autonomy for any such ethnic groups in plural societies. This component prescribes the delegation of as much decision making as possible to the separate segments. Lijphart suggests that all the decisions on the issues of common concern between the ethnic groups, such as foreign policy, should be made jointly by representatives of the segments in a grand coalition. However, in all other issues that concern the internal affairs of the ethnic group, such as education, the ethnic group has the right to decide on and manage them (Lijphart, 1987: 137). The underlying assumption of segmental autonomy is that the existence of a 'subcultural encapsulation and autonomy' can help reduce the prospects for the eruption of conflict between the ethnicities (Luther, 2001: 92). Lijphart (1977a: 42) contends that the aim of segmental autonomy 'is not to abolish or weaken segmental cleavages but to recognize them explicitly and to turn the segments into constructive elements of stable democracy'. The best form of segmental autonomy is the geographic separation of ethnic groups, since this can lead to the success of the 'consociational democracy' and ensure political stability (Lijphart, 1969: 219). Segmental autonomy can also be achieved through governmental or constitutional guarantees for the ethnic groups to preserve their distinct cultural heritage through ideological tools, such as schools and media, or through a federal system that can grant autonomy to each ethnic community to manage its internal affairs.

In addition to the two components discussed above, the consociational model includes a third component, the proportionality principle, which is based on the proportional distribution of state positions between ethnic groups. According to Lijphart, proportionality serves two main functions in divided societies. Firstly, it is a way of distributing state positions and revenues between the different communal groups (Lijphart, 1977a: 38). Secondly, it aims to delegate the important decisions to the leaders of the communal groups (Lijphart, 1977a: 40). The objective of proportionality is to guarantee fair representation of minorities in divided societies. As Lijphart (1995: 278) remarks, there are two positive implications of the proportionality principle for minorities: 'the over-representation of small segments and parity of representation (when the minority or minorities are over-represented to such an extent that they reach a level of equality with the majority or largest group)'. Parity and overrepresentation are tools aimed at ensuring protection and security to minorities (Lijphart, 1977a: 41).

The last component is the mutual veto. According to Lijphart (cited in Assaf, Noura, 2004: 10), the mutual veto is designed to guarantee 'to each segment that it will not be outvoted by the majority when its vital interests are at stake'. The aim of the mutual veto is therefore to guarantee for each ethnic group complete political protection from the undermining of its interests in the political system by other groups (Lijphart, 1977a: 36–7). It can be an informal agreement between the ethnic groups or a law that is stated in the constitution. Lijphart lists several characteristics of mutual veto that can help encourage ethnic groups to reach agreements on contestable issues. Firstly, the frequent use of the mutual veto by segmental groups is not likely since it might be used by other groups against them (Lijphart, 1977a: 37). When a certain group uses the veto to block, for instance, a government policy because the policy may undermine its interests, other groups may use the veto against it when the same segment wants to promote its own policy. Secondly, 'the very fact that the veto is available as a potential weapon gives a feeling of security which makes the actual use of it improbable' (Lijphart, 1977a: 37). Finally, each ethnic community will be aware of the dangers of the frequent use of the veto, since it might cause paralysis in the state institutions (Lijphart, 1977a: 37).

Background Conditions

The success of the consociational form of governance depends on the existence of a certain set of background conditions. However, the background conditions identified in the literature cannot be employed separately to assess the success or the failure of the consociational model in divided societies. This is because each scholar developed his or her list of conditions from examining specific cases. This seems to suggest the point that in every state there should be a certain set of background conditions that should exist to enhance the success of the model. The absence of a specific set of background conditions that ensures the success of the model also undermines the ability of the consociational theory to prescribe solutions for political instability and absence of democracy in divided societies.

Lijphart lists several background conditions that can enhance the success of the consociational model. These conditions are considered conducive for the success of the model, although they might not be necessary or sufficient. It is worthwhile quoting Lijphart (1977a: 54) in full on this crucial point:

> It is [. . .] worth emphasizing that the favorable conditions [. . .] are factors that are helpful but neither indispensable nor sufficient in and of themselves to account for the success of consociational democracy. Even when all the conditions are unfavorable, consociationalism, though perhaps difficult, should not be considered impossible. Conversely, a completely favourable configuration of background conditions greatly facilitates but does not guarantee consociational choices or success.

The negative impacts of the absence of the background conditions might be mitigated by the role of the politicians. Lijphart (1977a: 165) maintains that even when all the conditions are absent, Consociation-alism should not be considered impossible, because what really counts is the ability and willingness of the political elites to overcome 'the centrifugal tendencies inherent in plural societies and a deliberate effort to counteract these dangers'.

In his article, 'The Puzzle of Indian Democracy: A Consociational Interpretation', published in 1996, Lijphart listed nine background conditions that he considered as conducive to consociational governance in divided societies. He (1969, 1975, 1977a) developed those nine conditions after refining them over several years. The first background condition is the absence of a major ethnic group (Lijphart, 1996: 262). A major ethnic community might prefer pure majority rule and therefore might cause concerns for the minorities (Lijphart, 1996: 262). It might seek to dominate the political system instead of cooperating with the minorities. The second background condition is the absence of large socio-economic inequalities, since the existence of socio-economic differences between ethnic groups might lead 'to demands for redistribution, which constitute the kind of zero-sum game that is a severe challenge to elite cooperation' (Andeweg, 2000: 522). The third is the existence of a small number of ethnicities. A state that includes too many groups might make negotiations and agreement over the distribution of state positions and revenues almost impossible (Lijphart, 1996: 263).

The fourth background condition concerns the existence of ethnic groups that are of relatively the same demographic size which can create a balance of power between them, preferable the existence of at least three ethnic groups that are of roughly the same size (Lijphart, 1977a: 56). The fifth is a relatively small population. The political leaders '[i]n small countries [...] are more likely to know each other personally than in larger countries, [and] the decision-making process is less complex' (Lijphart, 1985: 123). The sixth is the existence of foreign threats which might promote internal unity (Lijphart, 1996: 263). External threats should be conceived as a common threat 'in order to have a unifying effect' (Lijphart, 1977a: 67). The seventh is the presence of overarching loyalties which aim to counter the effects of segmental loyalties (Lijphart, 1996: 262–3). The eighth concerns the geographical concentration of the groups (Lijphart, 1996: 263). With geographic separation, the 'subcultures with widely divergent outlooks and interests may coexist without necessarily being in conflict; conflict arises only when they are in contact with each other' (Lijphart, 1969: 219). The last background condition refers to pre-existing traditions of political accommodation which make political elites' behaviour moderate and cooperative (Lijphart, 1977a: 100).

Several scholars have discussed and elaborated on the background conditions listed by Lijphart. Adriano Pappalardo (1981), for instance, criticizes Lijphart's background conditions, especially the cases (Austria, Belgium and the Netherlands) that he investigated to develop his set of background conditions. Pappalardo argues that there are two main conditions that led to the success of the consociational model in these European states: stability among subcultures and elite predominance. Stability among subcultures means the ethnic groups' recognition of their diversity and therefore their readiness to accept each other as a reality which cannot be changed (Pappalardo, 1981: 369). Stability 'is both the guarantor of the status of the blocs and the truly important condition for elite cooperation' (Pappalardo, 1981: 369–70). By elite predominance, he means the existence of a 'powerful leadership' (Pappalardo, 1981: 381). The power of political elites is derived from the wide popular support that they enjoy from their constituencies. Such a type of leadership 'does not have to fear resistance from below and is highly likely to conduct and bring negotiation to a conclusion' (Pappalardo, 1981: 381). His focus on the role of elites is because Consociationalism demands powerful elites 'to whom has been attributed a maximum of moderation and/or negotiating ability in comparison with mass publics and sub-elite political activists' (Pappalardo, 1981: 381).

Gerhard Lehmbruch (1975) in turn offers to divide the background conditions to the success of Consociationalism into two main categories: (1) genetic conditions; and (2) sustaining conditions. He deduces this categorization from his analysis of several cases, such as Cyprus, Lebanon and Belgium. Genetic conditions are defined as conducive to consociational governance, while sustaining conditions can help explain its maintenance. According to Lehmbruch (1975: 380–1), the genetic conditions are: a tradition of elite accommodation, intensive formal and informal communication between elites, and the absence of a majority group. The only sustaining factor is a 'neutral' foreign policy that aims to avoid conflicts with neighbouring and international states which can help in preventing foreign powers' intervention in domestic politics (Lehmbruch, 1975: 381–4). To achieve a 'neutral' foreign policy, there should be no internal conflicts between subcultures that might entice foreign interference. For instance, if there is an internal ethnic conflict which has implications on neighbouring states, this might encourage the neighbouring countries to interfere which could fuel the conflict instead of resolving it (Lehmbruch, 1975: 382). However, Lehmbruch's classification of the factors is not completely clear. Lijphart (cited in Bogaards, 1998: 484) rightly remarks in this context 'a factor that is favourable for the *establishment* of a consociation will be also a positive condition for its *maintenance*'. For instance, the role of elite accommodation is necessary for both: establishing and maintaining the consociational form of governance. If the elite accommodation condition is absent after establishing the consociational model, the model will most likely fail.

In addition to the absence of a majority group condition suggested by Lehmbruch, Brendan O'Leary (1989: 574) adds three more conditions to secure the establishment and maintenance of the consociational model: 'a commonly perceived external threat, socioeconomic equality between the segments, and overarching society-wide loyalties'. His study of Northern Ireland concludes that the success of the consociational model depends on these four conditions, although he does not clarify why it is only these four that are needed (Bogaards, 1998: 485). He also maintains that the absence of the favourable factors does not necessarily mean that the consociational model will fail. He (1989: 574) argues that the political elites should 'engineer the conducive conditions' to facilitate the success of the consociational model. This point is supported by Lijphart (1975: 195) who claims that 'the crucial factor in the establishment and preservation of democratic norms and democratic stability is the quality of leadership'.

Critique of the Four Components of Consociationalism

The four components, as conceptualized by Lijphart, suffer from several weaknesses. They are often unable to achieve their objectives without the existence of background conditions. Furthermore, the ethnic conflicts exacerbated by the application of the four components can cause political instability. What is noticeable with the four components is that they sometimes have the same implications, such as entrenching ethnic identity. For instance, the proportionality and segmental autonomy components can both help entrench the sense of ethnic identity. For this reason, the following critical analysis might repeat the same point of weakness, like the point about ethnic identity, but it will provide different evidences and examples.

Grand Coalition

Several scholars have criticized the premises underlying the principle of the grand coalition component and have noted its inability to achieve its objectives (Barry, 1975a; Horowitz, 1985; Tsebelis, 1990). One of the points of criticism that can be levelled against Lijphart's definition of grand coalition is that it should include 'all significant segments'. The word 'significant' is used ambiguously in the definition without clearer indication of which segments are 'significant'. Noura Assaf raises several critical questions against Lijphart's definition of grand coalition. She (2004: 13) asks: 'What is not a significant segment of the divided society, and more importantly who/what decides what is not a significant segment of the divided society? What criteria determine significant segments as opposed to insignificant segments?' She argues that the word 'significant' may exclude certain minorities since the voting weight of these groups is limited and therefore they often cannot influence, for instance, the results of parliamentary elections. '[T]here is a tension between consociationalism's promise to secure the rights of minority groups (through the veto concept) and the use of the word "significant". Indeed, it is not clear how minority groups can exercise the veto right if they are not represented at the executive, decision-making level' (Assaf, Noura, 2004: 13).

In addition to the weakness in the definition, the success of the grand coalition is based on certain assumptions which sometimes do not materialize. Firstly, the existence of grand coalition might not lead to stability and cross-cultural elite agreement as Lijphart supposes. However, the formation of a grand coalition might become impossible when ethnic groups have divergent political orientations. For instance, the agreement between ethnic groups on a common threat is considered to be one of the background conditions that might facilitate the success of the model. The disagreement on a common threat sometimes leads to the formation of coalitions that include certain communities and exclude others. A certain political party which represents the majority of its ethnic group might seek to form a coalition with other ethnic political parties that share with them the same perspective towards foreign threats; while another party that represents the majority of its ethnic group which has a different perspective towards foreign threats might follow the same approach. Such ethnic coalitions might lead to vertical segmentation of the society and threaten the political stability of the political system. The grand coalition that is supposed to play the 'role of a cooperative, purposive, cross-segmental leadership group that could bring stability to culturally fragmented democracies' could lead then to political instability and deep ethnic fragmentation (Lustick, 1997: 95).

Secondly, the grand coalition might heighten rather than help reduce inter-ethnic conflict. Grand coalition appears to be based on the assumption that the political elites will maintain the peace and stability of the political system. Lijphart (1977a: 53) considers that:

> Consociational democracy entails the cooperation by segmental leaders in spite of the deep cleavages separating the segments. This requires that the leaders feel at least some commitment to the maintenance of the unity of the country as well as a commitment to democratic practices. They must also have a basic willingness to engage in cooperative efforts with the leaders of other segments in a spirit of moderation and compromise. At the same time they must retain the support and loyalty of their own followers.

The consociational model's reliance on political elites to promote democracy and stability is to some extent 'exaggerated'. Tsebelis criticizes this very elite approach of the consociational model. He (1990: 16–17) warns that the distribution of state positions between representatives of ethnic groups may provide motives for politicians to provoke conflict along ethnic lines in order to bolster their own bargaining position against other groups, in what he terms 'elite-initiated conflict'. Lieberman and Singh also emphasize the point that the institutionalization of ethnic differences can lead to ethnic conflict and violence. They (2012: 5) state that 'high levels of intergroup differentiation will increase the likelihood of violent conflict among relevant groups because boundary drawing generates emotional, conflict-prone dynamics'. In a similar vein, Horowitz (1991: 141) argues that '[t] here is no reason to think automatically that elites will use their leadership position to reduce rather than pursue conflict'. By initiating ethnic conflicts, the elites will be able to mobilize popular support from their ethnic groups, for instance, to gain their votes during the elections or to enhance their legitimacy as the main representatives of their ethnic communities.

Moreover, the political elites do not always represent the majority of their ethnicities, as Lijphart assumes, and they are often entangled in intra-ethnic conflicts which make the formation of 'effective' grand coalition almost impossible. Horowitz (1985: 575) considers that 'in democratic conditions, *grand* coalitions are unlikely, because of the dynamics of intraethnic competition. The very act of forming a multi-ethnic coalition generates intraethnic competition'. It is rare to have a set of politicians whose position represents the view of the entire ethnic group (Horowitz, 1985: 574). This contradicts Lijphart's (1977a: 25) point that the grand coalition should be formed of 'the political leaders of all significant segments in the plural society'. In the case of an ethnic community having more than one political leader, the politicians might fight to obtain state positions that are allocated for their communal group, such as cabinet seats. This will create obstacles to the formation of a grand coalition, so that the legitimacy of the governing grand coalition could be undermined and questioned.

Further to the wrong assumption mentioned above, Lijphart's grand coalition component is based on the assumption that the relationship between political leaders and the masses is based on mutual trust and on the premise that the political leaders' views and opinions really reflect the perceptions and views of their constituents. However, such a situation does not always materialize. Indeed, the political leaders might manipulate their representation to further their own interests rather than that of the community per se and therefore they may not reflect the views of their groups. They might also seek to change the opinion of their community. For instance, they might raise the sense of fear of their opponents among their followers so that those followers will support them to improve their share in the cabinet, although this might not always be in the interest of the community.

Segmental Autonomy

As conceptualized by Lijphart, the notion of segmental autonomy, like that of the grand coalition, suffers from several weaknesses. Lijphart bases his notion of segmental autonomy on the assumption that there is no possibility of communication between ethnic groups that is able to bridge the cultural differences. However, this assumption is not always correct. Cultural communities do not have fixed identities which cannot change over time. Ian Lustick and Dan Miodownik (2002: 25) argue that identities can change across time and space, and 'are malleable, tradable, and deployable'. These identities 'are activated differentially in response to changing incentive structures' (Lustick & Miodownik, 2002: 25). The rise of public awareness of the dangers of ethnic fragmentation and its impact on the stability and the development of the political system may encourage ethnic members to bridge their cultural differences through the formation of cross-ethnic political parties and common interest groups. In Lebanon, there are continuous calls to eliminate sectarianism and to secularize the political system by non-sectarian groups. Several large protests calling for the elimination of sectarianism took place in 2010, for instance, which included thousands of Lebanese citizens from all sectarian communities.

The segmental autonomy component may also help entrench a sense of ethnic identity since it recognizes each ethnic community as a political community that should have representatives in the political system. Granting autonomy for each ethnic community encourages vertical segmentation instead of horizontal contacts. The consociational model in this respect can be said to foster the permanent fragmentation of plural societies. As Geraint Parry (1969: 55–6) rightly remarks, 'horizontal contacts between members of the society break down and are replaced by vertical contacts between atomized individuals and the elite'. In such a situation, the consociational model legitimizes and strengthens segmental cleavages, and entrenches further the sense of ethnic identity. Vertical segregation of ethnic groups could weaken the loyalty of the citizen to the state institutions and the development of a shared sense of identity. If there is no common educational curriculum, for instance, the citizens may hold a weak sense of common identity. In such a situation, segmental autonomy can weaken the role of the state in divided societies and undermine its legitimacy.

instrumental to a larger strategic goal: the achievement of total power'
(Spears, 2002: 129). In such a situation, the power-sharing agreement
becomes a tool to achieve certain goals instead of being an instrument to
maintain stability between the ethnicities.

Moreover, power-sharing agreements and proportional distribution of
state positions cannot always build mutual trust between ethnic groups,
especially in states that were entangled in civil wars and/or were under
foreign occupation. Timothy Sisk (2008: 196) argues in this regard that
'while power-sharing may be desirable, and necessary, as an *immediate*
exit to deadly ethnic wars, power-sharing is not a viable *long-term*
solution to managing uncertainty in ethnically divided societies'. The
problems of hostility and lack of trust between ethnic groups might not
be resolved by a power-sharing agreement. Although more than 20 years
have passed since the end of the civil war in Lebanon, the sectarian
groups have not been able to build mutual trust. One of the examples
that reflect the lack of trust between these groups is their refusal to
eliminate confessionalism. Such a step might undermine their interests
in the state bureaucracy or could lead to the domination of a major
sectarian community on the political system.

The ethnic distribution of parliamentary seats might also encourage
ethnic parties to formulate electoral laws that suit their electoral
strategies, although electoral laws are essential instruments for deeply
divided societies to moderate ethnic divisions and motivate political
parties to adopt cross-sectarian perspectives (Horowitz, 2003; Reilly,
2002). Horowitz (1985: 628) claims in this regard that electoral laws
have an impact upon 'ethnic alignments, ethnic electoral appeals, multi-
ethnic coalitions, the growth of extremist parties, and policy outcomes'.
He (1985: 632) lists several goals of the electoral system in multi-ethnic
states:

(1) Fragment the support of one or more ethnic groups, especially a
     majority group, to prevent it from achieving permanent domination.
(2) Induce an ethnic group, especially a majority, to behave moderately
     toward another group and engage in interethnic bargaining.
(3) Encourage the formation of multiethnic coalitions.
(4) Preserve a measure of fluidity or multipolar balance among several
     groups to prevent bifurcation and the permanent exclusion of the
     resulting minority.

(5) Reduce the disparity between votes won and seats won, so as to reduce the possibility that a minority or plurality ethnic group can, by itself, gain a majority of seats.

The chosen electoral law might motivate political parties to moderate their positions. Several scholars argue that the formulation of an electoral law based on proportional representation (PR) with multi-ethnic districts will 'force' political parties to eliminate their ethnic identity and organize party members on a non-ethnic basis in order to secure their victory in elections. In his study of electoral laws in multi-ethnic African states, Andrew Reynolds concludes that there are several advantages of PR for divided societies. Firstly, it ensures that the political parties of the minority groups have parliamentary representation 'and this acts as an important confidence-building mechanism, assuaging minorities' fear (however constructed) that they will be submerged in the new democratic order' (Reynolds, 2004: 97). Secondly, it motivates political parties to create multi-ethnic and multi-regional electoral lists since they have to appeal to multi-ethnic constituencies, which reduces the incentives to adopt ethnic language and to endeavour to address exclusive ethnic interests (Reynolds, 2004: 97). Finally, the governments that are elected on PR systems can help reflect the 'realities' of the African states (Reynolds, 2004: 98), because the minorities will be able to have influence on the election results and the member of parliament (MP) candidates will be forced to address their views and interests.

Lijphart (2004) shares the view of Reynolds that electoral laws based on PR systems are the most appropriate electoral laws for such societies. He (2008: 169) states that societies divided along ethnic lines require harmony and conciliation, which implies the inclusion of ethnic groups in the decision-making process. Thus, an electoral law based on PR 'makes it possible for minorities to be fairly represented, and it encourages the development of a multiparty system in which coalition governments, based on compromises among the minorities, have to be formed' (Lijphart, 2008: 181). The first-past-the-post (FPTP) electoral system meanwhile is thought to exclude minorities and weaken their ability to influence election results. FPTP 'discriminates against minorities, and it tends to produce artificial majorities, two-party systems, and one-party governments' (Lijphart, 2008: 181).

However, the formulation of electoral laws based on PR in divided societies that have consociational systems often faces obstacles. The distribution of state positions along ethnic lines may encourage ethnic parties to formulate electoral laws that suit their electoral strategies. They may formulate electoral laws that secure their victory as the main representatives of their ethnicities, which will enable them to obtain the quota allocated for their communal groups in the state institutions and endow them with the veto power to block cabinet decisions that may undermine their interests.

What is noticeable is that Lijphart emphasizes the positive willingness of ethnic political parties and elites to formulate electoral laws based on PR. However, electoral laws are not often 'designed in a harmonious way, as conjured by the word "design". All too frequently they are a patchwork of incongruous compromises' (Taagepera, 2002: 249). The political parties and elites may not always seek to advance the interests of the people. Instead, they are often driven by their own interests and the interests of their communal groups. Thus, they will seek to formulate electoral laws that suit their interests and/or the interests of their respective communities. In a state plagued by ethnic conflicts and a deeply entrenched sense of ethnic identity, the ability of ethnic parties and elites to reach compromises on a reformed electoral law will be weakened. As the discussion in Chapter 6 will show, due to the inter- and intra-sectarian conflicts, several Lebanese political parties proposed an electoral law that entrenches sectarianism and does not seek to moderate sectarian divisions. Their positions were driven by their aim to secure their victory in the elections and improve their communities' influence on election results.

The selective formulation of electoral laws often has ramifications for the relationship between the different ethnic communities and entrenches lack of trust between them. The domination of a certain ethnic community on the political system due to the selective formulation of electoral laws will raise the fears of its ethnic peers. As Lijphart (1984: 22–3) argued above, 'minorities that are continually denied access to power will feel excluded and discriminated against and will lose their allegiance to the regime'. Horowitz (1990) also emphasizes the importance of the electoral laws to motivate the political elites to compromise and to appeal to other ethnic communities, which help build mutual trust between ethnicities. If a certain community feels that its influence on the decision-making process in the country is undermined because of the selective formulation of electoral laws which undermine its ability to secure the victory of its MP candidates, its loyalty to the state institutions would be weakened and this may contribute to its decision to secede from the state.

The selective formulation of electoral laws may also help entrench ethnic identities. The formulation of small electoral districts, for instance, might help an ethnic leader to cement close ties with his or her ethnic followers, especially when the electoral district is dominated by a certain communal group. Such laws may encourage politicians to employ intense ethnic language to mobilize popular support to secure his or her victory in the elections instead of employing political rhetoric that addresses national-level issues, such as socio-economic policies and democratic reforms. 'Electoral systems in which politicians depend on votes only from coethnics tend to reward ethnic extremists who assert maximal demands' (Esman, 1994: 258). Such electoral systems will lead to the emergence of ethnic extremists who are not able to reach compromises and formulate power-sharing agreements because of their deeply entrenched political positions. Thus, the electoral system should motivate politicians to 'appeal to members of more than a single ethnic community and [to] depend on their electoral support [...] [which helps] produce more moderate politics and reward accommodative politicians with cross-ethnic appeals' (Esman, 1994: 258).

The Mutual Veto

The mutual veto is another core component of Consociationalism. The above critical analysis shows how conflict between political parties and elites might lead them to veto government decisions in cases where they do not meet their interests. The different 'usages' of the mutual veto raise the question of how we can define it since Lijphart does not 'prescribe the form and forum it should take' (Halpern, 1986: 190–1). The absence of a clear and precise definition of mutual veto makes its application depend on the willingness and actions of political parties and elites on how to use it. The consociational theory should define when and under what conditions the mutual veto should be used. Its arbitrary 'usage' might exacerbate further ethnic conflicts and as such paralyse state institutions.

If a conflict erupts between political parties and elites, they may, for instance, manipulate the veto power to enforce their views. The more intense this conflict is, the more likely the veto power will be used, which would carry negative implications for the power-sharing agreement. It may lead to the 'tyranny' of minorities because of their ability to veto government and state decisions. This usually causes conflict within the governing grand coalition, one of the main components of the consociational form of governance. The Lebanese constitution, for instance, requires that the major sects (Sunni, Shiite, Druze and Christian) should be represented in the cabinet; otherwise the government would be considered illegitimate. This can grant each sectarian community a veto power as they can use the threat of resignation from the cabinet when they feel that their interests are at risk, which also makes the decision-making process slow. One of the main conflicts between sectarian political parties that has plagued government formations since 2005 concerns the March 8 Coalition request to have a blocking-third in the cabinet which entails the veto power.

The four components of the consociational model are inter-related and sometimes have the same implications. They have weaknesses and often cannot achieve their objectives without the existence of background conditions. These weaknesses create negative implications for political stability and the success of the power-sharing agreement. The grand coalition component sometimes cannot achieve its main objective to include all the leaders of the ethnic groups (Lijphart, 1977a: 25). The formation of grand coalition might lead to inter- or intra-ethnic conflicts and foster political instability. This is because of the absence of unitary leadership of each ethnic community and the competition between political parties and elites over the distribution of state positions and revenues. Furthermore, the notion of segmental autonomy may entrench a sense of ethnic identity. It grants each ethnic community the right to run its own internal affairs while the issues that are of common concern between ethnic communities are resolved between the representatives of these communities. The autonomy of ethnic communities often reinforces the loyalty of citizens to their respective communities rather than to the state institutions and as such weakens the sense of common national identity. Lastly, the mutual veto sometimes has negative implications for political stability, and may cause paralysis in the state institutions, although the aim of the veto is to provide political protection for each group.

Democratic Theory and Consociational Theory

The weaknesses are not only in the four components. The concepts of stability and democracy employed in the theory of Consociationalism also suffer from weaknesses. Lijphart's (1969: 216) definition of Consociationalism as a 'government by elite cartel designed to turn a democracy with a fragmented political culture into a stable democracy' combines two main concepts, stability and democracy, both of which Consociationalism aims to achieve. Both concepts suffer from vagueness as employed by Lijphart in the definition, which also undermines the explanatory power of the consociational theory.

The Consociational Theory and Stability

In his book, *Democracy in Plural Societies: A Comparative Exploration*, Lijphart (1977a: 4) defines political stability as:

> [A] multidimensional concept, combining ideas that are frequently encountered in the comparative literature: system maintenance, civil order, legitimacy, and effectiveness. The foremost characteristics of a stable democratic regime are that it has a high probability of remaining democratic and that it has a low level of actual and potential civil violence. These two dimensions are closely related; the latter can also be viewed as a prerequisite for, and as an indicator of, the former. Similarly, the degree of legitimacy that the regime enjoys and its decisional effectiveness are related both to each other and to the first two factors. Jointly and interdependently, these four dimensions characterize democratic stability.

The literature that Lijphart refers to in his definition of stability is Harry Eckstein's (1971) book, *The Evaluation of Political Performance: Problems and Dimensions*, and Leon Hurwitz's article, 'Contemporary Approaches to Political Stability' (Lijphart, 1977a: 4). Eckstein (cited in Van Schendelen, 1985: 158) evaluates and discusses the four dimensions of stability: system maintenance, civil order, legitimacy and efficiency. Hurwitz (1973) also discusses several conceptualizations of political stability including the absence of violence, governmental longevity/ endurance, the existence of a legitimate constitutional order, the absence of structural change and multifaceted societal attribute.

Van Schendelen raised several critical points against Lijphart's definition of stability, particularly regarding the literature to which Lijphart refers. Essentially, he considers Lijphart's definition as ambiguous and illusive. He (1985: 158) argues that Eckstein's four dimensions of stability and Hurwitz's definitions of political stability are taken for granted without further discussion and justification of why he refers to these two scholars. Also, Lijphart does not specify to which of Hurwitz's definitions of political stability he refers, although Hurwitz (1973: 461; Van Schendelen, 1985: 158) concludes that the concept of political stability 'remains as elusive as other abstract concepts in political science research'. Van Schendelen (1985: 158) concludes that Lijphart's 'concept of stability is neither developed out of his theory of consociationalism nor very useful for the evaluation of consociations'.

In addition to the ambiguity of Lijphart's definition of stability, several scholars have argued that the political stability that several multi-ethnic states enjoy stems from the cooperative role of political elites and not from the existence of the consociational model. Although the consociational model emphasizes the role of political elites for its success, their role is sometimes sufficient to ensure political stability without the need for other consociational components, such as the mutual veto or segmental autonomy. Seaver (2000: 254) considers that 'elite willingness to compromise is a better explanation for democratic stability in plural societies than are consociational devices, and that the determinants of elite cooperation are consequently more important in explaining stability than specific political mechanisms'. Barry's examination of states that Lijphart classified as consociational also concludes that it is not the consociational institutions that accommodate the contestable problems between the cultural groups but the roles of elites. For instance, he (1975b: 487) argues that in Switzerland the contestable issues are solved between the elites 'right at the stage of electoral competition when they aggregate support across the lines of cleavage. There is therefore nothing left to be done after the election: there are no parties elected on a solidary group basis facing one another.'

What might also lead to political stability in divided societies is the absence of hostility between the cultural groups. This is not, however, always due to the existence of the consociational components, such as proportionality and the mutual veto. The absence of contestable issues, such as conflicts over the distribution of state positions between ethnic groups, might lead to political stability and prevent the exacerbation of conflicts between cultural groups. Ethnic groups might 'not have incompatible aspirations such that the fulfilment of one section's aims would spell a threat to the material well-being, cultural survival or social honour of another' (Barry, 1975b: 486). Another factor that might lessen the hostility between ethnic groups is the existence of cross-cultural interest groups, for example labour movements. According to David Bohn (1980), in Switzerland, one of the prime cases that Lijphart classifies as consociational, there are several cross-cultural interest groups which have helped prevent conflicts between ethnic communities. The existence of these groups can help transcend ethnic divisions and lead public opinion towards the formulation of cross-cultural interests. Bohn (1980: 179) asserts that in Switzerland ' [n]ot only do the surface cleavages intersect, but there is *significant inter-ethnic contact, willingness to assimilate lingually and intermarry'*. Horowitz (1985: 572) also emphasizes this point by stating that 'the main political parties [in Belgium and Switzerland] are not organized along ethnic lines, and ethnic differences alternate and compete for attention with class, religious, and (in Switzerland) cantonal differences'.

The ambiguity of Lijphart's definition of stability and the weakness of the explanatory power of Consociationalism are not the only deficiencies in the theory. More seriously even, there are several multi-ethnic states that adopted Consociationalism and failed to reach stability, like Lebanon and Cyprus. Instead, the consociational model helped fuel civil wars. Hudson (1976), for instance, blames the consociational model for the eruption of the civil war in Lebanon. He argues that the consociational system in Lebanon was not able to cope with the changes in the demographic sizes of the sectarian communities and with the regional conflicts that impacted upon the Lebanese political system, especially the Arab–Israeli conflict. Therefore, he (1976: 119) concludes that the consociational model 'is inappropriate to the Lebanese situation because of its static characteristic it was unlikely to bring real stability, political normality, and above all political legitimacy back to the Lebanese political system'. Although the failure of several consociational states might be explained by the absence of several background conditions and problems in its implementation, it is clear that the consociational model cannot always be a successful solution to ensure political stability in deeply divided societies as Lijphart claims.

The Consociational Theory and Democracy

The weakness is not only in the definition of political stability. It is also in the definition of the concept of democracy. Lijphart (1977a: 4), in his book *Democracy in Plural Societies: A Comparative Exploration*, asserts that the concept of democracy 'virtually defies definition. Suffice it to say that it will be used here as a synonym of what Dahl calls "Polyarchy". It is not a system of government that fully embodies all democratic ideals, but one that approximates them to a reasonable degree.' Several critical points can be levelled against the democratic quality of Consociationalism. The consociational theory does not completely meet the criterion defined by Dahl. Van Schendelen levels such criticism against Lijphart's 'consociational democracy.' He argues that Lijphart's reliance on Dahl's definition to measure the democratic nature of 'consociational democracy' is problematic. '[T]he concept of polyarchy, if strictly taken, is incompatible with the consociational model [...] In a polyarchy, competition between elites is, more than anything else, essential; in a consociation, the antithesis of competition, i.e., intense collaboration, is crucial' (Van Schendelen, 1985: 157). Lustick as well raises critical questions concerning Lijphart's definition of democracy, in particular concerning the ambiguity of the definition itself. He (1997: 105) asks: 'what is meant by "reasonable"? What "democratic ideals" does he have in mind?'

In addition to the ambiguity of the definition, several other points listed by Dahl's criterion are not met by the consociational model. For instance, the fourth point in Dahl's list about the right of adults to run for *all* elective state positions does not exist in the consociational model. The distribution of state positions between the representatives of ethnic communities would make every state position exclusive for a certain ethnic community. In Lebanon, for example, state positions are distributed between the representatives of the sectarian communities. Therefore, such a distribution would undermine the principle of 'equality' between citizens, as raised by Dahl's criterion, to run for elective offices.

What further undermines its democratic nature is that it allows only limited public participation in the decision-making process. The focus on the role of elites to negotiate and reach compromises might prevent the public from participating in the decision-making process. Van Schendelen criticizes Lijphart's focus on the role of elites at the expense of popular participation. He (1985: 156) argues 'that in the inter-election period the relationship between electors and elected are almost non-existent or antagonistic; that elites' opinions and behavior are non-representative of the people's demands; and that elite-politics is full of secrecy and immune to popular control.' This point is also emphasized by Samuel Huntington (1981: 14) who contends that Consociationalism 'is democratic only in the sense that each communal group is represented and no significant decisions can be taken without the consent of those representatives', while democracy, as conceptualized by Dahl, 'involves competition as well as inclusiveness. Consociationalism achieves the latter by sacrificing the former.' Such a criticism undermines the democratic legitimacy of Consociationalism, since the public should audit and monitor the behaviour of political parties and elites in the state institutions.

Another weakness of 'consociational democracy' is the existence of weak political opposition or even the absence of political opposition (Lijphart, 1977a: 47). Although the consociational model might help prevent the emergence of societal cleavages by inhibiting the formation of opposition, it prevents the existence of one of the most important conditions that helps grant further legitimacy and transparency for the political system: political opposition and with it the possibility of power alternation. Several scholars, such as Seymour Lipset and Robert Dahl, strongly encourage the existence of opposition. Lipset (1959: 71) argues that in a case where an effective opposition is absent 'then the authority of officials will be maximized, and popular influence on policy will be at a minimum. This is the situation in all one-party states; and by general agreement, at least in the West, these are dictatorships.' As Dahl (1966: xvi) also observes, 'one is inclined to regard the existence of an opposition party as very nearly the most distinctive characteristic of democracy itself; and we take the absence of an opposition party as evidence, if not always conclusive proof, for the absence of democracy.'

Intervention of External Actors

The weaknesses are not only in the consociational theory itself, but they also reside in the consociational model's inability to ensure stability and engineer power-sharing agreements without foreign intervention. The above analysis criticized the model's flaws, while the following analysis will shift the focus to explore its ability to ensure stability without external support. It will also attempt to show that the consociational model is not often able to prevent foreign intervention.

Pretexts of Foreign Intervention in Consociational States

The stability of the consociational model rests largely on the agreement between the political parties and elites who are supposed to accommodate ethnic divisions and conflicts and reach compromises on contestable issues. However, conflicts between them might entice foreign states to interfere to manipulate any such conflicts to further their own interests.

Several factors encourage external actors to interfere in consociational states, which usually have negative implications for their political stability. Michael Kerr (2007: 249) defines negative foreign intervention as when 'the regional powers have a direct interest in destabilising the divided society's political institutions and possess the ability and desire to do so.' The first such factor concerns a situation whereby an ethnic conflict intersects with regional or international conflicts. Lehmbruch (1975: 382) argues that '[w]hen the internal conflicts between the subcultures correspond with cultural conflict between neighboring political units, this results in the internal replication of international conflicts, especially in the case of religious and ethnic conflicts.' This often happens in states that are located in turbulent regions, such as Lebanon and Iraq in the Middle East. The rise of the Sunni–Shiite conflict in the Middle East has plagued these two states due to their multi-sectarian composition. Foreign intervention in such cases might be further encouraged by the local political parties and elites themselves. Indeed, the intersection of internal and external conflicts might also encourage the local political parties and elites to manipulate the conflict and weave robust relations with foreign patrons to bolster their domestic positions. Seaver (2000: 249) argues that '[a]lthough consociational failure stems from the cessation of elite consensus, regional factors represent important antecedent variables that contribute to elite dissension and ultimately regime collapse.'

The intersection of internal and external conflicts might lead ethnic groups to have divergent perceptions of external threats. An ethnic groups' alliance with rival regional and international states might lead to their disagreement over the state's foreign policy, especially if the ethnic groups in question perceive their ethnic opponents' foreign alliances as an external threat. In such a situation, the absence of a common external threat can lead to the failure of unity and agreement between political parties and elites in consociational states. The civil war in Lebanon constitutes a vivid example of the political parties' and elites' divergent political orientations in defining foreign threats. During the civil war, many of the Lebanese Christian groups, such as the Kataeb Party, were allied with Israel with the pretext that they wanted to protect themselves against the armed Muslim groups, while Israel was considered the main enemy for the Muslim community. Instead of promoting unity between the sectarian groups as Lijphart argues, the divergent political orientations regarding external threats heightened the gap between them and therefore they accused each other of treachery. These parochial divisions made the Lebanese state 'highly vulnerable to foreign manipulation' (Hudson, 1985: 116).

The second factor that might encourage foreign intervention is the aim of a neighbouring state to widen its hegemony and place another state under its auspices, especially if the multi-ethnic state in question represents a threat to its national security. The neighbouring country may seek to interfere to stabilize the multi-ethnic state that is embroiled, for instance, in a civil war to prevent any spill-overs and adverse effects on its national security. The case of the Syrian military intervention in 1976 in Lebanon proves this point. One of the main reasons behind the Syrian intervention in the Lebanese civil war was Damascus' concern about the spill-over effects of the civil war on its own domestic stability. The violent conflict between the sectarian groups might entice Israeli military intervention, especially after the emergence of powerful armed resistance groups against Israel, that is, Palestinian groups. Indeed, as Raymond Hinnebusch (1998: 140) remarks, the Syrian intervention in the country was 'motivated by the grave security *threat* from the prospect that civil war and partition would open the door to Israeli penetration' in Lebanon and therefore cause threat and instability to Syria.

The third factor that might encourage foreign intervention is when political parties and elites feel that their ethnic communities are underrepresented in the state's institutions, so they would seek to weave robust relations with their ethnic fellows in other states, for instance, to ask for partition. Lehmbruch argues that the relationship between internal and external elites will be developed when the genetic conditions are not sufficiently developed. This is because the gap between domestic elites will be larger 'while the distance between the internal elites and the corresponding external elites (e.g. religious or ethnic leaders in the adjacent countries) will be smaller, and the identification with reference groups cutting across the borders of the political unit will prevail' (Lehmbruch, 1975: 383). In such a situation, internal and external parties will seek partition of the state since this will 'prevent a cumulative aggravation of both the internal and the external conflicts' (Lehmbruch, 1975: 383).

External ethnic conflicts might also encourage consociational states to interfere in multi-ethnic countries which can in turn create internal ethnic conflicts. The dispersion of an ethnic community in several countries may encourage the ethnic leaders to claim responsibility for their ethnic fellows in other states. The political leaders will feel compelled to interfere to save their ethnic fellows in case they are suffering from oppression or attack. This is because 'ethnic ties influence foreign policymaking [...] [S]upport for ethnic kin abroad can be a litmus test for a politician's sincerity on ethnic issues at home. Politicians lack credibility if they take symbolic stands on ethnic issues but do not follow up when an ethnically charged foreign event develops' (Saideman, 1997: 727). Ethnic leaders' support for their ethnic fellows in other states might lead to conflict on formulating the state's foreign policy. 'The level of conflictual relations between two states will be higher if both states contain group members from the same ethnic group, and one of the co-ethnics is politically and/or economically privileged in its society, but its brethren in the other state are not' (Davis & Moore, 1997: 174). The case of the Kurdish community in Syria, Iraq, Iran and Turkey supports this point. The Kurdish political elites in Iraq often condemn the Turkish military attacks on the Kurdish groups in Turkey, although Iraq has diplomatic relations with Turkey. This can help them to bolster their domestic positions against their political opponents and may create conflict with other ethnic and sectarian leaders

(Sunni and Shiite politicians) over the formulation of the state foreign policy with Turkey.

External Actors and Power-Sharing Agreements

Although foreign intervention can play a negative role by manipulating and exacerbating ethnic conflicts, the success of the consociational model in multi-ethnic states often hinges upon international commitment and interference. Indeed, international commitment is often necessary to put pressure on political parties and elites to reach a power-sharing agreement in the first place and to sustain it thereafter. For instance, the spill-over effects of ethnic conflicts (such as the smuggling of fighters and weapons to the neighbouring states might threaten their stability) may threaten the stability of the region which can encourage the regional states to seek a power-sharing agreement to end the conflict. External actors might also seek a power-sharing agreement in case their domestic allies are defeated by their ethnic opponents.

John McGarry and Brendan O'Leary's study of the case of Northern Ireland led them to highlight a lacuna in Lijphart's consociational theory. They (2004: 1–61) argue that the success of the consociational model in Northern Ireland can be largely explained by the intervention from the US, the UK and the Republic of Ireland. They criticize Lijphart's argument that the consociational institutions are capable of accommodating and solving ethnic conflicts in and of themselves. They (2004: 2) 'disagreed with Lijphart especially about the obstacles to a durable political settlement in Northern Ireland, and have insisted that such a settlement requires more than just consociational institutions.' Lijphart does not focus on the role of foreign factors in engineering a power-sharing agreement, since he listed eight out of the nine background conditions as endogenous while there is only one exogenous: the existence of external threat (McGarry & O'Leary, 2004: 4–5). McGarry and O'Leary's (2004: 4–5) criticism was that '[c]onventional consociational theory is overly "endogenous" or "internalist"; it has tended to treat states and regions as if they are sealed entities, relatively immune from exogenous forces.' They (2004: 5) argue that foreign intervention can enhance the enactment of consociational agreement by playing a positive rather than negative role through, for instance, mediation to exert pressure on conflicting parties to enact a power-sharing agreement. Lijphart's focus only on one external factor stemmed from his examination of specific cases, such as Belgium, the Netherlands, Switzerland and Austria, since these states were threatened by their neighbours and enacted consociational agreements (McGarry & O'Leary, 2004: 5).

Kerr's comparative study of Lebanon and Northern Ireland led him to the same conclusion that the external actors' role is often essential in engineering power-sharing agreements. He concludes that the success or failure of consociation in these two countries hinges upon the existence of positive exogenous variables. He (2006: 200) argues that:

> If such proactive and beneficial influences continue to buffer and stabilise consociation in Northern Ireland, then the prospects for power-sharing remain reasonably good. Conversely, if the Middle East remains the focal point of global Eastern and Western tension, and Syria maintains its pivotal role in the Arab–Israeli conflict, then a true Lebanese pact of consociation will remain a thing of the past.

He (2007: 248) states that foreign players would seek power-sharing agreements when their interests are at risk and regulating the conflict serves their policies. Also, Marie-Joëlle Zahar (2005: 235) in her study of foreign intervention in Lebanon argues that stability has rested on the existence of a foreign protectorate and has helped block the elimination of confessionalism.

However, imposing power-sharing agreements on the ethnic communities can also create negative implications in the long run. In a case when the consociational agreement is rejected by a certain segment, the prospects for the success of the agreement will be weakened. Lijphart (1977a: 137) argues that consociational solutions 'cannot be imposed against the will of one of the segments, especially if it is a majority segment.' The Ta'if Agreement is an obvious example. Almost all of the Christians rejected the agreement, which then led to their political marginalization during the Syria era. Thus, after the Syrian withdrawal in 2005, they called for amending the constitution to increase the powers of the main Christian positions, such as the presidency position, in the political system before eliminating confessionalism altogether. Their argument was that the Christian representation should be strengthened and empowered in the state institutions before transitioning to a non-confessional political system.

It can therefore be said that the success of international mediation efforts in enforcing a power-sharing agreement depends on several factors. According to Sisk (1996), several factors can make international mediation successful in ethnic conflicts. Firstly, it depends on the formula and options of the power-sharing agreement suggested by the international community. The intervening party should provide information to the negotiators 'and may provide face-saving exits from firmly entrenched positions' (Sisk, 1996: 97). Also, the mediators should be aware of the formulas of power-sharing agreements that will be suggested to solve the ethnic conflict (Sisk, 1996: 97). For instance, the distribution of state positions should reflect the numerical strength of each ethnic community. Secondly, the success of an international mediation initiative depends on the incentives provided to the conflicting parties to reach an agreement. The incentives 'can be tangible, such as the imposition of sanctions, military force, offers of guarantees [. . .] or side payments to parties' (Sisk, 1996: 101). Thirdly, the timing of the mediation initiative is important for the success of the mediators' efforts in reaching an agreement (Sisk, 1996: 108). The ethnic conflict should be 'ripe' (i.e. the conflicting groups are persuaded that violence will not achieve their objectives) so the rival groups will accept the mediation efforts to reach an agreement. Also, the intervention should be scheduled 'at an appropriate juncture in the development of a conflict' (Sisk, 1996: 108), for instance, to prevent the spill-over effects of the conflict to other neighbouring territories. In addition to the factors that Sisk lists, the role of the elites is important to the success of the international mediation efforts. The absence of the elites' willingness to compromise and negotiate to reach a power-sharing agreement will lead to the failure of the international efforts. As Lijphart emphasized, the success of the consociational form of governance depends largely on the role of elites to accommodate the ethnic conflicts and maintain the stability of the consociational model.

Political Parties in Consociational States

The 'need' for foreign intervention to secure the success of the power-sharing agreement is not the only weakness in the consociational model; this form of governance also has adverse effects on the behaviour of

domestic political parties and on democracy more broadly. Political parties in consociational states are usually entangled with ethnic outbidding to secure their political survival. The more the political party is able to address the interests of its ethnic community, the more it is able to mobilize popular support which will strengthen its ethnic leadership and enable it to ask for the quota allocated for its communal group in the consociational system.

Ethnic parties differ in their nature from the non-ethnic parties. A political party, as defined by Sigmund Neumann (1956: 396), is 'the articulate organization of society's active political agents, those who are concerned with the control of governmental power and who compete for popular support with another group or groups holding divergent views.' Edmund Burke (cited in Ware, 1996: 5) defines a political party as 'a body of men united for promoting by their joint endeavours the national interest upon some particular principles in which they are all agreed.' A more articulate definition is provided by Alan Ware (1996: 5): 'A political party is an institution that (a) seeks influence in a state, often by attempting to occupy positions in government, and (b) usually consists of more than a single interest in the society and so to some degree attempts to "aggregate interests".' Party systems are considered essential for modern democracies. Giovanni Sartori (1976: 58) argues that 'both party systems and party-state systems appear to be a requirement of modern political systems in that they provide a channelling system for the society.'

However, ethnic parties usually represent the interests of their ethnic communities and derive their popular support from their communal group. Horowitz (1985: 291–2) defines an ethnic party which 'derives its support overwhelmingly from an identifiable ethnic group (or cluster of ethnic groups) and serves the interests of that group. In practice, a party will serve the interests of the group comprising its overwhelming support or quickly forfeit that support.' Larry Diamond and Richard Gunther (2001: 23–4) identify several features of an ethnic party:

(1) Ethnic parties may be highly centralized around the personal leadership of a single leader, or may be more decentralized and federative in their structures.
(2) Candidate nomination may be determined by the hierarchical ethnic party leadership or by more localized ethnic elites.

(3) Electoral mobilization resembles more the clientelistic pattern of reliance on vertical social networks than the mass-based pattern of organization and programmatic communication.

(4) [T]he ethnic party stresses particularistic issues – both the narrow particularism of specific benefits that ethnic patrons promise to deliver to their clients and the wider particularism of competitive gains for the entire ethnic group.

(5) The ethnic party represents only the interests of a particular ethnic group and is, at best, aggregative only of the interests of subgroups encompassed by the wider ethnic identity.

(6) If the ethnic group is a majority, or nearly so, the ethnic party may aspire to form a government unilaterally.

(7) [T]he more purely a party is ethnic, the less it will integrate the citizen into a nationwide polity and breed identification with it.

The recognition of the consociational system of ethnic communities as political communities that should have representatives in the state institutions allows the emergence of ethnic parties that claim the representation of their ethnicities' interests. Kanchan Chandra (2005: 235) argues that 'the politicization of ethnic divisions inevitably gives rise to one or more ethnic parties. In turn, the emergence of even a single ethnic party "infects" the rest of the party system, leading to a spiral of extreme ethnic bids that destroy competitive politics altogether.' The ethnic party would seek to achieve the interests of its community, while dismissing the national interests. This is because of its ability to 'combine intraethnic interests, often very effectively. But it neither combines nor buckles nor takes a non-partial approach to the interests of various ethnic groups in a society. Its rationale is the incompatibility of those interests – and quite often their fundamental incompatibility' (Horowitz, 1985: 297). Ethnic parties may, for instance, block democratic reforms, such as the formulation of a new electoral law, in case they threaten to undermine their political positions. They will provide an ethnic interpretation for their position, especially if the new electoral law will weaken the ability of their communal groups to ensure the election of all their MP candidates. In such a situation, the ethnic parties will employ ethnic language to weave their position with the interests of their ethnicities and block democratic reforms.

Ethnic language is not only employed to convince the party followers of their decisions but also to mobilize popular support to win parliamentary elections. As Diamond and Gunther (2001: 23) write, '[t]he electoral logic of the ethnic party is to harden and mobilize its ethnic base with exclusive, often polarizing appeals to ethnic group opportunity and threat, and unlike virtually all other political parties (including nationalistic parties), electoral mobilization is not intended to attract additional sectors of society to support it.' The employment of ethnic language and inculcating a sense of fear may divert the attention of voters from focusing on the political platforms of the candidates to the candidate's ability to address the ethnic community interests. This point is stressed by Alvin Rabushka and Kenneth Shepsle (1972: 86) who argue that 'the free and open competition for the people's vote – is simply not viable in an environment of intense ethnic preferences. The demand-generating activity of ambitious leaders, the concomitant salience of primordial sentiments, and the politics of outbidding, weaken commitment to national values.'

If the ethnic party is able to mobilize the support of the majority of the ethnic community to secure its victory in parliamentary elections, this will empower its political position as the main representative of its communal group in the consociational system. As a result, this will endow it with the power to veto the government decisions and enforce its policy. In such a situation, the success of the power-sharing agreement would hinge on the consent of the ethnicity's main representative. The power-sharing agreement might reach a deadlock because of its inability to take decisions without the approval of one of the representatives of the ethnic communities. For instance, the formation of a coalition government in consociational states is essential. However, the functionality of the government would be undermined in a case where a certain ethnic party which represents the majority of its community vetoes a government decision because it does not meet its interests. This is because replacing the ethnic community representative with another one will be almost impossible due to the weak popular support that its intra-ethnic opponents enjoy.

Moreover, an ethnic party's position might be empowered or weakened if the country exists in a turbulent region, especially when the ethnic party has regional or transnational connections with their brethren in other states. The implications of any regional development that might influence their ethnic fellows might have major implications for the ethnic party's political behaviour. For instance, the rise of an ethnic group to power in a regional state might bolster the position of its fellows at the domestic level. This often results in more intransigence in the behaviour of the representatives of a certain ethnicity to reach compromises over, for instance, the formation of a new government, and also raises the fears of its political opponents about the aims and consequences of its foreign alliances. In such a situation, the conflicting ethnic parties might also seek to develop foreign alliances to empower their positions against each other. As discussed above, the external alliances of domestic parties would help exacerbate domestic conflicts, which usually have adverse effects on political stability and the power-sharing agreement.

In an environment of ethnic conflict and competition over the domination of the political system, the achievement of compromises and agreements between ethnic parties often becomes difficult. 'Ethnic parties make the mediation of group interests difficult, and this helps explain why ethnic party systems are often conflict prone' (Horowitz, 1985: 298). The endeavour of the political parties to obtain their interests and those of their ethnicities will be faced by their inter- and intra-ethnic political peers, which will spark an ethnic outbidding. Intra-ethnic outbidding is when ethnic parties which represent the same ethnic community 'seek to portray themselves as the true defenders of the group position while simultaneously undercutting the legitimacy of in-group rivals. Claim and counterclaim may result in an "ethnic auction", whereby attempts at inter-group rapprochement are made impossible by intra-group accusations of treachery and betrayal' (Gormley-Heenan & Macginty, 2008: 44). In such a situation, the rise of ethnic conflict will encourage the parties to manipulate it to mobilize popular support. According to Horowitz (2002: 197), ethnic parties that are 'pursuing ethnic conflict will generally find it difficult or unattractive to pursue settlement of the conflict.' Settling the political and ethnic conflicts might undermine the ability of ethnic parties to mobilize popular support from their groups on the basis that they are protecting and defending their interests. Thus, they will manipulate the ethnic conflict and raise the fears of their followers on the basis that their rival communal groups are attempting to marginalize them in the state institutions, which will help strengthen their popular support.

One of the major negative implications that ethnic outbidding has is that it may prevent the modernization of political parties. 'Party modernization refers to processes whereby political parties transform themselves from exclusive single-identity entities based on sectarian or ethnic membership to more pluralistic entities ready to engage on a wide range of issues and often employing modern methods to do so' (Gormley-Heenan & Macginty, 2008: 44). The emergence of ethnic parties due to the politicization of ethnic divisions will undermine their ability to modernize themselves. As Nordlinger (1972: 35) states, 'individuals belonging to a particular segment or conflict group will be adamantly and emotionally attached to "their" political party and parties', which undermines the ability of the political parties to mobilize followers from outside their ethnic communities. As mentioned previously, their ethnic nature will also threaten the stability of the state. In a case where each ethnic community has its representatives, this will lead to diversity of ethnic parties that hold different and sometimes contradictory aims, which would negatively influence political stability. Diamond, Linz and Lipset's (1995: 35) 26-nation study of democracy in developing countries concludes that a political system which has a small number of political parties 'with broad social and ideological bases, may be conducive to stable democracy.'

Conclusion

The consociational theory and model suffer from several weaknesses. There are flaws in the four components which often have negative implications for political stability and for its ability to engineer successful power-sharing agreements. Also, the consociational model cannot ensure that all citizens will be treated equally because of the distribution of state positions between ethnic groups. What undermines the model's democratic quality more is the 'absence' of political opposition. The importance of the opposition is in its ability to monitor and audit government decisions and policies. In addition, the consociational model's capacity to ensure stability in divided societies is often doubted. Political stability sometimes hinges on exogenous variables, making the model's ability to ensure stability in the long run almost impossible, especially if it is located in a turbulent region. What threatens the success of the power-sharing agreement further is the emergence of ethnic parties and the proportional distribution of state positions which 'stimulate' the ethnicities to compete over the domination of the political system. This can spark an ethnic outbidding that has adverse effects on political stability and the democratization process. As the following chapters will show, Lebanon's consociational system 'contributed' to the emergence of sectarian political parties. These parties are entangled in inter- and intra-sectarian conflicts and outbidding which have caused repercussions for political stability and the democratization process.

CHAPTER 2

WEAKNESSES OF LEBANON'S CONSOCIATIONAL MODEL IN THE POST-2005 ERA

Many of the weaknesses in the consociational model explored in the previous chapter also resonate with the Lebanese experience. Indeed, the consociational form of governance in Lebanon is often blamed for the absence of a democratic system and political stability, and for exacerbating sectarian conflicts (Elbadawi & Makdisi, 2011: 133; Haddad, 2009). Instead of facilitating a gradual democratization process and ensuring political stability after the Syrian withdrawal, the four components of the consociational model (i.e. a grand coalition, proportionality, confessional autonomy and mutual veto) have played a significant role in impeding democratic reforms and exacerbating sectarian conflicts in the country. During the Syrian era, Damascus used to ensure political stability and prevent the eruption of political and sectarian conflicts. However, after 2005, Lebanon witnessed a conflagration of political and sectarian conflicts which helped block the initiation of democratic reforms. As one prominent Lebanese journalist, Talal Salman (2011), argues, '[t]he nature of the country's political system prevents the Lebanese from ridding themselves of the shackles of quiescence and attaining their natural right of becoming citizens, and not just subjects or hapless followers of confessional leaders'.

This chapter will argue that the failure of Lebanon's consociational model to facilitate political stability and democratization in Lebanon after 2005 rests on two main factors. Firstly, it will be demonstrated that the weaknesses of the four components of the consociational model led to failure in achieving these objectives in the case of Lebanon. Secondly, it will be shown that the absence of several background conditions also contributed to its failure in Lebanon. By exploring the weaknesses in Lebanon's consociational model, the following chapters will show how the results of the failure of Lebanon's consociational model, such as its inability to shield the country from foreign intervention, could help exacerbate political conflicts and have implications for the democratization process.

Firstly, the chapter will provide a brief history and discussion of Lebanon and its consociational form of government, the major weaknesses in the National Pact (1943) and the Ta'if Agreement (1989), and the Syrian era (1990–2005). Secondly, it will provide an overview of the Lebanese political parties and their main political views. Thirdly, it will explore the major factors, such as the divergent political views of the political parties, which have undermined the ability of Lebanon's consociational system to achieve political stability in the post-2005 period. Fourthly, it will explore why the Lebanese model usually encourages foreign intervention, which undermines political stability. Finally, it will explore the major weaknesses in the Lebanese political parties. It will argue that Lebanon's consociational model encourages the formation of sectarian political parties that impair the ability of the model to promote political stability.

The National Pact and the Civil War

A House of Many Mansions, by the prominent Lebanese scholar Kamal Salibi (1988), is an accurate depiction of the nature of Lebanese society. Lebanon is characterized by deep sectarian divisions that have weakened its social cohesion and state institutions ever since its formation in 1920. During the Ottoman era, Lebanon was part of Greater Syria which also included present-day Jordan, Syria and Palestine. When the French occupied Lebanon (1918–43), the Christian Maronite community called for the formation of a Lebanese state to protect it and to ensure that it would not be absorbed into a Syrian Muslim state (Rigby, 2000; Makdisi, 2000). The Lebanese confessional (consociational) political system evolved from the *millet* system developed during the Ottoman reign. Simon Haddad (2009: 402) states that the Ottoman Turks, who institutionalized confessionalism in Lebanon, 'emphasized group differences in the Arab East generally, and particularly in what is now Lebanon, by compartmentalizing ethno-religious differences through the introduction of the "*millet* system". Non-Muslims were treated as second-class citizens and forced to pay a tax in exchange for protection'. Upon the request of the Christian community and as part of France's endeavour to create a regional ally, the French government created the Lebanese state by adding to Mount Lebanon, which was mainly dominated by Christians, the coastal cities of Tripoli, Tyre, Sidon and Beirut, and by removing the Bekaa Valley from Syrian jurisdiction and adding it to the frontiers of the new Lebanese state (Cleveland, 2009: 218–19). By adding these Muslim-dominated cities, the French aimed to ensure that the Christian Maronite community would be a minority (about 30 per cent of the total population) which would make it dependent on French support to bolster its domestic position (Cleveland, 2009: 225). Therefore, Lebanon from its inception has included a diverse constituency of religious groups that are geographically distributed (see Map 2). The Muslim community is mainly composed of four main sects: Sunni, Shiites, Druze and ʿAlawites. The Christian community in turn is composed of Maronite, Greek Orthodox, Greek Catholic, Armenian, Protestant and Anglican denominations.

After Lebanon gained its independence from French colonial rule in 1943, the two main Lebanese sects, Maronite and Sunni, represented by President Bechara al-Khoury and PM Riad al-Solh respectively, concluded an unwritten agreement called the 'National Pact' (*al-Mīthāq al-Waṭanī*). The National 'Pact was a reformulated continuation of an interconfessional political administration that had developed under the Ottoman *millet* system and the French Mandate' (Kerr, 2006: 124). The agreement recognized the fundamental rights of the different sectarian communities through which a confessional political system was established and each sectarian community was treated as a political community that had representatives in the state institutions. The agreement thus distributed the seats in parliament and government according to the population size of each recognized sect. The distribution of power was based on the relative population of each sect as measured in the 1932 census: Christians 52 per cent and Muslims 48 per cent (Rigby, 2000: 170).[1] Therefore, the census gave the Christians six representatives at any given level of government for every five Muslims, which came to be known as the 6:5 ratio (Rigby, 2000: 170). In addition, the main public offices (i.e. the political, military and security positions) were mainly controlled by Christians. Furthermore, the presidency was to be a Christian Maronite; the PM, a Muslim Sunni; the speaker of parliament, a Muslim Shiite; the minister of defence, an Orthodox Christian; the minister of the interior, a Muslim Druze; and the commander-in-chief of the armed forces, a Maronite Christian (Rigby, 2000: 170).

The constitution that was formulated during the French mandate in 1926 and adopted from 1943 until 1990 endowed the presidency with wide powers which cemented the domination over the political system of France's main ally, the Christians. The president had the authority to dissolve parliament if necessary, appoint the PM and had veto power in regard to all government decisions (Traboulsi, 2007: 245).[2] The government could not hold its meetings without the presence of the president. The president therefore had significant influence on the two main constitutional institutions: parliament and government.

However, the National Pact proved unable to prevent the eruption of civil war, with the outbreak of the conflict in 1975 being largely attributed to the weaknesses in the Pact. It proved unable to mitigate the impacts of internal and external factors and prevent the eruption of violence. The external factors concerned the political and military developments that took place after the 1967 war between Israel, Egypt, Syria and Jordan. Although the National Pact stated that Lebanon should follow a foreign policy which enjoys the support of its communal groups, it was not able to ensure the fulfilment of its objective.[3] Hudson (1985: 44) argues that '[t]he bargain between Sunnites and Maronites has proven increasingly difficult to maintain in the domain of foreign relations'. This is because of the support by the Muslim community of the Palestinian cause, in particular the Palestine Liberation Organization (PLO), which enjoyed the support of the Arab regimes against Israel. After the defeat of the Arab armed forces in the war of 1967 and the death of Gamal Abdel Nasser in 1970, new political leaders and parties emerged, such as Yasir Arafat, head of the PLO, the Ba'thist regimes in Syria and Iraq, and Gaddafi in Libya (el-Khazen, 2000: 11), which all supported the Palestinian cause and the PLO. This development was paralleled by the movement of the PLO from Jordan to Lebanon in 1970, complicating further the relations between the domestic parties. At the time the PLO was a militant organization and its military operations against Israel from Lebanese territories were legalized in the Cairo Agreement (1969), which was enacted between the Palestinian organization and the Lebanese government. Due to its military presence in Lebanon, it was considered by the Christian community as a movement to establish a Muslim state within the Lebanese state (Rigby, 2000: 173), especially as it had close alliances with Muslim parties and elites in the country.

In addition to the external factors, domestic factors also undermined the ability of the National Pact to ensure stability and ultimately helped spark the civil war. One of its main causes was the increase in the population of the Muslim community stimulating them to request an equal level of participation and share in the political system (Soffer, 1986). The change in their demographic size challenged the Christian privileges in the political system and therefore the Muslims requested constitutional amendments to re-distribute state positions equally between Muslims and Christians. According to Hudson (1988: 231), 'the uneasy (elite) agreement on the key question of the *distribution* of power among sects within the elite cartel came to be challenged both on the elite and mass levels'. The inability of the National Pact to ameliorate these conflicts rested on several incorrect assumptions contained within the Pact. It was based on the assumption that the demographic sizes of the sectarian groups would not change in the future. Therefore, it distributed the state positions according to the census of 1932. The Lebanese scholar and MP, Farid el-Khazen (1991: 39), states that there were two more faulty assumptions:

[A]n internal one based on the belief that elite consensus reflected grassroots communal support; and an external one derived from the assumption that the balance-of-power in the region would remain unchanged in the sense that it will always reflect the value system of the first generation of conservative pro-Western Arab nationalists. Future events showed that these faulty assumptions were at the root of conflict in Lebanon.

The Lebanese civil war had significant repercussions for Lebanon's demography and political life. Firstly, a significant portion of the Christian community migrated; about 100,000 Lebanese migrated from Lebanon, and most of them were Christians. It also caused the death of more than 100,000 Lebanese citizens and more than twice that number were wounded and maimed (Rigby, 2000: 169). The decline in the number of the Maronite community ranked them as third after the Sunni and Shiite communities, which made it difficult for them to claim the privileges that they had held before the civil war in the political system (Sirriyeh, 1998: 63). Secondly, during the civil war, several new political parties and elites emerged. A group of Shiite members separated from the Amal Movement, which was headed by the current speaker of parliament Nabih Berri (1992–present), and went on to form Hizbullah in 1982. Moreover, the Lebanese Forces Party (LFP) was formed as a loose coalition of Christian militias of the Kataeb Party, al-Ahrar, Guardian of the Cedars and other Maronite paramilitary units not affiliated to any political party or militia (Rowayheb, 2006: 312). In addition, the Christian political leader and former commander-in-chief of the armed forces, Michel Aoun, emerged as the most popular Christian leader due to his political and military opposition to the Syrian military presence in Lebanon and the Ta'if Agreement (Traboulsi, 2007: 242).

The Ta'if Agreement and its Constitutional Amendments

The Lebanese civil war eventually ended with the ratification of the Document of National Accord (the so-called Ta'if Agreement) in 1989. It was enacted in Ta'if, Saudi Arabia and under the auspices of the Arab League with the support of the US and France. The agreement redistributed the state administrative positions equally between the Muslim and Christian communities. Theodor Hanf identifies the main difference between the Ta'if Agreement and the National Pact. He (1993: 587) argues that '[t]he fundamental difference between the new coexistence pact of Ta'if and the National Pact of 1943 lay in the distribution of power. The old pact was a matter between two communities, the new one was between all communities on the basis of parity between Christians and Muslims.'

The Ta'if Agreement outlined the steps that were needed to complete the transition to a stable and democratic system. The agreement called for the transition to the Second Republic (from the First Republic 1943–90), which should ensure the implementation of the following steps. Firstly, the first elected parliament on a sectarian basis was supposed to form the so-called National Body for the Elimination of Confessionalism (Ta'if Constitution, 1989: Chapter 1, Part 2, Article G; Traboulsi, 2007: 244). This body should be formed with the agreement of all Lebanese sectarian communities and was to be tasked with the development of steps to eliminate confessionalism. Secondly, the Ta'if Agreement called for the formulation of a new electoral law, with the province (*Muḥāfaẓa*) as its electoral district, which would ensure equal and fair representation for all Lebanese factions (Ta'if Constitution, 1989: Chapter 1, Part 3, Article D). An electoral law based on large districts ensures that the majority of the electoral districts will be composed of more than one sectarian community, thus forcing parliamentary candidates to adopt a cross-sectarian and national rhetoric to mobilize popular support.

Thirdly, it stated that all Lebanese political groups should form a national unity government in accordance with the consociational principle of an elite cartel and grand coalition (Ta'if Constitution, 1989: Chapter 2). Fourthly, the term of the speaker of parliament was to be extended from one to four years to match the length of each parliament (Ta'if Constitution, 1989: Chapter 1, Part 2, Article A). After implementing these steps, Lebanon would complete its transition to the Third Republic. The Third Republic should witness the election of MPs on a non-sectarian basis. Also, a senate was to be formed that would include representatives of the sectarian communities. The agreement also suggested administrative reforms, in particular administrative decentralization (Ta'if Constitution, 1989: Chapter 1, Part 3, Article A). Each district or smaller unit would have an elected council aiming to enhance the socio-economic development of its district.[4]

However, the endorsement of the Ta'if Agreement was indeed based on the faulty assumption that national reconciliation between the communal groups had occurred. The formulation of the agreement 'presupposed that a national consensus existed in Lebanon at the end of the war, and that it was consecrating it with Syria as the godfather overseeing this process. So, in effect, Ta'if was based on the false premise that national reconciliation had occurred' (Kerr, 2006: 178). In his analysis of Lebanon's consociational model and the Ta'if Agreement, Kerr argues that Lebanon's main power-sharing Ta'if Agreement would not have happened without foreign support. He (2006: 178) concludes in his study that any solution to Lebanon's civil war would come second to the regional and international conflicts, so reaching a settlement in regard to the civil war had to wait until a regional agreement was in place. 'Thus, the timing of the agreement had little to do with the Lebanese, nor was it a symbol of Lebanon's capacity to transform its yearning for peace into a political settlement' (Kerr, 2006: 159).[5]

The main sectarian community which at the time opposed the Ta'if Agreement was the Christian community. Its opposition to the Ta'if Agreement rested on two grounds. Firstly, it argued that it weakened the main Christian position in the state, namely the presidency. Although it left the top three offices, president (Christian Maronite), PM (Muslim Sunni), and speaker of parliament (Muslim Shiite), unchanged, the Ta'if Agreement adjusted the powers that were endowed to each one of them. It transferred executive powers from the president to the cabinet, which was to be presided over by the PM rather than the president, which was different from the arrangement in the National Pact. In addition, the cabinet's powers were increased with the requirement that the appointment of the PM by the president should be made only after binding consultation with the MPs that nominate the PM (Ta'if Constitution, 1989: Chapter 1, Part 2, Article B). However, before the civil war, the president used to decide on the PM without the consultation of parliament. Secondly, the Christian parties at the end of the war were deeply divided (as was seen in the Aoun and Geagea military conflict in 1989) and 'defeated' by the Muslim parties (in particular the Progressive Socialist Party (PSP)) which were supported by the Syrian regime.[6] Thus, the 'legitimization' of the Syrian military presence in the Ta'if Agreement was interpreted by the Christians as a further tool to enhance the domination of Damascus' allies, that is, Muslim parties, on Lebanese politics.

In addition to the Christian 'grievances', the Ta'if Agreement suffered from several flaws (Salam, 2007). One of the main flaws was the inadequate distribution of power between the state institutions. Many of the president's executive powers were eliminated or weakened. For instance, the cabinet before the civil war could not take any decision without the approval of the president; however, the Ta'if Agreement limited the role of the president to attending cabinet meetings without the right to vote (Traboulsi, 2007: 245). Therefore, the political coalition that had the majority of the cabinet posts would be able to take decisions that sometimes met its interests because of the denial of the president's right to vote or to veto government policies. For instance, the government was able to ratify a draft law which requested that the United Nations form an international court to try those involved in the assassination of former PM Hariri, although the then president, Emile Lahoud (1998–2007), as well as Shiite ministers, protested against it. In addition, this agreement did not put time limits on the formation of the National Body for the Elimination of Confessionalism which left the time and period of its formation undetermined (Traboulsi, 2007: 244). As a result, this body has still not been formed, although more than 20 years have passed since the ratification of the agreement. Another important weakness is the fact that it did not put time limits on the formation of the government. Thus, government formation often takes several months, which usually causes paralysis in the state institutions.

The Road from Ta'if to the Syrian Military Withdrawal in 2005

The end of the Lebanese civil war and the ratification of the Ta'if Agreement were followed by Syria's dominance of domestic politics, which lasted for about 15 years (1990–2005). Syria, whose intervention was driven by its own interests, was able to legitimize its military presence through the Ta'if Agreement and the subsequent bilateral agreements between the two countries. It did not withdraw its military forces until the eruption of mass demonstrations against it after the assassination of Hariri on 14 February 2005, and under intense pressure from the international community.

Syria's Interests in Lebanon

Syria's interests in Lebanon are manifold and primarily involve security, economic and political interests. Lebanon's geographic proximity to Syria put Lebanon under Syria's direct sphere of influence and their common geographic borders have long made Lebanon a major security concern for Damascus. According to the former Syrian president Hafiz Assad (1971–2000) (cited in Dawisha, 1984: 229), 'it is difficult to draw a line between Lebanon's security in its broadest sense and Syria's security'. What concerns Damascus more is, however, that Lebanon has common borders with Israel, its staunchest enemy (Gambill, 2003).

Assad's justification for his military intervention in Lebanon during the civil war was that he did not want the Palestinians (in particular the PLO) to defeat the Christian parties, which might stimulate Israeli intervention to save its Christian allies (Salloukh, 2005). At the same time, he did not wish the Christian groups to form their own state in Lebanon, which might also trigger Israeli and other foreign military interventions (Salloukh, 2005). The Lebanese academic Asad AbuKhalil (1990: 7) argues that the 'Syrian military intervention in Lebanon and confrontation with the various sides was motivated by the Syrian attempt to prevent any side in the war from prevailing, and consequently from diminishing Syrian power in Lebanon'. Another security factor that encouraged Damascus to intervene in the Lebanese civil war was that victory for the PLO in the war might encourage the Sunni community in Syria to ask for greater influence in the state apparatus. As the scholar Richard Dekmejian (1978: 262) asserts, 'a leftist-Palestinian victory in Lebanon could have gone beyond an ideological challenge to Syria to assume religious overtones, i.e., a victory for Muslim Sunnite radicals which could in turn spill over into Syria and endanger the Assad regime, and threaten the dominant position of the Alawites in political life'.[7]

In addition to geographic proximity and the related security concerns, the economy of Lebanon was and is important for Syria. Firstly, hundreds of thousands of Syrian labourers work in Lebanon. For instance, about 1.4 million untaxed and unregulated Syrians were working in Lebanon between 1993 and 1995, who used to transfer billions of dollars annually to their home country (Gambill, 2001; Salloukh, 2005). Secondly, Lebanon's economy depends heavily on Syria since it is a key transit point for its exports to Jordan and the Arab Gulf states, which also benefit Syria in terms of the taxes and customs collected on Lebanese exports. It also gives Damascus leverage over the Lebanese government because of its ability to block this trade route. For instance, overland trade that was crossing the Syrian–Lebanese borders in 2005 was estimated to be worth between 600 and 700 million dollars, and Lebanon's own exports via this route only amounted to about 35 per cent of the total exports (Yacoubian, 2006: 2–3). Bassel Salloukh (2005), a Lebanese academic from the Lebanese American University (LAU), highlights the importance of Lebanon's economy for Syria. He states that Syrian domination of Lebanon 'created new opportunities for wealth production and investment outside Syria, allowed the regime to manage the informal economic sector, and enabled it to postpone introducing deeper economic liberalization measures with their inescapable effects on the regime's social welfare commitments'.

After the end of the civil war, another factor emerged which strengthened and increased the Syrian desire to intervene in Lebanese domestic politics. Damascus ensured that the foreign policies of the two countries were identical, in particular regarding the Arab–Israeli conflict which was known as *Talāzum al-Masārayn* (coordination/unity of the two tracks). An identical foreign policy coupled with the existence of an armed resistance (Hizbullah) against Israel served to strengthen the negotiating position of Damascus with Tel Aviv in case a peace agreement was reached between the two countries. 'Lebanon, firmly anchored in the Syrian orbit, served as Damascus's strategic depth', Emile el-Hokayem (2007: 38) argues, 'It guaranteed good-faith negotiations over the Golan Heights from a position of relative strength. The Western and Israeli assumption underlying Syrian–Israeli talks was that Damascus would constrain and eventually disarm Hizballah once peace was reached.'

The 'Legitimacy' of the Syrian Intervention after 1990

At the end of the civil war in 1990, Syria was supposed to withdraw its military forces from Lebanon. Although the pretext for its intervention did not exist after the end of the violent sectarian conflict in 1990, Syria was able to consolidate its power and gain official legitimacy from the Lebanese government for its military presence. Several factors 'legitimized' the Syrian military presence in Lebanon in the postwar period.

Firstly, the Ta'if Agreement granted legitimacy for the Syrian military presence with the pretext that the Syrian military forces were needed to ensure stability and prevent the eruption of future conflict between sectarian groups after the end of the civil war (Harik, 1997: 251). According to the Lebanese academic, Nawwaf Salam (2003), although Damascus did not attend the Ta'if negotiations, the agreement would not have reached a conclusion without its approval. Salam (2003: 41–2) maintains that the sections in the agreement dealing with the Syrian presence in Lebanon could not be amended by the Lebanese political parties because of the agreement between Damascus and the Arab Tripartite Committee which endowed Damascus with significant influence over Lebanese politics.[8] If they had rejected the articles in the agreement regarding the Syrian presence in Lebanon, the Ta'if Agreement would not have reached a conclusion (Salam, 2003: 41–2).[9] The Ta'if constitution (1989: Chapter 2, Article D) stated that:

> [T]he Syrian forces shall thankfully assist the forces of the legitimate Lebanese government to spread the authority of the State of Lebanon within a set period of no more than 2 years, beginning with the ratification of the national accord charter, election of the president of the republic, formation of the national accord cabinet, and approval of the political reforms constitutionally. At the end of this period, the two governments – the Syrian Government and the Lebanese National Accord Government – shall decide to redeploy the Syrian forces in al-Biqaa area from Dahr al-Baydar to the Hammana-al-Mudayrij-'Ayn Darah line, and if necessary, at other points to be determined by a joint Lebanese–Syrian military committee.

However, the Ta'if Agreement did not mention an enforceable timetable for the ultimate departure of Syrian forces from Lebanon. In fact, the ultimate withdrawal would come after the agreement of the governments of both states and contingent on the 'approval of the political reforms', which is an ambiguous condition since it is not clear what is referred to: is it the approval of these reforms in cabinet and parliament only or their implementation, for instance, the elimination of confessionalism and the election of a new parliament on a non-sectarian basis?

In addition to the vagueness of the agreement regarding the final departure of Syria's military forces, the Ta'if Agreement stated that Lebanon would not allow any aggressive action or threat to emanate from its territory against Syria. It (Ta'if Constitution, 1989: Chapter 4) stated that:

> Lebanon should not be allowed to constitute a source of threat to Syria's security, and Syria should not be allowed to constitute a source of threat to Lebanon's security under any circumstances. Consequently, Lebanon should not allow itself to become a pathway or a base for any force, state, or organization seeking to undermine its security or Syria's security.

This article secured confirmation for Damascus that Beirut would not threaten the security of its neighbour through, for instance, the emergence of anti-Syrian armed groups; in particular the security factor was one of the main factors that motivated Syria to interfere militarily in Lebanon.

Secondly, Damascus was able to extend and entrench its presence and legitimacy on Lebanese soil through a number of follow-up agreements that were signed between the two states. Beirut and Damascus signed more than 30 bilateral agreements after 1991 (SLHC, 1991). The most prominent of these was the Fraternity, Cooperation and Coordination Treaty (FCCT), signed in May 1991. This agreement strengthened further the relations between the two countries through the formation of joint councils that would elaborate and oversee implementation of policies regulating economic, political and military affairs (Harik, 1997: 251). The main council that was formed as part of the Agreement was the Syrian–Lebanese Higher Council (SLHC), headed by the presidents of the two countries (FCCT, 1991: Article 6, Section 1). The council 'shall set up the general policy of coordination and cooperation between the two states in the political, economic, security, military and other fields' (FCCT, 1991: Article 6, Section 1). In addition, a spin-off of the FCCT was the Defence and Security Agreement (DSA). The aim of this agreement was 'to examine the ways likely to preserve both states' security and propose joint measures to face up to any aggression or threat against their national security or any turmoil undermining the internal security of either state' (FCCT, 1991: Article 6, Section 5). However, this agreement neither mentioned whether the military troops of each country would be limited to their own borders, nor gave a timetable for the final withdrawal of the Syrian military troops (Thompson, 2002: 82).

Thirdly, Syria's consolidation of power and intervention in Lebanon was enhanced by the tacit Western acceptance of its military presence (Traboulsi, 2007: 245). The former Lebanese ambassador to the US, Abdullah Abu-Habib, argues that Washington was convinced that Lebanon would not be able to achieve internal peace without Syrian support (Abu-Habib, 1991: 107–63). 'US tacit support for a *fait accompli* in Lebanon is a policy the Syrian leadership has come to understand since the mid-1970s and has learned to turn to its advantage' (el-Khazen, 1998: 31). This conviction was reaffirmed when Damascus was granted full support from the international community to 'dominate' Lebanon as a reward for its support for the Gulf War in 1990 led by the US (Thompson, 2002: 88–90). Without tacit international support, Damascus would most likely have been unable to consolidate its power in Lebanon between 1990 and 2005.

The Syrian Military Withdrawal in 2005

Although Damascus had been able to 'legitimize' its presence in Lebanon for 15 years, it was forced to leave the country in April 2005. The Syrian military withdrawal would not have materialized without the intersection of two main factors: international and domestic.

On the international level, the conflict between the US and Syria which erupted after the Iraq War in 2003 played an influential role in encouraging Washington to exert pressure on Damascus to withdraw its forces from Lebanon. The Syrian regime's opposition to the Iraq War and its support for anti-US armed groups in Iraq escalated the conflict between the two countries. This provoked the US to request that Damascus cooperate against the smuggling of extreme groups to Iraq over its borders (Fisk, 2009). The US accused Syria of helping Saddam Hussein's military forces and Baʿth Party members, smuggling jihadists to Iraq to fight the American military forces, assisting organizations classified by the US as terrorist organizations, and developing weapons of mass destruction (Salhani, 2004: 4). As a consequence of the conflict between Washington and Damascus, the United States Congress (USC) promulgated the Syria Accountability and Lebanese Sovereignty Restoration Act in 2003 calling on Syrian military troops to withdraw from Lebanon (USC, 2003). It was not the only US attempt to put pressure on Damascus. In fact, the US and France also sponsored the United Nations Security Council (UNSC) issuance of Resolution 1559 in September 2004, which also called on the Syrian military troops to leave Lebanon (UNSC, 2004).[10]

The French position against Syria initially arose because of the constitutional amendment proposed by Syria's allies in parliament to extend the presidential term of Lahoud for three years; this was in September 2004. President Jack Chirac (1995–2007), who expressed his opposition to the constitutional amendment, became very critical of Syrian intervention after the assassination of his friend, Rafic Hariri, in 2005 (Blanford, 2006: 31; Fisk, 2009).[11] Before the assassination, several factors encouraged the French collaboration with the US against Assad. Washington and Paris accused the Syrian regime of supporting Hizbullah and the Palestinian armed groups in Lebanon politically and militarily, 'undermining the authority' of PM Hariri, and renewing the constitutional term of Lahoud (Baroudi & Salamey, 2011: 403). In addition to the aforementioned factors, France wanted to secure its foothold in Lebanon, especially as Lahoud was considered a very close ally of Syria. 'The French government wanted an understanding with Assad involving a degree of Lebanese independence and respect for French influence in Beirut, in exchange for French buttressing of Syria's position in the Levant' (Harris, 2005).

It was not only the US and France that requested Damascus' withdrawal from Lebanon. The assassination of Saudi Arabia's closest domestic ally, Hariri, was interpreted as undermining the Kingdom's influence in Lebanon. It 'was incensed at the callous dispatching of its Lebanese protégé, seeing in Hariri's death and the preceding months of humiliation and death threats a deliberate attempt to weaken the kingdom's influence in Lebanon' (Blanford, 2006: 148). Thus, Riyadh requested that the Syrian troops leave the country immediately. In a meeting between Bashar Assad and then Crown Prince of Saudi Arabia Abdullah in 2005, Abdullah 'advised' Assad to withdraw his troops from Lebanon without delay (Blanford, 2006: 158).

Domestic developments were also exerting pressure on the Syrian regime to withdraw its military forces. As the discussion in this chapter and the following chapters will show, the assassination of Hariri sparked popular uproar against the Syrian intervention in Lebanon and led to the formation of a multi-confessional coalition from the Sunni, Druze and Christian communities against the Syrian presence and the constitutional amendment of Lahoud's presidency, known as the March 14 Coalition in reference to the protest organized by anti-Syria parties on 14 March 2005. Nicholas Blanford (2006: 161) states that '[t]he March 14 rally was the climax of the month-long independence intifada and was deliberately intended to convey a message to the Shiites [i.e. Hizbullah] that, as far as other communities were concerned, the bulk of Lebanese wanted the Syrians gone and a new independent government installed'. This coalition exerted pressure on the pro-Syrian PM, Omar Karami, to resign and contributed to Assad's decision to withdraw from Lebanon in 2005 (Baroudi & Salamey, 2011: 406–7).

Overview of the Lebanese Political Parties

The Syrian withdrawal led to the emergence of new political parties which had either been prohibited during the Syrian era or were formed by political elites after 2005. The party political landscape in post-Syria Lebanon can be classified in two categories: pre- and post-2005 political parties. The main historical parties in Lebanon, which were formed before the Syrian withdrawal, are Hizbullah, the Amal Movement, the PSP, the LFP, the Kataeb Party, the el-Marada Party, the Syrian Social Nationalist Party (SSNP), the Lebanese Democratic Party (LDP) and the Tashnak Party. The political parties that emerged after 2005 are mainly the Christian Free Patriotic Movement (FPM) and the Sunni Future Movement.

The following discussion will focus mainly on the parties that have representatives in parliament, dividing them between the two main coalitions in Lebanon, that is, the March 8 and March 14 coalitions. Those political parties that are not represented in parliament will not be included in the discussion because their political significance is negligible. Table 2.1 outlines the number of eligible voters and number of MPs allocated to each sectarian community. It also shows the voting power of each communal group. Table 2.2 includes the size of the parliamentary blocs of each political party according to the results of the 2005 parliamentary elections. Table 2.3 and Table 2.4 include the number of MPs of each party and the size of the parliamentary blocs according to the results of the latest 2009 parliamentary elections.[12]

The March 8 Coalition, formed after a rally held on 8 March 2005 to show support for Syria, included several political parties that were closely allied to Damascus during its presence in Lebanon from 1990 until 2005. As highlighted above, the main parties that comprised this coalition are Hizbullah, the Amal Movement, the LDP, the SSNP and the el-Marada Party. The only Christian party which joined the alliance in February 2006 was the FPM, after it ratified an agreement with Hizbullah, commonly known as the 'Memorandum of Joint Understanding between Hizbullah and the Free Patriotic Movement' (ICG, 2008b: 31–3). This coalition does not, however, include a party or politician that represents a major portion of the Sunnis.

The most powerful party in the Coalition is Hizbullah. It is a Shiite-dominated party founded in 1982 and headed by its secretary general,

Table 2.1 Eligible Voters of each Sectarian Group and Allocated MPs (2005)[13]

	Sectarian Group	Eligible Voters	Allocated MPs
Islamic Sects	Sunni	795,233 (26.44%)	27 seats (21.09%)
	Shiite	783,903 (26.06%)	27 seats (21.09%)
	Druze	169,293 (5.63%)	8 seats (6.25%)
	'Alawite	23,696 (0.79%)	2 seats (1.56%)
Christian Sects	Maronite	667,556 (22.19%)	34 seats (26.56%)
	Greek Orthodox	236,402 (7.86%)	14 seats (10.94%)
	Greek Catholic	156,521 (5.20%)	8 seats (6.25%)
	Armenian Orthodox	90,675 (3.01%)	5 seats (3.91%)
	Armenian Catholic	20,217 (0.67%)	1 seat (0.78%)
	Protestant	17,409 (0.58%)	1 seat (0.78%)
	Minorities (Christians)	47,018 (1.56%)	1 seat (0.78%)
	Total	3,007,923 (100%)	128

Source: Salamey & Payne (2008: 457)

Table 2.2   Parliamentary Blocs (2005)[14]

Coalition	Parliamentary Bloc	No. of MPs
March 8 Coalition	Change and Reform Bloc (headed by the FPM)	21
	Liberation and Development Bloc (headed by the Amal Movement)	17
	Loyalty to the Resistance Bloc (headed by Hizbullah)	14
	Other Parties (Baath, SSNP, Kataeb, Nasserites)	4
	Total	56
March 14 Coalition	Future Bloc (headed by Future Movement)	39
	PSP Bloc	16
	LFP Bloc	4
	Qornet Shehwan Gathering (QSG)	7
	Tripoli Coalition	3
	Other Parties (The Democratic Left, Renewal Democratic)	2
	Total	71

Source: Salamey & Payne (2008: 460)

Sayyid Hassan Nasrallah, since 1992. It is an Islamist party that draws inspiration, as well as weapons and funds, from the Islamic Republic of Iran. It was the only Lebanese armed group to keep its arms after the end of Lebanon's civil war in 1990, doing so in order to combat Israel's occupation of southern Lebanon (1978–2000). Hizbullah did not participate in the government during the Syrian era.

The Amal Movement is another Shiite-dominated party headed by the speaker of parliament, Nabih Berri, and a close ally of Hizbullah since 2005. Founded in the mid-1970s by Imam Musa al-Sadr, the Movement was transformed into a close Syrian ally during the civil war and the Syrian tutelage era. While the Amal Movement previously competed with Hizbullah for Shiites' loyalty, the Movement has emerged in recent years as a strong supporter of Hizbullah's military wing. Together they represent more than 80 per cent of the Shiites in Lebanon (BCRI, 2010).

Table 2.3   Number of MPs for each Political Party (2009)

Coalition	Political Party	No. of MPs
March 8 Coalition	FPM	10
	Amal Movement	8
	Hizbullah	10
	el-Marada Party	1
	SSNP	2
	Tashnak Party	2
	Arab Baath Party	2
	Affiliated Independents	20
	Islamic Action	1
	LDP	1
	Total	57
March 14 Coalition	Future Movement	25
	LFP	8
	Kataeb Party	5
	PSP[15]	5
	Democratic Left Movement	1
	Ramagavar (Armenian Party)	1
	Al-Jama'a Al-Islamiyya Party	1
	Affiliated Independents[16]	22
	Hanchak (Armenian party)	2
	National Liberal Party	1
	Total	71

Source: IFES (2009: 1)

The Druze parties in the March 8 Coalition do not represent the majority of their sect. The main Druze party in the March 8 Coalition is the LDP, headed by Talal Arslan. The Arslan family, one of the main Druze political families, used to enjoy wide popular support within its community. However, since the civil war, its popularity among the Druze has declined dramatically. The LDP was formed in 2001 and has one MP in parliament. It established relations with Syria before 2005 and is a supporter of Hizbullah's military wing.[19]

The main non-sectarian party in the March 8 Coalition is the SSNP. It is a small party, founded in 1932 by Antoun Sa'adeh, a Greek Orthodox. Ideologically, the party adheres to a secular form of

Table 2.4   Parliamentary Blocs (2009)[17]

Coalition	Parliamentary Bloc	No. of MPs
March 8 Coalition	Change and Reform Bloc (headed by the FPM)	19
	Liberation and Development Bloc (headed by the Amal Movement)	13
	Loyalty to the Resistance Bloc (headed by Hizbullah)	13
	el-Marada Party	4
	Other Parties and Affiliated Independents (Baath, SSNP, Islamic Action Front, Lebanon Democratic Party)	8
March 14 Coalition	Future Bloc (headed by Future Movement)	29
	Democratic Gathering Bloc (headed by PSP)	11
	LFP Bloc[18]	5
	Kataeb Bloc	5
	Other Parties and Affiliated Independents (Liberal National Party, Democratic Left, Al-Jamaʿa Al-Islamiyya, Ramgavar, Hanchak)	21

Source: Corstange (2010: 288)

nationalism that calls for the creation of a 'Greater Syrian' state, consisting of much of Lebanon, Syria, Palestine, Iraq, Jordan, Cyprus and the Sinai Peninsula along with portions of Turkey (Pipes, 1988: 304–6). In reality, the party has been a close ally of the Syrian regime and a junior partner in the Hizbullah-led alliance.

The major Christian party in the March 8 Coalition is the FPM. It was founded in 2005 and led by General Michel Aoun, who was the head of the Lebanese army in the 1980s, and exiled during the Syrian era due to his political and military opposition to the Syrian military presence in Lebanon. He was also highly critical of Hizbullah's armed wing. However, he, paradoxically, allied himself with the Hizbullah-led March 8 Coalition in 2006 (ICG, 2007: 10–11). The FPM was originally part of the March 14 Coalition and in 2005 it defected from the coalition because of its conflicts with the Future Movement and the

LFP.[20] According to a poll by the Statistics Lebanon Company conducted in 2012, the FPM enjoys the support of about 24.16 per cent of Christians, which is the highest among the Christian parties (Ibrahim, 2012). The FPM is allied with two junior Christian parties and they are part of the FPM parliamentary bloc: el-Marada and Tashnak. The el-Marada Party was founded and is led by the Frangieh family, a Maronite political family from northern Lebanon. The current leader of the party is Sleiman Frangieh, a former interior minister and a close ally of the Syrian regime and Hizbullah. Sleiman Frangieh enjoys the support of about 3.76 per cent of the Christians (Ibrahim, 2012). The Tashnak Party, a major Armenian party, was founded in 1904 (Geukjian, 2009: 741), and is now closely allied with the FPM.

The March 14 Coalition is, by contrast, composed of anti-Syrian and anti-Hizbullah parties. Its main forces include the Future Movement, the Kataeb Party, the LFP and the PSP (2005–9). However, this coalition does not include a major representative of the Shiites, either a political party or a politician. The main party that heads the Coalition is the Future Movement. It is a Sunni-dominated party headed by Saad Hariri, the son of the assassinated former PM Rafic Hariri, who officially established it in 2007. The Future Movement won 25 seats in the 2009 parliamentary elections, making it the largest single party in parliament.[21] Its support is concentrated in the Sunni areas of West Beirut, northern Lebanon, and the southern city of Sidon. It is also a close ally of Saudi Arabia. As of 2010 about 63.4 per cent of the Sunni community expressed support for the Future Movement (BCRI, 2010).

There are no Christian parties in the March 14 Coalition which enjoy a popular support comparable to the FPM. The oldest Lebanese Christian party in the Coalition, the Kataeb Party, was founded by Pierre Gemayel in 1936. It is currently run by his son, the former president, Amin Gemayel (1982–8), who was exiled during the Syrian era from 1988 until 2000. The party had a primary role in the Ta'if Agreement and 'supported government policies [during the Syrian era] and established ties with Damascus' (el-Khazen, 2003a: 616).[22] However, it changed its perspective and became highly critical of Hizbullah's armed wing and the Syrian regime, especially after the Syrian withdrawal in 2005. According to a poll by the Statistics Lebanon Company conducted in 2012, the leader of the Kataeb Party, Amin Gemayel, enjoys the support of about 2.8 per cent of the Christian community (Ibrahim, 2012).

The military branch of the Kataeb Party, which used to be called the Lebanese Forces, split off in the late 1980s. In the early 1990s, the LFP was transformed into a political party. It is a Christian-dominated party led by Samir Geagea and has the support of about 23.84 per cent of the Christian community (Ibrahim, 2012).[23] Geagea was imprisoned during the Syrian era and was freed in July 2005, after parliament ratified an amnesty bill. The LFP is known for its opposition of the Syrian tutelage and Hizbullah's armed wing.

The main Druze party in the March 14 Coalition was the PSP. It is headed by the MP Walid Jumblatt and enjoys the support of the majority of the Druze. The PSP was part of the March 14 Coalition and a staunch critic of Hizbullah and Syria from 2005 until 2009, when Jumblatt changed his political orientation and left the March 14 Coalition (Rowayheb, 2011: 61–4). The PSP historically espoused Arabism and support for the Palestinian cause.

In addition to the political parties, the March 14 Coalition includes several non-partisan figures, such as the MPs Boutros Harb and Robert Ghanem. These independent politicians usually stand for election in joint electoral lists with political parties and thus many of them are members of parliamentary blocs headed by sectarian parties. The most powerful political figure in the March 14 Coalition is Michel Murr, a Greek Orthodox politician, former deputy PM and businessman. Driven by rivalry with Aoun, Murr formed a successful electoral alliance with the March 14 Coalition in the Christian Metn district in the 2009 parliamentary elections. Murr's son, Elias, held several ministerial positions (2000–11), such as minister of interior and municipalities, minister of defence, and deputy PM. He also survived an assassination attempt in 2005.

There are many non-partisan political figures and technocrats who are not affiliated with either of the two coalitions. The most influential is the former PM Najib Mikati (2011–13), a Sunni billionaire businessman from the northern city of Tripoli. He ran as an independent politician on a coalition list including March 14 Coalition figures in the 2009 parliamentary elections. He left the March 14 Coalition in 2009, however, and considered himself an independent politician not affiliated to either coalition. He held the premiership, replacing the current leader of the March 14 Coalition and the Future Movement, Saad Hariri, from 2011 until 2013. In addition to the independent politicians, there are several non-partisan political figures who are classified as technocrats, such as the former minister of the interior, Zayad Baroud, and the former minister of finance, Georges Corm. Unlike independent politicians, technocrats do not usually enjoy wide popular support.

Weaknesses of Lebanon's Consociational Model after 2005

The divergent views of the political parties regarding essential issues, such as the alliance with Syria, contributed to the weaknesses of Lebanon's model in terms of ensuring political stability. They led to the failure of consociational model to form successful grand coalitions to form the government, leading to its failure several times. The weaknesses in Lebanon's consociational model revolve essentially around two points. Firstly, there are flaws in the components of the consociational model which led to its failure to achieve political stability and help transition Lebanon to a stable democratic system as stated in the Ta'if Agreement, such as the flaws in the grand coalition component. Secondly, the absence of several background conditions has undermined the ability of the consociational model to ensure stability and democracy in Lebanon, such as the absence of agreement on state foreign policy.

Lack of Consensus on Fundamentals

One of the major weaknesses Lebanon's consociational model faces is the absence of agreement on fundamental constitutional and political issues which are essential for its functioning. There is an absence of agreement on the following issues: (1) proportional representation of sectarian groups in the state administrations; (2) Hizbullah's military wing; and (3) foreign policy and external threat.

Proportional representation of the sectarian groups in the state institutions is an essential component of the consociational model. In Lebanon, however, some of the sectarian groups are not yet satisfied with the current proportional distribution of state positions. The distribution of power between the main state positions is one of the main contentious issues in Lebanese politics. As mentioned above, the Christian community is calling for a redistribution of powers between state positions to empower the role of the presidency. This is because the Ta'if Agreement reduced the powers that were granted to the president before the civil war, which undermined Christian participation and influence on the political system. What augmented further the Christians' feeling of underrepresentation was their unequal representation in the state administration, such as the main posts in the ministries and security apparatus. During the Syrian era, the domination of the Muslim parties and politicians (such as Berri, Hariri and Jumblatt) over the state apparatus, paralleled with the absence of the main Christian parties, led these parties and politicians to distribute the state positions among them and their followers. This has meant that the number of Muslim employees in the state administrations is larger than that of the Christians. For this reason, the Christian Maronite Patriarch Bechara Boutros al-Rahi considers the current distribution of state administrative positions as 'unfair'. He calls for 'an equal distribution of posts between Christians and Muslims, and the need to fight the marginalization of Christians in the state bureaucracy' (Saab, 2012).

The demands of the Christian community for a widening of its influence in the state institutions conflict with those of the Muslim community. The current distribution of state positions in Lebanon does not truly reflect the numerical strength of the sectarian communities, and the increase in the demographic size of the Muslim community has not been met with a redistribution of state positions so as to really reflect the demographic size of each community. For instance, the distribution of parliamentary seats does not reflect the numerical strength of all sectarian groups. Although the demographic size of the Muslim community is far larger than that of the Christian community, the number of parliamentary seats does not reflect the numerical strength of each group since it divides parliamentary seats equally between Muslims and Christians. For this reason, parliamentary candidates who are running for elections in Muslim-dominated areas, for instance the Baalbeck-Hermal district, have to get three times as many votes to win a seat as those running in some Christian areas (Ciezadlo, 2005). Therefore, the result of the elections in political systems that are based on power-sharing agreements and proportional distribution of state positions between sectarian communities might not fairly reflect the people's will, since the minority and the majority groups (i.e. Muslims and Christians) each elect half of the MPs.

Apart from the conflict over the distribution of state positions, the inability of the Lebanese parties to reach an agreement on Hizbullah's military wing has entrenched mutual distrust between the political parties. Indeed, after the July War in 2006 between the Shiite party and Israel,[24] Hizbullah's military wing was heavily questioned by several political parties, in particular by members of the March 14 Coalition.[25] They became suspicious about its intentions and the 'merits' of its military wing, requesting the disarming of the group. On the other side, Hizbullah rejected their calls to disarm its military wing, stating that the Resistance is essential to protect Lebanon from Israeli attacks. What augmented the conflict over this issue further is the accusation the Special Tribunal for Lebanon (STL) levelled against Hizbullah of assassinating the former PM Rafic Hariri, which the Shiite party denied.[26] Questions surrounding the legitimacy of Hizbullah's military wing have re-emerged every time a new government is formed, since legitimizing it as a Resistance in the cabinet policy statement forces the government to recognize it and allow it to hold military weapons.

Further complicating relations between the Lebanese parties is the conflict over the country's foreign policy direction. Lebanon's political parties are deeply divided over this issue. Relations with Saudi Arabia, Syria, Iran, the US and France are among the basic issues that have divided the Lebanese political parties since 2005. The March 8 Coalition calls for the normalization of relations with Syria, while it is suspicious about strengthening the country's relations with the West. On the other side, the March 14 Coalition holds the opposite view, calling for strengthened ties with the West and for 'suspending' relations with Syria. One of the factors shaping these divisions over the state's foreign policy direction is the nature of the alliances between domestic and foreign players. Almost all of the Lebanese parties seek foreign support. Some of them already had established foreign alliances before the Syrian withdrawal in 2005 (Future Movement and Hizbullah), while others shuffled their foreign alliances after the departure of the Syrian troops (PSP and FPM). For instance, the hostility that erupted between the Future Movement and Syria after the assassination of Hariri led the major Sunni party to adopt a critical position towards the Syrian regime. '[F]rom 2005 on, the Sunnis joined the Christians in perceiving Lebanon as a final arrangement and in viewing Syria as a common enemy' (Haddad, 2009: 411). This has made the formulation of foreign policy since 2005 almost impossible. Each of the two coalitions attempted to formulate a foreign policy that reflects its political orientations.

The March 14 Coalition 'sought to realign Lebanon's international foreign policy in a pro-American direction' while the March 8 Coalition 'resisted this foreign policy realignment' (Salloukh, 2008: 308). Hudson criticizes the Lebanese political class and its inability to formulate a foreign policy. He (1988: 231) asks '[h]ow could a fragile, fractious coalition of notables, representative (in a flawed way) of sects but in terms of their social class position and interests not very representative of changing Lebanese society, steer Lebanon firmly through the shoals of regional politics?'

Confessional Autonomy

One of the factors that contributed to the lack of consensus on fundamental issues is the confessional autonomy that the sectarian groups enjoy. Indeed, confessional autonomy of sectarian communities in Lebanon has helped impede the prospects of building an overarching national identity and enabled the entrenchment of sectarianism. For instance, at present, there is no common educational curriculum. The private schools in Lebanon, often owned by religious sects which have their own education programmes, are blamed for the eruption of the Lebanese civil war. This is because 'the system gave those sects the ability to destroy the identity of the Lebanese and hence their integration, owing to the fact that certain religious sects taught in their schools materials contradictory to those by other religious sects' (Inati, 1999: 56). It is estimated that about 70 per cent of children in Lebanon are educated in the schools of their confessional groups (Rigby, 2000: 172). For instance, there is no common history book that is adopted by schools across the country which would instil a sense of common citizenship. According to Ussama Makdisi (1996: 23), a common history book would help redirect the Lebanese citizen 'towards a common national past and [replace] sectarian narratives that thrived during the recent war (civil war). [Its] ostensible goal is to urge the Lebanese to abandon their "premodern" loyalties of religion that are said to have inhibited the growth of a democratic, civil and secular society.'

The reason behind the absence of agreement between Lebanese sectarian communities and parties on a common history book is their divergent views on the interpretation of the events that have shaped the history of the country, such as the causes behind the civil war and the role of each sectarian community in its exacerbation. They also hold different views concerning the role of different political parties in protecting the state against foreign military threats, such as the role of Hizbullah in liberating southern Lebanon from Israeli occupation, since certain factions of the Christian community (e.g. LFP) consider Hizbullah a militia not an armed Resistance.

Confessional autonomy has also helped prevent intermarriages between members of different sectarian groups. The autonomy that Lebanese sectarian groups enjoy in managing their own personal affairs has played a significant role in widening the sectarian gap between these groups. According to a recent study conducted in 2013 by the Information International Research and Consultancy firm in Beirut, the percentage of intermarriages between Lebanese sects stands at about 15 per cent (173,883) of all marriages (*Assafir*, 2013). Only 10,797 marriages exist between Muslims and Christians, while the rest take place within each religious group. The low percentage of intermarriages stems from two main factors. Firstly, most of the sectarian groups have their own primary and secondary schools and religious institutions, which prevents the development of common education programmes that can instil a common sense of national identity and help overcome cultural differences. Secondly, the sectarian conflicts often lead to internal displacement of Lebanese citizens. For instance, the eruption of the conflict between the leaders of the Sunni and Shiite communities in Lebanon after the Syrian withdrawal in 2005 increased the migration of Sunni and Shiite citizens away from the geographic areas that are dominated by one of them. After 2005, a significant number of Sunnis left ʿAlawite- and Shiite-dominated areas, such as eastern Tripoli and the southern suburb of Beirut, because of the increased hostility between them (IDMC, 2010).

The Grand Coalition and Elite Behaviour

The abovementioned issues are not the only factors that have undermined the ability of the consociational model to ensure stability and democracy. The consociational model in Lebanon has also proven unable to secure the formation of an 'effective' and 'legitimate' grand coalition. This can be explained by the nature of the inter- and intra-sectarian divisions which undermines attempts to form such a coalition, contradicting its main assumption that sectarian groups would be united behind one leadership.

These intra-sectarian divisions are, for instance, evident in the Christian political parties, in particular the FPM and the LFP. Each one of these two parties considers itself the 'actual' representative of the Christian community and therefore lays claim to the main Christian positions in the political system. The conflict between these two parties emerges every time a new government is formed. For instance, after the FPM's victory in the parliamentary elections of 2005 with 21 MPs (which made it the largest Christian parliamentary bloc as its rival the LFP won only 4 MPs), the FPM declared itself the 'leader of the Christian community' (ICG, 2008b: 7). For this reason, it requested four posts in the government that was formed after the elections (BBC Arabic, 2005). However, it failed to reach an agreement with the March 14 Coalition, which had the majority in parliament, over the number of ministries the party should hold.[27] Therefore, the government included members from other Christian parties and did not really reflect the electoral results, which led some to question its legitimacy. Aoun, for instance, stated that the government 'lacks the comprehensive representation of the Lebanese people' (*Asharq al-Awsat*, 2006a).

Even in cases where a political party enjoys the support of the majority of its communal group, this does not mean that the prospects of forming an effective grand coalition are brighter. The party that represents the majority of its community can manipulate its popularity so as to promote its interests. As a consequence of the political conflict that erupted after the July War in 2006 between the March 8 and the March 14 coalitions, Hizbullah and the Amal Movement ministers who represented the Shiite community resigned from the government that was headed and dominated by the March 14 Coalition, which had the majority in government and parliament and did not include major representatives of the Shiite community. Hizbullah and its allies wanted to form a new government in which they would hold the blocking third that enables them to veto government decisions that are taken without their consensus.[28] The exclusion of a major sectarian community from the main governing coalition, that is, the March 14 Coalition, led to vertical segmentation of the Lebanese society between the Sunni and Shiite communities and undermined the legitimacy of the cabinet.

In addition to the weaknesses in the grand coalition component, the behaviour of Lebanese political parties does not always aim to promote stability or democracy. The grand coalition component developed by Lijphart is based on the assumption that the elites seek compromise and accommodate sectarian differences to promote stability and democracy. This does not always materialize. In Lebanon, political parties usually seek to promote their interests and the interests of their sectarian groups, regardless of whether this comes at the expense of democratic reforms. An example is the Future Movement veto of the proposed municipality electoral law for the districts of Beirut in 2010. This law was supposed to divide Beirut, which has a majority of Sunnis, into several districts. The Future Movement's argument was that such a law does not allow the Sunni community to elect its representatives (Bluhm, 2010). The division of Beirut into several districts in which each one includes diverse sectarian communities might undermine the ability of the Future Movement to win elections since the Sunni community would be distributed across several districts and its electoral strength would be weakened.

The Need for Foreign Intervention and Regional Stability

As the discussion of the formation of the Lebanese state and the weaknesses of Lebanon's consociational model has demonstrated, domestic Lebanese politics have suffered from foreign intervention ever since its formation. Three factors have encouraged foreign states to interfere in Lebanon since 2005: (1) the weaknesses of the consociational model; (2) the absence of a domestic arbiter; and (3) the location of the country in a turbulent region. These factors are tightly inter-linked. For instance, the weaknesses in Lebanon's consociational model coupled with the country's location in a turbulent region have made Lebanon subject to intensive foreign intervention.

Lebanon's consociational model plays a primary role in encouraging foreign intervention. According to the Lebanese politician and former leader of the Kataeb Party, Karim Pakradouni, 'the political system provides a space of freedom for the sectarian communities to build alliances with external actors'.[29] He argues that 'the sectarian groups are interested in external support to hold more power and external forces are interested in keeping sectarianism in order to sustain their interference in internal affairs'.[30] The consociational model's recognition of the sectarian communities as political communities encourages the latter to compete over the domination of the political system. This can be explained by reference to the absence of a stable balance of power between the sects, which exerts extensive pressure on them to seek means to empower their position against each other.[31] The sectarian communities 'are compelled by the situation to act as if they were states in an international environment' (Hudson, 1985: 9). This desire to build external alliances increases particularly during periods of political instability and conflicts, since they will be 'forced' to build alliances with foreign countries, which can provide 'protection' and support (Kerr, 2007: 238).

The inability of the Lebanese political parties to resolve their political and sectarian conflicts without foreign intervention and their dependence on foreign players to bolster their domestic positions can be explained by the absence of a conflict-regulating mechanism. Indeed, the Lebanese constitution does not provide a mechanism to solve political conflicts and prevent paralysis within the institutions of the state. The constitutional institutions, such as parliament and government, have been unable to accommodate political differences and conflicts without foreign intervention. The Lebanese jurist, Salim Jreissati (2011), argues that the Ta'if constitution cancelled the domestic arbiter role on the basis that governing the state is based on a power-sharing agreement meaning that no single position has the right to hold decisive authority.[32] The president must not hold wide-ranging powers, such as the right to dissolve parliament or government, because such far-reaching decisions should only be taken with the agreement of all the sectarian communities.[33] Therefore, a foreign arbiter has often been necessary to promote stability and inter-sectarian compromise. According to Zahar's (2005: 235) historical analysis of power-sharing arrangements in Lebanon, 'a foreign protectorate has been necessary – and perhaps sufficient – to secure domestic peace and stability, even without the support of all Lebanese communities'.

The absence of the 'arbiter role' has made the success of the power-sharing agreement dependent on external support. The pre- and post-2005 periods can shed light on this point. During its military presence in Lebanon, Syria used to ensure the 'agreement' between Lebanese political parties over the distribution of state positions between 1990 and its military departure in 2005. It used to interfere so as to distribute, for instance, cabinet posts between them. However, after its withdrawal in 2005, political parties were not able to reach agreement over the distribution of state positions which caused conflicts over their share. Thus, government formation often took several months because of the conflicts over the distribution of cabinet posts. Power-sharing agreements between political elites 'are inherently unstable or are contingent on long-term international commitments, and are therefore not always conducive to durable peace' (Spears, 2002: 129). Therefore, in the event that the international commitment was withdrawn, the power-sharing agreement might fail. '[I]n designing power-sharing arrangements, [foreign] protectors introduced procedural measures to convert politically charged issues into technically tractable matters; yet, this deliberate avoidance of the hard issues of Lebanon's statehood did not make these go away' (Zahar, 2005: 238).

In addition to the drawbacks of Lebanon's consociational model, the geographic position of the country in the turbulent Middle East exposes it to intensive foreign intervention. The endeavour of the domestic groups to seek foreign support often coincides with the intersection of the interests of external players. Bassel Salloukh says, 'the problem of Lebanon is that there is an intersection [of interests] between domestic and foreign players against domestic parties'.[34] He argues that 'the way the country is exposed to external intervention has to [do] with the behaviour of the internal actors'.[35] The Arab–Israeli conflict, the Palestinian refugee crisis and the long-standing Syrian interests in Lebanon have all made the country vulnerable to external interference, both politically and militarily. As Adham Saouli (2006: 708) states:

> The country's multipolar politics provides fertile ground for regional conflicts. In this context, regional and international pressure on either Syria or Israel is *displaced* to Lebanon. Authority in Lebanon was neither centralised in the hands of *one* political power, as in the case of Syria since 1970 or in Jordan, nor *institutionalised* sufficiently to include all political powers. This time lag facilitated the displacement of regional conflicts to Lebanon and provided the conditions for manipulating the domestic balance of power.

Weaknesses of Lebanese Political Parties

In addition to the weaknesses in Lebanon's consociational model and its 'need' for foreign intervention to promote stability, Lebanese political parties also suffer from several weaknesses. As a consequence of the confessional nature of Lebanese society and its consociational system, each sectarian community is headed by one or more sectarian political leader(s). The political leaders of the sects are often considered one of the main factors undermining democracy in Lebanon (Harik, 1998: 136–7). The recognition of each sectarian community as a political community led to the rise of *zu'mā'* (bosses, singular *za'īm*). The *zu'mā'* are the political leaders of their religious groups (such as Saad Hariri, Walid Jumblatt and Michel Aoun). They usually form their own political parties and demand obedience and blind allegiance from their co-religious members to whom they provide services and material awards. The Lebanese scholar, Samir Khalaf (1968: 253), defines fealty as 'the recognized obligation of a leader in return for the loyalty and unquestioned allegiance of a follower [. . .] fealty is sustained by personal commitments and a system of political obligations in which a powerful local leader or *za'im* is owed the personal loyalty of followers and servile dependents'. Therefore, those *zu'mā'* act as trustees and brokers, not as political decision makers. Many of the political leaders hold ministerial positions, in which government positions are often manipulated to obtain their interests.

Lebanese political parties also seek to provide socio-economic services to their followers and are considered the main domestic political players. They act as an agency for mobilizing popular support, and for obtaining the interests of their sects either in the consociational system or by providing socio-economic services, such as employment opportunities, to their religious followers (Cammett & Issar, 2010). 'Although no party in Lebanon reached power and ruled as parties do in parliamentary systems, parties have shaped parliamentary debates and participated in government, and party leaders, particularly those of established parties, are influential political figures' (el-Khazen, 2003a: 605). What is noticeable is that none of the Lebanese parties 'is powerful enough to impose its will upon all others' (Suleiman, 1967b: 690). This can be explained by the absence of a sectarian community that has an overwhelming majority of the Lebanese people. Several weaknesses characterize Lebanese political parties and their political behaviour: sectarianism, the absence of internal democracy, family-based parties, selective formulation of electoral laws to secure their victory in elections and cross-ideological electoral alliances.

The most significant weakness that characterizes Lebanese political parties is their sectarian nature. Most Lebanese parties claim to represent the interests of their sectarian groups. Unlike in Western democracies, where political parties claim to represent the national interests of the people, 'the sectarian element remains the most determining factor of party politics. Most parties/militias are associated with the interests of one single sect or one single ethnic group' (AbuKhalil, 1993: 60). Their sectarian nature has undermined their ability to raise national slogans, for instance to initiate democratic reforms, unless these reforms meet the interests of their groups. Lebanese political parties 'are generally too doctrinaire and the population is too fragmented to allow for adjustment and balancing of divergent views. Nor can they meaningfully link public demands to public policy since they are not in control of political power' (Suleiman, 1967b: 689). Their sectarian representation is often concentrated in certain districts, which has also led them to represent certain geographic areas (Suleiman, 1967a: 267). For instance, Tripoli and Akkar are predominantly Sunni and therefore they are represented mainly by the Future Movement, while the South is predominantly Shiite, represented by Hizbullah and the Amal Movement.

Although several Lebanese parties (such as the Future Movement, the PSP and the FPM) claim to be non-sectarian and secular, they have thus far failed to transform themselves into truly non-denominational parties. Their inability to transform themselves into secular parties can be explained to a large extent by the nature of Lebanon's consociational model, which treats sectarian groups as political communities. This encourages them to mobilize popular support on a sectarian basis as it is more effective than the political platforms, although the sectarian nature of the political parties sometimes runs contrary to their secular ideology (AbuKhalil, 1993: 60). As the following chapters will show, employing sectarian language and inculcating a sense of fear among their followers regarding other sects help widen their popular support within their communities, which can strengthen their negotiating position when asking for a larger share in the quota allocated for their communal groups. The employment of sectarian language to mobilize popular support from one party encourages its political peers to follow suit to similarly mobilize popular support. As Chandra (2005: 235) argues, the formation of one ethnic party can 'infect' the whole party system.

In addition to their sectarian nature, Lebanese parties are not internally democratic. Internal democracy 'involves the organization of free, fair and regular elections of internal positions as well as candidates for representative bodies' (Mimpen, 2007: 2). It also 'involves a different group of instruments that entail the equal and open participation of all members and member groups in such a way that interests are more or less equally represented' (Mimpen, 2007: 2). What inhibited the development of internal democracy is that the majority of Lebanese parties are formed by political families (PSP, Kataeb Party and el-Marada Party). The leadership of these parties is held by members of the founding families, which has prevented the alternation of leadership between the members of the same party. The leaders of these parties are sometimes the relatives of old or deceased leaders, for instance, Walid Jumblatt, the current leader of the PSP, is the son of the former leader of the party, Kamal Jumblatt (AbuKhalil, 1993: 61). Political parties are often established to preserve and spread the influence of the political leader within his sectarian group (AbuKhalil, 1993: 60). Thus, these parties are founded, funded, and have their political decisions taken by their party leaders, which has often made their continued existence dependent on their leadership.[36] The absence of internal democracy and the elitist nature of Lebanon's political parties have made sure that 'elitism in party structure cuts across ideological lines [...] all of these parties and organizations – left or right, sectarian or ostensibly secular – suffer from an unusually high allegiance to a personality cult of the party leader that hinders popular participation in the party's policy making' (AbuKhalil, 1993: 60). The significance of traditional political families in Lebanon was evident in the 2009 elections, when they were able to win 37 per cent of parliamentary seats (Haddad, 2010: 69).

Further to the weaknesses discussed above, Lebanese political parties have always sought to formulate electoral laws that suit their electoral strategies. As the discussion in the following chapters will show, the electoral laws of 1992, 1996, 2000, 2005, and 2009 were all formulated selectively so as to secure victory in the elections.[37] The importance of the electoral law for Lebanese parties is that it can help strengthen their ability to win the majority of seats in parliament that are allocated for their communities through, for instance, formulating electoral laws based on small districts.

The electoral laws that have been adopted since 1992 were all based on a winner-takes-all system with small districts which were often dominated by one main sect. This enhanced the ability of Lebanon's political parties to win elections with simple majorities. The International Institute for Democracy and Electoral Assistance (IDEA) Handbook of Electoral System Design classifies Lebanon's electoral system as the Block Vote (BV) system (Reynolds et al., 2008: 44). In BV systems, the voters are entitled to cast as many votes as there are seats in a certain district, as long as it meets the sectarian distribution allocated for that district. Therefore, voters have the right to add or subtract from the list of candidates of a certain party as long as the sectarian distribution of the list is not violated. In districts that are dominated by a certain sect the political party can win with a simple majority all seats allocated for the district by mobilizing the votes of its sectarian fellows without the need to appeal to other sectarian communities. Where this is the case, political parties are thus encouraged to employ extensively sectarian language to mobilize popular support without the need to adopt a certain political platform. '[E]lectoral laws in postwar Lebanon have served as a vehicle for the hardening of ethnic loyalties, rather than as a tool for ethnic engineering and moderation' (Salloukh, 2006: 641).

The formulation of electoral laws based on small districts which are dominated by a certain communal group secured for the political parties the ability to have the main influence on the formulation of the electoral lists in their districts. If the main sect in the district is represented by one main party, the candidates who represent the minority in the district are forced to weave alliances with the political representative of the main sect to secure their victory. For instance, the Christian politicians standing for election in districts where their community is a minority, such as the northern and southern Lebanon districts, have to build alliances with the main parties that represent the major sects in these districts. Such privilege enables the main political parties in these districts to extract concessions, such as political positions regarding certain issues, from the candidates representing the minorities. In his analysis of the electoral laws in Lebanon, Salloukh (2006: 640) argues that 'none of the postwar electoral systems created genuinely heterogeneous territorial constituencies with incentives for moderation-serving interethnic vote pooling. Instead, the electoral districts in all postwar elections have been purposefully gerrymandered to favour one political leader or another.'

If the electoral districts are not dominated by a certain sect or the sectarian community has more than one main representative, Lebanon's political parties seek to weave sectarian alliances with other parties. These alliances are often temporary, formed only to secure their victory in the polls. Electoral alliances have often been formed between intra-sectarian parties, although they might hold divergent views regarding, for instance, the role of religion in society, such as the alliance between Hizbullah and the more secular Amal Movement (Salloukh, 2006: 238). The electoral alliances have brought together groups with divergent views over essential issues, such as relations with Syria, the position towards the peace process with Israel and the status of Hizbullah's military wing. An example is the alliance of Hizbullah and the FPM in the 2009 parliamentary elections, although the FPM supports the peace process with Israel and Hizbullah completely rejects it. Lebanese parties have thus 'failed to promote national integration and were not able to establish mechanisms for cooperation — except on election day through the formation of temporary electoral alliances' (el-Khazen, 2003a: 606).

The Lebanese Association for Democratic Elections (LADE) identifies several flaws in Lebanon's parliamentary elections because of the behaviour of political parties. Firstly, political parties in certain districts are bribed by candidates to include them in their electoral lists (LADE, 2005: 27–8). As discussed above, the sects that dominate certain districts and are represented by one main party endow their representatives with the ability to formulate electoral lists of their districts because of their voting power. Secondly, the political parties manipulate their position and influence on state institutions to their benefit during the elections. For instance, they seek to provide employment opportunities in state institutions for their followers and/or manipulate their influence over the Ministry of Works to repair and pave the roads in their electoral districts (LADE, 2005: 31–2). Thirdly, they attempt to bribe voters through tangible (e.g. financial support) and intangible support (e.g. improving their employment conditions in state institutions) (LADE, 2005: 29). Fourthly, they often bribe domestic notables who have a significant influence on the voters (LADE, 2005: 30). This approach is frequently employed when the size of the district is too large for the candidate to approach the voters and mobilize them.

In addition to the problems with the behaviour of political parties, the electoral system suffers from the absence of official pre-printed ballots, which is heavily manipulated by the political parties to exert pressure on voters. Prepared ballots are usually distributed before or during election day by activists loyal to a certain party or through family members. LADE argues that prepared ballots serve the interests of the candidates in several ways. Firstly, they are usually written in a way that does not leave a space between the names of the candidates in the list, undermining the ability of the voter to add or subtract names (LADE, 2010: 21). Secondly, they enhance the ability of the candidates to identify who voted for them. Since they are written in a certain way, for example in a particular font, this can increase the chances of the candidates tracing votes back to the voters (LADE, 2010: 21), especially in cases where there is vote buying.

However, not all Lebanese political actors have party organizations. Non-partisan political figures also seek to have their influence on domestic politics, although they do not have the same magnitude of influence enjoyed by the political parties. Political elites are 'a minority of the population which takes the major decisions in the society. Because these decisions are of such wide scope, affecting the most general aspects of the society, they are usually regarded as *political* decisions' (Parry, 1969: 30). In her study of Lebanese elites, Rola el-Husseini, defines them as 'people who exercise power in society or who can be said to have a personal influence on national decision making' (el-Husseini, 2012: xvi–xvii). According to both definitions, a politician does not necessarily have to be a MP or minister. It is sufficient to have a significant influence on the national decision-making process. There are several members of political elites who are not MPs or in government (e.g. Elie Skaff). Those politicians seek to influence national decision making in Lebanon either directly (through their membership in a certain coalition) or indirectly through the pressure that they are able to exert on government. The characteristics of political elites in Lebanon are similar to those of political parties in terms of their claim of representing their communal groups in the consociational system. They compete with the sectarian political parties to improve their position in the consociational system and the position of their communities. They also form inter- and intra-sectarian electoral alliances to secure their victory in the elections (e.g. MP Michel Murr).

Some of them are wealthy businessmen (e.g. Mikati) who are able to provide socio-economic services for their followers and mobilize popular support. Moreover, the political elites seek to build foreign alliances. For instance, the former PM, Mikati, has close relations with Saudi Arabia and the Syrian regime.

Conclusion

This chapter has explored the major drawbacks of Lebanon's consociational model in the post-2005 period. It has argued that Lebanon's consociational model suffers from several weaknesses. These can be classified into two main groups: (1) weaknesses in the four components; and (2) the absence of several background conditions. The absence of agreement on fundamental issues, the confessional autonomy of the sectarian groups, and the nature of sectarian divisions and politicians' behaviour, coupled with weaknesses in the four components, have contributed to the failure of the consociational model in the post-2005 period. In addition, Lebanon's consociational model helps encourage foreign intervention due to the absence of a conflict-regulating mechanism. What has encouraged further foreign intervention in Lebanon is its geographic position in a turbulent region, the Middle East, which has exposed it to heavy external interference. Furthermore, Lebanon's consociational model has significant implications with regard to the sectarian nature of Lebanese political parties. Lebanese political parties have manipulated the sectarian nature of the political system to further their interests, which has then prevented the formation of powerful cross-sectarian parties that are able to promote stability and democracy. As will be shown in the following chapters, these weaknesses, such as the need for foreign intervention to engineer power-sharing agreements and the sectarian nature of political parties, have had considerable consequences for political stability and the democratization process.

CHAPTER 3

THE DEMOCRATIZATION PROCESS IN THE PRE- AND POST-SYRIAN WITHDRAWAL

The weaknesses in Lebanon's consociational model that were explored in the previous chapter have played an influential role in enhancing Syrian hegemony over Lebanon. Syria was able to use the sectarian groups' conflicts and divisions so as to enhance its influence and domination over Lebanese politics, which in turn adversely affected political freedoms and the democratization process. During the Syrian period, Lebanon did not witness significant progress towards reforming the political system, in particular formulating a new electoral law and eliminating confessionalism. It did witness attacks on political freedoms and civil liberties. Damascus imprisoned and exiled those who stood against its policy in Lebanon and so ensured the loyalty of the existing political class.

By comparing the two periods (pre- and post-2005), this chapter will argue that although the Syrian withdrawal in 2005 was a *necessary* condition for facilitating the success of the democratization process, it was not *sufficient*. It will argue that Lebanon's consociational model enhanced Syrian hegemony over Lebanon and helped spark political and sectarian conflicts in the post-2005 period. The aim of providing a comparative analysis of the two periods is to show how the Syrian withdrawal in 2005, which ended Syria's playing the 'arbiter role' to solve domestic conflicts, helped exacerbate political and sectarian conflicts and 'motivated' foreign intervention from diverse external players after 2005.

Firstly, the chapter will explore the behaviour of Lebanese political parties during the Syrian period. In doing so, the following sections in the chapter will be able to shed light on how the close alliance between the political class and Damascus impacted upon the initiation of the democratic reforms. Secondly, the chapter will discuss the Syrian era and its implications for the democratization process, as well as how the consociational model enhanced Syria's hegemony over Lebanon. Finally, it will briefly explore the post-Syrian era and the eruption of sectarian conflicts and divisions.

The Behaviour of Political Parties and Politicians during the Syrian Era

The presence of Syrian military forces, bilateral agreements, tacit Western support for Damascus and the Ta'if Agreement's 'legitimization' of its presence had made Damascus the most powerful player in Lebanon from 1990 until 2005. This led many Lebanese political parties to express their support for the Syrian military presence so as to secure their political survival, which to a large degree shaped their behaviour in this era.

Several factors help explain why Lebanese politicians at the time were willing to enact the bilateral agreements with the Syrian regime and cement their relations with it. Firstly, Damascus became a de facto power in Lebanon from 1990 onwards. The presence of more than 20,000 Syrian military troops and their intelligence forces endowed Damascus with wide political power. What further enhanced Syrian power and encouraged Lebanese parties to comply with it was the Ta'if constitution, which considered Syrian troops to be necessary to ensure stability. Secondly, several Lebanese parties, especially these political parties that represent the Muslim sects (Sunni, Shiites and Druze), such as the Amal Movement and the PSP, were supported politically and militarily by Syrian troops in their sectarian conflicts against the Christian armed militias during the civil war. This gave Damascus extensive political power and influence over them. Thirdly, Damascus was able to exert pressure and threaten Lebanese politicians who stood against it, for example forcing General Michel Aoun into exile.

The Lebanese political parties' and elites' alliances with Damascus were one of the main factors that secured their interests in the political system. Indeed, during this period, competition between political parties revolved mainly around strengthening their relationship with the Syrian regime. As el-Khazen (2003a: 623–4) asserts, '[i]n a political system that restricts foreign policy to a few slogans and domestic policy to constant feuding between politicians competing for privileged access to Damascus, political pluralism has a predetermined margin, and competition between government and opposition is confined to that margin'. Even the issues of 'governance, freedom of expression, human rights, and foreign policy do not figure on the agenda of political parties and, when they do, they are given low priority' (el-Khazen, 2003a: 618). In fact, it was not only Lebanon's political parties that sought to forge alliances with Damascus, but over 80 per cent of the non-partisan politicians who won parliamentary elections in 1992 and 1996 had robust relations with Syria (el-Khazen, 2003b: 69–70). The permanent alliance between the Lebanese domestic groups and Damascus reproduced almost the same political class from 1990 until 2005. '[T]here will only be one of two forms of elite circulation: members of the elite are chosen from within the pool of incumbents and a number of would-be incumbents ready to be co-opted' (el-Husseini, 2004: 261).

The close alliance of political parties and politicians with Syria turned Damascus into the main arbiter to solve conflicts between the Lebanese groups, endowing it with significant influence over their behaviour and decisions. Damascus' powerful arbiter role was used to enforce compromises when Lebanese political parties became intransigent and inflexible in regard to a political conflict, for instance over the distribution of cabinet posts. It used to represent a guarantee against the exacerbation of conflicts between the political parties and elites. '[T]he presence of a protector encouraged mutual intransigence on many issues by decreasing the painful consequences associated with hardened positions' (Zahar, 2005: 238). As the discussion of Syrian influence on the democratization process and political stability will show in the following section, the key influence of Syrian intervention on the behaviour of Lebanese politicians was its ability to enforce a compromise whenever there was a conflict between, for instance, the governing troika: former president, Elias Hrawi (1989–98), speaker of parliament, Nabih Berri, and former PM, Rafic Hariri (Hinnebusch, 1998: 150–1).

The political dominance of the 'loyal' political parties and politicians on state institutions helped them cement their dominance over their sects through funnelling state revenues and services to their followers. They manipulated state positions to improve their own status within their sects which 'reinforced political feudalism and blocked challenges to the elites' power. With the backing of the protectorate, these elites could quell all challenges to their own power in the guise of a defense of the power-sharing peace accord' (Zahar, 2005: 239). For instance, three main development and economic institutions were headed by Syria's allies in the post-civil war period and are still functioning in post-Syria Lebanon. These institutions were manipulated to provide socio-economic services (Ghosn & Khoury, 2011: 391), and to widen and strengthen the influence of political parties and leaders within their sects. The first such institution is the Central Refugees Fund, run by a figure close to Jumblatt's PSP and funded by the Lebanese government. This institution is supposed to fund and construct the houses and villages for Lebanese displaced due to the civil war. However, the funds were distributed to the supporters and followers of the Druze leader, Walid Jumblatt, although 70 per cent of the displaced in the Lebanese mountain region were Christians (el-Khazen, 2001). Thus, the 'same war leader [in reference to Jumblatt] who had played a role in the largest displacement (that from Mount Lebanon) was now given national responsibility for IDP (Internally Displaced Persons) return' (Assaf & el-Fil, 2000: 32). The Ministry of the Displaced, headed throughout the Syrian period by Jumblatt and his party members, spent 800 million US dollars between 1991 and 1999 (el-Husseini, 2012: 114–15). However, only 20 per cent of the displaced were able to return to their villages (el-Husseini, 2012: 114–15).

The second institution used for patronage purposes was the Council of the South, headed by one of Berri's deputies and tasked with reconstructing southern Lebanon due to the Israeli occupation (Nizameddin, 2006: 112). The Shiites' predominance in the South and their poverty 'make the region appealing to Shiite politicians who seek to establish leadership in their community, channel political and financial profits, and secure and enjoy unlimited Syrian backing' (Adwan, 2005: 11). Therefore, Berri secured control of the Council of the South which allowed him to funnel emergency aid and development projects to the Shiites of southern Lebanon (Adwan, 2005: 11). In his study of the politics of corruption in Lebanon, Reinoud Leenders (2004b: 187) states that 'Birri enjoyed near autonomy in running the reconstruction and relief program for the south, via the Council of the South.'

The last institution to mention here is the Council for Development and Reconstruction (CDR), headed by a figure close to Rafic Hariri and his son Saad. It is funded mainly by the Lebanese government to reconstruct areas devastated by the civil war. From 1992, the CDR 'grew into the government's main instrument for planning, financing, and implementing the country's reconstruction program' (Leenders, 2004a: 182). Many of the employees in the CDR were originally employees of the former PM Hariri and continued working for his private companies or as his private advisors (Leenders, 2004a: 183). The CDR operates mainly in Beirut, Hariri's main electoral district. Hariri's main focus on Beirut was because it is the capital and includes a large Sunni constituency. It is 'the city that gives most legitimacy to a Prime Minister not only because it is the capital but also due to its significant Sunni constituency' (Adwan, 2005: 9).

The Syrian presence not only entailed support for Damascus' allies, but also the marginalization of other religious groups and their political parties and leaders. One such group was the Christian community, whose marginalization led it to reject the transition to a de-confessionalized and fully fledged democracy in the pre- and post-2005 periods. Zahar (2005: 239) argues that 'the perceived bias on the part of the protector [in this case Syria] and the heightened insecurity among losers left the latter less willing to forgo power sharing for a non-confessional democracy [...] power sharing backed by a protector heightened suspicions and fed demands for still stronger power-sharing guarantees'. This case was apparent with the Christian community. The concept of 'al-ihbat al-Masihi [Christian hopelessness and discontent]' was coined to reflect the 'grievances' that the Christians suffered during the Syrian presence (Salloukh, 2009: 137–8; Zahar, 2005: 239–40). Their marginalization was mainly due to their opposition to the Syrian military presence in Lebanon. Accordingly, they rejected the 'transition to full democracy in favour of locking in guarantees through power sharing' (Zahar, 2005: 240). They requested improvements to Christian representation in the political system through, for instance, widening and increasing the Christian positions' power and the number of Christian employees in the state bureaucracy.

The Democratization Process and Syrian Intervention 1990–2005

After Syria was able to ensure a 'legitimate' presence in Lebanon as stipulated in the Ta'if constitution, the bilateral agreements, the tacit approval of the international community, and the 'compliance' of the domestic political class, it endeavoured to consolidate its power. This in turn had negative implications for the democratization process, in particular the implementation of the Ta'if constitution's recommendations regarding political reforms. It also led to the exclusion of the main representatives of a major sectarian community from Lebanese political life: the Christians. The persistence of the Syrian military presence and its negative implications for domestic politics can to a large extent be explained by the existence of Lebanon's consociational form of governance. The recognition of the sectarian groups as political communities represented by political parties and elites provided an opportunity for the Syrian regime to play them off against each other, using the conflicts between them, and thus play the role of the 'arbiter' to strengthen and entrench its presence.

The Weaknesses of the Sectarian Communities and the Syrian Role

The weaknesses from which the sectarian communities suffered during the Syrian era can be seen in two aspects of the Syrian influence. Firstly, the Christian community was politically 'marginalized' during the Syrian presence which weakened its ability to have an influence on domestic politics. Secondly, competition between representatives of the same sect was manipulated by Damascus to impose its arbiter role.

The most targeted community during the Syrian military presence in Lebanon was the Christian community. The weakness of the presidency coupled with several grievances led the Christian community to oppose Syrian intervention in Lebanon and boycott the first parliamentary elections after the end of the civil war in 1992. Its first 'grievance' was regarding the problem of the displaced Christians due to the Mountain War in 1983 between the Druze and Christian parties, which was shown to be a marginal issue for the governments that were formed after the ratification of the Ta'if Agreement because they did not put a plan in place for the return of the displaced people (el-Khazen, 1998: 14).

The second 'grievance' was the formation of cabinets with uneven representation, since the major Christian political parties and elites were not represented in the cabinets. Thus, the appointment of Christian figures loyal to Syria in the post-Ta'if governments 'did not help strengthen national unity; rather, they worked to reinforce the negative political atmosphere and lack of trust in the regime's proposals' (el-Khazen, 1998: 14), especially as one of the main Christian figures General Michel Aoun was exiled and not represented in the cabinet. The fourth grievance was the Christians' opposition to the electoral law that was adopted in 1992 which violated the Ta'if constitution (el-Khazen, 1998: 14). The Ta'if constitution stated that the electoral law should be based on large districts while the electoral districts for the 1992 elections were formed selectively to meet the interests of Syria's allies.

As a consequence of Christian opposition, the Syrian security apparatus targeted the Christian community. Most Christian parties and leaders were overtaken from within, dissolved, imprisoned and/or exiled. The leader of the Christian Kataeb Party, Amin Gemayel, for instance, was forced into exile in 1988 and pro-Syrian figures (such as Karim Pakradouni and George Saadeh) took over the leadership of the party. In addition, the Christian party, the LFP, was banned and its leader Samir Geagea imprisoned because he was convicted of assassinating the former PM Rashid Karami in 1987.[1] Furthermore, Damascus exiled and imprisoned several political leaders who were against its military presence. The most prominent anti-Syrian Christian figure, General Michel Aoun, fought against the Syrians in 1989 to force them to leave the country. After a battle in Beirut, Syrian military forces were able to quell his supporters and force him into exile in France in 1990 while many of his supporters were imprisoned. In so doing, the Syrian authorities weakened the ability of the Christian community to be effectively represented in the consociational system. The absence of the main Christian parties and politicians weakened its position to negotiate for a significant influence on the consociational system, such as its ability to shape the formulation of a new electoral law. However, the Christian political parties and leaders which represented the Christian community during the Syrian period enjoyed limited popular support within their sect, which undermined their negotiating position and their ability to veto government decisions.

The Christians were not the only community that suffered from internal divisions and Syrian manipulation, although they were the most targeted. Muslim sects were similarly targeted to ensure their compliance. For instance, Damascus was able to manipulate the conflict between the two rival Shiite parties, Hizbullah and the Amal Movement, especially during the violent conflict that erupted between them in 1988 which continued as a political contestation in Shiite areas in the post-Ta'if period (mainly southern Lebanon and the Bekaa Valley) (Hinnebusch, 1998: 146–7, 51). Syria aimed from this conflict to defeat Hizbullah because it considered the party to be an Iranian 'puppet' which was out of its control. This coincided with the Amal Movement's interest in dismantling its main Shiite political rival politically and militarily, which could strengthen its position in the consociational system as the main representative of its community. Thus, after the eruption of the conflict between them in 1989, Damascus did not exert pressure on its ally, the Amal Movement, to end the conflict until it had ensured that Syrian military forces had entered the southern suburb of Beirut (a Hizbullah-dominated area) and in return had allowed Hizbullah access to the South to fight Israel (Hinnebusch, 1998: 147). By allowing Hizbullah to fight on in the South, Damascus ensured that it had significant influence over it, since the route to smuggle weapons to the Shiite party from Iran was through Syria (Hinnebusch, 1998: 147).

What enhanced further Syrian influence on domestic politics was the absence of the role of arbiter, which the Lebanese president used to play before the ratification of the Ta'if Agreement. Before the Ta'if Agreement, the position of the presidency used to have wide-ranging powers, giving it the ability to play the arbiter role. As mentioned above, the president used to have the authority to veto any government policy, dissolve parliament and have the final decision when a conflict erupted among the political elites. However, the redistribution of powers in the Ta'if power-sharing agreement that were given to the speaker of parliament and the PM, at the expense of the presidency, helped the Syrians to strengthen their influence on Lebanese politics. For instance, the division of powers between a troika of Maronite president Elias Hrawi, Shiite speaker of parliament Nabih Berri, and Sunni PM Rafic Hariri, entailed the overlapping of the powers of the three offices to generate built-in competition, forcing these political leaders to refer to Syrian arbitration in cases of political conflict (Hinnebusch, 1998:

150–1). Whenever PM Rafic Hariri faced obstruction from the speaker of parliament, Berri, for his projects in parliament he used to resort to Syrian mediation to solve the conflict (Hinnebusch, 1998: 150). This led to important decisions being made in consultation with Syria (Hinnebusch, 1998: 150–1). The former minister and MP, and one of the founders of the Ta'if constitution, Albert Mansour (1993: 188–9), confirms the point that '[a]ll important and fundamental decisions were made outside the council of ministers, and later presented to it for ratification. As a matter of fact, decisions were not only made outside the council of ministers, but in place of it.' For instance, the decision to ratify the Defence and Security Agreement was taken outside the government and the Lebanese cabinet was not allowed to amend it (Mansour, 1993: 189). This agreement between Lebanon and Syria which was signed in September 1991 stated that the Lebanese government should pledge to '[p]revent any activity, act or organization in all the military, security, political and media fields that may cause prejudice to the other country' (DSA, 1991: Article 2, Section 211). The importance of this agreement for Damascus was that the Lebanese authorities were then obliged to prohibit any activity that might be 'interpreted' as targeting the Syrian military presence in the country.

With Lebanese political parties and elites complying with Syrian hegemony, Damascus ensured that the holders of key state positions were its allies, in particular the presidents and cabinet ministers. The election of Lebanese presidents was not to happen without Damascus' approval. The Lebanese president, according to the constitution, 'is the head of the state and a symbol of the unity of the country. He shall contribute to enhancing the constitution and to preserving Lebanon's independence, unity, and territorial integrity in accordance with the provisions of the constitution' (Ta'if Constitution, 1989: Chapter 1, Part 2, Article B). Yet the presidents that were elected during the Syrian era, Elias Hrawi and Emile Lahoud, were mainly chosen by Syria. Damascus also forced its allies and members in parliament to amend the constitution to extend the presidency periods of Hrawi and Lahoud by three years, beyond the six years outlined in the constitution (Salloukh, 2005: 20). Also, the appointment of government ministers used to be at the discretion of the Syrian intelligence officer in Lebanon: Lieutenant General Ghazi Kanaan (1983–2002) and subsequently, Brigadier General Rustum Ghazzali

(2002–5). Furthermore, the important and sensitive ministries (such as the ministries of defence, the interior, and foreign affairs) were headed by Syria's allies. In addition, the Lebanese intelligence apparatus was restructured to serve Syria's interests, which used to be called 'the common security Syrian–Lebanese apparatus'. Syrian security officers 'penetrated every nook and cranny of Lebanese life, and had the final say in appointments in almost all public institutions' (Salloukh, 2005: 20).

Political Freedoms during the Syrian Era

The intervention of Syrian authorities in Lebanese politics also carried negative implications for the expression of political freedoms. This is evident in the fact that Freedom House classified Lebanon as a non-Free State for several years between 1990 and 2004. Table 3.1 shows the status of political rights and civil liberties in Lebanon during the Syrian presence from 1990 until 2004. The scores of political rights and civil liberties were mostly between 5 and 6 which designate the country as not free. According to Freedom House (2002), the scores were low mainly because there were shortcomings in the electoral system which limited the right of Lebanese citizens to change their government, the judiciary being under severe Syrian political pressure, and because arbitrary arrest and detention were commonplace for those protesting against the Syrian presence in the country.

During the Syrian era, freedom of expression was severely limited. For instance, in 2002, a demonstration organized by the anti-Syrian Christian opposition group, the QSG, was cancelled by the Ministry of the Interior (Freedom House, 2003). In addition, several anti-Syrian demonstrations that occurred periodically during the same year were crushed by the police and led to several protestors being injured and detained (Freedom House, 2003). The Lebanese authorities were able to provide 'legal' cover for their steps against the opposition to Syrian interference due to the ratification of several bilateral agreements, including the DSA, which judges used 'to censor foreign publications and to indict journalists for critical reporting on Syria, the Lebanese military, the security forces, the judiciary, and the presidency' (Freedom House, 2003).

Elections and Electoral Laws during the Syrian Era

The limited political freedoms that Lebanon enjoyed during the Syrian presence along with the heavy Syrian intervention were two of the main

Table 3.1 Political Freedoms in Lebanon (1990–2004)[2]

1990			1991			1992			1993		
PR	CL	Status	PR	CL	Status	PR	CL	Status	PR	CL	Status
6	5	NF	6	4	PF	5	4	PF	6	5	PF

1994			1995			1996			1997		
PR	CL	Status	PR	CL	Status	PR	CL	Status	PR	CL	Status
6	5	PF	6	5	NF	6	5	NF	6	5	NF

1998			1999			2000			2001		
PR	CL	Status	PR	CL	Status	PR	CL	Status	PR	CL	Status
6	5	NF	6	5	NF	6	5	NF	6	5	NF

2002			2003			2004		
PR	CL	Status	PR	CL	Status	PR	CL	Status
6	5	NF	6	5	NF	6	5	NF

Source: Freedom House (2013)

reasons behind the absence of any democratic progress. The recommendations proposed in the Ta'if Agreement to reform the political system did not materialize, in particular the formulation of a new electoral law based on large districts, the elimination of confessionalism, and the formation of a senate.

One of the main impediments for the democratization process was the selective formulation of consecutive electoral laws during the Syrian era, which were formulated to secure the victory of Damascus' allies and weaken its opponents. The resentment of the Christian community against the Syrian presence in Lebanon had made it the main target of the Syrian authorities and their domestic allies from 1990 until 2005. Thus, consecutive electoral laws were formulated selectively to secure the victory of the Christian leaders who were allied with Damascus and undermine the ability of those who represented the majority of the Christian community to win the elections. In doing so, the Syrian authorities ensured that the Christian MPs would not be able to ask for a large share in the quota allocated for their community, veto government decisions or object to Syrian orders and instructions on the basis that they were not the main representatives of their sect.

One of the most important democratic reforms proposed for implementation in the aftermath of Ta'if was the formulation of a new electoral law based on large districts. Instead of formulating an electoral map which helps overcome confessionalism, the Syrian regime with its domestic allies formulated electoral laws that secured their victory and the marginalization of their sectarian opponents, in particular the Christians. The electoral laws of 1992, 1996 and the 2000 elections are clear examples. The electoral districts of the 1992 elections were divided to secure the victory of Damascus' allies and to exclude anti-Syrian groups. The electoral districts of the North, the South and Beirut were represented by 28, 23 and 19 MPs respectively, while the main Christian districts of Jbeil, Kisirwan and Baabda were represented by three, five and six MPs respectively (el-Khazen, 1998: 21–2). Moreover, the turnout in the 1992 elections stood at a mere 30 per cent, the lowest in Lebanon's history, mainly because of the Christian boycott (Salem, 1997: 27). In his evaluation of the electoral law of the 1992 elections, Hanf (1993: 629) argues that '[t]he new electoral law constituted a complete break with the Taif Agreement. Conceived primarily as an instrument to safeguard and consolidate a pro-Syrian policy, it profoundly disturbed the equilibrium between Christians and Muslims.' Even the timing of the elections was chosen to secure the Syrian military presence in Lebanon. The 1992 elections were held one month before the Ta'if stated deadline (21 September 1992) for the redeployment of the Syrian military forces to the Bekaa Valley. The aim of amending the timing of the elections was to ensure that the new elected parliament would withdraw demands for Syrian military redeployment (Salloukh, 2010: 210–11).

For the 1996 electoral law, the 1992 electoral law was adopted except for one major amendment. The three districts (North Bekaa, Zahle and West Bekaa) in the Bekaa Valley were combined into one main district. The aim of combining them into one district was to weaken the Christians' vote, as they are mainly concentrated in Zahle while other districts in the Bekaa Valley are overwhelmingly Muslim (see Maps 1 and 2). The reason behind this amendment was probably because several Christian political leaders decided to participate in the elections after their recognition that the Christian boycott would not lead to Syrian withdrawal (Khashan, 1997: 25). Instead, it would lead to further marginalization of the Christian community and to strengthening the hegemony of Muslim parties over the consociational system.

Hilal Khashan (1997: 35) notes three main flaws concerning the conduct of the 1996 elections: official manipulation of state institutions, for instance, to formulate electoral laws that suit the interests of the ruling elites; the absence of serious campaign issues; and vote-buying. Firstly, the biased distribution of the electoral districts secured the victory of Syria's allies. For instance, the division of the Mount of Lebanon into six districts, as was promulgated in the 1992 electoral law, secured the victory of Damascus' ally, the Druze leader Walid Jumblatt (Khashan, 1997: 36).[3] Secondly, the slogans that were raised in the elections were vague and did not promise a comprehensive political programme. Hariri's campaign slogan was 'moderation vs. radicalism.' However, he did not explain the differences between his 'moderation' and the 'radicalism' of his opponents (Khashan, 1997: 44–5). Thirdly, there were accusations of voters being bribed. These accusations were mainly against the wealthy businessman and politician Rafic Hariri, who was accused of bribing voters in his district, Beirut (Khashan, 1997: 42–4). The former MP Issam Naaman, who lost the elections to win the Druze seat in Beirut in the 1996 elections, considered the elections to be the worst elections since independence in 1943 since 'authority wedded itself to money' (Khashan, 1997: 42).

In a similar vein, the electoral law of 2000 was formulated by Major General Jamil al-Sayyed (1998–2005), then Director of Lebanon General Security Apparatus, who played a role in producing the draft law in coordination with Syrian authorities at Anjar, then the headquarters of the Syrian intelligence forces in Lebanon. Syria's allies in the cabinet endorsed the law automatically, despite its refutation by then PM, Salim el-Hoss (1998–2000) (Salloukh, 2006: 642). According to el-Hoss (2001: 61):

I was informed by President Lahoud that the Syrian brothers favoured the division of the *Muḥāfaẓāt* [large districts] into small districts, including Beirut, and then we received a project [for an electoral law] delivered to me and to President Lahoud by the Minister of the Interior Michel Murr. And it was well known that

General Jamil al-Sayyed, the Director of General security, played a
role in brokering the project in coordination with the Syrian
'marjīʿiyya' in Anjar [i.e. General Ghazi Kanaan].

Several examples show how the distribution of the electoral districts
and alliances was carried out so as to secure the victory of Damascus'
allies. For instance, the North of Lebanon district was divided in two in
order to weaken the voting power of the banned Christian LFP and at
the same time serve the electoral strategies of the Christian politician
Sleiman Frangieh, a close Syrian ally (Salloukh, 2006: 647). Another
example was that the number of electoral districts in Mount of Lebanon
was reduced from six (as was stated in the 1992 and 1996 elections) to
four, to secure the victory of Michel Murr, Syria's friend and President
Lahoud's ally (Salloukh, 2006: 646–7). In addition to flaws in the
electoral law, it has been estimated that about 200 million dollars were
spent to buy votes and to secure seats in the wining electoral lists
(Salloukh, 2006: 647).

The formulation of electoral laws to suit the interests of
Syria's allies was not the only policy pursued by Damascus.
The Syrian regime also used to force its domestic allies to include
pro-Syrian figures in their electoral lists and electoral alliances. The
Syrian intelligence chiefs in Lebanon, the late Kanaan and his
successor Ghazzali, as well as the Syrian vice-president, Abdul Halim
Khaddam, and the Syrian former chief of staff, Hikmat al-Shihabi,
excluded certain anti-Syria candidates from certain lists and exerted
pressure on its allies to include pro-Syrian candidates (Salloukh, 2006:
641). In the Baalbeck-Hermal district, for instance, Damascus exerted
pressure on Hizbullah to include in its electoral list for the 2000
elections the former advisor to President Bashir Gemayel (August–
September 1982) and former member of the LFP, Nader Sukkar, who
had become a pro-Syrian supporter (Salloukh, 2006: 649).
Furthermore, Damascus strove to control the electoral alliances of
its domestic allies. For instance, in northern Lebanon, it forced an
alliance between two erstwhile rivals, Sleiman Frangieh (a Christian
political leader) and Omar Karami (a Sunni political leader), to join in
a cross-sectarian alliance for the 1992 elections (Salloukh, 2006: 643).
Therefore, Damascus 'ensured that her allies controlled a substantial
percentage of parliamentary seats, and concomitantly held control

over presidential elections, cabinet formation and legislation'
(Salloukh, 2006: 641).

In addition to interventions in the formulation of subsequent
electoral laws, Syria also worked to forestall the formation of the
National Body for the Elimination of Confessionalism and the
establishment of a senate, which was supposed to be established after
the elimination of sectarianism. Syria and its domestic allies rejected
these political reforms because eliminating confessionalism and
forming the senate would have undermined the interests of Syria in
Lebanon. The existing consociational form of governance provided
the space for Damascus to manoeuvre and manipulate sectarian
divisions so as to ensure its political and military presence. During
the Syrian era, Lebanese politicians were not allowed to mention or
discuss the Ta'if Agreement in their political discourse and meetings
because the agreement called for a limited Syrian military presence in
Lebanon (Salloukh, 2005: 19). Thus, 'Syria stuck with the Lebanese
consociational system as it made government easier for Syria to control.
The communities remained divided and lacked any serious unified
Christian-Muslim opposition to Syrian hegemony, right up to the
assassination of Hariri' (Kerr, 2006: 199).

The Democratization Process in the Post-Syrian Era

The withdrawal of Syrian military forces in 2005 was supposed to lead
Lebanon to a stable democratic system. Syrian influence on Lebanon's
domestic politics was significantly weakened. However, contrary to
expectations at the time, Syrian withdrawal did not push the
democratic transition process forward. Instead, since 2005, Lebanon
has been embroiled in political and sectarian conflicts that have led to
political instability and adversely affected the prospects of any
meaningful democratic reform. Four main effects of Syrian withdrawal
on Lebanon's domestic politics can be identified: (1) the absence of the
arbiter role that Damascus used to play to distribute state positions and
revenues; (2) the emergence of Sunni–Shiite conflict represented by the
Future Movement and Hizbullah; (3) the participation of heavily armed
Hizbullah and the major Christian parties in the government; and
(4) intensive intervention from several external players in the country's
domestic politics.

Sectarian Conflicts and Political Instability in
Post-Syria Lebanon

One of the significant effects of Syrian withdrawal was the eruption of open sectarian conflicts (such as political assassinations and the surge of sectarian violence in northern Lebanon). As the discussion in the previous sections has shown, Damascus was the main political player in Lebanon. It was able to distribute state positions and revenues to sectarian communities, political parties and elites. This had prevented the eruption of open conflict between these groups and ensured political stability. However, the absence of the decisive Syrian role in post-2005 Lebanon led to the outbreak of conflicts between the Sunni, Shiite, Druze and Christian parties, which requested greater shares in the consociational system. This conflict over state positions was manipulated by the political parties to attract their sectarian followers on the basis that they were protecting the interests of their sectarian communities in the consociational system.

The existence of parties that represent the overwhelming majority of their sects, in particular within the Muslim sectarian communities, is one of the most significant features of post-Syria Lebanon. Before the eruption of the Lebanese civil war, there was within each sectarian community a wide array of political parties and elites that used to represent significant portions of their sectarian communities, but none of them used to represent the majority. This helped to prevent paralysis in the state institutions.[4] For instance, if the ministers that represent a Druze political party resigned from the government, the PM could nominate ministers from a different Druze political party. However, after the Syrian withdrawal in 2005 the sense of sectarian identity became more entrenched, which helped certain parties to mobilize wide popular support. For instance, the Future Movement became the main representative of the Sunni community in the post-2005 period. In such a situation, the PM is now forced to assign ministers to the principal party representing a certain sectarian community, otherwise its exclusion would mean the exclusion of the whole communal group from the cabinet which violates the proportional principle of the consociational model. The PM has to provide incentives and reach compromises to convince such a party to participate in the cabinet. Therefore, the sectarian political parties are able to veto government or parliament decisions in cases where they undermine their interests or the interests of their respective communities.

One of the implications of the existence of major parties aligned with religious groups was the eruption of the Sunni–Shiite conflict. Having one or two main political representatives of each sect meant that a conflict between those representatives would cause a major sectarian conflict. Since 2005, the conflict that has erupted between the Future Movement and Hizbullah has caused a deep Sunni–Shiite sectarian division.[5] This was manifest in the two major coalitions that emerged after the assassination of Hariri in February 2005. As discussed in the previous chapter, the main coalitions (March 8 and March 14) were headed mainly by Sunni and Shiite political parties respectively.[6] On 8 March 2005, a demonstration in favour of Syria, whose troops had been present in the country since the civil war and which was immediately suspected of the assassination of Hariri, took place. This protest was headed mainly by Hizbullah. As a response to this demonstration, large crowds gathered on 14 March to condemn the murder of Rafic Hariri and call for the withdrawal of Syrian troops. This demonstration on 14 March is also referred to as the 'Cedar Revolution', spearheaded mainly by the Future Movement. The March 14 Coalition accused Syria of assassinating Hariri and several anti-Syrian political figures and journalists, including Gebran Tueni, Walid Eido and Samir Kassir.

The eruption of sectarian conflict, in particular between the Sunni and Shiite sectarian parties, coupled with the existence of one or two major parties representing each sectarian community has had significant repercussions for political stability and the democratization process. The Lebanese academic, Ahmad Baydoun (2012: 64), argues that the 'absence' of political diversity within the religious groups has weakened the Lebanese political system, especially when a political conflict erupts between these groups, such as during the resignation of ministers who represent a major political party. This problem is exacerbated by the absence of an arbiter, a role taken by the president before the Ta'if Agreement, who was able to interfere to solve the sectarian conflicts (Baydoun, 2012: 64), and by Syria from 1990 until 2005. For instance, in 2006, the Shiite ministers (Hizbullah and Amal Movement ministers) resigned from the government, which was headed and dominated by the March 14 bloc, protesting against the government's call for the formation of an international court to try those involved in the assassination of Hariri.[7] It was also because of the

failure of Lebanese parties to form a new unity government which
would secure for Hizbullah and its allies the blocking third. The
resignation of the Shiite ministers from the cabinet undermined the
government's legitimacy and all its decisions were considered
illegitimate by Hizbullah and the Amal Movement. This was because
it violated the Ta'if Agreement's principle that the major sectarian
communities must be represented in the cabinet.

It was not the first time that conflict had erupted over state cabinet
posts. After the 2009 parliamentary elections, the March 8 Coalition
repeated the same request of holding more than a third of cabinet posts.
The reason behind the March 8 position was that the Ta'if constitution
states that the government is considered to have resigned when more than a
third of its ministers resign (Ta'if Constitution, 1989: Chapter 1, Part 2,
Article F). The March 8 bloc aimed to ensure that the government would
not adopt policies that it might oppose, such as a government decision to
disarm Hizbullah's military wing. However, before 2005 Hizbullah did
not participate in the cabinet since Damascus used to ensure that it did not
adopt policies that might target its military wing. After the Syrian
withdrawal, Hizbullah was 'forced' to participate in the government to
protect its military wing. The reason behind Hizbullah's participation in
post-2005 governments, according to one of its leaders, is that 'we never
had sought to be represented in government, because Syria was the
guarantor of the Resistance. After Syria's withdrawal, our governmental
presence became a requirement to preserve the Resistance' (ICG, 2010: 11).
Other new participants in government were the Christian parties in the
March 8 Coalition, in particular the FPM headed by Michel Aoun, which
requested more positions in cabinet on the basis that it represented the
majority of the Christians and as such had the right to hold the majority of
the Christian posts in the cabinet. The conflict over cabinet positions
erupted in 2006 after the resignation of Shiite ministers, in 2009 after the
parliamentary elections, and in 2013 after the resignation of the PM,
Mikati. The formation of these governments took several months and
involved regional engagement and intervention, mainly from Saudi Arabia
and Syria.

In addition to the conflict over state positions, the sectarian
communities cemented robust alliances with foreign powers. The
withdrawal of the major foreign political player from Lebanon in 2005
opened the political space for interference from regional and

international states, such as Saudi Arabia, Egypt, the US and France. The Syrian military presence in Lebanon was a de facto power that 'forced' the Lebanese groups to form alliances with it. However, after 2005, the inability of Lebanon's consociational model to provide a conflict-regulating mechanism to solve political and sectarian conflicts 'motivated' political parties to seek foreign support from different regional and international players to empower their position against their political opponents. According to Baydoun (2012: 103), foreign support for domestic groups increases when a conflict escalates between them, which justifies the intensive foreign intervention that the country witnessed after the end of the Syrian military presence. For instance, the Future Movement developed a strong alliance with Saudi Arabia and Egypt (during the Mubarak regime), while Hizbullah has cemented its relations with Syria and Iran. These alliances opened the opportunity for foreign states, such as Saudi Arabia and Syria, to interfere in Lebanese political life to promote their own political agendas.

The political and sectarian conflicts that erupted after Syrian withdrawal also significantly affected levels of political freedoms, although these levels improved compared to the Syrian era. The Syrian withdrawal led to improvements in the scores of political rights and civil liberties (cf. Tables 3.1 and 3.2). The reason behind the improvements of these scores was the withdrawal of direct foreign intervention. According to Freedom House (2006), '[t]he departure of Syrian military forces in April 2005 removed the single most powerful obstacle to freedom in Lebanon.' After 2005, the influence of the Syrian regime on the formation of cabinets, the organization of political groups, freedom of expression and media outlets, formulation of electoral laws and the right to criticize Syrian interference in Lebanese domestic politics was significantly weakened. This contributed to the improvements in the scores of political rights and civil liberties, as detailed below.

Nonetheless, Lebanon has not been classified as a Free State by Freedom House since 2005. Table 3.2 shows that between 2005 and 2012 Lebanon was considered Partly Free. The scores for political rights and civil liberties improved from 5 and 6 to between 3 and 5 respectively (Freedom House, 2013). According to Freedom House, the scores of political liberties and civil rights were low mainly because of foreign intervention in Lebanese domestic politics. 'The sectarian political system and the powerful role of foreign patrons effectively limits the accountability of elected officials to the public at large' (Freedom House, 2011). Also, there is widespread political and bureaucratic corruption in state institutions. 'Businesses routinely pay bribes and cultivate ties with politicians to win contracts, and anticorruption laws are loosely enforced' (Freedom House, 2011). In addition, the judiciary is heavily influenced by politicians (Freedom House, 2011).

Furthermore, the political and sectarian conflicts had significant implications for the democratization process. Lebanese politicians were not able to reach agreement on essential democratic issues, such as the formation of the National Body for the Elimination of Confessionalism and the election of a new president. The Christian community vetoed the formation of this body on the basis that the Christian representation should be strengthened first in the consociational system before the elimination of sectarianism, especially as its formation needs the consensus of all sectarian groups, as stated in the Ta'if Agreement. In addition, parliament was paralysed for about two years (2006–8). The head of the Amal Movement and the speaker of parliament, Nabih Berri, prevented the meeting of parliament for about one year (2006–7) because the March 14 Coalition MPs requested its meeting to ratify the STL draft law without the consensus of all Lebanese sectarian parties. From 2007 until 2008, parliament was also not able to convene to elect a new president after the end of the presidential term of Lahoud in November 2007. This was because political parties were not able to agree on a new president. Consequently,

Table 3.2   Political Freedoms in Lebanon (2005–12)

2005			2006			2007			2008		
PR	CL	Status	PR	CL	Status	PR	CL	Status	PR	CL	Status
5	4	PF	5	4	PF	5	4	PF	5	4	PF

2009			2010			2011			2012		
PR	CL	Status	PR	CL	Status	PR	CL	Status	PR	CL	Status
5	3	PF	5	3	PF	5	4	PF	5	4	PF

Source: Freedom House (2013)

the presidency remained vacant for several months until Lebanese political parties agreed on Michel Sleiman, the commander-in-chief of armed forces, as the new president in 2008, with the intervention of external players such as Qatar and Syria. Conversely, during the Syrian presence in Lebanon, Damascus used to interfere to prevent the escalation of these conflicts and had a decisive role in electing Lebanese presidents. Thus, from 1990 until 2005, the presidency did not witness any vacancies.

Parliamentary Elections and Electoral Laws in Post-Syria Lebanon

Two main features have characterized parliamentary elections in Lebanon since 2005. The first was the entry of new political players, in particular the Christian parties. The second was the absence of Syria's role in formulating electoral laws and forming electoral alliances. Nevertheless, the electoral laws that were adopted for the 2005 and 2009 elections were not designed to provide better representation of the Lebanese people and to push forward the democratization process. The endeavour of sectarian parties to improve their sectarian leadership as the main representatives of their sects in the consociational system motivated them to engineer selective electoral laws to secure their victory in the elections, although these laws entrenched further sectarianism.

Two parliamentary elections have been held since 2005 (2005 and 2009) and they were not based on large districts as had been set out in the Ta'if constitution. The parliamentary elections in 2005, which were considered the first free elections since 1972, were based on the 2000 electoral law.[8] They 'took place in spite of major internal divisions regarding the validity of the 2000 electoral law' which had been formulated for the 2000 elections, known as 'Kanaan Law' in reference to the former main Syrian military officer in Lebanon (Ajami, 2005: 635). As discussed above, the 2000 electoral law divided Lebanon into several districts to ensure the victory of Syria's allies. Damascus' former allies and the leaders of the March 14 Coalition, in particular the Future Movement and the PSP, tacitly supported the law because it promised to secure their victory in the elections. Clearly then, the elections, which are supposed to be one of the main steps in the democratization process, were based on an electoral law that entrenched sectarianism and did not provide a real representation of the Lebanese people.

Like the 2005 elections, the 2009 elections were based on an electoral law that did not help provide a real representation of the Lebanese people. Although four years had passed since the Syrian withdrawal in 2005, Lebanese political groups were not able to reach an agreement on an electoral law that could provide a fair and equal representation of the Lebanese people. The Maronite Church requested the adoption of the 1960 electoral law, which was based on small districts (*Qaḍāʾ*). The reason behind the Christian position was that the Christian community is distributed in small numbers in several districts and an electoral law based on large districts would force parliamentary candidates to comply with the interests of the major sectarian community in the district and prevent the Christians from electing deputies that shared their perspective. The Maronite Church's position regarding the electoral law was not opposed by the political parties. According to the former deputy of the speaker of parliament and the head of the Orthodox Gathering community, Elie Ferzli, the Maronite Church supported the adoption of the 1960 electoral law in 2009 because it was the best possible electoral law that enjoyed the support of political parties and at the same time improved the Christian representation in the consociational system.[9] The political parties that were supposed to lead the democratization process and make the transition to a stable democratic system after the Syrian withdrawal did not oppose this electoral law based on small districts since it helped them secure their victory in the elections. This type of electoral district allowed parliamentary candidates to cultivate clientalistic and patronage-based relations with their constituencies. Also, small districts are usually dominated by a major sectarian community, which help sectarian political parties to manipulate sectarian identity to mobilize popular support.

The electoral alliances in the 2005 and 2009 elections were basically still alliances between sectarian parties. After the Syrian withdrawal, Lebanon did not witness the emergence of cross-sectarian political parties able to push forward democratic reforms. Thus, the sectarian political parties once again cultivated strong inter-sectarian alliances during the election periods to secure their victory, although these alliances were reshuffled after 2005. As mentioned above, one of the examples that reflect the inter-sectarian alliances during the election period is the alliance of the Shiite party, Hizbullah, during the 2009 elections with the FPM, a Christian party, which was historically against Hizbullah's armed wing. Also, the Future Movement, a Sunni party, kept its close alliance with the PSP, a Druze party, which used to exist during the Syrian era. Thus, 'electoral alliances were inter-sectarian, but with a few exceptions: mainstream Sunnis and Shi'is were each heading a coalition [. . .] They each formed a coalition with Christians and Druzes' (Haddad, 2010: 62).

The following parliamentary elections were supposed to take place in June 2013. However, the Lebanese political parties amended the constitution to extend parliament's term for 18 months. As the discussion in Chapter 6 will show, the amendment was because of their inability to reach an agreement on a new electoral law. This was because both coalitions were relying on developments in the Syrian conflict to turn to their own advantage (Abu-Habib, 2013b). For the March 8 Coalition, Assad's defeat of the Syrian opposition would empower its negotiating position to enforce its electoral law. For the March 14 Coalition, toppling Assad's regime would empower its negotiating position and allow it to enforce its electoral law as well as weakening its main domestic opponent, Hizbullah. The amendment of parliament's term and the failure of sectarian political parties to agree on a new electoral law prove their inability to push forward the democratic reforms because of the political and sectarian conflicts, and their reliance on external factors.

Conclusion

The consociational model in both the pre- and post-Syrian withdrawal failed to advance the democratization process. The foreign intervention in Lebanon's domestic politics from 1990 until 2005 did not lead to a fully fledged democratic system. The Syrian regime was able to manipulate sectarian divisions and the distribution of state divisions and revenues to enhance and legitimize its intervention in Lebanon's domestic politics, and to ensure the compliance of the Lebanese political class to its own policies. Paul Salem (1998: 25) aptly summarizes the nature of Lebanon's 'democracy' during the Syrian presence, stating that:

> To say that Lebanon is a democracy in the sense that the people freely choose their representatives and decide on basic policy

directions is inaccurate; Lebanon is closer to an oligarchic system, with strong foreign backing, which uses the facade of democracy and constitutionalism to veil its control of public and private resources.

In the post-Syrian era, Lebanon's consociational model has also failed to ensure political stability and help promote the democratic reforms. 'Post-Syria Lebanon inherited the same contradictions of the post-war state inaugurated by the Ta'if Accord: a paralyzed state, penetrated by external actors, besieged by perpetual political crises, and divided by sectarian leaders into neopatrimonial fiefdoms' (Salloukh, 2009: 143). The absence of the Syrian arbitration role contributed to the failure of Lebanon's consociational model to ensure political stability. Post-Syria Lebanon witnessed several developments. Firstly, the participation of Hizbullah and the major Christian parties in the cabinet had significant impacts on the distribution of state seats. Secondly, religious groups, in particular the Muslim sects, had only one or two main representatives, which also helped exacerbate sectarian conflicts over the distribution of, for instance, cabinet posts. Thirdly, Lebanon witnessed intense foreign intervention that fuelled political and sectarian conflicts. The conflicts and reliance on external factors to bolster their domestic positions undermined Lebanese parties' ability to form the National Body for the Elimination of Confessionalism and to formulate a new electoral law that could have ensured better representation of the Lebanese people for the 2005, 2009 and 2013 parliamentary elections.

CHAPTER 4

DOMESTIC VARIABLES AND POLITICAL PARTIES SINCE 2005

As the discussion in the previous chapter showed, the Syrian intervention in Lebanon had significant implications for the behaviour of Lebanese political parties that adversely affected the prospects for democratic change, although Damascus did ensure political stability and prevent the eruption of overt political and sectarian conflicts. Contrary to the expectations raised by scholars and politicians that the Syrian withdrawal would encourage the Lebanese political parties to initiate genuine and sustainable democratic reforms, it has instead rendered their behaviour inflexible and they remain unable to reach compromises. The withdrawal of Damascus' military troops in 2005 motivated Lebanese political parties to employ extensively sectarian language to mobilize the popular support of their sectarian communities so as to win parliamentary elections and secure their political survival. This in turn entrenched the sense of sectarian identity further instead of weakening it and helped exacerbate political and sectarian conflicts, which undermined political stability and the democratization process.

This chapter seeks to explore the impact of inter- and intra-sectarian conflicts upon the behaviour of Lebanese political parties and the democratization process since the Syrian withdrawal in 2005. It will explore the reasons behind the inflexibility of Lebanese political parties and their inability to reach compromises whenever a political conflict has erupted between them in the post-Syrian era. It will argue that the current Lebanese consociational model, which treats sectarian communities as political communities, creates a built-in rivalry between and within sectarian groups to dominate the political system. This has often undermined the ability of Lebanese political parties to reach compromises over, for instance, the formulation of a new electoral law. It has also prevented them from initiating other democratic reforms that might undermine the interests of their sects, such as eliminating sectarianism in accordance with the Ta'if Agreement.

Firstly, the chapter will explore how inter- and intra-sectarian conflicts intersect in Lebanon. Secondly, it will focus on the influence of the rivalry *within* Lebanon's sectarian communities on the behaviour of Lebanese parties. Finally, it will examine the influence of the intersection of inter- and intra-sectarian rivalry on the behaviour of the country's political parties. In both sections, it will be argued that Lebanon's consociational model contributed to the emergence of these two factors and consequently hindered the initiation of democratic reforms.

The Intersection of Inter- and Intra-Sectarian Conflicts

The waning of Syrian influence on Lebanese domestic politics opened the door for new factors to play an influential role in the decision-making process of the country's political parties. Although the political parties used to mobilize popular support before Syrian withdrawal, their competition when mobilizing their sectarian followers was not as intense as in the post-2005 period. In the post-2005 period, Lebanese political parties employed extensively sectarian language to mobilise the support of their sects, fuelling the intensity of the existing inter- and intra-sectarian conflicts. Zahar (2005: 236) rightly argued that Syrian military withdrawal will 'put the stability of the post-Ta'if second Republic in jeopardy. Given the essential Syrian role in the implementation of the Ta'if accord – including the repression of political opponents and the silencing of counterelites – a Syrian military pullout would be likely to re-open the Pandora's box of civil violence.'

Lebanon's consociational model contributed to the emergence of two domestic factors that have impacted the decision-making process of political parties since 2005: (1) competition within sectarian groups; and (2) competition between sectarian groups. These two factors crippled the ability of Lebanese parties to widen their popular support beyond their sectarian groups. The politicization of the sectarian divisions by Lebanon's consociational model 'motivated' political parties to mobilize the support of their sectarian groups, which are usually concentrated in certain districts.[1] This has sparked inter- and intra-sectarian competitions and conflicts over the leadership of the sect and the distribution of state positions between communal groups. It has also motivated these groups and actors to reject democratic reforms that might undermine the interests of their respective sectarian communities. According to the journalist, Kassem Kassir, who is close to the March 8 Coalition and works at the Contemporary Islamic Thought Foundation for Research and Studies, the influence of the domestic factor on the behaviour of political parties 'became stronger than the external.'[2] External factors refer to the regional and international states' policies in Lebanon which aim to promote their interests, such as Saudi Arabia's policy to disarm Hizbullah's military wing. Although these two factors (i.e. domestic and external) used to exist during the Syrian era, domestic factors did not sway the behaviour of political parties to the same extent as the influence of the Syrian regime on them. Ahmad Baydoun explains how Lebanon's consociational model influences the behaviour of Lebanese political parties in the post-2005 period:

> Allowing the sectarian communities to participate in the political system would create internal pressure [within the sect], in the sense that if a particular party did not take the maximum [i.e. state positions and benefits] from the [consociational] system, it provokes forces within its sectarian community to take advantage of this weakness in order to mobilise the members of the religious group on the basis that they are able to gain more interests for the community in the system. Therefore, on one hand, the representative of the sectarian group feels that it has a significant space of freedom because the system cannot abandon it. And on the other hand, it feels that it is under pressure, if it does not request the maximum, its position within the community would be undermined.[3]

As the discussion below will show, conflicts between and within the representatives of the sectarian groups help shape the opinion of the sect and its political representatives. Karim Pakradouni, who was interviewed on the matter, states that the communal group 'forms the claim and the counter-claim in the face of the other sect, and political families within the sectarian community then form the political claim and the counter-claim. Hence, there are two levels of conflict: within the sectarian community and at the national level [i.e. between the sectarian communities].'[4]

Intra-Sectarian Rivalry

The nature of Lebanon's consociational model encourages political parties to use sectarian language to mobilize the support of their sectarian groups. Rivalries between the representatives of a sectarian community seeking to obtain state positions allocated by the consociational system for their respective sects are probably the most powerful factor in influencing the behaviour of Lebanese parties in the post-2005 era. Each party aims to rally the popular support of its community. To this effect, it employs two main strategies. Firstly, it employs sectarian language to address the interests of its community. The sectarian language is the political discourse adopted by political parties which addresses the interests of religious groups. Secondly, it often attempts to inculcate a sense of fear among its followers regarding its political rivals both within and outside its religious group so as to widen and strengthen the relationship with them. The fear-based approach is often employed when the intensity of the conflicts increases and before parliamentary elections. Therefore, their positions towards democratic reforms tend to be strongly correlated with their compatibility with their interests and the interests of their sects.

Intra-Sectarian Rivalry and Sectarian Rhetoric
Sectarian language sets limitations on the behaviour of political parties. Instead of promoting national interests and democratic reforms, political parties come to articulate their policies in a sectarian language solely aimed at their followers. The representation of sectarian groups in the consociational system sparks intra-sectarian conflicts in which they employ several approaches to mobilize popular support, such as imitating their intra-sectarian rivals' behaviour, accusations of treachery and resorting to violence. As the following discussion will show, a

political party is often unable to mobilize popular support from outside its sectarian group due to the intra-sectarian competition over the mobilization of its sectarian community.

The leaders of the political parties who used to criticize the Syrian presence in Lebanon and the distribution of state revenues among Syria's allies adopted sectarian language in order to mobilize their sectarian communities in the post-Syria period. Michel Aoun, head of the FPM, for instance, is one of the political leaders who adopted sectarian language to mobilize the support of the Christian community, although he used to denounce it before his return to Lebanon in 2005. In particular, his adoption of sectarian language was at variance with his previously secular-focused perspectives. Before his return to Lebanon from exile in France, he used to adopt a language which addressed the interests of all Lebanese people, such as the need to fight corruption in state institutions. In his first speech after his return from exile in May 2005, Aoun stated that 'if I employ sectarian language renounce me' (Sharaf, 2008). However, he paradoxically resorted to sectarian language to win the elections and to improve his negotiating position as the main representative of his community which can enable him to ask for a larger share in the quota allocated for the Christian community in the consociational system, for instance, in the cabinet. '[U]pon his return he rapidly adjusted to the sectarian dynamics, emerging as protector of the Maronites, indeed, their last line of defence' (ICG, 2005: 4). Although Aoun considers himself a secular politician, he was unable to form a cross-sectarian party. According to the Lebanese researcher Raed Sharaf (2010), his endeavour to participate in government and parliamentary elections after 2005 motivated him to adopt sectarian language. For instance, one of the main goals he campaigned on in parliamentary elections (2005 and 2009) was his aim of improving the level of Christian representation in state institutions, for example increasing the number of Christian employees in the state bureaucracy.

The intra-sectarian rivalry within the Christian community meant that its representatives (FPM, LFP and Kataeb) came to reject the formation of the National Body for the Elimination of Confessionalism. The veto power that is given to the sectarian communities by Lebanon's consociational system enabled the Christian parties to veto the formation of this body, although its formation is essential for the democratization process. The speaker of parliament, Nabih Berri, proposed the formation of this body, which does not eliminate sectarianism per se. It does, however, propose steps to eliminate it. Although he clarified that his 'initiative to form this committee, which will be headed by the president, doesn't mean that sectarianism will be eradicated the minute this committee is created' (*The Daily Star*, 2010), the Christian parties nonetheless rejected its formation outright. They argue that Christian representation should be strengthened first in the political system through, for instance, distributing state administrative positions equally between Christians and Muslims before eliminating confessionalism. The Christian political analyst, Michel Abou-Najem, who is close to the FPM and works at the Issam Fares Center for Lebanon, justifies the reason behind the Christian rejection of Berri's proposal to eliminate confessionalism. He states that proposing the 'elimination of political sectarianism by a sectarian party [i.e. the Amal Movement] may be aimed [...] to cancel the barriers for the dominance of this sectarian group on the system.'[5] The large demographic size of the Shiite community (see Map 2) will enhance its domination of the state system if sectarianism were to be truly eliminated, giving it significant voting power and influence over election results because of its sheer numerical strength.

However, the sectarian parties do not always agree on how to define and advance the interests of their sects, which often leads them to accuse each other of treachery and selling out their communities' interests, instead of competing over promoting the national interest, with issues such as democratic reforms. 'Such language often involves emotional appeals and may have particular resonance at the intra-group level since it can connect with a community-wide repository of myths, historical narratives and symbols' (Gormley-Heenan & Macginty, 2008: 49). The sectarian distribution of administrative positions in the state apparatus is often manipulated by these parties. For instance, the leader of the LFP, Samir Geagea, accused the FPM of undermining their community's interest in the political system because its ministers ratified the designation of a Shiite to be the Director of the General Security Apparatus, which was supposed to be held by a Christian (Lebanese Forces, 2013). A similar case is the LFP accusing the FPM of infringing 'Christian principles' by supporting Hizbullah's armed wing (*Asharq al-Awsat*, 2008). These Christian principles include the disarming of all armed groups, building a civil state, and protecting the sovereignty of the Lebanese state. This also happened within the Shiite community. The Shiite and anti-Hizbullah journalist from *al-Hayat* newspaper, Hazem al-Amin, accuses Hizbullah of mobilizing the Shiite community to support the Resistance, instead of acquiring more state positions and revenues proportional to the sect's demographic size.[6]

Intra-sectarian conflict can rapidly spiral out of control and leave deep sectarian divisions leading sometimes to violence. Accusations of treachery between political parties often augment the tensions to the point of encouraging violence, seriously undermining political stability. For instance, the former PM, Mikati, was accused of treachery because he replaced the former PM and head of the Future Movement, Saad Hariri, who represents the majority of the Sunnis.[7] As a consequence of his designation, riots erupted in Sunni areas, such as Tripoli, protesting against Mikati. Mikati's designation was then interpreted by the Future Movement and its supporters as a betrayal since Mikati was part of the March 14 Coalition in the 2009 parliamentary elections (France 24, 2011).

Another example that shows how intra-sectarian conflicts might develop into outright violence is the rivalry between Druze politicians. The rivalry between the PSP and Wiam Wahhab is intense and sometimes descends into violence. An instance that shows the intensity of the competition between the two parties is the violent conflict that erupted between supporters of the two parties in 2006 in Khalwat al-Kfier village in West Bekaa when Wahhab attended the funeral of a Druze citizen. The PSP MP, Wael Abou-Faour, stated that Wahhab seeks 'to spark conflicts anywhere. They want to stir up problems specifically within Jumblatt's popular base, his areas of influence and the Druze villages generally' (*al-Mustaqbal*, 2006a). Wahhab, on the other side, accused the PSP of planning the conflict in advance. He stated that 'he was subjected to an armed ambush which [was] deliberate and planned in advance by supporters of the Progressive Party, driven by their boss and MP Walid Jumblatt' (*Asharq al-Awsat*, 2006b).

The intra-sectarian rivalry is also evident within the Sunni community. The emergence of Salafi groups, which extensively employ sectarian language, forced the Future Movement to adopt more inflammatory sectarian language and express its support for them, although these groups are often critical of Hariri. If the Future Movement fails to mobilize the Sunni community, its ability to negotiate for the distribution of state positions allocated for its community in the consociational system will be weakened because it will not be the sole representative of its community and its intra-sectarian opponents will ask for a share proportional to their sectarian representation. The case of Shaykh Ahmad al-Aseer shows how the intra-sectarian rivalry and conflicts influence the behaviour of Lebanese political parties. Al-Aseer, a Salafi Sunni shaykh and imam of Bilal Bin Rabah Mosque in Sidon, southern Lebanon, has emerged since 2008 as an anti-Hizbullah figure. He accused Hizbullah of threatening the Sunni community in Lebanon because of its armed wing which inculcated a feeling of 'injustice and that its dignity is insulted' (*al-Akhbar*, 2012).[8] Thus, he organized a sit-in in his city, Sidon, for several months in 2012 to force Hizbullah to surrender its weapons. The sectarian language that he used against the Shiite party motivated the Future Movement to politically support these assertions, although al-Aseer has occasionally criticized it because it is not able to 'protect' the Sunnis in Lebanon. For instance, in one of his TV interviews he heavily criticized Saad Hariri's inability to take care of the affairs of the Sunni community in Lebanon and for his settlement outside the country away from his religious community after he left the PM position in 2011 (*al-Akhbar*, 2012).

The Future Movement support for al-Aseer became apparent after the violent clashes that erupted between al-Aseer and the Lebanese army in June 2013. As a consequence of his opposition to Hizbullah, al-Aseer supporters had several violent clashes with supporters and members from the Shiite party. For this reason, the Lebanese army established security checkpoints next to his mosque. This provoked al-Aseer to violently force the Lebanese army to leave military checkpoints, which led to the death of several army soldiers. In response, the Lebanese army sought to bring him to justice which led to military confrontation between the two sides. The confrontation led to the death of 18 army soldiers and more than 100 wounded, while 57 al-Aseer supporters also lost their lives and he fled to an unknown location (Khalil, 2013b: 3). As part of the Future Movement strategy to show that it seeks to 'protect' the Sunnis, the sister of the slain Rafic Hariri, Bahiyya, compared the attack on al-Aseer security square (i.e. under the control of al-Aseer armed supporters) to the tragedy that befell her with the assassination of her brother in February 2005 (Rizk, 2013). The former PM and MP from

Sidon, Fouad Siniora (2005–9), explained what happened to al-Aseer as being due to the existence of an armed party which is outside state hegemony, in reference to Hizbullah. He supported Shaykh al-Aseer's slogans, such as those calling for the disarming of Hizbullah. He stated that the slogans and demands initially raised by Shaykh Ahmed al-Aseer are legitimate, 'and these slogans and demands [represent the requests] of large portions of [Lebanese] people and the people of Sidon, who expressed their rejection for weapons and the control of Hizbullah's weapons on public life' (Khalil, 2013a).

Inculcating a Sense of Fear

Wherever the sectarian language approach fails to work for the interests of political parties, they revert to instilling a sense of fear among their followers. Lebanese parties not only accuse their political rivals within the sectarian community of being unable to protect the interests of their sect in the political system, they also accuse their sectarian opponents from rival sects of undermining the interests of their communities. Their main aim is hereby to inculcate a sense of fear among their followers. This tool is often referred to as 'Elite-Initiated Conflict' (Tsebelis, 1990: 16–17), or, as Covell refers to it in his study of Belgium politics, as 'Conflict Creation' (Covell, 1981: 210–12). The use of this tool can strengthen and widen the relationship between the followers and their representatives. As the following discussion will show, the consequences of adopting such behaviour are far reaching, including effects on the prospects for democratic reforms, and may have the following ramifications: entrenching the sense of sectarian identity, creating a lack of trust between members of sectarian groups, and bringing forth accusations of conspiring for the interests of the sectarian group.

What helps political parties to entrench a sense of fear among their followers is the nature of Lebanon's consociational model. Hudson provides an explanation of why the absence of mutual trust and the sense of fear exist among Lebanese sectarian communities. He (1985: 85) argues that '[t]he reason that communal identities remain so strong, reinforced rather than obliterated by the communications explosion, is the result of historic doctrinal differences and memories of oppression, both antique and recent.' However, it is not only this factor that has kept the sense of sectarian identity entrenched. Ahmad Baydoun explains how the consociational system and the political parties operating in it have created the sense of fear:

> The public has a dual feeling [towards the political system]. On one hand, it feels [...] that the system is disabled and there is no possibility to address this problem by the existing political framework. And on the other hand, they are afraid of the opposite sectarian group [...] The reasons for this dual feeling are: (1) the fear the sectarian groups have of each other, (2) the political parties inculcating this fear, (3) in addition, the system that feeds this fear. The [consociational] system makes people look at each other on a sectarian basis. The nature of the system's [sectarian] distribution of benefits and power [...] made the sectarian issue a major determinant of the political behaviour of citizens.[9]

One of the crucial domestic events in the post-2005 period that helped entrench the sense of fear among sectarian communities was the violence that erupted on 7 May 2008.[10] A violent conflict erupted between Hizbullah, the Amal Movement, and the SSNP on one side and the Future Movement and the PSP on the other side after the then government took a decision on 6 May 2008 to dismantle Hizbullah's private telecommunications network. The network was established for the sake of protecting its members from Israeli espionage, and it is not controlled or monitored by the Lebanese government. The government justified its decision by stating that Hizbullah's telephone network is 'illegal and unconstitutional' (Blanford, 2008). The then government was headed by the Future Movement leader, Fouad Siniora, and dominated by the March 14 Coalition.[11] The PSP leader accused Hizbullah 'of maintaining its own private telephone network, and of using security cameras to monitor Beirut airport with the possible aim of staging attacks or kidnappings' (Blanford, 2008). Thus, the government took its decision to dismantle Hizbullah's telecommunications network and dismissed the chief of the airport security apparatus General Wafiq Shuqair because of his close connections to Hizbullah and the March 8 Coalition.

The conflict between these two rival blocs culminated in an outbreak of violence, when Hizbullah used its military power to force the government to withdraw its decision to dismantle the network. Armed Hizbullah members took to the streets of Beirut and forced the evacuation of the offices of the Future Movement. The violence caused the death of at least 81 people and wounded 250 in four days of fighting in May 2008 (Macleod & Aysha, 2008). Subsequently, the government decision to dismantle Hizbullah's telecommunications network never materialized. It revoked its decisions after the eruption of the violence.[12]

The conflict raised the fears of Shiites and in particular Sunnis. Hizbullah's interpretation of the government decision at the time was that it was 'taken with the aim of causing a clash between the Resistance and the Army [which was supposed to implement the government decision] and sowing strife between Sunnites and Shiites' (Nasrallah, 2010). On the other side, this conflict deeply entrenched a sense of sectarian identity among Sunnis. The Future Movement effectively manipulated the conflict to strengthen its sectarian leadership. It portrayed Hizbullah's violent approach as an act of intimidation against the Sunni community. 'Sunni religious leaders sought to mobilise their constituency by resorting to an unprecedented form of sectarian rhetoric' (ICG, 2008a: 6). Thus, Hizbullah's attack on the Future Movement's offices in Beirut was heavily criticized by Sunni shaykhs labelling it as 'the enemy' (ICG, 2008a: 6). The Lebanese Sunni Mufti Muhammad Rashid Qabbani, who was close to the Future Movement, stated that Hizbullah has converted 'into an armed force to occupy Beirut and to violate its sanctities' (Qabbani, 2008). He went on: 'the Sunni Muslims are fed up with the encroachments and abuses [of Hizbullah] [. . .] They are not able to afford any more political and security adventures' (Qabbani, 2008).

The March 14 Coalition also heavily criticized Hizbullah's use of military power to force the government to revoke its decision and labelled the attack on the Future Movement offices a 'military coup against the state' (Abdallah, 2008). In a political statement, the March 14 Coalition criticized 'Hizbullah's claim that its arms were only targeted at Israel [since it] has proved false and invalid in the past two days, which witnessed the uses of such arms against the Lebanese people' (Abdallah, 2008). It compared its attack on the Future Movement offices to the Israeli occupation of Beirut in 1982, stating that 'Beirut did not fall to Israel in the past and will not fall to Hizbullah today' (Abdallah, 2008). Although the violent conflict forced the government to backtrack on its decision, it exacerbated the sectarian conflicts further and inculcated a sense of fear among sectarian groups.

The strategy of inculcating a sense of fear becomes more evident before parliamentary elections, when political parties desperately seek to mobilize popular support to secure their victory in the elections. Issues such as the May 7 violence and Hizbullah's armed wing were employed effectively by political parties during the parliamentary elections in 2009 to inculcate a sense of fear among their followers. Indeed, across the board, Lebanese political groups, instead of mobilizing popular support on the basis of their political programmes, which aim to push forward democratic reforms, usually simply manipulate the sense of fear to mobilize popular support. The Lebanese researcher, Kamal Dib (2009), states that 'the worst manifestation of the lack of true democracy in the current Lebanese elections is the total absence of platforms.' They focus almost exclusively on portraying themselves as protectors of their sects from their inter- and intra-sectarian political opponents. The Lebanese journalist and writer from *al-Akhbar* newspaper, Fidaa Itani, argues that 'the fear of the other forces [the citizen] to re-elect this political class.'[13] This point is also confirmed by Imad Salamey and Paul Tabar who conducted a poll about the behaviour of Lebanese citizens with regard to their loyalty to their sects and state institutions. They (2012: 507) concluded that 'sectarian leaders utilize their populism in order to prevent the emergence of a cross-confessional political agenda, instigating constant fear against other sects and their potential rise to power.'

Many of the speeches and political statements of the political parties before the parliamentary elections in 2009 provide clear examples. In an election gathering, the Druze parliamentary candidate, Wael Abou-Faour, warned against the victory of the March 8 Coalition in the parliamentary elections:

> The battle today is the battle of the [Lebanese] emigrants and the residents and [the election] is a referendum on the political choices of the country, and if we win we will justly rule [. . .] If we win our project is the security [of Lebanon] and the Lebanese army, economy, independence and stability. (Meghmas, 2009)

Furthermore, he warned against the victory of the March 8 Coalition since they 'disrupted the country and [. . .] sparked the May 7 [conflict]' (Meghmas, 2009). The Christian partisan leaders followed the same course. In an election gathering for the LFP Christian popular base in Batroun, Samir Geagea similarly warned against the victory of the March 8 Coalition. He stated that 'in the event of victory of the March 8 Coalition in the next election the [political] situation will not be a funny cartoon at all. However, it will be disastrous because Lebanon will turn quickly into a Banana Republic' (al-Mustaqbal, 2009a), and 'it will open new fronts in favor of Hizbullah and will suppress public and media freedoms' (The Daily Star, 2009).

The same approach was also adopted by the political parties of the March 8 Coalition in regard to the parliamentary elections in 2009. In a speech for an electoral gathering in southern Lebanon, the leader of Hizbullah, Nasrallah (2009a), reminded his followers that 'June 7 [i.e. election day] must be a day to thwart every conspirator and every schemer who thinks about colluding against the resistance.' It is noteworthy that Hizbullah's claim that its loss in elections would lead to the weakening of the Resistance, its military wing, is based on a solid argument. This is because its ability to protect its arms to continue defending the country against Israel is derived from the wide popular support that it enjoys from its community. Similarly, the speaker of parliament and the ally of Hizbullah, Nabih Berri, called on his followers to vote en masse for his joint electoral list with Hizbullah. He stated that 'those elections are a referendum on the resistance and development', in reference to the name of his electoral list 'development and liberation' (Zaatari & Zeineddine, 2009).[14]

It was not only Nasrallah and Berri who employed such an approach. The leader of the FPM warned against the effects of the elections on the political status of Christians. At an electoral gathering, Michel Aoun promised Christians that 'we are now at the door of the final liberation stage from the repressive methods', in reference to the marginalization of Christians in the pre- and post-2005 periods (Asharq al-Awsat, 2009). He was particularly referring to his exclusion from the government that was formed after the 2005 elections, although he represented a significant portion of the Christian community. Moreover, intra-sectarian rivalry may encourage politicians to 'demonize' their intra-sectarian opponents. At an electoral gathering, Aoun accused Geagea of being 'an executioner who was able to gather all his victims in a single electoral list [...] Our Christian belief urges us to forgive those who harmed us, but we should only forgive those who repent' (The Daily Star, 2009). In so doing, he referred to the crimes of which Geagea is accused, such as the assassination of the leader of the Liberal National Party, Dani Chamoun, whose brother, Dory, was part of the March 14 Coalition electoral list.

So, a clear political programme remained almost entirely absent from Lebanese political parties' speeches before parliamentary elections in 2009, with no party clearly stating its objectives in regard to democratic reform. In her report on the 2009 parliamentary elections, Melani Cammett (2009) argues that '[t]he election, and especially the campaign period, was remarkable for its lack of attention to issues of real substance.' Similarly, Dib (2009) criticizes the behaviour of Lebanese political parties, especially regarding their accusations of treachery:

> What fascinates the observer of the election campaigns are the daily barrages among top politicians, which contain high-brow and unbelievable accusations levelled against one another [. . .] Cries of corruption and unlawful activities surface every day on the airwaves and in newspapers, yet it does not seem that anyone, whether in the judiciary or otherwise, takes them seriously or at a minimum gathers information.

Inter-Sectarian Rivalry and Intersection with Intra-Sectarian Conflicts

The rivalry within sectarian communities is not the only factor that has determined the political behaviour and priorities of the Lebanese parties during the post-Syrian era, especially regarding democratic reforms. Lebanon's consociational model also 'encourages' sectarian parties to forge inter-sectarian alliances. The inability of sectarian political parties to dominate the consociational system encourages them to build inter-sectarian coalitions in order to win elections and to be able to form the government. This is because state positions are distributed between the communal groups and none of the sectarian communities has an overwhelming majority. Thus, '[c]ross-communal cooperation is essential to obtaining substantial power in Lebanon since all the sectarian groups are political minorities and cannot become a political majority without making coalitions with other groups' (Kota, 2010: 121). The representatives of the sectarian groups then manipulate intra-sectarian conflicts of their rival religious groups to build these alliances and to further their own interests. These alliances often lead political parties to make concessions, many of which come at the expense of democratic reforms. Also, these alliances reflect the vertical division of Lebanese society, mainly the Sunni–Shiite division. As the following discussion will show, this has weakened the ability of the grand coalition component, which is one of the main components of the consociational model, to secure the success of the power-sharing agreement.

By building these alliances, political parties will also be able to obtain the posts that are dominated by their rival sects, because not all state administrative and security positions are constitutionally distributed among sectarian groups. Although the Lebanese constitution stipulates that state administrative and security positions should be proportionally distributed among sectarian groups, the sectarian identity of each state position is not determined in the constitution, in particular administrative and security positions. Thus, the dominant coalition usually distributes the most influential positions, mainly the security positions, among its allies.

Cross-Sectarian Alliances and Intra-Sectarian Conflicts

As discussed in Chapter 2, the end of the Syrian presence witnessed the formation of two main coalitions, which included political parties from different sectarian communities. The Sunni and Shiite parties which constitute the core parties of the two coalitions manipulated the intra-sectarian conflicts in order to drag sectarian parties into their sphere of influence, in particular the parties of the Christian community, which has witnessed deep intra-sectarian conflicts since 2005. The Sunni, Shiite, Druze and Christian communities all witnessed intra-sectarian outbidding which was manipulated by the parties of rival sects, although the intensity fluctuated between the religious communities. The intersection between inter- and intra-sectarian rivalries and conflicts pushed several parties to extreme opposing sides, making them adopt positions that helped impede democratic reforms. What is noticeable is that these conflicts and alliances did not seek to push democratic reforms forward. They instead aimed to empower the position of the sectarian communities and their political parties.

The two main coalitions had to a large extent contradictory aims, especially regarding the status of Hizbullah's armed wing and relations with Syria. What is noticeable is that neither coalition set out a clear agenda for initiating democratic reforms, especially those that are stated in the Ta'if Agreement. Instead, their agendas were based on intersection of interests, such as formulating electoral laws that suit their electoral strategies, which were often at the expense of democratic reforms. As the following discussion will show, the grand coalition component failed to achieve its objective of bringing diverse sectarian groups into one coherent coalition to, for instance, form the government, with ramifications for its ability to secure the success of the power-sharing agreement and the democratization process.

The major coalition that emerged after 2005 was the March 14 Coalition, composed of several political parties that were historically on opposing sides. The parties of this coalition share common views and policies, such as their position against Hizbullah's armed wing and rejection of the Syrian presence. Nevertheless, the main factor that brought the parties of this coalition together was their mutual interest in, for instance, running elections in joint electoral lists, which imposed on them the need to make concessions, as will be shown in the following discussion.[15] The Future Movement, for instance, established a robust alliance with the LFP, although the leader of this party, Samir Geagea, was convicted of assassinating the former Sunni PM Rashid Karami during the civil war. Such an alliance between the Future Movement and a political figure (i.e. Samir Geagea), who was convicted of assassinating one of the most prominent Sunni figures, contradicts with its call for the 'Truth' about the assassination of Rafic Hariri and the defence of the Sunni community's rights in Lebanon. Within the Christian community, there were also similar alliances between conflicting parties. For instance, the Christian National Liberal Party, which joined the March 14 Coalition, formed an alliance with the LFP, although Samir Geagea stands accused of assassinating Dani Chamoun, the National Liberal Party's former leader and the brother of its current leader, Dory, during the civil war. What is noticeable is that a detailed reform programme was not the objective of the alliance, although it utilized national and reformist slogans, such as restoring and protecting the sovereignty of the country and building state institutions. As will be shown in the following chapter, this coalition accused Syria of failing to instigate the democratic reforms that are stipulated in the Ta'if Agreement. However, after it took power in 2005, the very same coalition did not seek to push forward the democratization process. Instead, it sought to protect and widen its interests in the consociational system through, for instance, formulating electoral laws that would secure its victory in subsequent parliamentary polls.

Like the March 14 Coalition, the alliance forged by the March 8 Coalition parties was also based on intersection of interests, which necessitated the making of concessions, although it is more 'homogenous' in its political vision and the policies of its parties, regarding its pro-Syrian leanings and its support for Hizbullah's military wing. This is because the majority of its parties were allied during the Syrian era and were closely allied with Damascus. The case of the FPM's alliance with Hizbullah is a clear example of how mutual interests brought these parties together, although they used to hold contradictory views and perspectives. The FPM, which joined the coalition in 2006, made concessions and even changed its political discourse and perspectives to be able to build this alliance. The 'Memorandum of Joint Understanding between Hizbullah and the Free Patriotic Movement' led the two parties to make two main concessions. The first concession was that 'the question of the Lebanese residing in Israel requires urgent action to enable their return to their country, taking into consideration all the political, security and living conditions surrounding this issue' (ICG, 2008b: 31), although Hizbullah used to be very cautious about this issue because these Lebanese families are families of alleged spies who stand accused of collaborating with Israel during its occupation of southern Lebanon. The second concession was its accentuation of the importance of the Resistance, Hizbullah's armed wing. One of the articles in the agreement stated that:

> Hezbollah's arms must be addressed as part of a comprehensive approach that falls within two parameters. The first parameter is reliance on justifications that reflect national consensus and constitute the sources of strength for Lebanon and the Lebanese in terms of preserving these arms. The second parameter is to objectively define conditions that would eliminate the reasons and justifications for keeping these weapons. (ICG, 2008b: 32)

These justifications are the continued Israeli occupation of the Shebaa Farms and defending Lebanon from Israeli attacks and military interventions (ICG, 2008b: 32). However, Aoun's support for the Resistance is somewhat surprising since he used to heavily criticize Hizbullah's armed wing before 2006.

The Memorandum between Hizbullah and the FPM did not include clear democratic reform objectives or a timetable to achieve them. It instead emphasized the importance of the current political system. The second article in the Memorandum stated that '[c]onsensual democracy remains the fundamental basis for governance in Lebanon, embodying the spirit of its constitution and the essence of the pact of coexistence' (ICG, 2008b: 31). However, the elimination of sectarianism 'will remain contingent on the realization of historical and social conditions necessary for real democracy, in which the citizen becomes a value in and of himself' (ICG, 2008b: 31). Regarding the electoral law, the Memorandum provided a vague statement that reads as follows '[r]eforming and organizing Lebanese political life require the adoption of a modern electoral law (of which proportional representation may be an effective form) that guarantees the accuracy and fairness of popular representation' (ICG, 2008b: 31). The Memorandum did not set out a clear timetable to achieve these objectives, that is, the elimination of confessionalism and the electoral law.

Several factors had paved the way for Hizbullah and the FPM to build their alliance and to negotiate these concessions. In one of his interviews, Aoun justified his support for the armed wing of Hizbullah by arguing that '[i]f Lebanon is subject to any aggression, the army cannot defend it or mount a sustained fight under the existing balances of power, especially against Israel. That is where the job of the resistance to liberate the land begins' (Kossayfi, 2012). The FPM alliance with the Shiite party can be explained by two main factors. As for the FPM, Hizbullah is an armed party and represents the majority of Shiites, which are among the largest sectarian communities in Lebanon. This enables the FPM, through its alliance with Hizbullah, to obtain a greater influence in the consociational system, including amongst others through more Christian posts in cabinet and better prospects of winning more Christian parliamentary seats in mixed areas that include Shiites. This in turn will increase the number of FPM Christian MPs and enable it to ask for a larger share in the quota allocated for Christians in the consociational system. According to the Lebanese journalist and media figure who works at the Lebanese Broadcasting Corporation (LBC), Khaled Saghieh, Aoun's justification for his alliance to the Christian community was that he wanted to widen and strengthen Christian participation in the consociational system.[16] As for Hizbullah, its conflict with the March 14 Coalition that erupted in 2005 over its armed wing left it without a major inter-sectarian ally. This encouraged it to build an alliance with the FPM, which represents a significant portion of the Christian community.

There are, however, different explanations for the alliances of the Christian parties (mainly the FPM and the LFP) across the sectarian divide. For the LFP, it was natural to weave an alliance with anti-Syrian and anti-Hizbullah forces, since it historically stood against Hizbullah's armed wing and the Syrian regime. However, the FPM changed its position regarding both Hizbullah and Syria. Khaled Saghieh provides an interpretation of the behaviour of the FPM and the LFP. He argues that there are two different visions held by the Christian parties regarding their alliances:

> There is a vision that considers that the Christians are able to regain their influence in the [consociational] system and this vision is championed by Aoun. [He] wove an alliance with the Shiites because historically [the Christians] did not have conflicts with them but the clash was always with the Sunnis over the distribution of powers between the president and the PM, and also to benefit from the Sunni–Shiite conflict to achieve the interests of the Christians. The second vision is that the recovery of this role [i.e. the Christian role] is not possible and [the Christians] should be satisfied with the current system [. . .] [This view] is represented by Samir Geagea. He is [. . .] convinced that the Christians are now a minority in Lebanon and in the region, and the maximum we [i.e. the Christians] can achieve is what is given to us [. . .] by Hariri and the Ta'if [Agreement], namely 50 per cent in state institutions albeit with limited powers.[17]

Both alliance strategies were aimed at protecting Christian interests in the consociational system. They did not, however, aim from these alliances to push forward democratic reforms, such as eliminating confessionalism and the electoral law. The Future Movement and Hizbullah for their parts sought to weave alliances with Christians in order to endow their interests and policies with more legitimacy and support, and to secure their victory in parliamentary elections. Former member of the FPM, Becharah Khairallah, argues that the Future

Movement and Hizbullah manipulated the Christian parties so as to give their vision and policies a national label rather than a narrow sectarian label.[18] Without cross-sectarian alliances their political positions would be weakened, and their perspective and policies would always be given narrow sectarian interpretations.

To ensure the persistence of these alliances (i.e. the March 8 and March 14 coalitions), political parties keep making concessions to their allies; otherwise, their allies' positions within their sectarian communities would be undermined and weakened. The Future Movement and Hizbullah have each faced this situation. Their attempts to keep their Christian allies within their sphere of influence have led them to make concessions and provide political support for them to empower their positions within the Christian community. Several cases show how the alliance between Hizbullah and the FPM motivated the former to make concessions and therefore influenced its political behaviour. For instance, it supported the FPM's electoral proposal of the Orthodox Gathering electoral law,[19] although an electoral law based on PR might make Hizbullah loses Shiite parliamentary seats.[20] In the event that anti-Hizbullah Shiite figures then won parliamentary seats, this would call into question the legitimacy of its military wing since it would show that it does not enjoy the overwhelming support of the Shiite community and weaken its position in the consociational system as the main Shiite representative. Its support for the FPM's electoral law proposal was, however, intended to empower its position within the Christian community, which would also secure the victory of the March 8 Coalition in the elections. What is noticeable is that Hizbullah initially supported the formulation of an electoral law based on large districts with PR. However, it changed its position after the insistence of its Christian ally, the FPM, on the Orthodox Gathering electoral law.

Furthermore, Hizbullah supported the FPM's requests to hold important ministerial positions in the governments that were formed after the May 7 conflict in 2008 and after the parliamentary elections in 2009,[21] although the FPM's shares in these two cabinets were at the expense of Hizbullah's share. For the 2008 government, the FPM requested a share in the cabinet proportional to its parliamentary bloc (21 MPs which is 16 per cent of parliamentary seats). 'Aoun unquestionably saw the post-Doha negotiations as the time to extract from his opposition peers the price of his political loyalty during the difficult months preceding' (Yadav, 2008). The FPM was awarded five cabinet posts out of 11 allocated for the opposition, which was the largest ministerial quota held by an opposition party. Out of these five, two are service portfolios and the deputy premiership (Yadav, 2008). 'Aoun no doubt recognizes that it may ultimately be the "service portfolios" – and the goods, services and jobs they distribute – that matter most in this caretaker cabinet' (Yadav, 2008). Hizbullah in turn held only the Ministry of Labour, a non-essential ministry. The FPM was also able to extract concessions from its Shiite ally in the government that was formed after the 2009 parliamentary elections. Out of ten ministers allocated for the March 8 Coalition, five ministries were held by the FPM parliamentary bloc, the largest ministerial quota held by a party from the March 8 Coalition, while Hizbullah held only two unessential ministries (Ministry of Agriculture and Ministry of Administrative Reform). The FPM was not able to hold five cabinet posts in these two cabinets without the support of Hizbullah. These posts empowered its position within the Christian community and provided further justification for its alliance with the Shiite party (Yadav, 2008).

The Future Movement followed the same approach with its Christian allies, although it was more intransigent and less flexible towards them. For instance, the Future Movement supported Geagea for the position of president, although Geagea was convicted of assassinating a Sunni PM. However, the Future Movement rejected several requests from the LFP. Firstly, it opposed the ratification of the Orthodox Gathering electoral law, although the Christian parties, including the LFP, agreed on this law and considered it to be an important step towards improving Christian representation in the consociational system. This law, if passed, would have significantly improved the stance of the LFP within the Christian community and strengthened its sectarian leadership's position when asking for a larger share in the quota allocated for its community in the consociational system. The Future Movement's rejection stemmed from its fear that it would lose the Christian parliamentary seats (about half of its parliamentary bloc) if the Orthodox Gathering electoral law was to be adopted.[22] Secondly, the Future Movement rejected the LFP's request to hold prominent cabinet posts (e.g. the Ministry of Works or Ministry of Finance) in the government that was formed by Saad Hariri in 2009 (Ibrahim, 2013).

Thirdly, the Future Movement rejected the LFP's request to put up candidates for parliamentary elections in 2009 in Akkar, a predominantly Sunni area, and al-Ashrafiyya, a Christian-dominated area, because it favoured independent Christian figures in the March 14 Coalition standing for election in these districts (Ibrahim, 2013). Fourthly, the leader of the LFP requested more MP seats from the Future Movement in areas dominated by Christians in the run-up to the 2013 parliamentary elections, which was also rejected (Ibrahim, 2013). Instead, the Future Movement re-initiated its financial support for the independent Christian politicians to prepare for the upcoming elections, excluding the LFP from its financial support (Ibrahim, 2013).[23]

What is noticeable in the behaviour of the Future Movement and Hizbullah is that the former was more intransigent with its Christian allies, while the latter was more flexible. The Future Movement's intransigence towards its Christian allies can be explained firstly by its alliance with a major inter-sectarian Druze party, the PSP, which represents the majority of its community and had a large parliamentary bloc. Secondly, none of the March 14 Christian parties represented the majority of their sects, and therefore had only small parliamentary blocs. On the other hand, the FPM was Hizbullah's main ally from outside the Shiite community. The FPM is 'Hizbollah's most important non-Shiite ally – and the key to its efforts to avoid a sectarian label' (ICG, 2007: 10). Although the Shiite party had alliances with other parties from different sectarian communities, the FPM brought with it the support of a large portion of its sectarian community and a large parliamentary bloc, while Hizbullah's other allies, like the Druze party, the LDP and the Druze political leader, Wiam Wahhab, do not enjoy the same popularity as the FPM within their sectarian communities.[24]

The conflict was not only over manipulating intra-Christian conflicts. The Future Movement and Hizbullah also sought to forge alliances with their opposing sectarian communities so as to weaken each other. For instance, the Future Movement appointed the Shiite figure, Ibrahim Shamseddine, who is against Hizbullah's policies, as a minister in the cabinet that was formed in 2008. Hizbullah employed similar tactics when it relinquished a Shiite seat in the cabinet that was formed in 2011 to a Sunni politician who was a rival of Hizbullah's main political opponent, the Future Movement, in Tripoli. It also assigned its MP and lawyer, Nawwar Sahili, to defend and free from prison the Sunni religious figure, Omar Bakri Fustoq, who opposes the Future Movement. Both parties have thus funded and defended their political allies, empowering the political positions of their allies from rival sects.

The main party that was able to benefit from the conflict between the two coalitions was the PSP. It left the March 14 Coalition in 2009, although it was a founding member in 2005. It was able to manipulate its alliance with this coalition to win the parliamentary elections in 2009. Its alliances are formed according to its interests, which is mainly to ensure that it holds the share allocated for its sectarian community in the consociational system. 'Jumblat's strategy of political alliance was not restricted by any ideological or sectarian considerations. It is apparent that Jumblat was willing to ally himself with anyone or any group if he believed that it was in his interest to do so' (Rowayheb, 2011: 64). The PSP ability to manipulate the conflict can be explained firstly by the fact that it represents the majority of Druze, making the formation of the cabinet almost impossible without its approval and participation, since it would undermine the legitimacy of the government and could be understood by the Druze community as excluding it from the cabinet. Secondly, the PSP had a large parliamentary bloc according to the 2009 parliamentary elections, meaning it would be able to change the balance of power between the two coalitions if it left a certain coalition. The March 14 Coalition has 61 MPs (48 per cent of all parliamentary seats) and the March 8 Coalition has 57 MPs (47 per cent), while the Democratic Gathering bloc headed by the PSP has seven MPs.[25] So, a change in the political alliances of the PSP would alter the balance of power between the two coalitions. For instance, if the PSP left the March 14 Coalition and joined the March 8 Coalition, the latter would have the majority (64 MPs) and the former would become a minority (61 MPs).

An example of how the PSP used the conflict between the two coalitions to further its interests and secure political survival was when it left the March 14 Coalition in 2009. Jumblatt's explanation for leaving the alliance was that the March 14 Coalition had been 'driven by the rejection of the opposition on sectarian, tribal and political levels rather than being based on a political platform' (Sakr, 2009). However, the PSP did not seek to provide a political platform or to bridge the gap between the two coalitions, in particular between the Sunni and Shiite parties. Instead, it sought to manipulate the conflict between the two conflicting parties to secure its share in state positions, in particular the Druze quota in the cabinet. It would not have been able to shift its alliances without having a significant parliamentary bloc and the existence of a Sunni–Shiite conflict, which it was able to manipulate to its benefit and to widen its influence outside its sectarian group. For instance, the PSP supported the March 8 Coalition government that was formed in 2011 which included ministers from its party,[26] although it did not completely break its relations with the Future Movement. Without PSP support, the government would not have been able to secure the parliamentary endorsement required.

The behaviour of the PSP can be explained by the fact that historically the Druze parties always sought to widen their influence outside their sect to be able to alter the balance of power between the conflicting religious groups. This is because the Druze community considers itself to be one of the founding sectarian groups of the Lebanese state. The scholar Marwan Rowayheb (2011: 47) argues that Jumblatt 'faced the limitations imposed on him by Lebanon's sectarian system in terms of acquiring a *de jure* strong or influential position within Lebanon's political system.' Although the PSP was more flexible with its alliances and able to exert pressure on both coalitions to advance democratic reforms because of its ability to change the balance of power between them, it still sought to secure its representation and the acquisition of cabinet seats in the government.

Political Parties with Overwhelming Sectarian Support

The previous section explored how inter-sectarian alliances motivated Lebanese parties to make concessions. The subsequent discussion will in turn explore how certain political parties, which enjoy the support of the overwhelming majority of their sects, used this popularity to further their interests. The politicization of the sectarian divisions by Lebanon's consociational model endowed political parties which enjoy wide popular support within their sects with the veto power that enabled them to block the government formation and impose their views, for instance, in the formulation of a new electoral law. Although this factor was employed to buttress the position of certain political parties, it was not manipulated to push forward democratic reforms. Instead, it helped entrench further the sense of sectarian identity and block the initiation of democratic reforms.

Political parties that enjoy the support of the majority of their sects can strengthen their negotiating position. Whenever the Lebanese parties which enjoy the support of the majority of their sects reject a government policy they effectively veto it. Baydoun (2012: 122) argues that the 'absence' of political diversity within the major sects (Sunni and Shiite communities) has made the exclusion of a party that enjoys wide support within its sect from the ruling coalition in the government seems 'an expulsion not for a political power but for the expulsion of the entire sectarian group that is represented by this political power from the circle of authority.' If there were a diversity of political parties within the sect which enjoy popular support, it would have helped prevent paralysis in state institutions. This is evident with the Muslim parties, that is, the Future Movement and the Hizbullah–Amal Movement alliance.[27] They benefited from representing the majority of their sectarian communities. For example, the sit-in organized by the March 8 Coalition in downtown Beirut in 2006 to force the government to resign was faced with indifference from the Future Movement.[28] This is because the majority of the Sunni community supported it. On the other hand, Shiite ministers in the cabinet resigned in 2006 because they did not reach an agreement with the March 14 Coalition to form a national unity government. The two Shiite parties were aware that PM Fouad Siniora was not able to assign new Shiite minsters without the approval of Hizbullah and the Amal Movement.

Another example that shows how the Future Movement and the Hizbullah–Amal Movement alliance benefited from their popular support within their sects was their ability to 'impose' their views in the Doha Agreement. The resignation of Shiite ministers in 2006 to force the government to resign did not materialize until the eruption of the violent conflict on 7 May 2008, which was followed by the Doha Agreement. Under the direct auspices of Qatar and the support of Saudi Arabia, Syria and Iran, the Lebanese parties reached an agreement to form a new government and adopt the 1960 electoral law for the 2009 parliamentary elections. The Future Movement and the March 14 Coalition were 'forced' to accept the acquisition of a Hizbullah-led alliance of the blocking third (11 out of 30 seats) in government, and to recognize Hizbullah's armed wing as a legitimate Resistance entity in the government policy statement. Conversely, Hizbullah had to accept an amendment to the 1960 electoral law dividing Beirut into three main electoral districts. Such an amendment guaranteed the victory of the Future Movement in the parliamentary elections in 2009. One of these districts has a majority of Sunnis, which secured the victory of ten MPs for the Future Movement (Haddad, 2010: 52). Holding the majority of the Sunni seats in parliament strengthens the Future Movement's position in the consociational system as the main representative of its community to ask for the Sunni community share in state institutions.

An important feature that characterized the Doha negotiations was the fact that the Future Movement, Hizbullah and the PSP were treated as the main representatives of their communities.[29] On the other side, the Christian community was represented by various political parties from both coalitions (FPM, LFP, Kataeb and el-Marada). The different and conflicting alliances of the Christian parties often undermined the Christian community's ability to obtain its interests in the consociational system, such as an electoral law that secures better representation of their community in parliament, unlike the Muslim parties which were able to impose their views because of the support of the majority of their sectarian groups. What is noticeable also is that these sectarian parties, including the Future Movement and Hizbullah, supported an electoral law which is based on small districts and a winner-takes-all voting system (i.e. the 1960 electoral law). This law secured their victory in the elections as the main representatives of their communal groups in the consociational system and helped block the emergence of cross-sectarian parties. The Future Movement and the Hizbullah–Amal Movement alliance did not manipulate the power that is endowed to them, which is due to the 'absence' of political diversity within their sects, to push forward democratic reforms.

The request for the third bloc in the cabinet did not only happen in 2008. The formation of the government in 2009 similarly required Hizbullah's approval. Although the political parties entered the parliamentary elections with completely different political slogans, the March 14 Coalition which had won a parliamentary majority in the 2009 elections had to grant the March 8 Coalition the blocking third in the cabinet. The 2009 parliamentary elections, which were the fiercest elections since the end of the civil war in 1990, had several major points of conflict in the electoral campaign. These were around three main issues: the international and regional alignments of the Lebanese state and political parties, the status of Hizbullah's military wing, and the number of representatives of each party in the government (Corstange, 2010: 286).[30] While the March 14 Coalition accused Hizbullah of facilitating Syrian and Iranian intervention in the country, using its weapons against its fellow citizens, and seeking to have the blocking third in the government, the March 8 Coalition accused the March 14 Coalition of inviting Western tutelage, and defended its weapons as necessary to defend Lebanon against Israel. However, after the parliamentary elections, both coalitions were 'forced' to seek compromises so as to form a new government. Therefore, the Future Movement and the March 14 Coalition had to accept Hizbullah's military wing as a legitimate resistance against Israel in the government policy statement.

The existence of political parties with the support of the majority of their sects might encourage other sects to unite behind one main leadership to empower their political positions in the consociational system. As discussed above, when a sectarian group has one main representative, its ability to extract concessions from its rival sects will be strengthened and it will also have greater influence and share in the sectarian distribution of the state positions in the consociational system. The endeavour of the communal groups to unite behind one main sectarian leadership often has negative implications for political stability and entrenches further the sense of sectarian identity. The ability of the Shiite community to unite behind the Hizbullah–Amal Movement alliance and the use by Hizbullah of its armed forces on 7 May 2008 created a sense of 'weakness' (al-Ghuban) among the rival sects, in particular within the Sunni community. This feeling of 'envy' is a common feature that characterizes the relationship between the sectarian groups, usually resulting in pressure coming to bear on the representatives of the religious communities to 'mimic' their rival sects. Ahmad Baydoun calls this behaviour 'mirror language.'[31]

A prominent example of how sectarian groups are attempting to unite themselves is the Sunni community, which is seeking to unite behind a single leadership and expel other Sunni members who oppose the viewpoints of the majority of the sect. For instance, the Future Movement attempted to expel the Sunni parties in Tripoli that stood against its hegemony on the Sunni community. The assassination of the head of the Information Branch, Wissam al-Hassan (a Sunni officer), in 2012, which enraged Sunni public opinion, motivated supporters from the Future Movement to take advantage of this event to attack the office of the Harakat al-Tawhid, a Sunni group which opposes the political orientations of the Future Movement. It also opposes mainstream Sunni public opinion regarding Hizbullah's military wing. The attack caused the death of a religious figure, Shaykh Abed el-Razzak al-Asmar. The same happened with Shaker Berjawi (a pro-Hizbullah Sunni figure), who was forced to leave the Sunni-dominated area in Beirut, Tarik al-Jdida, after an armed conflict with supporters and members from the Future Movement. On the other hand, there are sectarian communities which have attempted to unite behind one main leadership but have failed. The Christian community, for example, bemoans its political divisions, while also seeing this political diversity as advantageous. A Christian media figure and former consultant to the Lebanese president, who requested anonymity, put this point clearly: 'pluralism within the Christians is a source of richness for them as it is a source of weakness.'[32]

Conclusion

This chapter has explored and analysed how Lebanon's consociational model helped spark inter- and intra-sectarian conflicts between political parties after the Syrian withdrawal in 2005, which had negative implications for political stability and the democratization process. One of the main factors behind the eruption of these conflicts has been the political parties' endeavours to mobilize popular support and strengthen their sectarian leadership. This helps them to improve their political positions to ask for a larger share in the quota allocated for their respective sects in the consociational system. Also, the sectarian parties sought to weave inter-sectarian alliances to be able to form the cabinet and improve their negotiating position. These reflected the vertical and horizontal segmentation of Lebanese society and had repercussions for political stability and the democratization process. As the above analysis shows, the intersection of the two factors (inter- and intra-sectarian conflicts) motivated the political parties to employ sectarian rhetoric, inculcate a sense of fear among their followers, build cross-sectarian alliances which often entail concessions, reject the elimination of confessionalism and formulate electoral laws that suit their interests. Moreover, political parties with overwhelming sectarian support took advantage of the allocation of state positions among the communal groups in the consociational system which endowed them with the veto power to impose their policies and views. These conflicts entrenched further the sense of sectarian identity and mutual distrust between the sectarian groups, and helped block the initiation of democratic reforms.

CHAPTER 5

EXTERNAL VARIABLES AND POLITICAL PARTIES SINCE 2005

The previous chapter explored the influence of the inter- and intra-sectarian conflicts in shaping the decision-making process of Lebanese parties in the post-2005 era. However, domestic conflicts over state positions and resources are not the only conflicts that influence the behaviour of Lebanese parties and consequently the prospects of democratic reform. Indeed, the influence of external factors (foreign alliances and actors, as well as external events) on Lebanese politics has frequently intersected with domestic conflicts in shaping the behaviour of political parties, also having implications for political stability and the democratization process. Contrary to the expectation that the Syrian withdrawal would mark the end of foreign intervention in Lebanon, the intensity of foreign intervention in domestic politics from a diverse set of external players increased significantly in the post-2005 period, including most prominently Saudi Arabia, Syria, Qatar, the US, France and Israel.

This chapter will argue that Lebanon's consociational model 'encourages' political parties to seek foreign support to bolster their domestic positions. The intersection of foreign alliances with existing domestic conflicts (i.e. the inter- and intra-sectarian conflicts discussed previously) negatively influenced the behaviour of Lebanese political parties, increasing their mutual intransigence and distrust and having adverse implications for political stability and the democratization process. More specifically, it will be argued that the interventions of various external actors have had two main effects on the behaviour of Lebanese political groups since the Syrian withdrawal in 2005. Firstly, the intensity of foreign intervention has fuelled the inter-sectarian conflicts, which has encouraged them to become inflexible and stubborn when it comes to compromises. Secondly, foreign alliances and regional developments have fuelled the intra-sectarian conflicts. This in turn has also increased their intransigence and inflexibility, seriously undermining political stability and the democratization process.

Firstly, the chapter will discuss the forms of foreign intervention in Lebanon since the Syrian withdrawal, moving on to discuss the international and domestic political events that preceded and followed the Syrian withdrawal in 2005 to show in the later sections how Lebanon's political parties responded to these developments and how they shaped their behaviour towards one another and in regard to political reform. This second section will also explore the reasons behind the political parties' alliances with foreign actors. Thirdly, it will generally examine the influence of foreign alliances on inter- and intra-sectarian conflicts and on the behaviour of Lebanese parties, as well as on the prospects of initiating democratic reforms. Fourthly, it will focus on the main external factors that influenced the inter-sectarian conflicts in Lebanon in the post-2005 period (such as Resolution 1559 and the July War). Fifthly, it will explore the influence on intra-sectarian conflicts of those external factors studied in the previous section. In so doing, the last two sections will show that Lebanon's consociational model failed to shield the country from foreign intervention and ensure political stability. Instead, external interference which helped exacerbate inter- and intra-sectarian conflicts influenced the behaviour of Lebanese political parties and entrenched mutual distrust between them, which brought negative repercussions for political stability and the democratization process.

Forms of Foreign Intervention in Lebanon

Foreign intervention in Lebanon has taken many forms. Since 2005, Lebanon has witnessed many interventions from diverse external players. These players have employed different means to intervene in the domestic politics of the country. As the discussion in the following sections will show, the increase in the intensity of domestic and regional conflicts has led foreign patrons to widen and diversify their forms of support to bolster the position of their domestic allies against their opponents.

Baydoun classifies three main forms of foreign support for Lebanese groups. The first form constitutes *physical* support. This usually includes financial and military support, such as weapons, intelligence information, and training (Baydoun, 2012: 100), and has increased significantly since the Syrian withdrawal in 2005. Political parties, such as the Future Movement and the PSP, have all received large amounts of money from their foreign patrons. These financial resources were largely spent on supporting the parliamentary election campaigns in 2005 and 2009. For instance, Saudi Arabia and the US are both known to have funded the Future Movement to combat Hizbullah in case a sectarian conflict erupted between the two communities (Hersh, 2007). As is well known, Hizbullah also regularly receives financial and military support from Iran.

The second form of support is *political*. Baydoun defines political support as 'the use of the capabilities and influence of an outside party in the regional or international networks and systems to support its domestic Lebanese ally's positions and requests (which constantly coordinates with the objectives of the [foreign] sponsor) and to protect it' from its political opponents (Baydoun, 2012: 100). The political influence of foreign patrons is often employed via international institutions, such as the United Nations, and geared towards the protection of domestic allies in Lebanon. For instance, the US and France both proposed several resolutions in the UNSC to support their March 14 Coalition ally in 2006 after the resignation of the Shiite ministers, which undermined the legitimacy of Siniora's government, such as Resolutions 1680 (17 May 2006), 1664 (29 March 2006) and 1686 (15 June 2006). According to Sami Baroudi and Imad Salamey (2011: 411), these resolutions aimed to put pressure on the Syrian government and indirectly on its domestic March 8 Coalition ally to reduce their opposition to the March 14 Coalition.[1]

The third form of support is *cultural and educational* in nature. It includes a web of traditions, values, practices and slogans which have an educational influence in organizing and mobilizing Lebanese citizens (Baydoun, 2012: 101). Such support is less common among Lebanese political groups. Although this factor may not directly influence domestic politics, it helps strengthen the political ties that bring the domestic and external players together. The most evident example of this form of support is Iran's support for Hizbullah. The Islamic Republic of Iran represents a spiritual and ideological inspiration for Hizbullah (Qassem, 2010).

Political Parties' Foreign Alliances since 2005

The waning of the main foreign player (i.e. Syria) in Lebanon has led to a reshuffling of the foreign alliances pursued by Lebanese parties. The timing of the Syrian withdrawal in 2005 coincided with an intense conflict between the two main axes in the Middle East (Iranian- and American-led axes), especially after the Iraq War in 2003. The regional conflict ran in parallel with the emergence of a Sunni–Shiite conflict in Lebanon, which helped fuel it.

The International Scene since 2005 and the Arab Revolutions

The Syrian withdrawal in 2005, supposed to mark the end of foreign intervention in Lebanon, was followed by a significant rise in the degree and intensity of external interference in Lebanon's domestic politics. As the report of the International Crisis Group (ICG) (2005: 8–12) stated: 'Lebanon shifted from Syrian tutelage to Western umbrella'. According to the ICG's (2005: 8) analysis:

> Lebanon today falls under the auspices of a remarkable array of UN senior envoys and resolutions. No fewer than four senior UN envoys are involved: Geir Pedersen, the Secretary General's Personal Representative for Lebanon; Terje Roed-Larsen, his representative for compliance with Security Council Resolution 1559 concerning Syria's withdrawal and the disarmament of militias; Alvaro de Soto, the UN Special Coordinator for the Middle East peace process; and Detlev Mehlis, who is responsible for investigating Hariri's assassination. This is in addition to the multinational forces of UNIFIL.[2]

The ICG report refers to the several resolutions taken by the United Nations since 2004. Resolution 1595 (7 April 2005) requested the establishment of 'an international independent investigation

Commission ("the Commission") based in Lebanon to assist the Lebanese authorities in their investigation of all aspects of this terrorist act [i.e. Hariri's assassination]' and to '[e]njoy the full cooperation of the Lebanese authorities, including full access to all documentary, testimonial and physical information and evidence in their possession that the Commission deems relevant to the inquiry' (UNSC, 2005a). Resolution 1636 (31 October 2005) stated that the Security Council '*[i]nsists* that Syria not interfere in Lebanese domestic affairs, either directly or indirectly, refrain from any attempt aimed at destabilizing Lebanon, and respect scrupulously the sovereignty, territorial integrity, unity and political independence of this country' (UNSC, 2005c). Resolution 1614 (29 July 2005) warned the Lebanese government that the presence of UNIFIL is interim and would be withdrawn if it did not deploy its army on the southern borders with Israel (ICG, 2005: 9; UNSC, 2005b).[3] As mentioned in Chapter 2, the most significant resolution was Resolution 1559 (2 September 2004) because it called for foreign forces to withdraw from Lebanon and the demilitarization of the armed groups. Articles 2 and 3 in this Resolution called for '*all* remaining foreign forces to withdraw from Lebanon' and '*the* disbanding and disarmament of all Lebanese and non-Lebanese militias' (UNSC, 2004). These two articles referred to the Syrian military presence, the Palestinian armed groups and the armed wing of Hizbullah. Article 5 of Resolution 1559 also called 'for a free and fair electoral process in Lebanon's upcoming presidential election conducted according to Lebanese constitutional rules devised without foreign interference or influence' (UNSC, 2004).

However, these resolutions were not the only measures taken by the international community to exert pressure on Syria and Lebanon. As mentioned in Chapter 2, the USC promulgation of the Syria Accountability and Lebanese Sovereignty Restoration Act in 2003 was a significant international effort to call for the Syrian withdrawal from Lebanon and to demilitarize the armed groups. The Act stated that Syria should cease its support for 'terrorism' and 'declare its total renunciation of all forms of terrorism, and close all terrorist offices and facilities in Syria, including the offices of Hamas, Hizballah, Palestinian Islamic Jihad, the Popular Front for the Liberation of Palestine, and the Popular Front for the Liberation of Palestine – General Command' (USC, 2003: Section 3, Article 1). It also called on the government of Syria to immediately withdraw its military forces from Lebanon, including military and security forces (USC, 2003: Section 3, Article 2). Furthermore, it stated that the government of Lebanon should deploy its armed forces in southern Lebanon and 'should evict all terrorist and foreign forces from southern Lebanon, including Hizballah and the Iranian Revolutionary Guards' (USC, 2003: Section 3, Article 4).

The promulgation of these resolutions reflected a change in the international scene which emerged after the Iraq War in 2003. The demise of the Iraqi regime widened Iranian influence in the region. Vali Nasr (2006: 66) argues that Iran 'welcomed' the demise of the Iraqi regime 'because Iraq had been a preoccupation of Iranian foreign policy for much of the five decades since the Iraqi monarchy fell to Arab nationalism in 1958'. The rise of Shiite parties in Iraq was paralleled with their alliance with Iran. This is what the Jordanian King Abdullah called the 'Shiite Crescent', ranging from Bahrain to Lebanon (Hizbullah) through Syria, Iraq and Iran. The rise of Iranian influence in the Arab world encouraged certain other Arab countries, in particular Saudi Arabia, Egypt (under the Mubarak regime) and Jordan, to seek to undermine Tehran's influence in the region. This was met with US intentions to undermine Syrian and Iranian influence in the Middle East after the Iraq War (Mearsheimer & Walt, 2006: 59–62).

What further complicated the conflict between the two axes was the eruption of the Arab Revolutions in 2011, which influenced the balance of power between regional and international players. Indeed, the toppling of several Arab regimes led to structural changes in the regional balance of power between the pro-American and pro-Iranian axes. The Syrian conflict threatened one of the main pillars of the Iranian axis and Hamas' 'withdrawal' from the Iranian orbit weakened the position of the Syrian regime. On the other side, the demise of the Mubarak regime dealt a major blow to the American-led axis in the region. However, the short-lived Muhammad Mursi presidency (2012–13) and his successors, Adly Mansour (2013–14) and Abdel Fattah el-Sisi (2014–present), adopted a 'moderate' tone towards the US and Israel, thus signalling that Cairo will not join Tehran's sphere of influence.[4] The foreign policy of Egypt since 2011 has as yet not witnessed any radical changes in regard to the major issues in the region, such as the Arab–Israeli conflict, Egyptian–Israeli relations, or its cooperation with the US against 'terrorism'. What is noticeable in these revolutions then is the way that they have led to major changes at the domestic level of the revolutionary states, while their foreign policies have not undergone radical changes.

Lebanon's Political Parties and Foreign Alliances

As mentioned previously, the Syrian withdrawal in 2005 was accompanied and followed by major regional and international developments. These developments left their mark on Lebanese political parties' foreign alliances. Indeed, since 2005, several Lebanese political parties have defected from the Syrian orbit and joined the American-led axis in the region. The Sunni–Shiite conflict has shaped the foreign alliances of Lebanese parties since 2005. The increase in the intensity of the regional and international conflicts between the two main axes was reflected in Lebanon by the conflict between the two communities: Sunni and Shiite. Meanwhile, the Druze and Christian parties manipulated the Sunni–Shiite conflict to promote their interests and accordingly built their own external alliances.

The Syrian military withdrawal led many political parties to capitalize on its consequences. The intense pressures from Western powers and Arab states (such as Saudi Arabia and Egypt) on the Syrian regime, which culminated after the assassination of Hariri, led both parties (pro- and anti-Syrian) to capitalize on these consequences at the domestic and regional levels. Each party had its own interpretation of the Syrian withdrawal, especially regarding future relations with Syria and the status of Hizbullah's armed wing. According to the Lebanese media figure, Muhammad Obied, who is close to the March 8 Coalition and a former member of the Amal Movement:

> The March 8 Coalition was formed to affirm that the withdrawal will not change Lebanon's choices regarding the Resistance and the alliance with Syria, and the March 14 [Coalition] was formed to oppose the March 8's propositions and to confirm that a portion of the Lebanese people became linked directly with the American project through their support for Resolution 1559. It also aimed to confirm that the Syrian withdrawal will weaken Syria's domestic allies and in particular the Resistance.[5]

The different interpretations of the consequences and aims of the Syrian withdrawal coupled with the absence of agreement on the post-Syrian

order encouraged Lebanese groups to seek and strengthen their foreign
alliances so as to bolster their domestic positions vis-à-vis their inter-
and intra-sectarian rivals. Khaled Saghieh argues that:

> After 2005, every sect who felt 'intimidated' resorted to external
> players to protect itself, and the external players also wanted to
> intervene, particularly during the 2005 period at the climax of the
> American project in the Middle East and the occupation of Iraq.
> There was an American desire to intervene, especially after the
> collapse of the relations between Saudi Arabia and Syria after
> Hariri's assassination, and there was also an Iranian desire to keep
> its influence in Lebanon after the Syrian withdrawal.[6]

The withdrawal of Syrian military forces during 'abnormal' circumstances encouraged the two Muslim parties, the Future Movement and
Hizbullah, to strengthen the alliances they had established before the
Syrian withdrawal in 2005. In addition to its alliance with Saudi Arabia,
which was established before 2005, the Future Movement's aim to
disarm Hizbullah's military wing and weaken Syrian influence in
Lebanon intersected with the same interest of Egypt, the US, the UK
and France, which subsequently helped strengthen its alliances with
them.[7] For Hizbullah, the endeavour of the Future Movement and the
March 14 Coalition to disarm its military wing encouraged it to
strengthen its external alliance.[8]

On the other side, the two Christian parties, the LFP and the
Kataeb Party, did not change their foreign alliances. The leaders of
these two parties kept their close alliances with the West, in particular
with the US and France, which were established before the Syrian
withdrawal. What further encouraged the leader of the LFP,
Samir Geagea, to strengthen the party's foreign alliances is that he
envisioned, according to Khaled Saghieh, that the interests of the
Christians would be served by an alliance with the major Sunni party,
the Future Movement.[9] An alliance with a Sunni party, which has close
connections with major Arab Sunni states, would enhance the ability
of the LFP to build an alliance with Arab Sunni countries, including
Saudi Arabia and Egypt. What further enhances the LFP's ability to
build these alliances with these Sunni states is their shared position
against Hizbullah's military wing.

While the foreign alliances of the Future Movement, Hizbullah, the LFP and the Kataeb Party have remained the same since 2005, those of the Christian party, the FPM, and the Druze party, the PSP, have not. The FPM initiated a significant change in its foreign alliances in 2005. Before 2005, it was a close ally of the US and France. However, after 2005 it became critical of Western intervention in Lebanon. This criticism was voiced after it left the March 14 Coalition before the parliamentary elections in 2005, which were supported by the West. As discussed in the previous chapter, the leader of the FPM, Aoun, reasoned that the interests of the Christian community in Lebanon would be best served through an alliance with the Shiite party, Hizbullah,[10] which by extension implied an alliance with the Syrian regime.

The foreign alliances of the Druze PSP in turn witnessed a total of three significant changes. The first such change occurred after the assassination of Hariri in 2005, when the party adopted a highly critical political discourse towards Syria and Hizbullah. This was replaced by the adoption of a more moderate political discourse towards Syria in 2009. The third change then commenced with the eruption of the Syrian conflict in 2011. Again, the PSP became highly critical of the Syrian regime, although it retained a moderate stance towards Damascus' domestic allies. Its support for the Syrian opposition stems from the fact that it cannot stand against the Sunni majority of Syria and the Arab world.[11] The support of Saudi Arabia and the Arab Gulf states for the Syrian opposition and their significant influence upon Lebanese domestic politics motivated it to stand against the Syrian regime so as to maintain its relationship with these Sunni states. Khaled Saghieh attributes Jumblatt's unstable alliance-seeking behaviour to the small size of the Druze community, which always aims to preserve its political status and position within the political system due to what he calls 'minority fears'.[12]

External Factors and Inter- and Intra-Sectarian Conflicts

As the discussion above showed, after the Syrian withdrawal, the rivalry between the sectarian political parties over state positions encouraged them to seek foreign support in order to bolster their domestic positions. Such foreign alliances usually fuel inter- and intra-sectarian conflicts and further entrench the sense of sectarian identity and lack of trust, both of which carry adverse implications for the prospects of democratic reform. According to Karim Pakradouni, the initiation of democratic reforms in Lebanon requires 'reconciliation and harmony' between the political parties before implementing the reforms,[13] since the Lebanese political system is based on a power-sharing agreement.

The increase in the intensity of conflict between the political parties has made them heavily dependent on their foreign patrons to bolster their domestic positions. Zahar (2012b: 56) argues that it would 'be wrong-headed to deny Lebanese factions' and politicians' own role in increasing their country's dependence on the outside world'. The more the domestic player is entangled in an alliance with external parties, the more the foreign patron has influence over its domestic client and the more it will feed the suspicions and mutual distrust of political opponents. In such a situation, the domestic party with external alliances will invariably encourage its inter- and intra-sectarian opponents to strengthen their foreign alliances too. This becomes evident when there are political and sectarian conflicts since parties will desperately seek foreign support to bolster their positions against their domestic opponents. Baydoun (2012: 104) argues that an external player manipulates Lebanese domestic clients to put pressure on its domestic and regional opponents, which often involves violence through its domestic allies' attempts to quell its opponents, albeit without involving itself directly in the conflict.

The developments at regional and international levels which have implications at the domestic level, such as the passage of UNSC Resolution 1559, influence the behaviour of Lebanese political parties, since they capitalize on its repercussions which has implications on their ability to reach compromises. This in turn further restricts the prospect for democratic reforms. The rise in the intensity of foreign intervention usually raises the fears and suspicions of domestic parties towards one another and blocks the prospect of initiating genuine democratic reforms in the country. As Zahar (2012a: 77) argues, '[t]he intervention of outsiders has rendered the deconfessionalisation of Lebanon's political system as elusive as ever. It has also contributed to reawakening sectarian feelings and stoking up sectarian tensions in society.' This point is also confirmed by Karim Pakradouni who asserts that 'the experience of Lebanon with foreign intervention has proved that the domestic reforms are not a priority for foreign states; what they are interested in is the subordination of the political class [to their will]'.[14]

Intersection of External Factors with
Inter-Sectarian Conflicts

External players often seek to cement alliances with the largest sects. Lebanon's consociational model frequently gives large sects more influence over domestic politics than smaller ones because of their numerical strength and voting power. It does so although the system is based on a power-sharing agreement which in theory does not allow certain parties to dominate the political system. For this reason, foreign powers usually seek to cement alliances with the largest sects in order to secure and increase their influence over domestic politics, in particular the Sunni and Shiite communities (the two largest communities). As the discussion below will show, the foreign powers' quest to increase their influence intersected with the inter-sectarian conflicts in Lebanon. Saudi Arabia supports the main Sunni party, the Future Movement, while Iran supported and continues to support the Shiite party, Hizbullah. This has entrenched the mutual distrust between the two parties and the sense of sectarian identity, making the initiation of democratic reforms almost impossible without foreign support.

Several examples show how the intersection of interests between domestic and external players shaped the political priorities of the Lebanese political parties, entrenched mutual distrust and suspicion, and negatively affected political stability. As the following discussion will show, Resolution 1559, the assassination of former PM Hariri, the July War, the Fatah al-Islam conflict, and the manipulation of Hizbullah's external alliances all left their mark on political stability and the democratization process. The case of the Doha Agreement can also shed light on how the external players were able to sponsor the Doha Agreement and engineer a power-sharing agreement between the domestic parties when they felt that their interests were at risk. This demonstrates the heavy influence of the external players on the domestic parties in agreeing upon essential democratic issues, such as electoral law and the election of a new president. These events and developments also show how Lebanon's consociational model 'motivated' the political parties to seek foreign support and to capitalize on the implications of external events, which had adverse effects on their behaviour and undermined their ability to reach compromises on essential democratic issues and engineer power-sharing agreements.

UNSC Resolution 1559 and the Assassination of Hariri

Resolution 1559, issued on 2 September 2004, one day before the Lebanese presidential elections, has had significant implications for Lebanese domestic politics in the post-2005 period and far-reaching effects on the stability of the power-sharing agreement, fuelling tensions at political and sectarian levels. The political parties manipulated the Resolution to further their own interests, which entrenched their suspicions of each other. Their capitalization on the Resolution was because they expected that it would force Damascus to leave the country and lead to the formation of a new power-sharing agreement. This Resolution and the assassination of Hariri fed the inter-sectarian conflicts and contributed to the failure of the power-sharing agreement that was engineered after the 2005 parliamentary elections and the formulation of a new electoral law.

The first group of parties to capitalize on the implications of the Resolution were the Christian parties. The formulation of UNSC Resolution 1559 raised the hopes of the Christian parties, who sought to bolster their political opposition and to force the Syrian military to withdraw from Lebanon (Abu-Habib, 2013a). The withdrawal of Syria would enable them to have influence over the distribution of state positions that are allocated for their community in the consociational system; Damascus had prohibited the Christian parties and elites from holding these positions. Thus, they helped found the main opposition gathering in 2004, the so-called Bristol Gathering, which later became the March 14 Coalition, after it organized the anti-Syria protest on 14 March 2005. It included political parties which met in December 2004 at the Bristol Hotel in Beirut. They were against the Syrian military presence in Lebanon and the extension of the presidential term of Lahoud, and called for the formulation of a 'fair' electoral law (Choucair, 2005: 2). In addition to the QSG, the Bristol Gathering included the FPM, the PSP, the Democratic Forum and the Democratic Leftist Movement, as well as members of Rafic Hariri's parliamentary bloc (Choucair, 2005: 2).

The Druze leader, Walid Jumblatt, was one of the first Muslim politicians who defected from the Syrian orbit and joined the American-led alliance, that is, the Bristol Gathering. He was aware that UNSC Resolution 1559 marked a change in US policy towards Syria (Ross, 2005). According to the Lebanese journalist Nicolas Nassif (2011),

Jumblatt changed his position after he received assurances from American officials that the Syrian regime would be toppled through Resolution 1559, the assassination of Hariri and the formation of the STL. Because of his betting on there being dramatic regional developments to follow the issuance of the Syria Accountability Act and UNSC Resolution 1559 to force Syria to withdraw from Lebanon, he rejected the Syrian request to amend the constitution to extend the presidential period of Lahoud by three years (Assaf, Nayla 2004). As a consequence of his and the March 14 Coalition opposition to this extension, they boycotted Lahoud. Jumblatt stated that 'as long as the president remained in power, the work of any cabinet will be hindered' (Raad & Assaf, 2005).[15] Jumblatt's behaviour after the issuance of Resolution 1559 can be explained by his expectation that Lebanon would witness a radical change in its foreign policies towards Syria and the US, which would eventually lead the West, and in particular Washington, to be the new external player in Lebanese domestic politics. This would imply a new power-sharing agreement and a new distribution of state positions among sectarian groups. Thus, his support for the US call on Syria to withdraw its military forces and the resignation of Lahoud was to secure his future share in the quota allocated for his community in the consociational system under the auspices of the new external player.

However, the Sunni leadership, in particular erstwhile PM Rafic Hariri, was more cautious in terms of his position towards Syria, Hizbullah and Resolution 1559, although he expected a dramatic change in the role of Syria in Lebanon, which would yield a new power-sharing agreement. Thus, he started approaching the Lebanese opposition to the Syrian presence. Hariri agreed on ratifying the constitutional amendment to comply with the Syrian will to extend the presidential term of Lahoud in September 2004. He was aware that Articles 2 and 3 in Resolution 1559, which asked for Hizbullah's military wing to be disarmed and called for the Syrian withdrawal, would be 'humiliating' for Damascus and would not realistically materialize (Blanford, 2006: 104). After Hariri stepped down as PM in October 2004, he started approaching the Christian- and Druze-led opposition, the Bristol Gathering, although he did not officially call for the Syrian forces to withdraw. According to Blanford (2006: 6), 'Hariri was wary of losing the support of his constituency if he was seen moving too close to the more outspoken of Syria's Lebanese adversaries.' The Sunni leadership was more cautious because it did not want to spark a violent Sunni–Shiite conflict. Saouli (2006: 712) justifies Hariri's position in the following terms:

> Hariri's response to regional changes was more cautious, largely due to the delicacy of his position within the Lebanese political structure and a leadership that emanated from the Sunnite community, which traditionally supported Syria. Within the opposition, Hariri participated partially by delegating a Christian member of his parliamentary block to the opposition camp, while two pro-Syria members of his block resigned. At the same time, Hariri maintained his relations with pro-Syrian forces in Lebanon and Syria itself.

On the other hand, Hariri's cautious position towards Syria, Hizbullah and UNSC Resolution 1559 raised fears in the pro-Syria camp about his intentions. He was accused by the pro-Syria camp of tacitly supporting the Resolution. The Lebanese government, headed by PM Omar Karami (2004–5) at the time, accused him of supporting UNSC Resolution 1559 (Choucair, 2005: 2–3). Damascus also accused Hariri 'of plotting with the US and France against Syria and of deviating from the joint Lebanese–Syrian stand' (Blanford, 2006: 92). The pro-Syrian camp view was that UNSC Resolution 1559 complies with the 'American and Israeli objectives of disarming Hizbullah and weakening the regional states that support it (i.e. Syria and Iran). Therefore, it accused the then opposition (i.e. the Bristol Gathering) of encouraging foreign intervention in Lebanon. The pro-Syria camp considered Resolution 1559 to be, in the words of the pro-Syrian figure and former PM Omar Karami, 'a fitna decision which will divide the Lebanese' (Samad, 2009).[16]

The intensive foreign intervention in Lebanese politics, as well as the promulgation of several UNSC resolutions (1595, 1636 and 1559) and the assassination of Hariri, raised the suspicions of Hizbullah regarding the Lebanese opposition. Hariri's death marked the end of the Syrian presence in Lebanon and therefore the end of the main political protector of the Resistance. Zahar (2012a: 70) states that 'UNSC Resolution 1559 is perceived by the Shia, particularly by Hizbollah, as proof that they are the target of a concerted campaign for political marginalization and even physical elimination'. In his speech on the 8 March protest which was aimed to show support for Syria and denounce Resolution 1559, Nasrallah (2005) stated that:

> Who accepts from the opposition [i.e. the March 14 Coalition] that the regulation and the presence of [the Syrian] withdrawal will be only on the basis of the Ta'if Agreement we agree with him. However, he who is capitalising on Resolution 1559 – we tell him that we see [your capitalization on Resolution 1559] as a coup on the Ta'if Agreement and its terms, which means a coup on the national consensus.

Resolution 1559, which was followed by several political assassinations of March 14 Coalition members (see Table 5.1), further entrenched the fears of Hizbullah and increased its intransigence in regard to reaching agreements on debatable issues, such as the STL, which put the stability of the power-sharing agreement at risk and reflected a deep cleavage over the formulation of state foreign policy. PM Siniora's position that 'Lebanon cannot confront the international community by refusing to comply with UN Security Resolution 1559' raised the fears of Hizbullah towards the March 14 Coalition (Abu-Rizk, 2005). Hizbullah's relations with the March 14 Coalition were further complicated by the government's approval of the STL draft law after the assassination of Gebran Tueini in December 2005. The March 14 Coalition took the Tueini assassination as an opportunity to urgently discuss the draft law on the STL. The government decision was based on the vote of the majority of ministers and not on consensus. Thus, Hizbullah and the Amal Movement protested against it and their ministers suspended their participation in the government in December 2005.

Initially, the stated reason of the two Shiite parties was the marginalization of Shiite ministers from debates and discussions in government. At a later stage, however, they requested that the government re-affirm the status of Hizbullah's military wing as a Resistance entity, as stated in the cabinet policy statement. Their request was motivated by their fears that the March 14 Coalition was becoming more entangled with its external alliances with Western states.

Hizbullah and the Amal Movement 'needed reassurance that even if foreign pressure to apply the resolution [i.e. Resolution 1559] increased, the cabinet would not relinquish solidarity with the Shiite faction' (Fakhoury-Mühlbacher, 2009: 378). Their suspension undermined the legitimacy of the government because the distribution of state positions was according to the power-sharing agreement. In a case where one of the sectarian groups is not part of the cabinet, one of the components of the consociational system (the proportional representation of the sects) is undermined and cabinet legitimacy would be questioned. What further fuelled the government crisis was that the Lebanese president at the time, Emile Lahoud, refused to attend cabinet meetings without the participation of the Shiite ministers. The conflict that erupted after the suspension of the Shiite ministers further entrenched the tensions between the two coalitions. Walid Jumblatt, for instance, declared his suspicions regarding the loyalty of Hizbullah to Lebanon. He stated that 'to those who hold the rifle today we say, "thank you, the South is free", to whom is your allegiance now, Lebanon or other countries', in reference to the close alliance of Hizbullah with Syria and Iran (Hatoum, 2006). Their suspension did not end until February 2006 when the PM Siniora declared in a speech in parliament that 'the national resistance in Lebanon was never and will never be called anything but resistance' (Choucair, 2006).

These developments clearly carried ramifications for the initiation of democratic reforms. The popular uproar after the assassination of Hariri forced Omar Karami's government to resign in late February 2005. Lebanese parties were not able to agree on a new government until Saudi Arabia and Syria had agreed, in mid-April 2005, about one month before the deadline for parliamentary elections, on Najib Mikati forming the new cabinet which included representatives from both parties (pro- and anti-Syrian forces) (Haddad, 2005: 308). Although Hizbullah and the FPM requested the formulation of a new electoral law (which could imply the postponement of the elections for at least several weeks until they agreed on a new law),[17] the March 14 Coalition rejected their request. This rejection can be explained by the wide popular support that the Coalition enjoyed after the assassination of Hariri, paralleled with formidable foreign pressure, in particular from the US, to hold the elections on time (May 29–June 19) (Norton, 2007b: 482). Such a law secured their sectarian leadership, in particular for the

Future Movement. The Future Movement could claim to be the main representative of the Sunnis and ask for the quota allocated for its community in the consociational system.

Not only had the formulation of a new electoral law been blocked, but Hizbullah also became more intransigent regarding its military wing. As discussed above, the intensive foreign intervention after the assassination of Hariri and the close alliances of the March 14 Coalition with Western powers raised its fears and suspicions about its domestic opponents. It feared 'that its domestic rivals will seize on foreign demands to strengthen their own negotiating position' (Leenders, 2006). Leenders (2006) writes of Hizbullah's refusal to make concessions in the National Dialogue meetings in 2006 that it was 'in no mood to compromise while the US and France [were] breathing down its neck [...] [T]he US and France are drumming up UN support for their demands while institutionalizing their pressures by sending an ever increasing stream of UN investigators and rapporteurs.'[18]

The July War in 2006 and the Fatah al-Islam Conflict

Resolution 1559 was not the only external factor that fuelled inter-sectarian conflicts in Lebanon and threatened the stability of the power-sharing agreement and the prospects of democratic reforms in the country. The July War of 2006 also had deep political and sectarian implications, leading to paralysis in the main legislative state institution, parliament, and a vacancy in the presidency position, undermining the stability of the power-sharing agreement and contributing to the eruption of the Fatah al-Islam conflict. The war erupted when Hizbullah kidnapped two Israeli soldiers on the Lebanese border with Israel on 12 July 2006, which was followed by a massive attack from Israel on Hizbullah and the country's infrastructure. The war did not end until the UNSC promulgation of Resolution 1701 (11 August 2006). The Resolution called for 'a full cessation of hostilities based upon, in particular, the immediate cessation by Hizbollah of all attacks and the immediate cessation by Israel of all offensive military operations' (UNSC, 2006d: 2). This resolution also called on the Lebanese government to send its armed forces to southern Lebanon to help ensure security. Over the course of 33 days, more than 1,109 Lebanese were killed, the majority of them being civilians (HRW, 2009: 79). After the end of the war, Hizbullah considered its ability to withstand the Israeli attack as a 'divine victory'.

in Paris 'to continue the work that was launched at the Paris I and Paris II donor conferences, which focused on helping Lebanon cope with its crippling public debt' (Baroudi & Salamey, 2011: 412).[23] The Paris III Donor Conference was held on 25 January 2007, at which Arab and other foreign donors pledged over 7 billion dollars in aid (Ministry of Finance, 2007: 4). This happened two months after the resignation of the Shiite ministers and followed the opposition-led strike on 23 January 2007, which led to clashes between supporters of the two coalitions that left at least six dead and several wounded (*al-Mustaqbal*, 2007a, 2007b). According to a former US senior intelligence official, '[w]e are in a program to enhance the Sunni capability to resist Shiite influence, and we're spreading the money around as much as we can' (Hersh, 2007).

On the other hand, the March 14 Coalition heavily criticized Hizbullah for its part in the July War. Both the Future Movement and the March 14 Coalition accused Hizbullah of sparking the conflict with Israel in order to mitigate international pressure on Syria and Iran after the assassination of Hariri in 2005. They also accused it of being a 'state within the state' because of its military arsenal and called for its military wing to be disarmed. Jumblatt heavily criticized it for monopolizing state decisions in regard to war and peace. He stated that the establishment of a powerful state is 'through the integration of the Resistance in the army, and that the decision of war and peace should be under the command of the state' (*al-Mustaqbal*, 2006b). He questioned the loyalty of Hizbullah's military resistance, asking: 'is the Resistance Lebanese or is it a tool of the Syrian–Iranian axis on Lebanese soil?' (*al-Mustaqbal*, 2006b). In a similar vein, the Christian leader, Samir Geagea, criticized Hizbullah's declaration of victory after the July War. He stated that '[w]e are the victors because it was us who were demanding the [Lebanese] Army's deployment [in southern Lebanon], backed by UNIFIL [peacekeepers], while they [i.e. Hizbullah] were opposed' (*The Daily Star*, 2006). He also criticized the military wing of Hizbullah, asking: 'how can a strong state be built with a statelet within its midst? How can it be done with arms and ammunition continuing to flow in, when they force the state to follow their own schedule?' (*The Daily Star*, 2006).

The rise of the military power of Hizbullah due to its ability to withstand the Israeli attack, and the exacerbation of political and sectarian tensions, motivated the Lebanese political parties to arm themselves (Bathish, 2007; Picard, 2012: 100). One of the groups that was rumoured to be targeted by the Future Movement to be its armed wing was the Palestinians, in particular the Fatah al-Islam group that was settling in the Palestinian refugee camp, Naher al-Bared, near Tripoli, in northern Lebanon (Fisk, 2007; Knudsen, 2011: 100–2).[24] According to the journalist Seymour Hersh (2007), this group was part of the pro-Syrian group Fatah al-Intifada, and when it changed its position against the Syrian regime, it received financial and military support from the Future Movement and Saudi Arabia. The reason behind the Future Movement's support for the Fatah al-Islam group was probably to balance the military power of Hizbullah. If a violent conflict erupted between the two Sunni and Shiite parties, the Future Movement would not be able to withstand the military power of Hizbullah unless it had an armed wing, which the Fatah al-Islam group was supposed to be.

The military presence of this group was eventually terminated when the Lebanese army attacked Naher al-Bared camp in May 2007.[25] The clashes between the group and the Lebanese army erupted when a bank was robbed near Tripoli in May 2007 by members of the Fatah al-Islam group, which led to clashes in the streets with Lebanese security forces, leaving two members of the group dead. In revenge, the militant group killed at least 15 Lebanese soldiers near the refugee camp, which provoked the army to attack the camp to capture those responsible. About 222 Islamist militants were killed in a 15-week battle, more than 202 were captured and an unknown number were buried in mass graves in the refugee camp (Bayoumy, 2007). In addition, at least 42 civilians and 163 soldiers were killed (Bayoumy, 2007). It is considered the worst internal violent conflict in Lebanon since the end of the civil war (Bayoumy, 2007). The head of the army accused the militant group of being directly linked to al-Qaeda.

The violent conflict undermined political stability and the country's security, and enflamed tensions between the March 8 and March 14 coalitions. Both sides accused each other of supporting the group. The Future Movement accused the Syrian regime of funding and training its members, while the March 8 Coalition accused the Future Movement and its regional ally (Saudi Arabia) of supporting and funding it to combat Hizbullah in case a Sunni–Shiite violent conflict erupted. The conflict with Fatah al-Islam encouraged the Siniora government to call upon the US to increase its military support for the Lebanese army.

This move was criticized by Nasrallah 'as a marker of widening US intervention in Lebanon' (Quilty, 2007). In short, the conflict had deep political and security implications. The rise of extreme groups raised the fears of Hizbullah and its followers, entrenched the lack of trust between the two coalitions and affected political stability and the country's security detrimentally.

Hizbullah's Foreign Alliances

While Hizbullah was heavily influenced by the foreign alliances of the March 14 Coalition, its domestic opponents manipulated its external alliances to widen their popularity and question its loyalty to the Lebanese state. Hizbullah's foreign alliances with Syria and Iran heavily bolstered its domestic position and helped widen its popularity within its sectarian community, mainly due to their political, financial and military support. Its wide popular support gave it the ability to ask for the quota allocated for its community in the consociational system and to veto state institutions' decisions when they did not comply with its policies and perspectives.

Hizbullah is an ideological party that draws its political views from the Iranian cleric Imam Khomeini's *Wilāyat al-Faqīh*.[26] As Norton (2007b: 477) states, '[f]or Iran, the creation of Hezbollah represented the realisation of the revolutionary state's zealous campaign to spread the message of the self-styled "Islamic revolution"'. Although Hizbullah no longer aims to form its own Islamic state in Lebanon,[27] its ideological links have raised 'suspicions' among its domestic opponents. The ideological link between Hizbullah and Iran is regarded by some Lebanese parties as a sign that the party was promoting the establishment of an Islamic state in Lebanon. In a newspaper article, the former MP and member of the Future Movement, Mustafa Alloush (2011), argues that:

> It was clear that the Wilāyat al-Faqīh party [i.e. Hizbullah] benefited from the absence of law during the civil war to enforce its presence [...] based on political ideology associated with the project of Wilāyat al-Faqīh [...] The entry of Wilāyat al-Faqīh Party to the Lebanese political game after the issuance of a religious fatwa from the infallible guardian [i.e. the Supreme Leader of Iran Sayyid Khamenei] was not to recognise the state and

its laws, but it was a dissimulation exercise and constant quest to demolish the state in order to establish the project of the party in its place.

It is not only the ideological links of Hizbullah with Iran that have been manipulated by its opponents. Hizbullah's participation in the government since 2005 has also been considered by its opponents as filling the political vacuum that was left by its regional ally, Syria, which used to ensure that Lebanon's foreign policy concurs with its policy and also used to provide political protection for Hizbullah's military wing.[28] 'Hizballah's actions since the 2005 Syrian withdrawal from Lebanon are often presented as an extension of Syrian and Iranian policy' (el-Hokayem, 2007: 44). One of the manifestations of these accusations is the Future Movement's accusation that Hizbullah was receiving orders and instructions from Damascus when it took its decision with its allies to resign from the Hariri government in January 2011. In a political statement, the Future Movement stated that the decision of Hizbullah to resign from the government 'was based on a direct order from Bashar Assad which Sayyed Hassan Nasrallah executed in Beirut along with the formation of a new Cabinet that still functions under his [Assad's] supervision' (*The Daily Star*, 2013a), in reference to the government that was formed after the forced resignation of Hariri; the majority of the ministers in this government were from the March 8 Coalition.

The resignation of Hizbullah and the March 8 Coalition ministers from the government in 2011 was in protest at the March 14 Coalition decision to fund the STL that indicted four members of Hizbullah of Hariri's assassination. The STL decision was supported by the March 14 Coalition which also accused Hizbullah's regional ally, the Assad regime, of the assassination. The conflict over the STL entrenched the tensions between the two communities (Sunni and Shiite). Hizbullah rejected the arrest of its members. Nasrallah warned that '[m]istaken is the one who thinks that we will allow the arrest or detainment of any of our mujahideen [fighters]. We will cut off the hand that tries to get to them' (Sakr, 2010). He heavily criticized the credibility of the STL and considered it a tool in the hands of the West and in particular the US to dismantle its military wing, after their failure to do so through the July War in 2006. Nasrallah warned that '[t]hose who again place wagers on the Americans are wrong. When the American power was at its peak, it failed them and today the Americans are lost' (Sakr, 2010). On the other side, the leader of the Future Movement, Saad Hariri, called on Hizbullah to extradite the four members because its intransigence would further inflame sectarian tensions. He stated that 'Hizbullah entrenched the [Sunni–Shiite] tensions when it refused to extradite those accused of Hariri's assassination' (Naharnet, 2013).

The Doha Agreement and the Role of External Players

The above discussion shows that external players often seek to fuel inter-sectarian conflicts to further their own interests. However, they might also 'force' their domestic allies to engineer power-sharing agreements, when they feel that their interests are at risk. These agreements are often at the expense of democratic reforms. An example of external players' influence on domestic parties was their ability to exert pressure on them to ratify the Doha Agreement, which ended the violence that erupted on 7 May 2008. The agreement was enacted on 21 May 2008 under the auspices of their external allies,[29] in which the domestic parties agreed on the election of the president, the formation of a new cabinet and the formulation of a new electoral law.

The violence that erupted between the Lebanese parties in May 2008 would not have reached a peaceful settlement without the support and agreement of their foreign patrons. The Doha Agreement was enacted under the auspices of the main external players at the time (Saudi Arabia, Syria, Qatar, the US and France). The foreign players who funded and supported their domestic allies to combat their opponents were able to bring them together to reach a power-sharing agreement on the election of the president, the formation of a new cabinet and a new electoral law. Jim Quilty's (2008) analysis of the factors that led to the violence that erupted on May 7 and the role of external players in it, states that 'Washington's responsibility resides in the culture of intransigence it has helped to cultivate in the Siniora government since the 2006 war and its consistent rejection of dialogue with the opposition.' The reasons behind the support of these states, in particular Saudi Arabia, for the agreement were their fears that the inability of the Future Movement to withstand Hizbullah's military attack might lead the Shiite party to take over state institutions, such as the government, and undermine their influence in Lebanon. For Hizbullah and its regional allies, their aim was to force the government to revoke its decision regarding the telecommunications network and form a new government with the third bloc for Hizbullah and its allies, after the resignation of the Shiite ministers in November 2006.

In the end, the external players were able to enforce an agreement on decisive issues. The Lebanese parties agreed to: (1) elect the head of the army, Michel Sleiman, as the Lebanese president; (2) form a national unity government; (3) adopt Qaḍāʾ as an electoral district for the 2009 elections; (4) abstain from resuming violence; and (5) initiate the National Dialogue meetings between Lebanese parties under the aegis of the newly elected president (ICG, 2008b: 26). As was mentioned earlier, the agreement reinforced the sectarian nature of the electoral law by adopting the 1960 electoral law. After the ratification of the agreement, the Hizbullah-led alliance ended the sit-in in Beirut which had lasted for more than 16 months (December 2006– May 2008).

What is noteworthy here is that although parliament had been paralysed for about two years (2006–8), there had been regular incidences of sectarian violence, government legitimacy had been questioned and the presidency had been vacant for several months, the external players did not interfere until they felt their interests were at risk when violence erupted on 7 May 2008. It can thus be concluded that these states were happy to widen the gap between the Lebanese parties as long as the conflict served their interests and that they only 'forced' them to reach agreements when they felt a growing risk to their own interests. The March 14 Coalition's foreign allies' desire to disarm Hizbullah's military wing through Resolution 1559 and the July War, as well as through their influence on their domestic allies encouraging them to curb the dialogue with Hizbullah, widened the gap between the Lebanese sectarian groups which culminated in the violence that erupted in May 2008. Clearly then, democratic reforms in Lebanon hinge to a large extent on the agreement of external players. If they agree to push these reforms forward, they can play an influential role in exerting pressure on domestic parties to initiate political reforms. Ahmad Baydoun emphasizes the significance of foreign states in this regard. He argues that the initiation of democratic reforms needs regional agreement between the main external players in Lebanon because of the significant influence they have over domestic parties.[30]

Intersection of External Factors with Inter- and Intra-Sectarian Conflicts

While the previous section explored the influence of external interventions on inter-sectarian conflicts, what follows explores its influence on intra-sectarian conflicts. As mentioned in the previous chapter, Lebanon's consociational model 'motivates' Lebanese political parties to employ sectarian language and manipulate domestic conflicts to instil a sense of fear that then mobilizes the popular support of their sects. In so doing, political parties strengthen their sectarian leadership and secure their victory in elections and in the acquisition of the share allocated for their sects in the consociational system, such as cabinet seats and security positions. In addition to the domestic conflicts, the external alliances of the domestic parties and direct foreign interventions, such as in the July War in 2006, were heavily manipulated by the Lebanese political parties to mobilize popular support and inculcate a sense of fear, especially before parliamentary elections.

The sense of fear and elite-initiated conflict discussed in the previous chapter were significantly exacerbated after 2005. The assassinations that took place in the period between 2004 and 2013 (see Table 5.1), and the eruption of violent conflicts in the country were all manipulated by various Lebanese political groups to mobilize the support of their followers. The Future Movement and the March 14 Coalition accused Syria and its domestic allies of the assassinations. 'The many assassinations raised conflict levels and confessional concerns now took centre stage and disposed people to take refuge in their own sect' (Knudsen, 2010: 16). Table 5.1 shows the assassinations of March 14 Coalition figures which have taken place in Lebanon since 2004:

The most prominent assassination was that of former PM Rafic Hariri on 14 February 2005, which deeply threatened the Sunni community and ultimately resulted in Syrian military withdrawal.[32] Hariri was a wealthy businessman and the most powerful Sunni political leader in the country. His 'political, economic, and social works and activities made him a cult figure in Lebanon, especially among the Sunni Muslims [...] [he] was undoubtedly a truly important figure in not only his country but also the region and even the world' (Ajami, 2005: 637). His death was interpreted by many in the Sunni community as an attack on the entire community (Blanford, 2006: 139–73; ICG, 2010: 7). The assassination

Table 5.1   Assassinations of March 14 Coalition Figs (2004–13)[31]

2004	• Marwan Hamade (attempt), MP
2005	• Rafic Hariri, former PM
	• Basil Fuleihan, former economy minister
	• Samir Kassir, journalist
	• Georges Hawi, former leader of the Communist Party
	• Gibran Ghassan Tueni, editor-in-chief (*Annahar* newspaper) and MP
	• Ali Ramez Tohme (attempt), journalist
	• May Chidiac (attempt), journalist and news anchor
	• Elias Murr (attempt), deputy PM, defence minister
2006	• Samir Shehadeh (attempt), police colonel, senior investigator of Hariri's assassination
	• Pierre Amin Gemayel, industry minister and MP
2007	• Walid Eido, MP
	• Antoine Ghanem, MP
2008	• Wissam Eid, Captain, internal security forces
2012	• Wissam al-Hassan, head of Information Security Branch, senior investigator of Hariri's assassination
2013	• Muhammad Shatah, academic and former minister of finance

Source: Knudsen (2010: 5)

awakened Sunnis' deep 'grievances' against the Syrian regime, such as their 'resentment at Syria's ability to thwart Hariri's project; discomfort at the lack of any credible alternative; and anxiety stemming from a more general sense of vulnerability. The end result was a massive, overpowering instinct of communal solidarity' (ICG, 2010: 7).[33]

As a consequence of the assassination of Hariri and the unprecedented rise in the popularity of his son, Saad, the Hariri family endeavoured to portray a sense of an enemy targeting the Sunnis in order to mobilize their popular support and strengthen its sectarian leadership which would improve its position in the consociational system as the main representative of its communal group. This was done in clear contradiction of the party's national and moderate slogans. In one of his speeches, the new leader of the Future Movement, Saad Hariri, confirmed that 'we are a civilian political current, moderate, democratic, and no one and nothing will be able to drag us to a sectarian position or violence or extremism' (*al-Mustaqbal*, 2013). Contrary to these slogans, the Hariri family nevertheless developed a set of new concepts like 'al-Ḥaqīqa' (the truth about Hariri's assassination) and 'we will not forget', which later became slogans for parliamentary elections. In short, '[w]hat had started as a spontaneous outcry against Hariri's death grew in scope to encompass a program for political reform, national unity and full sovereignty [...] the truth [al-haqiqa] about Hariri's death was linked to the declaration's calls for freedom [huriyya] in the political system and independence [istiqlal] from Syria' (Haugbolle, 2010: 209). The insistence on the 'Truth' 'became the single most popular slogan in the demonstrations [i.e. the March 14 protests]' (Haugbolle, 2010: 209). In addition, they were able to skilfully manipulate these concepts in the media, such as the Future Channel (owned by the Future Movement) and Christian-owned media outlets, the LBC and *Annahar* newspaper (Haugbolle, 2010: 213), so as to inculcate a sense of fear and challenge the Syrian regime and its domestic allies. Ultimately, Hariri's death and the ability of his family to manipulate the implications of his assassination led '[t]housands of voters [to give] Saad their votes out of loyalty and respect to his late father and because of his potential capability to fill the void left by the assassination' (Ajami, 2005: 637).

It was not only the sense of fear approach that was adopted by the Future Movement and its allies to mobilize popular support. They also manipulated the fact of the Syrian military presence in Lebanon from 1990 until 2005 in order to accuse Damascus of being responsible for the absence of democratic reforms. The March 14 Coalition that emerged against Syrian hegemony raised national and reform slogans, such as protecting the country's sovereignty and implementing the reforms that are stipulated in the Ta'if Agreement. This movement was able to manipulate these slogans and accuse Damascus regarding the absence of political reforms. Fidaa Itani argues that to be able to mobilize popular support 'to push Syria to withdraw, this group [i.e. the March 14 Coalition] started to talk about the civil state, political reform, the electoral law, and lowering the voting age to 18' and thus blamed Damascus for the absence of these reforms.[34] The rise in the popularity of the March 14 Coalition 'strengthened the [sectarian] leadership of Jumblatt and Saad Hariri'.[35] Thus, the anti-Syria political parties did not initiate democratic reforms after they took power in 2005 because these reforms would most likely undermine their sectarian leadership. For instance, eliminating confessionalism, which is one of the basic reforms stipulated in the Ta'if Agreement, would weaken the pretext of the political parties that they seek to protect their sectarian community's interests in the consociational system.

The death of Hariri was not the only event that was manipulated by the Lebanese parties to inculcate a sense of fear among their followers. The July War too had deep sectarian implications and increased the popularity of certain political parties. For Hizbullah, two main factors increased its popularity within its sect after the July War. Firstly, it was able to withstand the Israeli attack and keep the Israeli prisoners. Secondly, the March 14 Coalition's 'tacit' support for the war entrenched the impression among the Shiites of Lebanon that the March 14 Coalition was conspiring against them to weaken their position in the political system. Nasrallah's (2006a) speech after the July War clearly reflected the deep resentment that the party had towards the March 14 Coalition:

> During the war, we heard much that was injurious [. . .] After the war, political rivalry continued and so too the media attacks and political assaults against the Resistance and us [. . .] We patiently withstood the political media assault on the resistance in Lebanon during the war, but after the war it reached an extent tolerable only by prophets, and we are not prophets.

On the other hand, the July War increased the popularity of the Future Movement among Sunni citizens. The massive destruction of Lebanon's infrastructure and Hizbullah's 'denunciation of Future Current leaders as traitors further radicalised the Sunni base' (ICG, 2010: 11). What further stoked Sunni fears was the military might that Hizbullah showed during the July War. In this vein, 'many of its domestic opponents saw this as an acute threat. Sunnis in particular worried that the now more politically active and far better armed Shiites would be tempted to impose their rule' (ICG, 2010: 12).

The July War and the sit-in organized by the March 8 Coalition after the war entrenched further the sense of fear within the Sunni community. While the sit-in adversely affected the fortunes of the March 8 Coalition, it significantly helped improve the political position of the Future Movement. The March 8 Coalition 'was largely dominated by

Shiites, and its actions (a sit-in in the centre of Beirut, the heart of Rafiq al-Hariri's reconstruction efforts; blocking the prime minister's office) were seen by Sunni members of March 14 as targeting quintessentially Sunni symbols' (ICG, 2007: 2). The Sunni Mufti, Muhammad Rashid Qabbani, issued a statement denouncing the sit-in. He stated that 'we will not allow others to harm Beirut's grandeur' and criticized the March 8 Coalition's 'anarchy' as hurting Beirut's 'dignity' (Qabbani, 2007). Ibrahim al-Masri, al-Jamaʿa al-Islamiyya deputy general secretary, argued that '[t]he resignation of Shiite ministers, Hizbollah's rejection of the government and the fact that it organised a general strike at the heart of Sunni areas is unacceptable. Hizbollah has become a fifth column that serves foreign interests and we cannot tolerate that' (ICG, 2007: 9). The sit-in was faced with intransigence from then PM, Fouad Siniora. According to Khaled Saghieh, the reason behind the PM's intransigence was the wide popular support that he enjoyed from his Sunni community:

> The sit-in protest, which took place in 2006, helped the March 14 Coalition to entrench the Sunni polarisation. This sit-in provoked the feelings of the Sunni community and Siniora took advantage of this sentiment, especially in Lebanon there is no possibility to topple a president [i.e. the PM] in case his sect is united and supported him. In addition, the March 8 Coalition was not allied with a powerful Sunni party to support its position.[36]

Moreover, domestic political players often manipulated the external alliances of their opponents to mobilize popular support from their sects which helped fuel inter- and intra-sectarian conflicts. The external alliances of the domestic parties were heavily manipulated in the intra-sectarian conflicts discussed in the previous chapter. For instance, Shaykh Ahmad al-Aseer accused Hizbullah of attempting to establish an Islamic state which complies with its ideological perspectives. In a television interview with the LBC, he criticized it because it represents 'a project that aims to dominate the country under a sectarian label which is linked to the Wilāyat al-Faqīh, and this is what makes [the people] feel offended' (al-Akhbar, 2012). Similarly, the PSP MP, Wael Abou-Faour, accused Wahhab of collaborating with the Syrian regime to destabilize Lebanon and spark the conflict that erupted in Khalwat al-Kfier in 2006. He stated that what happened 'is part of a Syrian political decision to spark domestic [conflicts] in Lebanon, [by sparking] political and security riots' (al-Mustaqbal, 2006a). The same political discourse and accusations are employed within the Shiite community. The Shiite cleric, Sayyid Ali al-Amin, who is close to the March 14 Coalition, heavily criticizes Hizbullah because of its external alliances. In an interview, al-Amin stated that the 'performance of the political front (Hizbullah) that controls the state of affairs within the Shiite community is not in harmony with the community's aspirants [...] Such a performance isolates the Shiite community and implies that the community is a source of fear or concern to others' (Nehme, 2008). He stated that its behaviour 'implies that the Shiite community is linked to regional agendas and not interested in national agendas', in reference to its close alliance with Iran (Nehme, 2008).

The implications of these external alliances and the July War were intensively manipulated by the Lebanese political parties before the parliamentary elections in 2009, with the aim of inculcating a sense of fear among their followers. In a speech in an election gathering in Baalbeck, Nasrallah warned against the implications of a loss for Hizbullah and the March 8 Coalition in the parliamentary elections of 2009. He (2009b) stated that 'we are facing an election in which the US administration is directly involved, they form candidacy lists, deal with arising obstacles [...] even resorting to utilizing the highest political level possible, not only the US Secretary of State has been used but the US Vice President in person'. This was in reference to the visit to Lebanon, before the elections in 2009, of the US vice president Joe Biden, who held meetings with March 14 Coalition parties and linked US support for Lebanon to the outcome of the elections. In another election gathering in southern Lebanon, Nasrallah also urged the southern citizens to vote for Hizbullah. He (2009a) warned against a weak turnout in the elections:

> Some seek to project elections as a referendum on the resistance and its arms. The most concerned people about the resistance and its arms, are the citizens of the South, why? [...] [B]ecause the South is most present in the circle of 'Israeli' ambitions, threats and dangers [...] Therefore, whose concerns are the aggressions

and their confrontation? Who is under threat? Who is in the circle of 'Israeli' ambitions? Who is under daily threat of having their resources plundered, their homes destroyed and of being displaced, they are primarily the citizens of the South.

On the other hand, the March 14 Coalition employed the same approach. The leaders of this coalition used the implications of the July War, the assassinations and the external alliances of their opponents to mobilize popular support. In an election gathering in northern Lebanon, the leader of the Future Movement, Saad Hariri, warned that the elections were fateful for Lebanon. He stated that:

> The capital of the North [i.e. Tripoli] has been targeted during the past four years as Lebanon was also targeted [. . .] [Its] Arab identity, freedom, moderation, independence and economy were targeted to replace them with an alternative project [in reference to the Syrian hegemony over Lebanon] which PM Rafic Hariri was assassinated for. For this reason it is important to support [the March 14 Coalition] to win the majority of the MPs and to ensure the continuity of the project of sovereignty and independence (al-Mustaqbal, 2009b).

In an election gathering for the PSP in the Druze village of Rashaya, which took place one week before the election day on 7 June, Walid Jumblatt also warned against the loss of the March 14 Coalition in the elections and considered the elections as a battle for independence from Syria. He stated that the election results 'will decide the fate of Lebanon in the third independence battle, since the first one was in the Rashaya castle, and the second one was in the liberation of the South of Lebanon and the third is due after one week to continue the march of the March 14 Coalition' (al-Mustaqbal, 2009c); this was in reference to the Druze attack on Rashaya Castle in 1925 to liberate it from the French military forces.

Christian partisan politicians took the same approach. During a speech by the Kataeb Party parliamentary candidate in the North of Matin district, Elie Karame reminded his supporters that the March 8 Coalition 'plunged the country into a devastating war [i.e. the July War] and disrupted commercial markets in Beirut [in reference to the sit-in]' (al-Mustaqbal, 2009d). He also made accusations that the March 8

Coalition had paralysed 'the Chamber of Deputies, the cabinet and the election of the president of the republic; and intimidated Bkirki [i.e. the Maronite Church] and the presidency, and attacked the international tribunal which we insisted on having established for the sake of truth so we could know who killed Shaykh Pierre Gemayel' (al-Mustaqbal, 2009d). Also, a speech by the head of the Kataeb Party, Amin Gemayel, at the commemoration of Hariri's death on 14 February 2009, warned that 'the elections are fateful to complete the march of the Cedar Revolution and prevent undermining all the positive accomplishments and national achievements in the past four years' (Bazzi, 2009). He stated that this election 'is not a choice between candidates belonging to two national camps competing on the service of the state and nation and the people. However, it is a choice between candidates belonging to two contradictory projects: a project that aims to complete the march of sovereignty, independence and economic renaissance' and a project that 'aims to bring back foreign tutelage' (Bazzi, 2009), in reference to the Syrian tutelage. Gemayel stressed that 'victory in this election is the real punishment of the killer, whether it is a people or organisation or a regime or a state' (Bazzi, 2009).

Conclusion

This chapter has explored and analysed how Lebanon's consociational model failed to prevent foreign intervention in Lebanon. It has also examined the ramifications of regional and international developments, which affected political stability and the prospects of democratic reforms. The sectarian political parties were motivated to seek foreign support as part of their endeavours to strengthen their own domestic position, with the aim of gaining more positions in the consociational system, especially those allocated for their sects. This was met with external players' willingness to widen and strengthen their intervention in Lebanon. In so doing, external intervention fuelled inter- and intra-sectarian conflicts and undermined political stability and the democratization process, especially after the passage of Resolution 1559 and the assassination of Hariri. As a consequence, the Lebanese political parties became more reluctant to initiate democratic reforms and reach compromises over, for instance, the electoral law or the election of the president without external intervention. This was evident after the end of the July War and the ratification of the Doha Agreement. After the war, Lebanese parties were not able to reach an agreement on the election of a new president until the external players intervened to engineer a power-sharing agreement.

Also, the resignation of Shiite ministers from the government undermined one of the main pillars of the consociational model, namely the proportional distribution of state positions, and threatened the stability of the power-sharing agreement. This led to the government's legitimacy being questioned by Hizbullah and its allies. At the same time, the influence of external factors and the foreign alliances of the political parties fuelled the intra-sectarian conflicts. The various foreign influences were used by the domestic parties to inculcate a sense of fear among their followers and therefore strengthen their sectarian leadership, which would help them secure their share in the quota allocated for their sects in the consociational system. This was often at the expense of democratic reforms which, as a result, were almost entirely absent from the platforms of the political parties.

CHAPTER 6

THE 2013 PARLIAMENTARY ELECTIONS AND THE SYRIAN CONFLICT

The previous two chapters explored how the Lebanese consociational model influenced the behaviour of Lebanon's political parties, affected political stability and helped block the initiation of democratic reforms. This chapter will demonstrate, by means of a case study, how the intersection of the three factors (inter- and intra-sectarian conflicts and external factors) explored in the previous two chapters have influenced the behaviour of Lebanese parties. The case study will explore the implications of the Syrian conflict on the behaviour of Lebanese political parties regarding the formulation of a new electoral law and the postponement of parliamentary elections that were supposed to be held in June 2013. It will demonstrate how the Lebanese political parties' failure to reach an agreement on a new electoral law for the 2013 parliamentary elections due to inter- and intra-sectarian conflicts intersected with the implications of the Syrian conflict and led them to postpone the elections for 18 months.

While previous electoral laws were formulated only after the intervention of external players, Lebanese political parties were not able to agree on a new electoral law for the 2013 parliamentary elections. The absence of direct foreign intervention and the Lebanese parties' betting on the outcome of the Syrian conflict contributed to their failure to agree on a new electoral law and led them to postpone the elections.[1] As will be shown below, all Lebanese political parties were hoping to capitalize on the outcome of the Syrian conflict to feed into their interests; for example, there was the expectation that toppling the Assad regime would weaken the negotiating position of its domestic allies in formulating a new electoral law.

It is widely argued that in the case of Lebanon an electoral law based on PR would help mitigate the implications of sectarian differences and conflicts (Jaafar, 2007; LADE, 2006). Firstly, PR with large provinces, as stated in the Ta'if Agreement, would 'force' political parties to employ cross-sectarian language, such as developing political platforms, because they would be appealing to diverse constituencies. Secondly, such an electoral law would ensure a sense of security for the minorities; as Reynolds (2004: 97) states, PR is a 'confidence-building mechanism', in particular for the Druze and the Christian communities. This is because they would have influence on the election of the candidates that represent their electoral districts (Jaafar, 2007: 296–300). However, the existing electoral law allows candidates to win elections with a simple majority through the votes of their sects because it is based on small districts with a dominant sectarian group.

Abdo Saad, head of the Beirut Center for Research and Information (BCRI) and a specialist in the study of Lebanese parliamentary elections, argues that an electoral law based on PR would help overcome confessionalism. He identifies several advantages of PR in large electoral districts system. Firstly, it would strengthen the social cohesion of the Lebanese people because large districts include diverse sectarian groups and therefore there would be greater opportunity for interaction between the diverse sects and their parliamentary candidates (Saad, 2007). Secondly, it would ensure the representation of all political parties and each according to its popular weight (Saad, 2007). Thirdly, it would force candidates to adopt a national and cross-sectarian political discourse. Saad (2007) states that candidates standing for election in diverse districts would be forced to adopt a national-level discourse and political platform, which would be positively reflected in the behaviour of the voter who would then vote along these lines. This would help with bringing 'about a departure from the darkness of confessionalism and localism and entering the vast realm of citizenship and nationalism' (Saad, 2007). Finally, and most importantly, it would help weaken the influence of sectarian leaders, since new cross-sectarian political parties would emerge. Ultimately, it 'would diminish political confessionalism by indirectly contributing to the elimination of the spoils sharing. This would be achieved by weakening the pillars of this system namely the traditional sectarian leaders' (Saad, 2007). However, as the following discussion will show, the prospects of formulating a new electoral law that provides better representation of the Lebanese people are weak. This is because the Lebanese political parties are driven by their interests and the interests of their sects, which undermine attempts to reform the electoral law.[2]

This chapter will firstly explore the influence of domestic conflicts on the behaviour of political parties and how this shaped their respective positions on the formulation of a new electoral law. Secondly, it will explore the influence of the Syrian conflict on the inter- and intra-sectarian conflicts. Thirdly, it will explore how the intersection of domestic conflicts and the implications of the Syrian conflict together influenced the behaviour of Lebanese parties in regard to formulating a new electoral law and how it 'motivated' them to postpone parliamentary elections. In so doing, the chapter will show how Lebanon's consociational model contributed to the failure of Lebanese parties to reach an agreement on a new electoral law and led them to postpone the elections.[3]

Domestic Inter- and Intra-Sectarian Conflicts

The debate between Lebanese political parties over the formulation of a new electoral law, initiated a few months before the specified deadline for the June 2013 poll, was aimed at replacing the existing law that had been adopted for the 2009 elections and which had been based on small districts (in fact, on the 1960 electoral law) with majoritarian rule. The main parties that endeavoured to replace the law were the March 8 Coalition and the Christian parties in both coalitions. The March 8 Coalition's rejection of the existing law was based on the fact that the law as it stood did not ensure its victory in parliamentary elections. For the Christian parties, in turn, their desire to strengthen their community's representation in the consociational system led them to ask for a new electoral law. By supporting the formulation of a new electoral law that would improve the influence of Christian voters on the election results, the Christian parties would increase their popularity within their sect and thus strengthen their sectarian leadership, which could help them when asking for their share in the quota allocated for their sect in the consociational system.

Thus, several electoral laws were proposed by the political parties to replace the existing 2009 law. As will be shown below, the Christian parties proposed the so-called 'Orthodox Gathering' electoral law, which was the only law that was submitted to parliament for debate and consideration. There were other electoral laws proposed by the Future Movement and the LFP, which were based on a hybrid system (majoritarian and PR systems). Also, Hizbullah proposed an electoral law based on PR with large provinces as electoral districts. However, these laws were not submitted to parliament because they did not enjoy sufficient support from amongst the sectarian political parties to secure their approval.[4] As concerns the Orthodox Gathering electoral law, it was put before parliament because it enjoyed the support of the March 8 Coalition, the LFP and the Kataeb Party. Parliamentary arithmetic shows that, had there been a vote on it, it would have passed in parliament, despite the Future Movement's and PSP's opposition.

The Orthodox Gathering electoral law was proposed by Lebanese Orthodox leaders and supported by the Christian parties. It was supported throughout by the FPM, the Kataeb Party and the el-Marada Party, while the LFP initially supported the law and later changed its position. It proposes that each sectarian community has the right to elect its MPs based on PR with Lebanon as one electoral district. Their aim in supporting this law was to improve Christian representation in the political system, since, if adopted, it would secure the election of all MPs allocated for the Christian community in the consociational system by Christian voters (Kossayfi, 2013). According to Ferzli, the proposed law can take all the Christian MPs out of the influence of the Muslim parties, since they will be elected by Christian voters only.[5] Such an electoral law would take them out of the Sunni, Shiite and Druze parties' influence. According to Saad, the current electoral law (i.e. the 1960 law) allows the Sunnis and Shiites to elect 75 per cent and 70 per cent of their MPs, respectively, while the Christians are able to elect only 26 per cent of their MPs (Bassil, 2013). This is because they are distributed throughout several electoral districts with small demographic sizes. Thus, the dominant sectarian group in the electoral district has a decisive influence over district-level election results.

The competition among the Christian political parties for the support of their sectarian community led the FPM, Kataeb and el-Marada parties to favour the Orthodox Gathering electoral law. The basis of the FPM and the el-Marada Party support for the law was threefold: if adopted it would (1) improve Christian representation in the political system; (2) improve their sectarian leadership; and (3) secure the victory of the March 8 Coalition with a majority of parliamentary seats.[6] The LFP, initially advocated the law, and Kataeb supported it because it promised to improve the level of Christian representation in the political system. Had they rejected the law, they would have been accused of undermining their community's interests in the consociational system, although this law might lead to the loss of the parliamentary elections for the March 14 Coalition. The LFP and the Kataeb Party took their decision because 'if the Christian vote is not "liberated" in the upcoming June elections, the March 14 alliance will be massacred at the polls because of the harsh feelings stirred up among the Christians by' the leader of the FPM, Michel Aoun, and the head of the Maronite Church, Patriarch Bechara Boutros al-Rahi (Hajj, 2013). These 'grievances' are the need of the Christians to elect their candidates.

However, as was mentioned earlier, the LFP did come to alter its position and eventually withdrew its support for the Orthodox Gathering electoral law when parliament convened to vote on it on 15 May 2013, leading to the fall of the law due to lack of quorum. According to Michel Aoun, the LFP did not vote for the law because of the offer from the Future Movement to nominate Geagea for the next presidential elections in 2014 and to grant the LFP more seats in the March 14 Coalition parliamentary bloc in the next parliamentary elections (NNA, 2013). The Future Movement's offer thus served to offset the possible loss of the LFP's seats in Christian-dominated districts because of its loss of Christians' popular support after it took the decision to stand against the proposed law.[7] Geagea justified his party's position against the law by stating that 'the priority of the LF {i.e. the LFP} has always been on securing a voting system that enjoys national backing in order to replace the current legislature governing the polls – the amended version of the 1960 law' (*The Daily Star*, 2013b).

As a consequence of the intra-sectarian rivalry over the mobilization of the Christian community, the FPM accused the LFP of selling out the Christian community's interests to satisfy its inter-sectarian allies, in reference to the Future Movement. The FPM framed the refusal by the LFP to sign up to the Orthodox Gathering electoral law as undermining the position of Christians in the consociational system, portraying the LFP's position against the law as a 'coup d'état' against Christians and accusing it of treachery (Reda, 2013). This is because the main Christian parties (FPM, LFP, Kataeb and el-Marada) reached an agreement under the auspices of al-Rahi on supporting the Orthodox Gathering electoral law for the next elections.[8] Aoun considered Geagea's rejection another concession made at the expense of Christian interests, since the first concession was made at the Ta'if Agreement (NNA, 2013), in reference to the limited powers the agreement endowed to the position of presidency. He stated that Geagea 'made concessions which did not gain the approval of the Christians [in reference to the Christian parties] gathered under the auspices of Bkirki' (NNA, 2013). The FPM minister, Gebran Bassil, stated that 'the position of the Lebanese Forces [Party] caused a setback for the Christians' (al-Akhbar, 2013a), since it represented an opportunity for them to strengthen their representation in parliament and reduce the Muslim parties' influence over Christian MPs.

The rise in the popularity of Aoun due to his support for the Orthodox Gathering electoral law motivated the Future Movement, the PSP, the LFP and the Kataeb Party to support the postponement of parliamentary elections that were supposed to be held in June 2013. Indeed, it was feared that the rise in Aoun's popularity would have allowed him to win the majority of Christian seats in parliament and to declare himself the main leader of the Christian community. Such a victory would then improve Aoun's chances of running for the main Christian position in the consociational system, the presidency, and improve the chances of gaining a larger share in the Christian quota in the cabinet and state security and administrative positions. This would be achieved at the expense of the LFP and the Kataeb party's shares. As one FPM MP pointed out with regard to the reason behind the extension of the term of parliament that it 'stems from the fear of the "Lebanese Forces [Party]" and "Phalange [i.e. the Kataeb Party]" and the "Future Movement" and MP Walid Jumblatt from a new tsunami [i.e. massive victory] for Michel Aoun if elections were held according to any [electoral] law', in reference to Aoun's large Christian parliamentary bloc in the 2005 parliamentary elections

(Younes, 2013). This point is also confirmed by Elie Ferzli who argues that the refusal of the LFP to support the proposed law, which made it lose some of its popularity within its community, and the rise in the popularity of Aoun encouraged it to postpone the elections.[9] Abdullah Abu-Habib (2013b) clarifies the concerns of the Christian parties regarding the extension of parliament's term:

> [T]he Lebanese Forces Party implicitly favors extension [i.e. the extension of parliament's term] because it wants to give its supporters enough time to digest its flip-flopping from being a proponent to an opponent of the Orthodox Gathering Law [. . .] In contrast, Gen. Michel Aoun maintained his call for elections to be held on time, in order to safeguard currently applicable laws, while hoping that his staunch support for the Orthodox Gathering Law would result in an electoral tsunami similar to the one he enjoyed in 2005.

In addition to the rise in Aoun's popularity, there are two other domestic factors that led the PSP to postpone the elections. Firstly, the size of its parliamentary bloc allowed it to create political capital from the conflict between the two main Muslim parties, the Future Movement and Hizbullah. As mentioned in Chapter 4, the Druze parties have long sought to play a 'mediation' role between the sectarian communities. So the PSP expects that in the next parliamentary elections both coalitions, in particular the Future Movement and Hizbullah, will seek to weaken its ability to win a large parliamentary bloc because of its ability to 'blackmail' both coalitions. The PSP 'endorses extending parliament's term because it wants to retain its role as a political linchpin. This role allows the Druze to switch sides while maintaining the balance of power necessary to safeguard the perpetuation of that role' (Abu-Habib, 2013b). Secondly, the PSP was seeking to postpone the elections because of the next presidential elections. The PSP with its current parliamentary bloc would have an influence on the nomination of the next president who was going to be elected in May 2014.

For the Future Movement it was its fear that the Salafi groups might win the elections which meant it wanted them postponed. Several factors led to the gradual emergence of these groups in the post-2005 period. Firstly, the assassination of Hariri created a sense of 'vulnerability' among Sunnis, and these groups were seen as a way to fill the vacuum that was left by the absence of his leadership (Abdel-Latif, 2008: 2). Secondly, the 7 May violence was manipulated by these groups and presented by them as targeting the entire Sunni community in Lebanon. Thus, they raised the slogan 'defending *Ahl al-Sunna*' (Abdel-Latif, 2008: 2). Thirdly, they manipulated the 'grievances' of their fellow Sunnis in Syria after the eruption of the Syrian civil war; this helped widen their popularity within their community, as the discussion in the following section will show. According to Farid el-Khazen, 'the Future Movement did not want to open the door [i.e. to run the elections on time] to compete with the Islamic fundamentalist movements which became very strong'.[10] He adds another factor which is the broken alliance between the Future Movement and Mikati and Safadi, two of its main Sunni allies in Tripoli.[11] Elie Ferzli also confirms the point that one of the factors that pushed the Future Movement to postpone the elections in 2013 was the weakness and fragmentation of its Sunni popular base.[12] If the Salafi groups had been able to win large parliamentary blocs, they would have been able to compete with the Future Movement over the leadership of their community and the quota allocated for it in the consociational system.

The Syrian Conflict and Inter- and Intra-Sectarian Conflicts

In addition to the domestic factors, the Syrian conflict has also had repercussions for the behaviour of political parties and contributed to their position on the formulation of the electoral law and the postponement of the 2013 elections in Lebanon. All parties are trying to capitalize on the implications of the conflict to improve their own domestic positions. Officially, the Lebanese government has 'dissociated' itself from the conflict in Syria and does not support either side in the conflict. However, the Sunni, Shiite, Druze and Christian parties have all tried to take advantage of the Syrian conflict to improve their domestic positions. Firstly, the Lebanese groups saw it as an opportunity to undermine the position of the regional allies of their domestic opponents in a way that would then lead to weakening their opponents at the domestic level. Secondly, the Lebanese groups sought to use this conflict in their neighbouring country to strengthen their sectarian leadership. The political parties manipulated the 'grievances' of their sects so as to mobilize popular support and strengthen their sectarian leadership, which entrenched sectarian identities further and widened the political gap between the sects, especially after the intervention of the Future Movement and Hizbullah in the Syrian crisis. Thirdly, it fuelled intra-sectarian conflicts, particularly within the Christian community.

For the Sunni community, the Future Movement stood with the Syrian opposition against the Assad regime and attempted to use events to strengthen its sectarian leadership. Indeed, the Syrian conflict presented an opportunity for the Sunni parties to weaken the influence of the Assad regime in Lebanon even further and undermine its domestic allies. If Assad were to be toppled, Hizbullah's political and military power would be severely weakened, which might lead to the group losing its popular support within the Shiite community. Thus, its ability to veto government decisions and ask for a larger share in the consociational system would be undermined. The Lebanese scholar Paul Salem (2012: 5) explains the Sunni community's position on the Syrian conflict by stating that the 'Sunnis in Lebanon feel increasingly marginalized and humiliated by an all-powerful Hezbollah. They saw the uprising in Syria as an opportunity [...] to bring down a regional power that stood behind Hezbollah's power in Lebanon.'

Moreover, the Future Movement attempted to manipulate the grievances of the Sunni communities in Lebanon and Syria to widen its popular support, which had repercussions for political and security stability at the domestic level. The intra-sectarian outbidding motivated the Future Movement to adopt a more critical discourse against the Syrian regime and employ sectarian language so as to be able to mobilize popular support, especially after the rise of the Salafi groups in northern Lebanon which also usually employ sectarian language.[13] During the first four months of the Syrian conflict, the Future Movement distanced itself from the conflict and did not support either side. Although it belatedly developed a more critical political discourse against the Assad regime, it was blamed by several Sunni extremist groups for not financially and militarily backing the Syrian rebels.[14]

Therefore, many MPs from the Future Movement called for protecting Sunni areas housing Syrian opposition activists. The clashes between the Lebanese army and pro-Syrian opposition militants in Arsal provide a telling example. Muhammad Kabbara, an MP in the Future

Movement parliamentary bloc, warned against targeting the areas supporting the Syrian opposition in Lebanon, in particular Arsal.[15] He warned that 'if Arsal is besieged, we will besiege the whole country and we call to punish all those responsible for the killing of our Sunni people in Lebanon' (al-Seyassah, 2013). Furthermore, the Future Movement is accused of funding and arming the Syrian opposition (Mortada, 2012a, 2012b), although it has denied these accusations. These accusations include, for instance, that it has opened an office in Tripoli to recruit Sunni fighters to fight in Syria and to send arms and weapons to the anti-Assad opposition (Mortada, 2012a), and that it is using Turkey as a hub to smuggle weapons to support the Syrian opposition fighters (ICG, 2012: 21).

On the other hand, the main Shiite party, Hizbullah, expressed its support for the Assad regime. It considered the Syrian conflict a plot to topple the regime in Damascus and disarm its military wing. In a speech, Nasrallah (2011) justified his party's support for the regime in Damascus by stating that:

> We are with the reform in Syria, and we stand with a regime [i.e. the Syrian regime] which [. . .] supported the resistance movements, and we say yes to address all the causes and manifestations of corruption or defects, yes to all reforms which in fact have been accepted by the Syrian leadership and advocated by the Syrian people. But there are those who do not want reforms in Syria, no security, no stability, no civil peace, [and] no dialogue. There are those who want to destroy Syria.

Like the Future Movement, Hizbullah is also intervening militarily in Syria. The regular attacks from Syrian militant groups on the inhabitants of the Shiite villages, which are located on the Syrian–Lebanese borders in northern Bekaa, an area politically represented by Hizbullah, led it initially to give military support to the inhabitants of these villages. At a later stage, however, it started aiding the Syrian regime in its fight against militant opposition groups, supporting the regime's attacks in Qusayr city and in other areas inside Syria, which eventually led to the defeat of the opposition and the Syrian army's conquest of the city.[16] In one of his speeches, Nasrallah (2013b) justified his party's military intervention by stating that 'Takfiri groups' [i.e. extreme militant groups] control over Syria and especially in border areas with Lebanon poses a great danger for the Lebanese Muslims as well as Christians [...] [i]f Syria falls in the hands of the Takfiris and the US, the resistance will be trapped and "Israel" will enter Lebanon. If Syria falls, the Palestinian cause will be lost.' To mitigate the effects of Hizbullah's intervention in Syria on the Sunni–Shiite conflicts, Nasrallah (2013b) stated that '[w]e do not evaluate matters from a Sunni or Shiite perspective, but from a perspective joining all Muslims and Christians together, since they are all threatened by this Takfiri plot financed by the US'.[17]

While the positions of the main parties of the Sunni and Shiite communities are clear on the Syrian crisis, the Druze and the Christian parties have been deeply divided over it. The Druze community is divided between the PSP, which called on the Druze of Syria to join the Syrian opposition, and the LDP and Wahhab, who expressed their support for the regime in Damascus. The PSP MP, Akram Shouhayib, justifies his party's position by stating that it is not acceptable for the 'Druze to stand with the regime [i.e. Assad's regime] against the revolution of [the Syrian] people, and to be a tool for the suppression of their fellow Syrians [...] Therefore, it was our duty to call on them to join the revolution alongside their brothers who are struggling to reach a democratic Syria' (Akkoum, 2012). The PSP support for the Syrian opposition stems from two main factors. Firstly, it accuses the Syrian regime of assassinating Kamal Jumblatt, the father of its current leader, Walid Jumblatt. Secondly, it sought to strengthen its external alliances with influential regional states in Lebanon, mainly Saudi Arabia, which supports the Syrian opposition, especially after Riyadh broke its relations with the PSP; this was because of its support for the March 8 Coalition government in 2011 that excluded the Future Movement and the March 14 Coalition. If Assad's regime were to be overthrown, the influence of Saudi Arabia on Lebanese domestic politics would be increased; in particular the position of Hizbullah would be weakened and a new Sunni leadership, which might be close to the Saudi Kingdom, would take power in Syria.[18] This would entail a new power-sharing agreement and a redistribution of state positions.

Meanwhile, the PSP's Druze rivals, the LDP and Wahhab, expressed their support for the Syrian regime. If the regime in Damascus were toppled, the domestic positions of the LDP and Wahhab would be heavily weakened, especially as the position of their main domestic ally, Hizbullah, would be dramatically undermined. This would weaken their ability to ask for the share allocated for their sect in the consociational system. The member in the parliamentary bloc of LDP, Fadi al-Awar, justified his party's position by stating that 'the position of the Druze of Lebanon stems from the position of Syrian Druze who are supporters of the Syrian regime and its president, and they cannot stand with the Salafi forces that are killing the people in the name of the revolution' (Akkoum, 2012). A firmer stance still was taken by the Druze politician, Wiam Wahhab, who expressed his staunch support for Assad. He stated that 'if Syria {i.e. the Assad regime} asked us to fight against the West {i.e. the Syrian opposition} we will fight with Syria, and if the Druze of Jabal al-Arab {an area dominated by Druze in Syria} asked us to support them, we will do' (Akkoum, 2012).

The intra-sectarian rivalry was even more intense within the Christian community. The FPM and the LFP provided very different interpretations and perspectives on the Syrian conflict. The FPM stood with Assad's regime, while the LFP expressed its support for the Syrian opposition. This can be explained with reference to the intense intra-sectarian outbidding within the Christian community. Defeating the Assad regime would drastically improve the position of the LFP and its ally, the Future Movement, which would enable it to obtain a larger share of its community's quota in the consociational system. What would further improve the LFP position if Assad is toppled is that the position of its Christian rival, the FPM, would be greatly weakened because the domestic position of its main inter-sectarian ally, Hizbullah, would be undermined. The FPM's argument was that overthrowing the Syrian regime would allow the Muslim Brotherhood to take power and form their own 'Islamic state', which might treat Christians as *Dhimmīs* (second-class citizens). In a press conference, Michel Aoun justified his support for the Syrian regime by arguing that 'the purpose of the war in Syria is not the [implementation of the] reforms, but the persecution of minorities, primarily the Christians', in reference to the violence against the Syrian Christians (Lebanon Files, 2013).

On the other side, the LFP supported the Syrian opposition because of the role of the Syrian regime in weakening and marginalizing the Christian community in Lebanon and the imprisonment of its leader,

Samir Geagea, during its military presence in the country. Thus, it supported the Muslim Brotherhood's pursuit of power in Syria. In a television interview, Geagea called on Christians in Syria 'not to be afraid [of extremism] and to seek to achieve what they believe in and in particular justice and freedom and democracy and equality and a true citizenship. This is the only exit for their salvation and not to be protected by dictatorial regimes' (al-Jazeera, 2012). He stated that the Syrian regime was culpable because it harmed 'Christians not only in Syria [but] in Syria *and* in Lebanon' (al-Jazeera, 2012).

One of the implications of the Syrian conflict for Christian intra-sectarian rivalry was the ability of the FPM to manipulate the Syrian refugees issue in Lebanon, and the grievances of its fellow Christian in Syria, to mobilize the popular support of its community. According to the minister of the interior, Marwan Charbel (2011–13), the number of Syrian refugees in Lebanon stands at about 1,200,000 including Palestinians in mid-2013, which is expected to rise as long as the conflict in Syria continues (*al-Akhbar*, 2013b). Thus, the FPM member and Minister Gebran Bassil called for the Syrian–Lebanese borders to be closed in order to block the flow of Syrian refugees because Lebanon is not able to afford the economic burden associated with them. However, his position was not justified solely with reference to economic reasons. He framed this issue in such a way as to mobilize popular support of the Christians in his electoral district (Batroun) after he had failed twice in the previous parliamentary elections (2005 and 2009). What motivated the FPM to manipulate the Syrian refugees issue is the Christian grievances regarding the Palestinian refugees' settlement in Lebanon, since 'the Christians of Lebanon were the party most concerned about the settlement of Palestinians – the majority of whom are Muslims – in Lebanon, for fear of disrupting the political and numerical balance there' (Chararah, 2013). If the number of Syrian and Palestinian refugees increased dramatically and/or become armed, they might become a source of instability as was the case with the Palestinian refugees during the civil war (Chararah, 2013; Salem, 2012: 8), because they might be recruited by extreme groups with the aim of carrying the Syrian conflict into Lebanon (Chararah, 2013; Salem, 2012: 21). The Lebanese journalist Jean Aziz (2013b), who is close to the FPM, argues that the problem of the Syrian refugees is not about their committing crimes 'but the existence of organized armed groups'. He supports his argument by reference to the clashes between Lebanese security forces and Syrian armed groups in several Lebanese cities and villages, such as Akkar, Tripoli, Beirut and Arsal (Aziz, 2013b). These fears were confirmed through the presence of extremist groups in the armed Syrian opposition, which tortured many Syrian Christians and destroyed several churches, further supporting the FPM's position against these groups in Syria.

The Syrian conflict has also had implications for the position of the Christian parties regarding the future of the country's electoral law. The intersection of an external factor (i.e. the Syrian conflict) and their inter-sectarian conflicts led the two Christian parties (FPM and el-Marada) to adopt the so-called Orthodox Gathering electoral law. In addition to their endeavour to strengthen the Christian representation in the political system, the two Christian parties' support for the proposed law was also motivated by the attacks on Christians in Syria by Sunni militant groups. What further stoked their fears was the Sunni militant groups' political and military activities in northern Lebanon (Tripoli and the Syrian borders), with a growing sense that the Sunnis might then seek to form their own *Umma* state. This is because the current electoral law (2009 electoral law) gives the Future Movement the ability to have a large parliamentary bloc although about half of its MPs are non-Sunnis. Thus, one of the factors that led the two Christian parties to support the law in question, which helps reduce the number of Future Movement MPs and consequently undermine its influence on domestic politics, was their fears that the rise of a Sunni leadership in Syria would embolden and strengthen the domestic position of the Sunni community in Lebanon (ICG, 2012: 12). This might lead to its hegemony over the political system and the marginalization of the Christian community. An FPM activist interviewed by ICG expressed his party's concern about the rise of Sunni leadership in Syria. He stated that '[t]he Syrian regime halted Sunni aspirations in Lebanon. If Sunnis were to rule Syria, they would ally themselves with those in Lebanon. Nothing would then stop Sunni domination over the country' (ICG, 2012: 12). This point is also confirmed by Farid el-Khazen who argues that the Syrian civil war 'played a role in supporting any [electoral law] proposal that enhances the protection of the Christians', especially after the rise of extreme groups in Syria which targeted them.[19]

The Intersection of Domestic Conflicts with the Syrian Conflict

The intersection of the inter- and intra-sectarian conflicts with the repercussions of the Syrian conflict contributed to the failure of Lebanese political parties to reach an agreement on the electoral law, which then led them to postpone the parliamentary elections that were supposed to be held in June 2013. All the main parties (Future Movement, Hizbullah, Amal Movement, PSP, LFP, Kataeb Party and el-Marada Party), except the FPM, supported the constitutional amendment to extend the term of parliament for 18 months, until November 2014.[20]

On the domestic level, as was mentioned above, the intra-Christian competition encouraged the LFP and the Kataeb Party to postpone the elections after the failure of the political parties to vote for the Orthodox Gathering electoral law on 15 May, a few weeks before the date of the elections which were supposed to take place on 9 June. Their position can be explained by their fears that the FPM would win a massive victory in the elections which would improve its sectarian leadership and improve its negotiating position when asking for a larger share in the quota allocated for its community in the consociational system. The rise in the FPM's popularity within its community stems from four main factors: (1) its staunch support for the Orthodox Gathering electoral law; (2) its objection to the rise to power of the Muslim Brotherhood in Syria; (3) its denunciation of the Syrian opposition attacks on the Christians; and (4) its party's manipulation of the Syrian refugee issue in Lebanon. Also, the Future Movement and the PSP position of trying to prevent the FPM from having a massive victory in the elections was one of the factors that led both parties to postpone the elections. In addition to this, there are two other domestic factors that led the PSP to advocate the postponement of parliamentary elections. Firstly, its current parliamentary bloc allowed it to play off the conflict between the two main Muslim parties, the Future Movement and Hizbullah, which was especially significant as these two parties are likely to seek to weaken the PSP in the next elections. Secondly, its current parliamentary bloc endowed the PSP with a significant influence on the election of the next president who was to be elected in May 2014.

On the external level, the Future Movement's and Hizbullah's support for postponing the elections was mainly because of their hopes that the Syrian conflict would strengthen their domestic positions to an extent that would allow them to formulate a new electoral law which could secure their victory in parliamentary elections and improve their sectarian leadership. This would enable them to ask for the share of their sects and their rival sects in the consociational system. Hizbullah's intervention in Syria in May 2013, and its ability together with the Syrian army to defeat the Syrian opposition in Qusayr, improved its domestic position. Thus, the Future Movement supported the postponement of the elections until the opposition's position against the Assad regime improved, while Hizbullah was focused instead on its immersion in the Syrian conflict. Abu-Habib (2013b) explains the positions of the two political parties regarding the extension of parliament's term for 18 months:

> While the Shiite duo (Hezbollah and Amal) might benefit from that [i.e. postponement of the elections] as a result of Hezbollah's immersion in the Syrian quagmire [. . .] [The Future Movement], on the other hand, favors extension as a means to galvanize and organize its electoral 'machine', which proved capable of transporting home tens of thousands of expatriate voters during the 2009 elections.

The reasons behind Hizbullah and the March 8 Coalition's decision to support a postponement of the elections was mainly because of Hizbullah's military intervention in Syria, as Abu-Habib states. In the event that the Syrian regime won the war against the opposition, the March 14 Coalition's aspirations of weakening their domestic rival (i.e. Hizbullah) through toppling Assad would fade and this would weaken their negotiating position for formulating a new electoral law. Hizbullah and the March 8 Coalition were therefore betting 'on winning the battle in Qusair and several other strategic Syrian territories. Thus, Hezbollah and its political allies are buying time until the war shifts in their favor' (Saab, 2013).

However, the Future Movement's decision to support a postponement of the elections was not only informed by the lack of 'preparation', as Abu-Habib argues. In fact, the March 14 Coalition and especially the Future Movement did not insist on having parliamentary elections in June 2013, because they were awaiting developments in Syria. If the regime were overthrown, the Future Movement and the March 14 Coalition would be in a powerful position to negotiate a new electoral law, which would secure their victory in the polls, especially as the positions of their domestic rivals would be weakened. After the conquest of Qusayr by Hizbullah and the Syrian regime, the position of the Syrian opposition was drastically weakened. Thus, the Future Movement and its domestic allies capitalized on the anti-Assad regional players, such as Saudi Arabia, in order to 'offset' the loss of Qusayr. The Future Movement and the March 14 Coalition therefore considers that it is in their 'interest to also postpone elections until the Qusair loss is assimilated and its results and repercussions dissipated, both in Lebanon and Syria; or until the presumed international revenge for the fall of the city matures, which would lead to better Lebanese electoral conditions for the Hariri coalition' (Aziz, 2013a). Farid el-Khazen also argues that their failure to topple the regime in Syria encouraged them to postpone the elections.[21] As for the PSP, as discussed in the previous section, the external factor that contributed to its support for delaying the polls was that if the Syrian regime were defeated, Saudi Arabia's influence on domestic politics would increase, which would help improve the PSP's domestic position and secure it significant influence on the formulation of a new electoral law and the power-sharing agreement that would be enacted under the auspices of the new regional sponsor, that is, Saudi Arabia.

Conclusion

This chapter has explored the implications of the Syrian conflict on domestic politics and the postponed parliamentary elections. It has attempted to show how Lebanon's consociational model helped spark inter- and intra-sectarian conflicts that intersected with the repercussions of the Syrian conflict which then led Lebanese political parties to postpone the elections. The case study shows two main failures of Lebanon's consociational model. Firstly, the sectarian distribution of the state positions sparked inter- and intra-sectarian conflicts. Secondly, the model 'encourages' domestic parties to capitalize on the ramifications of external factors to bolster their domestic positions against their opponents.

The sectarian representation of the communal groups in the political system helped spark intra-sectarian conflicts. This was particularly evident within the Christian and Sunni communities. Their endeavour to improve their community's representation in the consociational system led them to adopt an electoral law that further entrenches sectarianism. As a consequence of their conflict over the electoral law, the LFP and the Kataeb Party supported the postponement of the elections to prevent their Christian rival, the FPM, from winning the elections and therefore strengthening its sectarian leadership; such a victory would also have helped the FPM to ask for the quota allocated for their sect in the consociational system. For the Future Movement, its fears of the rise of Salafi groups if the elections had been held on time encouraged it to postpone the polls.

The Christian community's intra-sectarian conflict intersected with the inter-sectarian conflicts. What contributed to the Future Movement and PSP endeavour to postpone the elections was their aim of preventing the FPM from wining a massive victory in the elections. Furthermore, one of the factors that led the PSP to postpone the elections was its endeavour to secure its domestic position as the main player able to change the balance of power between the two coalitions. In addition to the domestic factors, the positions of the Future Movement and Hizbullah were significantly influenced by the Syrian conflict. Both parties bet on its developments to strengthen their domestic positions to negotiate for the formulation of a new electoral law which would secure their victory in the elections. The intersection of inter- and intra-sectarian conflicts with the Syrian conflict subsequently motivated Lebanese political parties to postpone the parliamentary elections.

What is noticeable is that the absence of direct foreign intervention weakened the ability of Lebanese parties to formulate a new electoral law. The electoral laws of the previous elections (1992, 1996, 2000, 2005, and 2009) were all formulated under direct foreign aegis. This shows once again the inability of Lebanon's consociational model to push forward democratic reforms and ensure political stability without direct foreign intervention. The last point that can be concluded from this case study is that the popular support of a political party within its sect is not enough to help push forward democratic reforms, whether it enjoys the support of the majority of its sect or only a small portion of it. The tense nature of the competition between the Christian parties led them to support an electoral law which entrenches sectarianism, while the PSP, enjoying the support of the majority of its sect, supported the postponement of the elections simply to secure its domestic position.

CONCLUSION

This book has examined how Lebanon's consociational model has impeded the democratization process since Syrian military withdrawal in 2005. It has argued that Lebanon's consociational model helped provoke inter- and intra-sectarian conflicts that intersected with external factors to adversely affect the behaviour of political parties and the democratization process. The sectarian distribution of state positions often encouraged political parties to widen their popular support within their communal groups in order to win elections as the main representatives of their communities, which can enhance their ability to obtain the quota allocated for their respective communities in the consociational system. Thus, they employed several approaches to secure their victory in polls, such as employing extensively sectarian language and inculcating a sense of fear among their followers to mobilize them. As a consequence, their ability to reach compromises and initiate democratic reforms has been weakened because of their deeply entrenched positions. The intra-sectarian outbidding motivates political parties to adopt extreme positions regarding the interests of their communal groups in the consociational system. This has often undermined their willingness to make concessions and reach compromises because their intra-sectarian opponents will accuse them of sacrificing their communities' interests. In such a situation, the sectarian parties' positions regarding democratic reforms will be shaped by their compatibility with their sects' interests. In a case where democratic reform undermines their communities' interests in the consociational system, they will reject it.

While intra-sectarian conflicts have implications for the behaviour of Lebanon's political parties, the inter-sectarian conflicts and alliances have a similar influence. The existence of mixed electoral districts has often imposed on sectarian parties the need to build inter-sectarian alliances during parliamentary elections to secure their victory. These alliances have often had adverse ramifications on the ability of political parties to initiate democratic reforms. The political parties were forced to make concessions to their inter-sectarian allies to be able to build the alliance and secure their victory in the elections, such as in the case of Hizbullah's support for the FPM's electoral law proposal (i.e. Orthodox Gathering electoral law) for the 2013 parliamentary elections.

In cases where the electoral district is comprised of one main sect and is united behind one main political leadership, its political representative has often been able to form the electoral list and to choose all MP candidates. This has frequently forced candidates who are representing minorities to support the political positions of the main party in the district in order to secure their inclusion in its electoral list, which often contradicts their communities' political perspectives. In such a situation, the legitimacy of the power-sharing agreement is repeatedly questioned by the minorities which have limited influence on the selection of their candidates and election results.

What has fuelled these conflicts further is political parties' pursuit of foreign support to bolster their domestic positions against their rivals. The waning of the Syrian influence on Lebanese politics since 2005 has intersected with the willingness of regional and international states to interfere and widen their influence in Lebanon. External players have manipulated the inter- and intra-sectarian conflicts to promote their policies. The main sectarian division in Lebanon since 2005 has been the Sunni–Shiite division, which intersects with a regional sectarian conflict between Saudi Arabia and Iran. Several events have taken place since 2005 which were sparked and/or fuelled by the external players and have had consequences on the initiation of democratic reforms. The assassination of Hariri, Resolution 1559, the July War, the Fatah al-Islam conflict and the Syrian conflict all had implications for political stability and for the ability of political parties to initiate democratic reforms.

Lebanon's political parties have manipulated their external alliances and the alliances of their opponents to bolster their domestic positions against their inter- and intra-sectarian rivals. They have regularly received political, financial and military support from their external patrons. They have also manipulated the external alliances of their rivals and the assassinations that took place in Lebanon since 2005 to inculcate a sense of fear among their sectarian followers and secure their victory in the elections instead of mobilizing popular support on the basis of their political platforms. As a consequence, foreign states' intervention have further inflamed these inter- and intra-sectarian conflicts, which has increased the reluctance of political parties to reach compromises and initiate democratic reforms.

Further to the points discussed above, the Christian community, which was marginalized during the Syrian military presence, rejected democratic reforms on the basis that Christian representation in the consociational system should be strengthened first. All the main Christian parties rejected the formation of the National Body for the Elimination of Confessionalism and called for the formulation of a new electoral law that improves their community's influence on the election results. The marginalization of the main Christian parties and politicians during the Syrian period, coupled with the limited powers given to the main Christian position in the consociational system, the presidency, encouraged the Christian parties to call for strengthening and widening the powers that are granted to the positions allocated for their community before initiating genuine democratic reforms.

The case of the electoral law that was supposed to be adopted for the parliamentary elections in June 2013 is a pertinent example of how the intersection of external factors with inter- and intra-sectarian conflicts influences the behaviour of Lebanese political parties in relation to democratic reforms. The Syrian conflict has brought significant changes at political and sectarian levels. The conflict within the Christian community over the electoral law intersected with the inter-sectarian conflict, mainly between Sunni and Shiite parties, which are both seeking to capitalize on the unfolding Syrian conflict. The events in Syria further encouraged their intransigence in regard to formulating a new electoral law, with both parties now waiting until the developments in Syria turn to their advantage. As a consequence, they were not able to reach an agreement on a new electoral law and this led them to postpone the elections for 18 months.

The case of the electoral law and the Syrian conflict demonstrates which factor is more influential in terms of the behaviour of political parties. The nature of the effect of a certain factor on the behaviour of Lebanese political parties depends on the position of the party within its sectarian community. Certain conditions determine the influence of a certain factor on the behaviour of political parties:

(1) If the intra-sectarian competition within a small sectarian community is intense and the party does not enjoy the support of the majority of its sect, this will have a significant influence on the parties' behaviour, as in the case of the Christian parties and their position on the electoral law.

(2) If the political party represents a small sectarian community and enjoys wide popularity within its sect, it will be more influenced by inter-sectarian conflicts. In such a situation, the political party will seek to secure its interests and the interests of its sect, as was seen with the PSP and its position on the electoral law and the 2013 parliamentary elections.

(3) If the party enjoys wide popular support from one of the largest sects, it will be influenced by inter-sectarian conflicts and external factors because of its endeavour to ensure that it has a powerful influence over state institutions, as in the cases of the Future Movement and Hizbullah.

The failure of the consociational model in Lebanon can be explained by the weaknesses in the four components and the absence of several background conditions. The four components failed to achieve their objectives in Lebanon. The grand coalition component failed to ensure the formation of effective coalitions. The vertical division between the Sunni and Shiite communities and the intra-sectarian conflicts between the Christian parties undermined the ability of the component to ensure the formation of 'legitimate' governments. This was evidenced in the governments that were formed in 2005 and 2011 respectively. This can be explained by the fact that this component is based on the faulty assumption that the sects are united and represented by one main political representative. Secondly, the confessional autonomy that the sectarian groups enjoy also helped widen the gap between them.

The right of religious communities to manage their own affairs, such as private schools owned by the sects and the absence of a common history book, helped widen the gap between them and weakened any sense of national identity.

Thirdly, the proportional representation of the sects was based on the notion that the political parties will willingly seek to formulate electoral laws that provide better representation of the Lebanese people. However, Lebanon's political parties formulated electoral laws that secured their victory as the main representatives of their sects to be able to obtain the quota allocated for their respective communities in the consociational system. Also, the proportional representation component is not often able to 'fairly' distribute the state positions and the powers that are allocated to them between the different sects. For instance, the Christian community is not yet satisfied with the current distribution of power between the main state positions (i.e. presidency, speaker of the parliament and PM) and it is calling for a constitutional amendment to widen the powers that are given to the presidency position. Fourthly, the veto component was manipulated by the parties, especially those that represent the majority of their sects. This was evident with the main Muslim parties: the Future Movement, Hizbullah and the PSP. These three parties were able to manipulate the veto component to secure their interests in the political system, which sometimes led to paralysis in the state institutions and undermined their ability to reach compromises.

What is particularly noticeable in the study of the behaviour of the Lebanese political parties and the implications for the democratization process is that none of the Lebanese parties is able to solely push forward the democratization process. The success of the democratization process in Lebanon depends on the agreement of the sectarian political parties. Thus, political stability and the absence of sectarian and violent conflicts are essential for the success of the democratization process. The democratic reforms that are stated in the Ta'if Agreement were supposed to be implemented by the Lebanese political class after the end of the civil war. However, these reforms remain in stasis. Although new political parties participated in post-2005 governments which enjoy wide popular support and were not part of the 'corrupt' ruling class of the Syrian period, mainly Hizbullah and the FPM, they have still not aimed to push forward the democratization process. On the contrary, Hizbullah's participation in the government has mainly been aimed at protecting the Resistance, while the FPM has chiefly endeavoured to widen and strengthen Christian influence in the consociational system.

Nevertheless, the most pertinent question for the Lebanese public is how to push forward democratic reforms. There is actually no agreement among scholars or Lebanese politicians on which approach should be adopted. One of the approaches that may shape the path towards the elimination of confessionalism depends on the existence of two concurrent factors. The first of these is the aim of formulating a new electoral law that is based on PR with large districts. As discussed in the previous chapter, such an electoral law would allow the emergence of cross-sectarian political parties and weaken the influence of the existing sectarian leaders. A new political class, which is less influenced by the inter- and intra-sectarian conflicts and competition, might have the ability to initiate democratic reforms, which should eventually eliminate confessionalism. The second factor is the existence of a positive regional environment. A positive regional environment entails an agreement between the main external players in Lebanon on the importance of the initiation of democratic reforms and ensuring political and security stability. The case of the Doha Agreement is an example of how regional and international states were able to engineer a power-sharing agreement between Lebanese political parties, although the agreement did not aim to push forward democratic reforms.

On the theoretical level, the study of Lebanon's consociational model shows that the consociational model suffers from weaknesses, which have stark implications for political stability and the democratization process. The analysis shows that this form of governance is apt to spark inter- and intra-ethnic conflicts. The distribution of state positions between ethnic groups motivates political parties to compete over the representation and interests of their ethnicities, which can then lead to the failure of the power-sharing agreement and even descend into violence. Ethnic parties will seek to strengthen and widen their ethnic leadership to be able to obtain the quota allocated for their respective communities in the consociational system. This often entails employing ethnic language and accusing their inter- and intra-ethnic opponents of undermining their communities' interests to mobilize popular support, which would help spark ethnic conflicts. Thus, the ethnic outbidding between the parties will be concerned with addressing the interests of their communities in the consociational system. Also, the ethnic competition which might develop into ethnic violence would put the stability of the country at risk and undermine their ability to reach compromises because of their deeply entrenched positions. Furthermore, the endeavour of ethnic parties to secure their victory in the elections encourages them to build temporary inter-ethnic alliances, which necessitate making concessions for their allies that are sometimes at the expense of democratic reforms. As a consequence, the initiation of democratic reforms will be almost impossible due to the absence of agreement between the representatives of the ethnicities or due to the concessions that they make for their ethnic allies.

The book also shows that the consociational model in the post-occupation periods might fail to shield the country from foreign intervention which intersects with inter- and intra-ethnic conflicts. Because of the political vacuum left by the occupation force, domestic parties will desperately seek to cement new external alliances to protect their domestic positions against their domestic opponents. The endeavour of ethnic parties in seeking foreign support is to replace the alliance with the former main external player in the country. External alliances are sometimes considered essential for domestic parties since foreign patrons can provide political, financial, and military support for them to bolster their positions against their opponents. What may increase the willingness of foreign actors to intervene is the existence of the consociational state in a turbulent region. Regional players might seek to promote their interests through building alliances with domestic parties to weaken the influence of their regional and international rivals in the country. This would help fuel further inter- and intra-ethnic conflicts which can have adverse implications for political stability and the democratization process.

Moreover, the groups that were marginalized during the occupation period are likely to reject democratic reforms until their representation is strengthened in the consociational system. During the occupation period, the ethnic groups that are closely allied with the occupation force will dominate the consociational system and marginalize its ethnic opponents. Thus, the marginalized ethnic groups will lose their trust in their ethnic peers and will seek to strengthen their ethnic representation in the consociational system after the withdrawal of the foreign forces. Their position regarding democratic reforms will be therefore shaped by their compatibility with their interests in the consociational system.

Several lessons can be concluded from the study of Lebanon's consociational model for the multi-ethnic and multi-sectarian Arab states that are witnessing democratic uprisings and civil wars. Firstly, the consociational model is not, as Lijphart argues (1989: 41), always a 'strong medicine', to manage the ethnic and sectarian conflicts, especially for states that are located in turbulent regions, since it encourages foreign intervention from regional states seeking to widen and strengthen their regional influence. Secondly, the formation of a consociational political system in states like Syria and Iraq which have diverse ethnic and sectarian compositions will most likely lead to political instability and violent conflicts. However, a non-sectarian political system, which does not allocate state positions on ethnic and sectarian bases and protects the cultural heritage of the communal groups, can be a better alternative. As discussed in the case of Lebanon, the consociational model can help spark inter- and intra-ethnic conflict which can have repercussions for political stability and democracy.

Syria and Iraq have several features in common with Lebanon which undermine the likelihood of the consociational model succeeding in their cases. Firstly, they are located in a turbulent and unstable region, the Middle East, which will mean they face intense intervention from external players. These states are often portrayed as an arena for conflict between the main regional axes (Iranian- and American-led axes), which will help fuel the tensions between a state's ethnic and sectarian communities, especially when these communities have transnational connections like the Sunni and Shiite communities. The nature of ethnic and sectarian conflicts in these states intersect with regional sectarian conflicts, like the Saudi–Iranian conflict, which can help to further entrench the sense of ethnic and sectarian identity and widen the political gap between the communal groups. In such a situation, the recognition of these communities as political communities will put the stability of the country at risk since the outcome will eventually come to hinge on the agreement of the main external players, as the case of Lebanon shows.

Secondly, the consociational form of governance in these countries might fail because of its weaknesses, such as its ability to help spark inter- and intra-ethnic conflicts especially after the end of civil war or an occupation era. The defeat or the marginalization of a certain community in a civil war or during an occupation period might lead it to lose its trust in its ethnic peers. The ongoing conflict in Syria is sometimes portrayed by its warring parties as a sectarian conflict between the ʿAlawites who are dominating the regime and the Sunnis who are the majority of the Syrian people. Thus, the formation of this form of governance in Syria after the end of the war may entrench further the sense of ethnic and sectarian identities, because of their politicization, and may raise the fears of the communities about their shares in the political system. In such a situation, ethnic and sectarian parties may manipulate the repercussions of the previous era (i.e. the Assad era), such as the 'marginalization' of the Sunnis, to mobilize popular support on the basis that they aim to strengthen their community's representation in the consociational system; this may help spark inter- and intra-ethnic conflicts. This was evident in the case of Lebanon after 2005. The Christian parties manipulated the marginalization of the Christian community during the Syrian period to mobilize popular support on the basis that they were seeking to strengthen their community's representation in the consociational system, which helped fuel the tensions between the sects. They also rejected the initiation of genuine democratic reforms, such as eliminating confessionalism, because of their incompatibility with their interests in the consociational system.

NOTES

Introduction

1. The former head of the army, Michel Aoun, was forced to leave the country in 1990 because of his political and military opposition to the Syrian military presence.
2. Geagea was imprisoned because he was convicted of assassinating the former PM Rashid Karami in 1987.
3. Democratic reforms, which are stated in the Lebanese constitution, refer to the elimination of confessionalism, formation of a Senate which includes representatives from sectarian communities and the formulation of a new electoral law based on large districts. These reforms will be discussed in further details later in this book.
4. Several definitions of democracy have been developed by scholars in the field. However, Dahl's definition is a more detailed and clear-cut definition compared to the definitions provided by the following scholars. Dahl's definition shares the basic principles of democracy mentioned by those scholars, such as 'equality of citizens', 'inclusion of people under state's jurisdiction', 'protection against the state's arbitrary action' and 'mutually binding consultation' (Tilly, 2007: 14–5). Charles Tilly (2007: 13–14), for instance, defines a democratic regime's status as revolving around 'the degree that political relations between the state and its citizens feature broad, equal, protected and mutually binding consultation'. Samuel Huntington provides a more detailed definition. He (1984: 195) argues that '[a] political system is defined as democratic to the extent that its most powerful collective decision-makers are selected through periodic elections in which candidates freely compete for votes and in which virtually all the adult population is eligible to vote'. David Beetham (1994: 28) provides a similar definition, stating that democracy is: 'concerning the collectivity binding decisions about the rules and policies of a group, association or society. It claims that such decision-making should be, and it is realized to the

extent that such decision-making actually is, subject to the control of all members of the collectivity considered as equals. That is to say, democracy embraces the related principles of *popular support* and *political equality*.'

5. This book will use the term 'religious community' as a synonym for 'sectarian', 'sect' and 'communal', and the term 'divided society' as a synonym for 'plural', 'vertically segmented' and 'communally divided'. Ian Lustick (1979: 325) defines a society as a plural society 'if ascriptive ties generate an antagonistic segmentation of society, based on terminal identities with high political salience, sustained over a substantial period of time and a wide variety of issues. As a minimum condition, boundaries between rival groups must be sharp enough so that membership is clear and, with few exceptions, unchangeable.'

6. This book will use the term 'confessionalism' as a synonym for 'sectarianism'. Sectarianism is the recognition of religious communities as political communities that should have representatives in the political system (Makdisi, 2007: 24).

Chapter 1   Consociation

1. This chapter will provide a critique of the corporate type of the consociational model since that is the type applied in Lebanon.

Chapter 2   Weaknesses of Lebanon's Consociational Model in the Post-2005 Era

1. The last official consensus conducted in Lebanon was in 1932. Since then, the figures given for the numerical size of each sect have been estimations.

2. The 1926 Constitution witnessed few amendments in 1943; especially the articles related to the powers and role of the mandate state were deleted from the constitution. In theory, the president was supposed to play the role of the arbiter. However, many of the Lebanese presidents were biased in their political positions.

3. The National Pact stated that Lebanon should follow foreign policy which does not contradict with the demands of its sectarian groups. Bassel Salloukh (2008: 285) summarizes this point by stating that the National Pact ensured a balance 'between Christian and Muslim expectations of Lebanon's foreign policy to maintain cordial relations with the Arab states, a Muslim demand, but not at the expense of Lebanon's sovereignty and independence, a Christian demand'.

4. The constitutional amendments that are stated in the Ta'if Agreement were ratified by the Lebanese Parliament in November 1989.

5. One of the main factors that led to the ratification of the agreement was the fall of the Soviet Union which left many of its domestic allies without political and financial support. This also reduced the tensions between the main superpowers (US and Soviet Union) in the region which enhanced the enactment of the agreement (Salam, 2003: 40).

6. The violent conflict between Aoun, who was the head of the army, and Geagea erupted in February 1989 after the former called on Geagea to disarm his militia and Geagea rejected this request. It was also caused by their conflict over control of one of Beirut's main ports. In March 1989, Aoun declared the 'war of liberation' against the Syrian military presence in the country. The clashes led to the defeat of Aoun, forcing him to leave the country in 1990.

7. Damascus' military intervention was officially sanctioned by the Arab summit convened in Riyadh, Saudi Arabia, in October 1976 to end the violent sectarian conflict (Ellis, 1999: 11). Therefore, an Arab Deterrent Force (ADF), a 30,000-strong peacekeeping force, was created to bring security to Lebanon, composed mainly of Syrian military troops (Thompson, 2002: 76). After the end of the civil war in 1990, the number of the ADF was reduced to about 20,000 soldiers and was only composed of Syrian military forces.

8. The Arab Summit held in Casablanca, Morocco, in 1989 formed the Arab Tripartite Committee which was composed of King Fahd of Saudi Arabia, King Hassan II of Morocco, and President Shadli Ben Jedid of Algeria. This Committee aimed to solve the Lebanese crisis. The reason behind Saudi Arabia's endeavour to end the war was that country's desire to secure its influence in Lebanese domestic politics, although Syria was the main external player. The Kingdom 'wanted to limit Syrian dominance in Lebanon, position itself as the second Arab power vis-à-vis Syria, gain a role as peace broker in the Middle East and reinstate the traditional elites to power in Lebanon, particularly the Sunni community' (Kerr, 2006: 169). For this reason, it pledged to provide monetary aid to Lebanon after the war through the Sunni leader, Rafic Hariri (Kerr, 2006: 169).

9. The Syrian influence was enforced because of Damascus' alliance with the main Muslim parties (the Amal Movement, the PSP, and the Sunni Nasserite parties), and the presence of its military forces which ended the military conflict with Aoun and restored stability to eastern Beirut (a Christian-dominated area). This gave it heavy influence over Lebanese parties, which made the ratification of an agreement to end the civil war almost impossible without its consent.

10. The implications of the Syria Accountability Act and Resolution 1559 on Lebanese domestic politics will be discussed in more detail in Chapter 5.

11. Hariri essentially stood against the constitutional amendment and declined to form the new government in October 2004. According to former minister Fares Bouez, who met Hariri after the Syrian regime took its decision to extend the presidential term of Lahoud, Hariri's eventual approval of the constitutional amendment was given because if he refused to comply with the Syrian will 'it would be the final break between me [i.e. Hariri] and the Syrians and I can't afford to do that' (Blanford, 2006: 101). Bashar Assad's justification for his decision to extend Lahoud's presidential term was that it 'was taken as a defensive measure against the inevitable UN resolution', in reference to UNSC Resolution 1559 (Blanford, 2006: 105). He stated that Lahoud was 'a man of

principles and sincerity', and he 'was the best choice for fighting the battle with us, as subsequent events proved' (Blanford, 2006: 105).

12. The focus on the 2009 parliamentary elections is because it clearly reflected the political and sectarian divisions in Lebanon. In 2005, the Future Movement, Hizbullah, the Amal Movement, the PSP and the LFP entered the elections on common electoral lists. The outcome of the elections was a massive victory for the March 14 Coalition. After the elections, they jointly formed the cabinet which had the majority of its posts from the March 14 Coalition. The divisions and conflicts between them surfaced after the elections. However, in the 2009 polls, these parties entered the elections on different electoral lists with different political programmes and slogans.

13. To be eligible to vote, a Lebanese citizen must be aged 21 or over.

14. The former MP Pierre Dakkash is not mentioned in the table because he was an independent candidate and did not join either of the two coalitions. The Tripoli Coalition was composed of Sunni figures who were closely allied to the Future Movement. The Kataeb Party was part of the March 8 Coalition because its leadership had pro-Syrian leanings. QSG is an anti-Syrian gathering of Christian parties and leaders, established in April 2001. It included the National Liberal Party, the 'unofficial' Kataeb Party loyal to Amin Gemayel and Elie Karame, the LFP and the National Bloc, in addition to several independent politicians (el-Khazen, 2003a: 622).

15. The PSP left the March 14 Coalition in August 2009. This point will be discussed in Chapter 4.

16. The non-partisan MPs, Najib Mikati and Ahmad Karami, left the March 14 Coalition in August 2009, and they 'declared themselves as "centrists"' (IFES, 2009: 1). Also, the MP Muhammad Safadi left the March 14 Coalition after the 2009 elections.

17. The number of MPs in the parliamentary blocs is often more than the number of the MPs of political party that heads the bloc. This is because a major political party might enter the elections with alliances from non-partisan candidates and form a parliamentary bloc that includes partisan and non-partisan MPs.

18. Three independent MPs who ran for elections in Zahle district joined the LFP parliamentary bloc after the elections in 2009.

19. Another Druze political party emerged after 2005, Hizb al-Tawhid al-Arabi. This party was founded by its current leader, Wiam Wahhab. It is a supporter of Hizbullah's armed wing and a close ally of the Syrian regime. It has no representatives in parliament.

20. This point will be discussed further in this chapter and in the following chapters.

21. Although the Future Movement represents the majority of the Sunnis, there are other Sunni parties, such as Salafis and al-Jama'a al-Islamiyya (an Islamic party which won a seat in the 2009 parliamentary elections), which are closely allied with the Future Movement.

22. The change in the position of the Kataeb Party towards Syria and Hizbullah was after Gemayel assumed the position of 'higher leader' in 2001.

23. Notably, the poll shows that 34.8 per cent of Christians do not see the current Christian political parties and leaders as their representatives (Ibrahim, 2012). This point will be discussed in Chapter 4 to show how the absence of a major Christian party influenced the inter- and intra-sectarian outbidding and - conflict.

24. The July War erupted between Hizbullah and Israel when Hizbullah kidnapped two Israeli soldiers on 12 July 2006. It lasted for 33 days. The abduction operation aimed to swap the Israeli soldiers with Lebanese prisoners in Israel. The July War will be discussed in more detail in Chapter 5.

25. Christian parties and leaders (such as Michel Aoun and the LFP) called on Hizbullah to disarm its military wing after the Israeli military withdrawal in 2000. Muslim parties and leaders (such as Rafic Hariri and the PSP) did not call on it to disarm its military wing until the eruption of the July War in 2006.

26. This point will be discussed further in Chapters 5 and 6.

27. What encouraged further the March 14 Coalition to exclude the FPM from the new government was the existence of other Christian parties and leaders in the March 14 Coalition, such as the LFP. Although the FPM was part of the March 14 Coalition, it left the Coalition after the return of Aoun to Lebanon in 2005. This is because of its rivalry with the LFP and its close alliance with the Future Movement. It was also because of the electoral alliance that was formed between the Future Movement, Hizbullah, the Amal Movement, the PSP and the LFP in 2005, which marginalized the FPM.

28. This point will be discussed in further detail in the following chapters.

29. Interviewed on 4 May 2012, Beirut, Lebanon.

30. Ibid.

31. The sectarian communities and their representatives seek to acquire the means of power to be able to obtain their interests in the political system. The main factors that determine the power of the sectarian community are 'social cohesion, demographic strength, economic power and foreign alliances' (Haddad, 2001: 131). The social cohesion and foreign alliances are to a large extent the responsibility of the representatives of the sectarian group. Social cohesion is the unity of the sectarian group behind one political leader or party. The ability of a political party or leader to cultivate the support of the majority of his religious group can improve his negotiating power, which will help increase the community's share in the political system. This is because he is the main representative of his group, and therefore the government's legitimacy would be undermined if he is not holding the posts allocated for his community (Baydoun, 2012: 122). In addition to the social cohesion factor, foreign alliances can improve the political position of the religious group. The more powerful the external patron the more powerful is the domestic political position of the sectarian group and its representatives (Baydoun, 2012: 107–8).

32. The Lebanese president used to play the arbiter role before the ratification of the Ta'if Agreement. The wide powers that this position used to enjoy, such as dissolving the government, prevented paralysis in state institutions and ensured that whenever a political conflict erupted between the political parties, he would be able to intervene and force a settlement between them.

33. This point is also supported by one of the Ta'if constitution founders, Albert Mansour (interviewed on 2 May 2012, Beirut, Lebanon), who argues that the Lebanese constitution lacks a conflict-regulating mechanism because it stands against the notion of the Ta'if Agreement's principle of confessional coexistence.

34. Interviewed on 15 May 2012, Beirut, Lebanon.

35. Ibid.

36. Two parties are not 'owned' by a certain political leader: Hizbullah and the SSNP.

37. One of the features that also characterizes the formulation of electoral laws in Lebanon is that they were formulated after heavy foreign intervention. This point will be discussed in further details in the following chapters.

Chapter 3   The Democratization Process in the Pre- and Post-Syrian Withdrawal

1. The Lebanese militia leaders who participated in the civil war are not yet prosecuted. On the contrary, they participated in the political process after 1990, except for some selective legal trials such as imprisoning Samir Geagea, and exiling Amin Gemayel and Michel Aoun. This has created a sense of injustice among Christians.

2. PR: Political Rights Score; CL: Civil Liberties Score; NF: Not Free; PF: Partly Free. Each point total corresponds to a rating of 1 to 7, with 1 representing the highest and 7 the lowest level of freedom.

3. If the Mount of Lebanon had been one electoral district, Jumblatt might have lost the elections. This is because the Druze leader fought the Christians in the Lebanese mountain during the civil war and forced the migration of thousands of Christians from the areas that were under the control of his party (Khashan, 1997: 36).

4. Although the existence of diverse political parties can help prevent paralysis in state institutions, intra-sectarian competition in such a situation might be become intense and contribute to the intransigence and stubbornness of the political parties because any concession that a sectarian party makes will be manipulated by its intra-sectarian opponents to suggest they are selling out their community's interests. This point will be discussed in further detail in the following chapter.

5. The conflict between the two parties (Future Movement and Hizbullah) was over several issues, including the status of Hizbullah's armed wing and relations

with Syria. Also, this conflict echoed the conflict between their regional allies: Saudi Arabia (a Sunni state) and Iran (a Shiite state).

6. Although the Future Movement and Hizbullah are the major parties representing the overwhelming majority of their sects, this does not exclude the fact that intra-sectarian conflicts within the Sunni and Shiite communities influence their behaviour. The next chapter will explore how intra-sectarian conflicts and rivalry within these groups influenced the behaviour of the political parties.

7. The STL was formed as an international court that aimed to investigate the assassination of Hariri, after the request of the Lebanese government, headed by the March 14 Coalition, for the tribunal to be formed. The UNSC promulgated Resolution 1757 on 30 May 2007 which stated that the agreement between the Lebanese government and UNSC to form the tribunal 'would enter into force. The Council sought to bypass the need for parliamentary approval by invoking Chapter VII of the UN Charter' (Sriram, 2012: 50). The agreement between the Lebanese government and the UN regarding the formation of the Tribunal was not ratified by parliament and was considered to be constitutionally illegitimate by the March 8 Coalition. The STL accused four members of Hizbullah of assassinating Hariri, while Hizbullah denied its involvement in the assassination and rejected their extradition.

8. The reasons behind adopting the electoral law of the 2000 parliamentary elections for the 2005 parliamentary elections will be discussed in Chapter 5.

9. Interviewed on 27 November 2014, Hazmieh, Lebanon.

Chapter 4   Domestic Variables and Political Parties since 2005

1. What further encourages political parties to use sectarian language is the geographic distribution of the religious groups. In Lebanon, the geographic distribution of sectarian groups has meant that a sectarian group is concentrated in almost every electoral district, especially in small districts (*Qaḍā'*). For instance, the North of Lebanon district has a Sunni majority, while the Baalbek-Hermal district has a majority of Shiites (see Map 2). This has made candidates for elected office seek to address the interests of the major sectarian community in his or her electoral constituency as a means to mobilize votes.

2. Interviewed on 11 April 2012, Beirut, Lebanon.

3. Interviewed on 21 April 2012, Beirut, Lebanon.

4. Interviewed on 4 May 2012, Beirut, Lebanon.

5. Interviewed on 25 April 2012, Beirut, Lebanon.

6. Interviewed on 18 April 2012, Beirut, Lebanon.

7. In January 2011, Mikati was nominated by the March 8 Coalition and the PSP as a designate PM to replace Saad Hariri. Hariri's government was forced to resign after the third of its members who were from the March 8 Coalition

resigned. Their resignation was because of the political tensions which arose due to the funding for the STL and their request to reinvestigate the false witnesses in Hariri's assassination, especially as the STL was expected to accuse members of Hizbullah of Hariri's assassination.

8. Al-Aseer became popular after the attack of Hizbullah on the Future Movement's offices in Beirut in May 2008 which was considered by several Sunni parties as an attack from a Shiite party on the Sunnis. He heavily manipulated the Sunnis 'grievances' against Hizbullah which cultivated wide popular support for him within his community.

9. Interviewed on 21 April 2012, Beirut, Lebanon.

10. The external factors were influential in inculcating the sense of fear among sectarian groups. As will be shown in the next chapter, Lebanese political parties manipulated the implications of the July War that erupted between Hizbullah and Israel in 2006 and the assassinations that took place in Lebanon to inculcate the sense of fear among their followers.

11. Hizbullah was not represented in the government due to the resignation of its ministers after the inability of Lebanese parties to reach an agreement on a new unity government after the July War in 2006.

12. The conflict was resolved after the intervention of external players, in particular Qatar. It was able to engineer a power-sharing agreement between the warring parties, known as the Doha Agreement. This point will be discussed in more detail in the following chapter.

13. Interviewed on 8 and 15 May 2012, Beirut, Lebanon.

14. The elections in the Shiite areas, mainly Baalbeck-Hermal and South of Lebanon districts, are often portrayed as a referendum on the armed wing of Hizbullah: if Hizbullah and the Amal Movement lose the elections, it would undermine the legitimacy of the Resistance.

15. The influence of their antagonism towards Syria on the formation of this coalition will be discussed in the next chapter.

16. Interviewed on 21 April 2012, Beirut, Lebanon.

17. Ibid. Rafic Hariri is considered one of the founders of the Ta'if Agreement.

18. Interviewed on 11 May 2012, Mount of Lebanon, Lebanon.

19. The Orthodox Gathering electoral law is proposed by the Lebanese Orthodox Gathering which is composed of several political leaders and headed by Elie Ferzli. It states that each sectarian community has the right to elect its MPs based on PR with Lebanon as one electoral district. The FPM support for this law was because it secures the election of all Christian MPs by Christian voters, ensuring that Christian MPs will be out of the sphere of influence of Muslim parties, such as the Future Movement, Hizbullah and the PSP. One of the main disadvantages of this law is that it will entrench further the sense of sectarian identity and prevent the emergence of MPs with cross-sectarian views and policies. This point will be discussed in further detail in Chapter 6.

20. Hizbullah's opponents within the Shiite community would be able to win the parliamentary elections if the Orthodox Gathering electoral law was adopted

because it is based on PR, unlike the electoral laws that were adopted in the previous elections which were based on a winner-takes-all system.

21. The government that was formed after the May 7 conflict will be discussed in further detail in this chapter and the following chapter.

22. The refusal of the Future Movement to support the law and its ability to put pressure on the LFP to abstain from voting for the law in parliament have influenced the LFP's popularity within the Christian community. As a consequence, the LFP supported the postponement of the 2013 parliamentary elections. The position of the Future Movement and the LFP on the electoral law will be discussed in more detail in Chapter 6.

23. The LFP requests and the Future Movement's financial support for the independent Christian politicians happened before parliament took its decision to extend its term for 18 months.

24. There is an external factor that also enforced the alliance between Hizbullah and the FPM, which is the July War. The FPM's support for Hizbullah during the war made Nasrallah declare that those who stood with the Resistance during the war are 'partners in victory' (al-Akhbar, 2006).

25. After the PSP had decided to leave the March 14 Coalition in 2009, four MPs left its parliamentary bloc and joined the March 14 Coalition parliamentary bloc. As of 2011, the Democratic Gathering bloc has actually become composed of seven MPs only. After the withdrawal of the PSP parliamentary bloc and three MPs (Najib Mikati, Ahmad Karami and Muhammad Safadi), the size of the March 14 Coalition parliamentary bloc has reduced to 61 MPs.

26. The PSP support for the March 8 Coalition government that was formed in March 2011 can be explained by its recognition that the government would be temporary until the parliamentary elections in June 2013 so it could satisfy and strengthen its relations with Hizbullah. At the same time, the Future Movement was not able to completely break its relations with it because of their electoral alliance. If this alliance was broken, the Future Movement would lose several MP seats in Druze-dominated districts, in particular in the Mount of Lebanon districts.

27. The PSP was also able to manipulate its popularity to impose its policies. As discussed in the previous section, one of the factors that strengthened the political position of the PSP was its wide popular support within its community.

28. The March 8 Coalition organized the sit-in in Beirut after the July War to force the government, which was headed by the Future Movement, to resign. This point will be discussed in further detail in the following chapter.

29. The PSP did not attempt to impose its view on the distribution of the electoral districts because the division of the districts according to the 1960 electoral law suited its electoral strategies.

30. The influence of the external factors, such as foreign alliances, on parliamentary elections will be discussed in the following chapter.

31. Interviewed on 21 April 2012, Beirut, Lebanon.

32. Interviewed on 11 May 2012, Beirut, Lebanon.

Chapter 5 External Variables and Political
Parties since 2005

1. Resolution 1680 called on Syria to delineate the geographic borders with Lebanon and to establish full diplomatic relations with the Lebanese government. It also called on the Lebanese and Syrian governments to prevent the smuggling of weapons to Lebanon (UNSC, 2006b: Article 5). Resolution 1664 approves the request of the Lebanese government to form the STL to try those involved in the assassination of Hariri in February 2005 (UNSC, 2006a). Resolution 1686 supports the government call to expand the mandate of the mission of the International Independent Investigation Commission to cover 'the other terrorist attacks' in Lebanon since October 2004, since its only mission was to investigate the assassination of Hariri (UNSC, 2006c: 1). It also approves the government request to extend the term of the Commission for one year (UNSC, 2006c).
2. UNIFIL (United Nations Interim Forces In Lebanon) was established in 1978 to ensure Israel's withdrawal and to help the government of Lebanon to spread its authority in the South.
3. After the Israeli military withdrawal in 2000, the Lebanese army was not deployed in the South. The Lebanese government's justification was that the army is not able to withstand Israeli attacks and only Hizbullah can defend the South.
4. The former Egyptian president and member of the Muslim Brotherhood, Muhammad Mursi, was toppled after the eruption of anti-Muslim Brotherhood protests and the army intervention to force him to resign in July 2013. Adly Mansour, the head of the supreme constitutional court, assumed the position of the presidency until the election of the new president in 2014.
5. Interviewed on 1 May 2012, Beirut, Lebanon.
6. Interviewed on 21 April 2012, Beirut, Lebanon.
7. One of the main factors that also led to the emergence of the Sunni–Shiite conflict in Lebanon is that the demographic sizes of both communities are almost equal which put them in conflict over the distribution of state positions and revenues. Khaled Saghieh (interviewed on 21 April 2012, Beirut, Lebanon) argues that 'the internal Sunni–Shiite conflict was going to happen without external intervention, but external intervention has fueled this conflict'.
8. Interview with the Lebanese academic from the LAU, Bassel Salloukh, on 15 May 2012, Beirut, Lebanon.
9. Interviewed on 21 April 2012, Beirut, Lebanon.
10. Ibid.
11. Ibid.
12. Ibid.
13. Interviewed on 4 May 2012, Beirut, Lebanon.
14. Ibid.

15. The conflict between Hariri, Jumblatt and Lahoud was before the extension of Lahoud's presidential term. The conflict was mainly over the socio-economic policy of the government.

16. Fitna is an Arabic term which refers to causing conflicts and problems between people and attempting to create a chaotic situation.

17. The reason behind Hizbullah and the FPM's request to postpone the elections was because the 2000 electoral law would secure the victory of the March 14 Coalition. Also, the 2000 electoral law defragments and weakens the voting power of Christians.

18. The National Dialogue meetings were convened after the eruption of the conflict between the two coalitions in March 2006. The meetings used to be held in parliament and not in the presidential palace because of the conflict between the March 14 Coalition and the former president, Lahoud. After the election of President Michel Sleiman, the National Dialogue meetings were moved to the presidential palace. The main participants were the Future Movement, Hizbullah, the Amal Movement, the PSP, the FPM, the LFP, the Kataeb Party, the el-Marada Party, representatives of the Orthodox community and civil society, the president, the speaker of parliament and the PM. The main issues for discussion were the national defence strategy to replace Hizbullah's armed wing, diplomatic relations with Syria and the STL, although any emerging issue could be discussed in the meetings, such as the eruption of violence in northern Lebanon. Several rounds of meeting were held between 2006 and 2012. However, the National Dialogue meetings did not reach an agreement on decisive issues, such as the national defence strategy.

19. Interviewed on 1 May 2012, Beirut, Lebanon.

20. Ibid.

21. The reason behind Hizbullah's call for a new government was firstly because the government which was formed in 2005 was headed and dominated by the March 14 Coalition. Secondly, Hizbullah sought to include the FPM in the new government and have a blocking third which would enable the March 8 Coalition to veto government decisions.

22. Saudi Arabia provided hundreds of millions of dollars as financial assistance to the March 14 Coalition for the parliamentary elections in 2009 to be able to win the elections and combat Hizbullah and the March 8 Coalition (Worth, 2009).

23. The first two conferences were held in Paris on 27 February 2001, and 23 November 2002, at the invitation of the former president of France, Jacques Chirac (Baroudi & Salamey, 2011: 412). Former PM, Rafic Hariri, represented Lebanon at both meetings.

24. The head of this group was Shaker al-Absi, a Palestinian who served in the Jordanian army. He escaped a death sentence in Jordan and was imprisoned for three years in Syria after he was accused of smuggling weapons to the Golan Heights (Abdel-Latif, 2008: 18). After he was freed, he left for Lebanon and started training members from Fatah al-Intifada. In November 2006, he left the

group, took its offices in Naher al-Bared camp and formed the Fatah al-Islam group (Abdel-Latif, 2008: 18).

25. More than 400,000 Palestinian refugees are settling in Lebanon and reside in refugee camps, which are out of the Lebanese government's security and political control.

26. *Waliyya al-Faqīh* (jurist-theologian) is a person who holds religious qualifications and 'who defines the general politics of a nation's life' and the 'role of the charged [i.e. who is in power] in executing holy judgements' (Qassem, 2010: 114). His authority 'represents a continuation of that of the Prophet and the infallible Imams (PBUT) insofar as its role is concerned' (Qassem, 2010: 116).

27. In its political manifesto published in 2009, Hizbullah recognized Lebanon's consociational model, considering it as the most appropriate system until the Lebanese sects agree to eliminate sectarianism (Hizbullah, 2009).

28. According to Hizbullah deputy secretary-general Shaykh Naim Qassem: 'It is only natural that Hizbullah's views concur with those of Syria, for no one is safe from Israel's ambitions' (Qassem, 2010: 398). He argues that '[w]e do not consider the relationship with Syria to be either mandatory or accidental, but rather the cornerstone for facing major regional obligations [. . .] [and] so far [it has] proven its utility and necessity' (Qassem, 2010: 399).

29. It is worth noting that both coalitions accused each other of sparking the conflict in May 2008 to serve the interests of their external allies. Geagea, for instance, considered that the 'armed and bloody coup which is being implemented aims to return Syria to Lebanon and extend Iran's reach to the Mediterranean' (Abdallah, 2008). On the other side, Nasrallah (2010) considered the government decision to dismantle his party telecommunications network as an 'American-inspired' decision.

30. Interviewed on 21 April 2012, Beirut, Lebanon.

31. The assassinations of Wissam al-Hassan and Muhammad Shatah are added by the author.

32. There were also assassinations of non-March 14 Coalition members. Three assassinations of the March 8 Coalition took place: Imad Mughniyah, Hizbullah's military leader (2008), Saleh al-Aridi, a senior LDP party official (2008), and Hassan Lakkis, a Hizbullah military leader (2013); and Francois al-Hajj, an army officer (2007).

33. Hariri's 'project' was to rebuild state infrastructure and improve the economic conditions of the Lebanese people after the end of the civil war. Hariri's 'project' is a term coined by the leaders and supporters of the Future Movement after his assassination.

34. Interviewed on 8 and 15 May 2012, Beirut, Lebanon.

35. Interview with the Lebanese journalist and media figure who works at the LBC, Khaled Saghieh, on 21 April 2012, Beirut, Lebanon.

36. Ibid.

Chapter 6   The 2013 Parliamentary Elections and the Syrian Conflict

1. What is noticeable is the absence of a direct foreign intervention to exert pressure on domestic parties to reach an agreement on a new electoral law as was the case in the formulation of the previous electoral laws. This can, in part, be explained with the immersion of the main foreign players in Lebanon (Syria, Saudi Arabia and Qatar) in the Syrian conflict and their betting on its consequences which may endow them with greater influence over Lebanese domestic politics at a later stage. For instance, it is in the interest of Saudi Arabia to topple the Syrian regime which will weaken the position of its domestic opponents, in particular Hizbullah.

2. Although reforming the electoral law is essential for the success of the democratization process in Lebanon, it is not sufficient by itself. Reforming the electoral law should be followed by implementing the reform steps stated in the Ta'if Agreement, such as forming the National Body for the Elimination of Confessionalism and the senate.

3. Elements of this chapter have been previously published in: Assi, AF & Worrall, J, 2015, 'Stable Instability: The Syrian Conflict and the Postponement of the 2013 Lebanese Parliamentary Elections', *Third World Quarterly*, Vol. 36, No. 10, pp. 1944–67 (http://www.tandfonline.com), and formed part of the evidence basis drawn upon in the article.

4. Hizbullah's electoral law proposal was rejected by the March 14 Coalition because it secures the victory of the March 8 Coalition in the elections. What also led Hizbullah to change its position regarding the electoral law was the insistence of its ally, the FPM, on the Orthodox Gathering electoral law.

5. Interviewed on 27 November 2014, Hazmieh, Lebanon.

6. The Orthodox Gathering electoral law, which is based on PR, if adopted, would lead to the victory of the March 8 Coalition. The political opponents of the Future Movement within the Sunni community, such as Nasserites who are close to the March 8 Coalition, would be able to win parliamentary seats, since the Future Movement represents about 63.4 per cent of the Sunni community (BCRI, 2010). Furthermore, the Future Movement parliamentary bloc would lose about half of its MPs, who are non-Sunnis. Thus, the March 14 Coalition ability to win the majority of the parliamentary seats would be weakened.

7. Elie Ferzli (interviewed on 27 November 2014, Hazmieh, Lebanon) also confirms the point that the LFP received an offer from the Future Movement to reject the Orthodox Gathering electoral law, which involved an increase in the number of the LFP MPs in parliament in the next parliamentary elections.

8. Interview with the scholar and MP in the FPM parliamentary bloc, Farid el-Khazen, on 9 December 2014, Beirut, Lebanon. El-Khazen attended the Christian parties' meetings in Bkirki (the residence of the Maronite Patriarch) to discuss the electoral law.

9. Interviewed on 27 November 2014, Hazmieh, Lebanon.

10. Interviewed on 9 December 2014, Beirut, Lebanon.

11. Ibid.

12. Interviewed on 27 November 2014, Hazmieh, Lebanon.

13. These groups became very active after the eruption of the Syrian conflict. The conflict represented an opportunity for them to strengthen their sectarian leadership. Thus, they forcefully employed sectarian language, for example defending the rights of Sunnis in Syria and Lebanon against Hizbullah and the Syrian regime. For Sunni Islamist groups, the Syrian conflict is an opportunity to topple Assad's regime and to undermine the political and military power of its domestic ally, Hizbullah (ICG, 2012: 3). Their 'hatred' for Assad's regime is because they accuse it of their repression in Lebanon during its military presence and the repression of their religious fellows in Syria (ICG, 2012: 3).

14. It was rumoured that some of the Sunni militant groups sought to form their own independent area in northern Lebanon in order to support the Syrian opposition (al-Amin, 2012).

15. Clashes erupted between the Lebanese army and pro-Syrian opposition fighters in Arsal when the Lebanese army attempted to capture Khaled Hmayyad who is accused of terrorist offences. These clashes left two military officers dead and several wounded on 1 February 2013. Arsal, a Lebanese village, is located next to the Syrian–Lebanese border and has mainly Sunni inhabitants.

16. Qusayr is a Syrian city located next to the Syrian–Lebanese border.

17. Nonetheless, Hizbullah's military intervention had implications for Sunni–Shiite relations. The Sunnis in Lebanon considered its intervention in aid of the Assad regime as targeting and undermining the rise to power of the Syrian Sunnis. Saad Hariri accused Nasrallah of receiving orders from Damascus and Tehran to interfere in Syria to rescue and help Assad's regime combat the opposition. He stated that 'Nasrallah chose [...] to stand in the ranks of the oppressors and declares his commitment to defend until death the regime of Bashar Assad, and to follow the Iranian [orders] [...] and the fatwa issued by the Waliyya al-Faqīh [...] to prevent the fall of this regime' (al-Quds, 2013). Several suicide bombings took place in Lebanon after Hizbullah's intervention in Syria. Jabhat al-Nusra and Abdullah Azzam Brigades, both of which are extreme militant groups opposed to the Assad regime, claimed responsibility for these attacks. Their aim in the suicide bombings was to exert pressure on Hizbullah to withdraw its armed forces from Syria.

18. The former deputy of the speaker of parliament and head of the Orthodox Gathering, Elie Ferzli, interviewed on 27 November 2014, Hazmieh, Lebanon.

19. Interviewed on 9 December 2014, Beirut, Lebanon.

20. Parliamentary elections in Lebanon usually take place every four years, in June, and parliament was supposed to postpone the elections for one year so they could be held in June 2014. However, due to the presidential elections which were supposed to take place in May 2014, parliament delayed parliamentary

elections until November 2014; particularly as the previous presidential elections in 2007 had taken more than seven months until Lebanese parties agreed on the election of Michel Sleiman as president. The Lebanese parties once again postponed parliamentary elections (until 2017) in November 2014, using the pretext that the security situation is not stable and that the election centres might be targeted by terrorist groups.

21. Interviewed on 9 December 2014, Beirut, Lebanon.

BIBLIOGRAPHY

Abdallah, H 2008, 'Day 3: Hizbullah, Amal take West Beirut', *The Daily Star*, May 10, viewed on: 02-12-2013, available on: http://www.dailystar.com.lb/ News/Lebanon-News/2008/May-10/48912-day-3-hizbullah-amal-take-west-beirut.ashx#axzz2lxQbVUsk.

Abdel-Latif, O 2008, *Lebanon's Sunni Islamists – A Growing Force*, No. 6, Carnegie Middle East Center, Carnegie Endowment for International Peace, Beirut, viewed on: 06-03-2013, available on: http://www.carnegieendowment.org/files/ CMEC6_abdellatif_lebanon_final.pdf.

Abu-Habib, A 1991, *Al-Dawa' Al-'Asfar: Siyāsat America Tijāh Lubnān*, Sharikat Al-Maṭbū ʿāt li-l-Tawzīʿ wa-Nnashar, Beirut.

——— 2013a, 'Khiṭāb Al-Qiyādāt Al-Ssiyāsiyya Al-Masīḥiyya fī Waqt Al-'Azamāt', *Al-Akhbar*, February 2, viewed on: 02-02-2013, available on: http://www.al-akhbar.com/node/176744.

——— 2013b, *Postponing Lebanon's Elections Assures Political Chaos*, Al-Monitor, May 30, viewed on: 18-10-2013, available on: http://www.al-monitor.com/pulse/ politics/2013/05/lebanon-extension-parliament-elections-politics.html.

Abu-Rizk, Z 2005, 'Hizbullah's Crisis of Confidence', *The Daily Star*, November 25, viewed on: 07-12-2013, available on: http://www.dailystar.com.lb/News/ Lebanon-News/2005/Nov-25/6223-hizbullahs-crisis-of-confidence.ashx#ixzz 2mmbwwfzs.

AbuKhalil, A 1990, 'Syria and the Shiites: Al-Asad's Policy in Lebanon', *Third World Quarterly*, Vol. 12, No. 2, pp. 1–20.

——— 1993, 'The Study of Political Parties in the Arab World: The Case of Lebanon', *Journal of Asian and African Studies*, Vol. Fall, pp. 49–64.

Adwan, C 2005, *Corruption in Reconstruction: The Cost of 'National Consensus' in Post-War Lebanon*, The Lebanese Transparency Association, Beirut, viewed on: 26-02-2013, available on: http://depot.gdnet.org/newkb/fulltext/adwan.pdf.

Ajami, J 2005, 'Lebanese Elections 2005 Version: Land Liberation or Mind Liberation?', *American Behavioral Scientist*, Vol. 49, No. 4, pp. 634–9.

Ake, C 1975, 'A Definition of Political Stability', *Comparative Politics*, Vol. 7, No. 2, pp. 271–83.

Akkoum, C 2012, 'Al-Druze fī Lubnān bayn Al-Dda'awā 'ilā Al-Nniḍāl Ḍidda Niẓām Asad wa-l-'Ist'dād li-l-Qitāl Ma'ahu', *Asharq Al-Awsat*, February 24, viewed on: 12-11-2013, available on: http://www.aawsat.com/details.asp?section=4&issueno=12141&article=665119&search=%E6%E5%C7%C8%20%CC%E4%C8%E1%C7%D8%20%C7%E1%CF%D1%E6%D2&state=true#.UnVc9flSgmQ.

Al-Akhbar 2006, 'Nasrallah 'an Al-'Akthariyya: Bila Qalbin wa-Bila 'Aqal', *Al-Akhbar*, September 13, viewed on: 31-05-2013, available on: http://www.al-akhbar.com/node/162214.

———— 2011, 'Milyāray Dollar min Al-Ssu'ūdiyya li-14 'Athār', *Al-Akhbar*, March 28, p. 11.

———— 2012, 'Al-Aseer: Saad ḥattā 'Ski' ma Bya'rf', *Al-Akhbar*, March 16, viewed on: 24-10-2013, available on: http://www.al-akhbar.com/node/45684.

———— 2013a, 'Bassil: Al-Quwwāt 'Aṭāhat Al-Waḥda Al-Masīḥiyya', *Al-Akhbar*, May 17, p. 7.

———— 2013b, 'Milyuwn wa-200 'Alf Nāzaḥ Sūrī fī Lubnān', *Al-Akhbar*, July 18, viewed on: 17-10-2013, available on: http://www.al-akhbar.com/node/187298.

Al-Amin, I 2012, ''Imārat 'Ahl Al-Sunna fī Al-Shshamāl', *Al-Akhbar*, May 5, p. 3.

Al-Jazeera 2012, *Samir Geagea ... Al-Mashhad Al-Ssyāsī Al-Llubnānī (Interview)*, Al-Jazeera Channel Website, November 10, viewed on: 06-03-2013, available on: http://www.aljazeera.net/programs/pages/b62fb67e-90ba-485b-980a-b16a568ab594#L6.

Al-Mustaqbal 2006a, 'Abou-Faour: Mā Ḥaṣala Jiz'un min Qarār Sūrī bi-Tafjīr Al-'Awḍā'', *Al-Mustaqbal*, April 12, p. 5.

———— 2006b, 'Khādim Al-Ḥarmayn Al-Shsharīfyan Yushīd bi-'Wdat Al-Janūb li-l-Ddawla ... Wa-'Istahjān 'Arabī Wasa' li-Kalām Ra'īys Al-Ssūrī', *Al-Mustaqbal*, August 18, p. 18.

———— 2007a, 'Al-Ththulāthā' Al-'Aswad: Dawlat 'Hizbullah' Tuḥāṣir Lubnān', *Al-Mustaqbal*, January 24, p. 15.

———— 2007b, 'Ḥaẓar Tajuwwal fī Beirut ba'da 'Istibāḥatihā min Mīlīshayāt Al-'Inqilābiyīn', *Al-Mustaqbal*, January 26, p. 20.

———— 2009a, 'Geagea: 'Idhā Fāzat Al-Mu'āraḍa Saytaḥuwwal Lubnān Jumhūriyyat Mawz', *Al-Mustaqbal*, May 31, p. 4.

———— 2009b, 'Hariri: Da'm Fawz Al-'Akthariyya Yu'ammn Al-'Istimrāriyya li-Takrīs Mashrū' Al-Ssiyāda', *Al-Mustaqbal*, May 31, viewed on: 28-12-2013, available on: http://www.almustaqbal.com/storiesprintpreview.aspx?storyid=349957.

———— 2009c, 'Jumblatt Yajūl fī Manṭaqaty Hasbaya wa-Rashaya: Ma'rakat Al-'Istiqlāl Al-Ththālitha fī 7 Ḥuzayrān', *Al-Mustaqbal*, June 1, p. 6.

———— 2009d, 'Sami Gemayel: Al-'Awlawiyya li-Binā' Al-Ddawla wa-l-Jjayash wa-Ḥaṣar al-Ssilāh', *Al-Mustaqbal*, May 31, p. 4.

———— 2013, 'Hariri: Hizbullah laysa Shi'a wa-l-Ssilāḥ 'Ummu Al-Mashākal', *Al-Mustaqbal*, February 15, p. 18.

Al-Quds 2013, 'Hariri: Hizbullah Yajurrū Lubnān 'ila Al-Kharāb min 'Ajal Bashar Assad', *Al-Quds*, May 1, viewed on: 18-10-2013, available on: http://www.alquds.co.uk/?p=39525.

Al-Seyassah 2013, 'Arsal fī Qabḍat Al-Jjayash Al-Llubnāny wa-Tashdud fī Mulāḥaqat Al-Maṭlūbīn', *Al-Seyassah*, February 5, p. 42.

Alagha, J 2005, *Hizballah After the Syrian Withdrawal*, No. 237, MERIP Middle East Report, pp. 34–9.

——— 2006, *The Shifts in Hizbullah's Ideology: Religious Ideology, Political Ideology, and Political Program*, Amsterdam University Press, Isim, Leiden.

Alloush, M 2011, 'Limādha Yas'ā Ḥizb Wīlāyat Al-Faqīh 'ila Hadm Muqawwimāt Al-Ddawla', *Al-Mustaqbal*, December 24, p. 4.

Andeweg, RB 2000, 'Consociational Democracy', *Annual Review of Political Science*, Vol. 3, pp. 509–36.

Armanazi, G 2005, 'Syria's Withdrawal from Lebanon: An Interim Postscript', *Middle East International*, Vol. 755, No. July 22, pp. 28–9.

Asharq Al-Awsat 2006a, 'Aoun Yuḥmmal Al-Ḥukūma Mas'ūliyyat "I'ādat Al-Bilād 'ila Siyāsat Al-Mḥāwar", *Asharq Al-Awsat*, October 16, viewed on: 02-11-2013, available on: http://www.aawsat.com/details.asp?section=4&issueno=10184& article=387573&search=%E3%ED%D4%C7%E1%20%DA%E6%E4&state= true#.UnVULfiSgmQ.

——— 2006b, 'Ṭarafā Ḥadath Khalwat Al-Kfier Yu'ṭūn Riwāyatyan Mutanāqiḍatyan', *Asharq Al-Awsat*, April 12, viewed on: 05-11-2013, available on: http://www.aawsat.com/details.asp?issueno=9896&article=357893#.UnV2p PlSgmQ.

——— 2008, 'Qā'id Al-Quwwāt Al-Llubnāniyya Yaḥmal bi-'Unf 'alā Aoun wa-Hizbullah wa-Yu'alan 'Al-Ththwābat Al-Ttārīkhiyya li-l-Masīḥīyin' Nuqṭat 'Irtikāz li-Wḥdatihim', *Asharq Al-Awsat*, September 22, viewed on: 26-12-2012, available on: http://www.aawsat.com/details.asp?issueno=10626&article= 487912.

——— 2009, 'Hariri Yushdad 'alā Al-Munāṣafa bayn Al-Masīḥīyin wa-l-Muslimīn. Wa-Aoun 'Munfatah' 'alā Al-Muḥīṭ', *Asharq Al-Awsat*, May 31, viewed on: 24-10-2013, available on: http://www.aawsat.com/details.asp?issueno=10992& article=521331.

Assaf, G & El-Fil, R 2000, 'Resolving the Issue of War Displacement in Lebanon', *Forced Migration Review*, Vol. 7, pp. 31–3.

Assaf, Noura 2004, 'Consociational Theory and Democratic Stability, A Re-Examination Case Study: Lebanon', Unpublished PhD Thesis, University of Warwick.

Assaf, Nayla 2004, 'Lebanese MPs Give Lahoud 3 More Years', *The Daily Star*, September 4, viewed on: 08-02-2013, available on: http://www.dailystar.com.lb/ News/Politics/Sep/04/Lebanese-MPs-give-Lahoud-3-more-years.ashx#ixzz2K J2Di87n.

Assafir 2013, 'Dirāsa li-Al-Dduwaliyya li-l-Ma'lūmāt: 173 'Alf Zawāj Mukhtalaṭ', *Assafir*, April 2, p. 5.

Aziz, J 2013a, *Lebanese Politics Affected by Syrian Battle for Qusair*, Al-Monitor, May 23, viewed on: 03-12-2013, available on: http://www.al-monitor.com/pulse/ originals/2013/05/qusair-fall-affect-lebanese-politics.html.

——— 2013b, *Syrian Armed Groups Among Those Displaced in Lebanon*, Al-Monitor, January 11, viewed on: 21-01-2013, available on: http://www.al-monitor.com/ pulse/originals/2013/01/syrians-infiltrating-lebanon.html.

Baroudi, SE & Salamey, I 2011, 'US-French Collaboration on Lebanon: How Syria's Role in Lebanon and the Middle East Contributed to a US–French Convergence', *Middle East Journal*, Vol. 65, No. 3, pp. 398–425.

Barry, B 1975a, 'The Consociational Model and its Dangers', *European Journal of Political Research*, Vol. 3, No. 4, pp. 393–412.

——— 1975b, 'Political Accommodation and Consociational Democracy', *British Journal of Political Science*, Vol. 5, No. 4, pp. 477–505.

Bassil, P 2013, 'Saad: Al-'Intishār Al-Masīḥī ʿalā Msāḥt Al-Waṭan Yudʿaf Tamthilahum.Wa-Nnisby Yuquwwīhī', *Ath-Thabāt*, January 18, p. 8.

Bathish, HM 2007, 'All Sides Repeat Denials of Training for War, But … ', *The Daily Star*, September 26, viewed on: 17-12-2012, available on: http://www.dail ystar.com.lb/News/Politics/Sep/26/All-sides-repeat-denials-of-training-for-war-but-.ashx#ixzz2FK5Y7W5V.

Baydoun, A 2012, *Lubnān: Al-'Iṣlāḥ Al-Manshūd wa-l-Kharāb Al-Mardūd*, Dar Al-Saqi, Beirut.

Bayoumy, Y 2007, *Lebanon Says 222 Militants Killed in Camp Battle*, Thomson Reuters, September 4, viewed on: 03-02-2013, available on: http://www.reuters. com/article/2007/09/04/idUSL04786404.

Bazzi, Y 2009, 'Baʿda 4 Sanawāt. Taẓāhura Milūniyya Jadīda', *Al-Mustaqbal*, February 15, p. 20.

BBC Arabic 2005, *'Istimrār Masāʿī Tashkīl Al-Ḥukūma Al-Llubnāniyya*, British Broadcasting Corporation – Arabic, July 4, viewed on: 24-09-2013, available on: http://news.bbc.co.uk/hi/arabic/middle_east_news/newsid_4648000/ 4648185.stm.

BCRI 2010, *Al-'Ittijāhāt Al-Ssayāsiyya w-l-'Ijtimāʿiyya fī Lubnān*, May–June, Beirut Center for Research & Information, Beirut, viewed on: 26-12-2012, available on: http://www.beirutcenter.net/Default.asp?ContentID=800&menuID=46.

Beetham, D 1994, 'Key Principles and Indices for a Democratic Audit', in Beetham, D (ed.), *Defining and Measuring Democracy*, Sage Publications, London, pp. 25–43.

Blanford, N 2006, *Killing Mr Lebanon: The Assassination of Rafik Hariri and its Impact on the Middle East*, I.B.Tauris, London.

——— 2008, 'A Cell Phone Civil War in Lebanon', *Time*, May 7, viewed on: 02-12-2013, available on: http://content.time.com/time/world/article/ 0,8599,1738255,00.html.

Bluhm, M 2010, 'Political Rifts Complicate Municipal Election Reforms', *The Daily Star*, January 21, viewed on: 11-01-2013, available on: http://www.dailystar. com.lb/News/Politics/Jan/21/Political-rifts-complicate-municipal-election-reforms.ashx.

Bogaards, M 1998, 'The Favourable Factors for Consociational Democracy: A Review', *European Journal of Political Research*, Vol. 33, No. 4, pp. 475–96.

Bohn, DE 1980, 'Consociational Democracy and the Case of Switzerland', *Journal of Politics*, Vol. 42, No. 1, pp. 165–79.

Cammett, M 2009, *Democracy, Lebanese-Style*, August 18, MERIP Middle East Report Online, viewed on: 10-12-2011, available on: http://www.merip.org/ mero/mero081809.

——— 2014, *Compassionate Communalism: Welfare and Sectarianism in Lebanon*, Cornell University Press, Ithaca, New York.

Cammett, M & Issar, S 2010, 'Bricks and Mortar: Clientelism, Sectarianism and the Logics of Welfare Allocation in Lebanon', *World Politics*, Vol. 62, No. 3, pp. 381–421.

Chandra, K 2005, 'Ethnic Parties and Democratic Stability', *Perspectives on Politics*, Vol. 3, No. 2, pp. 235–52.

Chararah, N 2013, *Lebanon Struggles to Manage Palestinian, Syrian Refugees*, Al-Monitor, January 10, viewed on: 12-01-2013, available on: http://www.al-monitor.com/pulse/originals/2013/01/palestinian-syrian-displacement.html.

Choucair, J 2005, *Lebanon's New Political Moment*, March, Carnegie Endowment for International Peace, Washington, viewed on: 11-03-2013, available on: http://carnegieendowment.org/files/PO14.Choucair.FINAL.pdf.

Choucair, W 2006, 'The Shiites' Return to Cabinet Ends a Period of Political Deterioration', *The Daily Star*, February 4, viewed on: 06-12-2013, available on: http://dailystar.com.lb/News/Lebanon-News/2006/Feb-04/6867-the-shiites-return-to-cabinet-ends-a-period-of-political-deterioration.ashx#axzz2mi066Ud2.

Ciezadlo, A 2005, 'Lebanon's Election: Free but Not Fair', *The Washington Post*, May 22, viewed on: 26-01-2012, available on: http://www.washingtonpost.com/wp-dyn/content/article/2005/05/20/AR2005052001868.html.

Cleveland, W 2009, *A History of the Modern Middle East*, 4th edn, Westview Press, Boulder, Colorado.

Conteh-Morgan, E 1997, *Democratization in Africa: The Theory and Dynamics of Political Transitions*, Praeger Press, Connecticut & London.

Cordell, K & Wolff, S 2009, *Ethnic Conflict: Causes, Consequences, and Responses*, Polity Press, Cambridge.

Corstange, D 2010, 'The Parliamentary Election in Lebanon, June 2009', *Electoral Studies*, Vol. 29 No. 2, pp. 285–9.

Covell, M 1981, 'Ethnic Conflict and Elite Bargaining: The Case of Belgium', *West European Politics*, Vol. 4, No. 3, pp. 197–218.

Dahl, R 1971, *Polyarchy: Participation and Opposition*, Yale University Press, New Haven & London.

——— 1982, *Dilemmas of Pluralist Democracy: Autonomy vs. Control*, Yale University Press, New Haven & London.

——— (ed.) 1966, *Political Oppositions in Western Democracies*, Yale University Press, New Haven.

Dakroub, H 2006, 'Hezbollah Urges Protests Against Gov't', *The Washington Post*, November 19, viewed on: 04-03-2013, available on: http://www.washingtonpost.com/wp-dyn/content/article/2006/11/19/AR2006111900590.html.

Davis, DR & Moore, WH 1997, 'Ethnicity Matters: Transnational Ethnic Alliances and Foreign Policy Behavior', *International Studies Quarterly*, Vol. 41, No. 1, pp. 171–84.

Dawisha, A 1984, 'The Motives of Syria's Involvement in Lebanon', *Middle East Journal*, Vol. 38, No. 2, pp. 228–36.

Dekmejian, RH 1978, 'Consociational Democracy in Crisis: The Case of Lebanon', *Comparative Politics*, Vol. 10, No. 2, pp. 251–65.

Diamond, L & Gunther, R 2001, 'Types and Functions of Parties', in Diamond, L & Gunther, R (eds), *Political Parties and Democracy*, Johns Hopkins University Press, Baltimore & London, pp. 3–39.

Diamond, L, Linz, JJ, et al. (eds) 1995, *Politics in Developing Countries: Comparing Experiences with Democracy*, 2nd edn, Lynne Reinner Publishers, Boulder & London.

Dib, K 2009, 'Lebanese Elections: When Faking Democracy Works', *The Daily Star*, June 1, viewed on: 06-11-2013, available on: http://www.dailystar.com.lb/

News/Lebanon-News/2009/Jun-01/54996-lebanese-elections-when-faking-democracy-works.ashx#axzz2jscSeqj7.

DSA 1991, *Defence and Security Agreement*, Lebanon–Syria, 1 September 1991, Syrian Lebanese Higher Council, Damascus, viewed on: 29-09-2013, available on: http ://www.syrleb.org/docs/agreements/02DEFENSE_SECURITYeng.pdf.

El-Hokayem, E 2007, 'Hizballah and Syria: Outgrowing the Proxy Relationship', *The Washington Quarterly*, Vol. 30, No. 2, pp. 35–52.

El-Hoss, S 2001, *Li-l-Ḥaqīqa wa-l-Ttārīkh: Tajārub Al-Ḥukum bayn 1998-2000*, Sharikat Al-Maṭbūʿāt li-l-Tawzīʿ wa-Nnashar, Beirut.

El-Husseini, R 2004, 'Lebanon: Building Political Dynasties', in Perthes, V (ed.), *Arab Elites: Negotiating the Politics of Change*, Lynne Rienner Publishers, Boulder, pp. 239–66.

———— 2012, *Pax Syriana: Elite Politics in Postwar Lebanon*, Syracuse University Press, New York.

El-Khazen, F 1991, *The Communal Pact of National Identities: The Making and Politics of the 1943 National Pact*, October, Centre for Lebanese Studies, University of Oxford, viewed on: 08-09-2012, available on: http://lebanesestudies.com/wp-content/upl oads/2012/03/8b844d712.-The-Communal-Pact-of-National-Identities-The-Making-and-Politics-of-the-1943-National-Pact-Farid-el-Khazen-1991.pdf.

———— 1998, *Lebanon's First Postwar Parliamentary Election 1992: An Imposed Choice*, February, Centre for Lebanese Studies, University of Oxford, viewed on: 03-05-2012, available on: http://lebanesestudies.com/wp-content/uploads/2012/04/b23a9af8.-LEBANON-N-FIRST-POSTWAR-PARLEMANTARY-ELECTION-AN-IMPOSED-Farid-el-Khazen.pdf.

———— 2000, *The Breakdown of the State in Lebanon 1967–1976*, I.B.Tauris, London & New York.

———— 2001, 'Lebanon: Independent No More Disappearing Christians of the Middle East', *Middle East Quarterly*, Vol. Winter, pp. 43–50, viewed on: 14-02-2013, available on: http://www.meforum.org/16/lebanon-independent-no-more.

———— 2003a, 'Political Parties in Postwar Lebanon: Parties in Search of Partisans', *The Middle East Journal*, Vol. 57, No. 4, pp. 605–24.

———— 2003b, 'The Postwar Political Process: Authoritarianism by Diffusion', in Hanf, T & Salam, N (eds), *Lebanon in Limbo: Postwar Society and State in an Uncertain Regional Environment*, Nomos Verlagsgesellschaft, Baden–Baden, pp. 53–74.

Elbadawi, I & Makdisi, S 2011, *Democracy in the Arab World: Explaining the Deficit*, Routledge, London.

Ellis, KC 1999, 'Lebanon: The Struggle of a Small Country in a Regional Context', *Arab Studies Quarterly*, Vol. 21, No. 1, pp. 5–25.

Esman, MJ 1994, *Ethnic Politics*, Cornell University Press, New York.

Fakhoury-Mühlbacher, T 2007, 'The July War and its Effects on Lebanon's Power-Sharing: The Challenge of Pacifying a Divided Society', *Journal of Peace Conflict & Development*, Vol. 10, No. March, pp. 1–14.

———— 2009, *Democracy and Power Sharing in Stormy Weather: The Case of Lebanon*, VS Verlag fur Sozialwissenschaften, Wiesbaden.

FCCT 1991, *Fraternity, Cooperation and Coordination Treaty Between the Republic of Lebanon and the Syrian Arab Republic*, Lebanon–Syria, 22 May 1991, Syrian

Lebanese Higher Council, Damascus, viewed on: 23-03-2012, available on: http://www.syrleb.org/docs/agreements/01TREATYeng.pdf.

Fisk, R 2007, 'Scores Dead as Lebanese Army Battles Islamists in Bloodiest Day since Civil War', *The Independent*, May 21, p. 2.

―――― 2009, 'Who Killed Mr Lebanon?': The Hunt for Prime Minister Rafiq Hariri's Assassins', *The Independent*, January 11, viewed on: 30-10-2013, available on: http://www.independent.co.uk/voices/commentators/fisk/who-killed-mr-lebanon-the-hunt-for-prime-minister-rafiq-hariris-assassins-1231542.html.

France 24 2011, *Najib Mikati Yanāl Taʾīd Ghālibiyyat Al-Nnuwwāb wa-ʾAnṣār Hariri Yahtajjūn bi-ʿUnf*, France 24 News Channel, January 25, viewed on: 26-12-2012, available on: http://www.france24.com/ar/20110125-lebanon-hariri-hezbollah-miqati-demonstrations-parliament.

Freedom House 2002, *Freedom in the World 2002: Lebanon*, Freedom House, Washington, viewed on: 29-09-2011, available on: http://www.freedomhouse.org/template.cfm?page=22&year=2002&country=1560.

―――― 2003, *Freedom in the World 2003: Lebanon*, Freedom House, Washington, viewed on: 26-04-2013, available on: http://www.freedomhouse.org/report/freedom-world/2003/lebanon.

―――― 2006, *Freedom in the World 2006: Lebanon*, Freedom House, Washington, viewed on: 19-11-2013, available on: http://www.freedomhouse.org/report/freedom-world/2006/lebanon.

―――― 2011, *Freedom in the World 2011: Lebanon*, Freedom House, Washington, viewed on: 29-09-2011, available on: http://www.freedomhouse.org/report/freedom-world/2011/lebanon.

―――― 2013, *Freedom in the World Country Ratings: 1973–2013*, Freedom House, Washington, viewed on: 30-04-2013, available on: http://www.freedomhouse.org/report-types/freedom-world.

Gambill, GC 2001, 'Syrian Workers in Lebanon: The Other Occupation', *Middle East Intelligence Bulletin*, Vol. 3, No. 2, viewed on: 30-09-2013, available on: http://www.meforum.org/meib/articles/0102_l1.htm.

―――― 2003, *The Syrian Occupation of Lebanon*, May 13, Middle East Forum, viewed on: 01-02-2012, available on: http://www.meforum.org/546/the-syrian-occupation-of-lebanon.

Geukjian, O 2009, 'From Positive Neutrality to Partisanship: How and Why the Armenian Political Parties Took Sides in Lebanese Politics in the Post-Taif Period (1989–Present)', *Middle Eastern Studies*, Vol. 45, No. 5, pp. 739–67.

Ghazal, R 2005, 'Protesters Celebrate Victory and Ready for Next Step in Battle for Independence', *The Daily Star*, March 1, viewed on: 17-09-2011, available on: http://www.dailystar.com.lb/News/Politics/Mar/01/Protesters-celebrate-victory-and-ready-for-next-step-in-battle-for-independence.ashx#axzz1YEo4j81O.

Ghosn, F & Khoury, A 2011, 'Lebanon after the Civil War: Peace or the Illusion of Peace?', *Middle East Journal*, Vol. 65, No. 3, pp. 381–97.

Gilley, B 2004, 'Against the Concept of Ethnic Conflict', *Third World Quarterly*, Vol. 25, No. 6, pp. 1155–66.

Gormley-Heenan, C & Macginty, R 2008, 'Ethnic Outbidding and Party Modernization: Understanding the Democratic Unionist Party's Electoral Success in the Post-Agreement Environment', *Ethnopolitics*, Vol. 7, No. 1, pp. 43–61.

Green, DP & Seher, RL 2003, 'What Role Does Prejudice Play in Ethnic Conflict?', *Annual Review of Political Science*, Vol. 6, pp. 509–31.

Haddad, S 2001, 'Christian–Muslim Relations and Attitudes Towards the Lebanese State', *Journal of Muslim Minority Affairs*, Vol. 21, No. 1, pp. 131–48.

——— 2005, 'The Lebanese Parliamentary Elections of 2005', *The Journal of Social, Political, and Economic Studies*, Vol. 30, No. 3, pp. 305–31.

———2009, 'Lebanon: From Consociationalism to Conciliation', *Nationalism and Ethnic Politics*, Vol. 15, No. 3, pp. 398–416.

——— 2010, 'The Political Consequences of Electoral Laws in Fragmented Societies: Lebanon's 2009 Elections', *The Journal of Social, Political, and Economic Studies*, Vol. 35, No. 1, pp. 45–78.

Hajj, E 2013, *Lebanon's Electoral Law and the Regional Crisis*, Al-Monitor, January 18, viewed on: 02-02-2013, available on: http://www.al-monitor.com/pulse/originals/2013/01/lebanon-region-may-disintegrate.html#ixzz2JlEF28eS.

Halpern, SM 1986, 'The Disorderly Universe of Consociational Democracy', *West European Politics*, Vol. 9, No. 2, pp. 181–97.

Hanf, T 1993, *Coexistence in Wartime Lebanon: Decline of a State and Rise of a Nation*, The Centre for Lebanese Studies & I.B.Tauris, London.

Harik, J 1997, 'Syrian Foreign Policy and State/Resistance Dynamics in Lebanon', *Studies in Conflict & Terrorism*, Vol. 20, No. 3, pp. 249–65.

——— 1998, 'Democracy (Again) Derailed: Lebanon's Ta'if Paradox', in Brynen, R, Korany, B & Noble, P (eds), *Political Liberalization and Democratization in the Arab World*, Lynne Rienner Publishers, London, Vol. 2, pp. 127–55.

Harris, W 2005, 'Bashar al-Assad's Lebanon Gamble', *Middle East Quarterly*, Vol. Summer, pp. 33–44, viewed on: 30-10-2013, available on: http://www.meforum.org/730/bashar-al-assads-lebanon-gamble.

Hatoum, M 2006, 'Jumblatt Questions Hizbullah's Allegiance', *The Daily Star*, January 9, viewed on: 06-12-2013, available on: http://www.dailystar.com.lb/News/Lebanon-News/2006/Jan-09/7282-jumblatt-questions-hizbullahs-allegiance.ashx#ixzz2mi3G6fXl.

Haugbolle, S 2010, *War and Memory in Lebanon*, Cambridge University Press, Cambridge.

Hersh, SM 2007, 'The Redirection: Is the Administration's New Policy Benefitting Our Enemies in the War on Terrorism?', *The New Yorker*, Vol. March 5, viewed on: 03-02-2013, available on: http://www.newyorker.com/reporting/2007/03/05/070305fa_fact_hersh?printable=true#ixzz2Jqc3QGcp.

Hinnebusch, R 1998, 'Pax-Syriana? The Origins, Causes and Consequences of Syria's Role in Lebanon', *Mediterranean Politics*, Vol. 3, No. 1, pp. 137–60.

Hizbullah 2009, *Sayyed Nasrallah: Hizbullah's New Political Manifesto. We Want Lebanon Strong & United*, Al-Ahed News Website, viewed on: 01-02-2013, available on: http://english.alahednews.com.lb/essaydetailsf.php?eid=9632&fid=54.

Hokayem, E 2012, 'Syria and its Neighbours', *Survival*, Vol. 54, No. 2, pp. 7–14.

Horowitz, DL 1985, *Ethnic Groups in Conflict*, University of California Press, London.

——— 1990, 'Making Moderation Pay: The Comparative Politics of Ethnic Conflict Management', in Montville, JV (ed.), *Conflict and Peacemaking in Multiethnic Societies*, Lexington Books, Toronto, pp. 451–75.

——— 1991, *A Democratic South Africa? Constitutional Engineering in a Divided Society*, University of California Press, Berkeley & London.

———— 2002, 'Explaining the Northern Ireland Agreement: The Sources of an Unlikely Constitutional Consensus', *British Journal of Political Studies*, Vol. 32, No. 2, pp. 193–220.

———— 2003, 'Electoral Systems: A Primer for Decision Makers', *Journal of Democracy*, Vol. 14, No. 4, pp. 115–27.

HRW 2009, *Why They Died: Civilian Casualties in Lebanon During the 2006 War*, Vol. 19, No. 5, Human Rights Watch, viewed on: 07-12-2013, available on: http://www.hrw.org/sites/default/files/reports/lebanon0907.pdf.

Hudson, M 1976, 'The Lebanese Crisis: The Limits of Consociational Democracy', *Journal of Palestine Studies*, Vol. 5, No. 3, pp. 109–22.

———— 1985, *The Precarious Republic: Political Modernisation in Lebanon*, 2nd edn, Westview Press, Boulder & London.

———— 1988, 'The Problem of Authoritative Power in Lebanese Politics: Why Consociationalism Failed', in Shehadi, N & Mills, DH (eds), *Lebanon: A History of Conflict and Consensus*, The Centre for Lebanese Studies & I.B.Tauris, London, pp. 224–39.

Huntington, S 1981, 'Reform and Stability in a Modernizing, Multi-Ethnic Society', *South African Journal of Political Studies*, Vol. 8, No. 2, pp. 8–26.

———— 1984, 'Will More Countries Become Democratic?', *Political Science Quarterly*, Vol. 99, No. 2, pp. 193–218.

Hurwitz, L 1973, 'Contemporary Approaches to Political Stability', *Comparative Politics*, Vol. 5, No. 3, pp. 449–63.

Ibrahim, R 2012, ''Istiṭlā'a li-l-R'ay: Al-Masīḥiūn lā Yashkūn Hizbullah', *Al-Akhbar*, November 7, viewed on: 05-12-2012, available on: http://al-akhbar.com/node/171039.

———— 2013, 'Al-Ddā'ira Al-Ḥamrā' wa-Ttayyār Al-'Azraq 'Al-Quṣṣa Mish Rummāna'', *Al-Akhbar*, February 23, viewed on: 24-02-2013, available on: http://www.al-akhbar.com/node/178102.

ICG 2005, *Lebanon: Managing the Gathering Storm*, No. 48, International Crisis Group, Brussels, viewed on: 11-05-2013, available on: http://www.crisisgroup.org/~/media/Files/Middle%20East%20North%20Africa/Iraq%20Syria%20Lebanon/Lebanon/Lebanon%20Managing%20the%20Gathering%20Storm.pdf.

———— 2007, *Hizbollah and the Lebanese Crisis*, No. 69, International Crisis Group, Brussels, viewed on: 19-11-2011, available on: http://www.crisisgroup.org/~/media/Files/Middle%20East%20North%20Africa/Iraq%20Syria%20Lebanon/Lebanon/69_hizbollah_and_the_lebanese_crisis.pdf.

———— 2008a, *Lebanon: Hizbollah's Weapons Turn Inward*, No. 23, International Crisis Group, Brussels, viewed on: 05-05-2013, available on: http://www.crisisgroup.org/~/media/Files/Middle%20East%20North%20Africa/Iraq%20Syria%20Lebanon/Lebanon/b23_lebanon_hizbollahs_weapons_turn_inward.pdf.

———— 2008b, *The New Lebanese Equation: The Christian's Central Role*, No. 78, International Crisis Group, Brussels, viewed on: 19-11-2011, available on: http://www.crisisgroup.org/~/media/Files/Middle%20East%20North%20Africa/Iraq%20Syria%20Lebanon/Lebanon/e_new_lebanese_equation___the_christians__central_role_english_web.pdf.

———— 2010, *Lebanon's Politics: The Sunni Community and Hariri's Future Current*, No. 96, International Crisis Group, Brussels, viewed on: 15-02-2013, available on: http://www.crisisgroup.org/~/media/Files/Middle%20East%20North%

20Africa/Iraq%20Syria%20Lebanon/Lebanon/96%20Lebanons%20Politics%
20-%20The%20Sunni%20Community%20and%20Hariris%20Future%20Cu
rrent.ashx.

——— 2012, *A Precarious Balancing Act: Lebanon and the Syrian Conflict*, No. 132,
International Crisis Group, Brussels, viewed on: 10-10-2013, available on: ∼ /
media/Files/Middle%20East%20North%20Africa/Iraq%20Syria%20Lebanon/
Lebanon/132-a-precarious-balancing-act-lebanon-and-the-syrian-conflict.
pdf">http://www.crisisgroup.org/ ∼ /media/Files/Middle%20East%20North
%20Africa/Iraq%20Syria%20Lebanon/Lebanon/132-a-precarious-balancing-
act-lebanon-and-the-syrian-conflict.pdf.

——— 2013, *Too Close For Comfort: Syrians in Lebanon*, No. 141, International Crisis
Group, Brussels, viewed on: 07-12-2013, available on: http://www.crisisgroup.
org/∼/media/Files/Middle%20East%20North%20Africa/Iraq%20Syria%
20Lebanon/Lebanon/141-too-close-for-comfort-syrians-in-lebanon.pdf.

IDMC 2010, *No New Displacement but Causes of Past Conflicts Unresolved*, December 30,
International Displacement Monitoring Centre, Geneva, viewed on: 10-07-2013,
available on: http://www.internal-displacement.org/8025708F004BE3B1/
(httpInfoFiles)/ADA51C6E3FB628FFC1257809004FD417/$file/Lebanon_
Overview_Dec2010.pdf.

IFES 2009, *The Political Affiliation of Lebanese Parliamentarians and the Composition of
the Different Parliamentary Blocs*, September, International Foundation for
Electoral Systems, Washington, viewed on: 29-12-2012, available on: http://
www.ifes.org/∼/media/Files/Publications/IFES%20News%20in%20Brief/
2009/1528/lebanon_parliament_elections_200909.pdf.

Inati, SC 1999, 'Transformation of Education: Will it Lead to Integration?', *Arab
Studies Quarterly*, Vol. 21, No. 1, pp. 55–68.

Jaafar, R 2007, 'Democratic Reform in Lebanon: An Electoral Approach', in
Choueiri, Y (ed.), *Breaking the Cycle: Civil Wars in Lebanon*, Stacey International,
London, pp. 285–305.

Jabbra, JG & Jabbra, NW 2001, 'Consociational Democracy in Lebanon: A Flawed
System of Governance', *Perspectives on Global Development and Technology*, Vol. 17,
No. 2, pp. 71–89.

Jreissati, S 2011, 'Kalimat Al-ʾUstādh Salim Jreissati', paper presented to Dawr
Riʾāst Al-Jumhūriyya wa-Dustūr Taʾif, March 2, Issam Fares Center for
Lebanon, Beirut, viewed on: 26-01-2013, available on: http://www.if-cl.org/
Library/Files/uploaded%20Files/Minbar%202011/6%20-Jraysati.pdf.

Kerr, M 2006, *Imposing Power-Sharing: Conflict and Coexistence in Northern Ireland and
Lebanon*, Irish Academic Press, Ireland & Oregon.

——— 2007, 'The Philosophy of Lebanese Power-Sharing', in Choueiri, Y (ed.),
Breaking the Cycle: Civil Wars in Lebanon, Stacey International, London,
pp. 237–54.

Khalaf, S 1968, 'Primordial Ties and Politics in Lebanon', *Middle Eastern Studies*,
Vol. 4, No. 3, pp. 243–69.

Khalil, A 2013a, '14 ʾAdhār Taktashf ʿAl-ʾAʿyish Al-Wāḥid fī Al-Janūb", *Al-Akhbar*,
July 8, viewed on: 24-10-2013, available on: http://www.al-akhbar.com/node/
186616.

——— 2013b, 'Al-Jjayash Yafukkū ʾAsra Saida', *Al-Akhbar*, June 25, viewed on:
15-09-2013, available on: http://www.al-akhbar.com/node/185727.

Khashan, H 1997, 'Lebanon's 1996 Controversial Parliamentary Elections', *Journal of South Asian and Middle Eastern Studies*, Vol. 20, No. 4, pp. 24–49.

——— 2013, 'Will Syria's Strife Rip Lebanon Apart?', *Middle East Quarterly*, Vol. Winter, pp. 75–80, viewed on: 10-12-2013, available on: http://www.meforu m.org/3462/syria-civil-war-lebanon.

Knudsen, A 2010, 'Acquiescence to Assassinations in Post-Civil War Lebanon?', *Mediterranean Politics*, Vol. 15, No. 1, pp. 1–23.

——— 2011, 'Nahr El-Bared: The Political Fall-Out of a Refugee Disaster', in Knudsen, A & Hanafi, S (eds), *Palestinian Refugees: Identity, Space, and Place in the Levant*, Routledge, London & New York, pp. 97–110.

Kossayfi, H 2012, 'Michel Aoun: Elections or Doom', *Al-Akhbar*, September 22, viewed on: 23-12-2012, available on: http://english.al-akhbar.com/content/ michel-aoun-elections-or-doom.

——— 2013, 'Al-Muqābala: Aoun li-Sleiman Satakhsar Al-Ṭṭaʿan fī Al-Ortho-doxy', *Al-Akhbar*, February 15, viewed on: 28-02-2013, available on: http://al-akhbar.com/node/177613.

Kota, S 2010, 'Undemocratic Lebanon?: The Power-Sharing Arrangements After the 2005 Independence Intifada', paper presented to World Congress for Middle Eastern Studies, July 21, Barcelona, viewed on: 25-12-2012, available on: http://www.ritsumei.ac.jp/acd/re/k-rsc/hss/book/pdf/vol04_06.pdf.

LADE 2005, *Al-ʾinfāq Al-ʾintikhābī*, Lebanese Association for Democratic Elections, Beirut, viewed on: 20-05-2014, available on: http://www.lade.org.lb/ getattachment/ffbcc23e-50e3-418e-ace2-0767bf2a148d/%D8%AA%D9% 86%D8%B8%D9%8A%D9%85-%D8%A7%D9%84%D8%A7%D9%86% D9%81%D8%A7%D9%82-%D8%A7%D9%84%D8%A7%D9%86%D8% AA%D8%AE%D8%A7%D8%A8%D9%8A.aspx.

——— 2006, *Al-Ttamthīl Al-Nnisbī*, Lebanese Association for Democratic Elections, Beirut, viewed on: 22-05-2014, available on: http://www.lade.org.lb/ getattachment/35f04f26-b244-4817-b3b4-52b4ad507fd7/%D8%A7%D9% 84%D8%AA%D9%85%D8%AB%D9%8A%D9%84-%D8%A7%D9%84% D9%86%D8%B3%D8%A8%D9%8A.aspx.

——— 2010, *Taqrīr Al-Jamʿiyya Al-Llubnāniyya min ʾjal Dimocrātiyyat Al-ʾintikhbāt*, Lebanese Association for Democratic Elections, Beirut, viewed on: 20-05-2014, available on: http://www.lade.org.lb/getattachment/a4c92bf4-84be-42fe-bb90-57bc8c8a4a40/%D8%AA%D9%82%D8%B1%D9%8A% D8%B1-%D9%85%D8%B1%D8%A7%D9%82%D8%A8%D8%A9-%D 8%A7%D9%84%D8%A7%D9%86%D8%AA%D8%AE%D8%A7%D8% A8%D8%A7%D8%AA-%D8%A7%D9%84%D9%86%D9%8A%D8%A 7%D8%A8%D9%8A%D8%A9-2009.aspx.

Lebanese Forces 2013, *Geagea Yuwʾakkid ʾAnna Al-Quwwāt Tataʾraḍ li-Ḥarb ʾIlghāʾ wa-Yatawajjah li-Aoun: Lā Tataʿdda ʾAlaynā wa-ʾillā fa-l-Maʿraka Maftūḥa walan Naskut ʿan Kadhibik*, Lebanese Forces Party Official Website, May 16, viewed on: 04-11-2013, available on: http://www.lebanese-forces.com/2013/05/ 16/geagea-lf-faces-an-elimination-war/.

Lebanon Files 2013, *Kalimat Michel Aoun baʿda ʾIjtimāʿ Takttul Al-Ttaghīr wa-l-ʾIṣlāḥ*, Lebanon Files News Website, January 3, viewed on: 08-02-2013, available on: http://www.lebanonfiles.com/news/486442.

Leenders, R 2004a, 'Nobody Having Too Much to Answer For: Laissez-Faire, Networks and Postwar Reconstruction in Lebanon', in Heydemann, S (ed.),

Networks of Privilege in the Middle East: The Politics of Economic Reform, Palgrave Macmillan, New York, pp. 169–200.

———— 2004b, 'The Politics of Corruption in Post-War Lebanon', Unpublished PhD Thesis, School of Oriental and African Studies, University of London.

———— 2006, *How UN Pressure on Hizballah Impedes Lebanese Reform*, May 23, MERIP Middle East Report Online, viewed on: 22-01-2013, available on: http://www.merip.org/mero/mero052306.

Lehmbruch, G 1975, 'Consociational Democracy in the International System', *European Journal of Political Research*, Vol. 3, No. 4, pp. 377–91.

Lieberman, ES & Singh, P 2012, 'The Institutional Origins of Ethnic Violence', *Comparative Politics*, Vol. October, pp. 1–24.

Lijphart, A 1969, 'Consociational Democracy', *World Politics*, Vol. 21, No. 2, pp. 207–25.

———— 1975, *The Politics of Accommodation: Pluralism and Democracy in the Netherlands*, 2nd edn, University of California Press, Berkeley.

———— 1977a, *Democracy in Plural Societies: A Comparative Exploration*, Yale University Press, New Haven & London.

———— 1977b, 'Majority Rule Versus Democracy in Deeply Divided Societies', *Journal of Political Studies*, Vol. 4, No. 2, pp. 113–26.

———— 1984, *Democracies: Patterns of Majoritarian and Consensus Government in Twenty-One Countries*, Yale University Press, London.

———— 1985, *Power-Sharing in South Africa*, Institute of International Studies, University of California, Berkeley.

———— 1987, 'Consociational Democracy', in Bogdanor, V (ed.), *The Blackwell Encyclopaedia of Political Institutions*, Blackwell Reference, Oxford & New York, pp. 137–9.

———— 1989, 'Democratic Political Systems: Types, Cases, Causes, and Consequences', *Journal of Theoretical Politics*, Vol. 1, No. 33, pp. 33–48.

———— 1995, 'Self-Determination versus Pre-Determination of Ethnic Minorities in Power-Sharing Systems', in Kymlicka, W (ed.), *The Rights Of Minority Cultures*, Oxford University Press, Oxford, pp. 275–87.

———— 1996, 'The Puzzle of Indian Democracy: A Consociational Interpretation', *The American Political Science Review*, Vol. 90, No. 2, pp. 258–68.

———— 2004, 'Constitutional Design for Divided Societies', *Journal of Democracy*, Vol. 15, No. 2, pp. 96–109.

———— 2008, *Thinking About Democracy: Power Sharing and Majority Rule in Theory and Practice*, Routledge, London & New York.

Lipset, SM 1959, 'Some Social Requisites of Democracy: Economic Development and Political Legitimacy', *The American Political Science Review*, Vol. 53, No. 1, pp. 69–105.

———— 1960, *Political Man: The Social Bases of Politics*, 1st edn, William Heinemann Limited, London.

Lustick, IS 1979, 'Stability in Deeply Divided Societies: Consociationalism versus Control', *World Politics*, Vol. 31, No. 3, pp. 325–44.

———— 1997, 'Lijphart, Lakatos, and Consociationalism', *World Politics*, Vol. 50, No. 1, pp. 88–117.

Lustick, IS & Miodownik, D 2002, 'The Institutionalization of Identity: Micro Adaptation, Macro Effects, and Collective Consequences', *Studies in Comparative International Development*, Vol. 37, No. 2, pp. 24–53.

Luther, KR 2001, 'Consociationalism', in Clarke, PB & Foweraker, J (eds), *Encyclopedia of Democratic Thought*, Routledge, London, pp. 91–4.

Macleod, H & Aysha, R 2008, 'Lebanese Troops Withdraw as Violence Resumes', *The Guardian*, May 12, viewed on: 01-03-2013, available on: http://www.gu ardian.co.uk/world/2008/may/12/lebanon1.

Makdisi, U 1996, *Reconstructing the Nation-State: The Modernity of Sectarianism in Lebanon*, No. 200, MERIP Middle East Report, pp. 23–6.

—— 2000, *The Culture of Sectarianism: Community, History and Violence in Nineteenth-Century Ottoman Lebanon*, University of California Press, Berkeley.

—— 2007, 'Understanding Sectarianism', in Hovespian, N (ed.), *The War on Lebanon: A Reader*, Arris Books, Gloucestershire, pp. 20–7.

Mansour, A 1993, *Al-'Inqilāb 'alā Ta'if*, Dar Al-Jadīd, Beirut.

McGarry, J & O'Leary, B 2004, *The Northern Ireland Conflict: Consociational Engagements*, Oxford University Press, Oxford.

—— 2006, 'Consociational Theory, Northern Ireland's Conflict, and its Agreement: What Consociationalists Can Learn from Northern Ireland', *Government and Opposition*, Vol. 41, No. 1, pp. 43–63.

Mearsheimer, JJ & Walt, SM 2006, 'The Israel Lobby and U.S. Foreign Policy', *Middle East Policy*, Vol. 13, No. 3, pp. 29–87.

Meghmas, A 2009, 'Abou-Faour: Al-Ma'raka fī 7 Ḥuzayrān 'alā Khāyarāt Lubnān wa-Mustaqbalihī', *Al-Mustaqbal*, May 31, p. 4.

Mill, JS 1991, *Considerations on Representative Government*, Prometheus Books, New York.

Mimpen, J 2007, 'Intra-Party Democracy and its Discontents: Democratization in a Volatile Political Context', paper presented to NIMD Expert Meeting on Intra-Party Democracy, April 12, Netherlands Institute for Multiparty Democracy, The Hague, viewed on: 26-02-2013, available on: http://www.nimd.org/documents/I/intra-party_democracy_and_its_discontents_mimpen.pdf.

Ministry of Finance 2007, *International Conference for Support to Lebanon – Paris III: Third Progress Report*, September 28, Ministry of Finance, Republic of Lebanon, Beirut, viewed on: 01-02-2013, available on: http://www.rebuildlebanon.gov.l b/images_Gallery/Paris%20III-Third%20Progress%20Report.pdf.

Mortada, R 2012a, 'Ḥmā'im Saad Hariri fī 'Al-Ththawra Al-Ssūriyya", *Al-Akhbar*, October 19, pp. 4–5.

—— 2012b, 'Sakr Yudīr Ghurfat 'Amāliyyāt bayn Lubnān wa-Turkiyya', *Al-Akhbar*, November 30, pp. 2–3.

Naharnet 2013, *Hariri Yu'kkid 'Anna 'Al-Ssilāh wa-Al-Ddawla lā Yaltqiyyān': Lan Nushārik fī Al-Ḥukūma fīhā Hizbullah wa-Na'arid 'Alayhī 'allā Nushark Naḥnu 'Aydan*, Naharnet News Website, August 2, viewed on: 06-12-2013, available on: http://www.naharnet.com/stories/ar/92971.

Nasr, V 2006, 'When the Shiites Rise', *Foreign Affairs*, Vol. July/August, pp. 58–74.

Nasrallah, H 2005, *Kalimat Al-'Amīn Al-'Aām fī Al-Masīra Al-Ḥāshida Tandīdan bi-l-Qarār 1559 wa-Wafā'an li-Sūriyya wa-Da'aman li-l-Muqāwama*, March 8, Beirut, Moqawama Website, viewed on: 06-12-2013, available on: http://www.moqawama.org/essaydetails.php?eid=2094&cid=142.

—— 2006a, *Sayyed Hassan Nasrallah Speech at the Divine Victory Rally Held in Beirut*, September 22, Beirut, Al-Ahed News Website, viewed on: 12-12-2012, available on: http://english.alahednews.com.lb/essaydetails.php?eid=709& cid=447.

——— 2006b, *Sayyid Nasrallah fī Al-Llayala Al-Ssābi'a li-l-'Itisām Al-Maftūḥ li-Qiwā Al-Muā'raḍa Al-Waṭaniyya Al-Llubnāniyya*, December 7, Beirut, Moqawama Website, viewed on: 05-03-2013, available on: http://www.moqawama.org/essaydetails.php?eid=2143&cid=142.

——— 2009a, *Sayyed Nasrallah Speech in Nabatieh: Execute Spies Starting with Shiite Collaborators*, May 22, Nabatieh, Al-Ahed News Website, viewed on: 24-10-2013, available on: http://english.alahednews.com.lb/essaydetails.php?eid=8521&cid=450.

——— 2009b, *Sayyed Nasrallah's Speech at Baalbek: Opposition to Build a Strong State & Army, 'Israel' is Afraid*, May 29, Baalbeck, Al-Ahed News Website, viewed on: 14-10-2013, available on: http://english.alahednews.com.lb/essaydetails.php?eid=8550&cid=450.

——— 2010, *Sayyed Nasrallah Full Speech on Martyr's Day*, November 11, Beirut, Al-Ahed News Website, viewed on: 12-12-2012, available on: http://english.alahednews.com.lb/essaydetails.php?eid=12621&cid=451.

——— 2011, *Al-'Amīn Al-'Aām li-Hizbullah fī Al-Masīra Al-'Āshūrā'iyya Al-Kubrā fī Al-Ḍḍāḥya*, December 6, Beirut, Moqawama Website, viewed on: 06-02-2013, available on: http://www.moqawama.org/essaydetails.php?eid=22614& cid=138.

——— 2013a, *Sayyed Nasrallah: Ahmad Qassir's Operation Marks the Beginning of Victories*, November 11, Beirut, Al-Ahed News Website, viewed on: 11-11-2013, available on: http://english.alahednews.com.lb/essaydetails.php?eid=24772&cid=445.

——— 2013b, *Sayyed Nasrallah: I Promise You Victory Again*, May 25, South of Lebanon, Al-Ahed News Website, viewed on: 17-10-2013, available on: http://english.alahednews.com.lb/essaydetails.php?eid=23208&cid=445.

Nassif, N 2011, 'Jumblatt bayn ma Qālaḥū li-l-Asad 'an Qurb wa-'an Bu'ad', *Al-Akhbar*, July 28, pp. 2–3.

Nehme, D 2008, *Sayyed Ali Al-Amin Urges Hizbullah Not to Lead Lebanon 'To the Bottom'*, Naharnet News Website, February 15, viewed on: 05-11-2013, available on: http://old.naharnet.com/domino/tn/NewsDesk.nsf/getstory?op enform&E728F0B7E0634CF5C22573F00065ED89.

Neumann, S 1956, *Modern Political Parties: Approaches to Comparative Politics*, University of Chicago Press, Chicago.

Nizameddin, T 2006, 'The Political Economy of Lebanon Under Rafik Hariri: An Interpretation', *The Middle East Journal*, Vol. 60, No. 1, pp. 95–114.

NNA 2013, *Aoun: Geagea Qaddama Tanāzulāt lam Taḥza bi-Muwāfaqat Al-Masīḥīyin*, National News Agency, May 18, viewed on: 08-10-2013, available on: http://www.nna-leb.gov.lb/ar/show-news/34908/.

Nordlinger, EA 1972, *Conflict Regulation in Divided Societies*, Center for International Affairs, Harvard University, Cambridge, Massachusetts.

Norton, AR 2007a, *Hezbollah: A Short History*, Princeton University Press, Princeton & Oxford.

——— 2007b, 'The Role of Hezbollah in Lebanese Domestic Politics', *The International Spectator*, Vol. 42, No. 4, pp. 475–91.

O'Leary, B 1989, 'The Limits to Coercive Consociationalism in Northern Ireland', *Political Studies*, Vol. 37, No. 4, pp. 562–88.

O'Loughlin, E 2005, 'Cedar Revolution Moves Towards Free Democracy', *Sydney Morning Herald*, May 28, viewed on: 16-09-2011, available on: http://www.smh. com.au/news/World/Cedar-Revolution-moves-towards-free-democracy/2005/ 05/27/1117129897892.html.

Pappalardo, A 1981, 'The Conditions for Consociational Democracy: A Logical and Empirical Critique', *European Journal of Political Research*, Vol. 9, No. 4, pp. 365–90.

Parry, G 1969, *Political Elites*, George Allen and Unwin Ltd, London.

Picard, E 2012, 'Lebanon in Search of Sovereignty', in Knudsen, A & Kerr, M (eds), *Lebanon After the Cedar Revolution*, Hurst & Company Ltd., London, pp. 83–103.

Pipes, D 1988, 'Radical Politics and the Syrian Social Nationalist Party', *International Journal of Middle East Studies*, Vol. 20, No. 3, pp. 303–24.

Qabbani, MR 2007, *Taṣrīḥ Samāḥat Muftī Qabbani fī Ḥisār Beirut 'Ithra 'Iḍrāb Al-Muʿārḍa*, January 23, Dar Al-Fatwa fī Al-Jumhūriyya Al-Llubnāniyya, Beirut, viewed on: 14-02-2013, available on: http://www.darfatwa.gov.lb/ content.aspx?NewsID=179&CatID=45.

———— 2008, *Risālt Muftī Al-Jumhūriyya Shaykh Muḥammad Rashīd Qabbani*, May 7, Dar Al-Fatwa fī Al-Jumhūriyya Al-Llubnāniyya, Beirut, viewed on: 01-03-2013, available on: http://www.darfatwa.gov.lb/content.aspx?NewsID=650& CatID=43.

Qassem, N 2010, *Hizbullah: The Story from Within*, 3rd edn, Saqi, Beirut.

Quilty, J 2007, *Winter of Lebanon's Discontents*, January 26, MERIP Middle East Report Online, viewed on: 19-01-2012, available on: http://www.merip.org/ mero/mero012607.

———— 2008, *Lebanon's Brush with Civil War*, May 20, MERIP Middle East Report Online, viewed 19-01-2012, available on: http://www.merip.org/mero/ mero052008.

Raad, N & Assaf, N 2005, 'Opposition Will Accept 'Neutral' Cabinet', *The Daily Star*, March 2, viewed on: 06-12-2013, available on: http://www.dailystar.com.l b/News/Lebanon-News/2005/Mar-02/5013-opposition-will-accept-neutral-cabinet.ashx#ixzz2mi61JWov.

Rabushka, A & Shepsle, KA 1972, *Plural Societies: A Theory of Democratic Instability*, Charles E. Merrill Publishing Company, Columbus, Ohio.

Reda, N 2013, 'Muwājaha 'Masīḥiyya' bayn Geagea wa-Aoun Tastaʿīd Adabiyyāt Al-Ḥarb.Wa-Al-Rahi Yadkhul ʿalā Khaṭ Al-Tahdi'a', *Asharq Al-Awsat*, May 19, viewed on: 08-10-2013, available on: http://www.aawsat.com/details.asp?s ection=4&issueno=12591&article=729076#.UlMa_VBJMmQ.

Reilly, B 2002, 'Electoral Systems for Divided Societies', *Journal of Democracy*, Vol. 13, No. 2, pp. 156–70.

Reynolds, A 2004, *Electoral Systems and Democratization in Southern Africa*, Oxford University Press, Oxford.

Reynolds, A, Reilly, B, et al. 2008, *Electoral System Design: The New International IDEA Handbook*, International Institute for Democracy and Electoral Assistance, Stockholm, viewed on: 16-05-2014, available on: http://www.idea.int/publ ications/esd/upload/ESD_Handb_low.pdf.

Rigby, A 2000, 'Lebanon: Patterns of Confessional Politics', *Parliamentary Affairs*, Vol. 53, No. 1, pp. 169–80.

Rizk, M 2013, 'Bahhiyya Hariri Tarithu Al-Aseer: "Amirat Al-Jamaaʿa", *Al-Akhbar*, July 12, viewed on: 25-02-2014, available on: http://www.al-akhbar.com/node/186927.

Ross, D 2005, 'US Policy Toward a Weak Assad', *The Washington Quarterly*, Vol. 28, No. 3, pp. 87–98.

Rowayheb, MG 2006, 'Lebanese Militias: A New Perspective', *Middle Eastern Studies*, Vol. 42, No. 2, pp. 303–18.

——— 2011, 'Walid Jumblat and Political Alliances: The Politics of Adaptation', *Middle East Critique*, Vol. 20, No. 1, pp. 47–66.

Saab, AG 2012, 'More Mediation Needed on Appointments', *The Daily Star*, January 12, viewed on: 15-03-2013, available on: http://www.dailystar.com.lb/News/Lebanon-News/2012/Jan-12/159594-more-mediation-needed-on-appointments.ashx#axzz2nHPBp2V9.

——— 2013, 'West Fears Postponement of Lebanon's Elections', *The Daily Star*, May 28, viewed on: 30-12-2013, available on: http://www.dailystar.com.lb/News/Politics/2013/May-28/218585-west-fears-postponement-of-lebanons-elections.ashx#axzz2oyhYBKEr.

Saad, A 2007, 'The Shortfalls of Lebanon's Electoral System', *The Daily Star*, January 18, viewed on: 30-11-2013, available on: http://www.dailystar.com.lb/News/Lebanon-News/2007/Jan-18/45892-the-shortfalls-of-lebanons-electoral-system.ashx#axzz2lyhw8EDG.

Saideman, SM 1997, 'Explaining the International Relations of Secessionist Conflicts: Vulnerability versus Ethnic', *International Organization*, Vol. 51, No. 4, pp. 721–53.

Sakr, E 2009, 'Jumblatt Says it's Time to Part Ways with March 14, Slams Electoral Platform', *The Daily Star*, August 3, viewed on: 15-12-2012, available on: http://www.dailystar.com.lb/News/Politics/Aug/03/Jumblatt-says-its-time-to-part-ways-with-March-14-slams-electoral-platform.ashx#ixzz2F8mgUsHW.

——— 2010, 'Nasrallah: We Will not Allow Arrest of Fighters', *The Daily Star*, November 12, viewed on: 06-12-2013, availabe on: http://www.dailystar.com.lb/News/Lebanon-News/2010/Nov-12/59886-nasrallah-we-will-not-allow-arrest-of-fighters.ashx#ixzz2miMHijOl.

Salam, N 2003, 'Ta'if Revisited', in Hanf, T & Salam, N (eds), *Lebanon in Limbo: Postwar Society and State in an Uncertain Regional Environment*, Nomos Verlagsgesellschaft, Baden-Baden, pp. 39–51.

——— 2007, 'Ta'if's Dysfunctions and the Need for Constitutional Reform', in Choueiri, Y (ed.), *Breaking the Cycle: Civil Wars in Lebanon*, Stacey International, London, pp. 307–23.

Salamey, I & Payne, R 2008, 'Parliamentary Consociationalism in Lebanon: Equal Citizenry vs. Quotated Confessionalism', *The Journal of Legislative Studies*, Vol. 14, No. 4, pp. 451–73.

Salamey, I & Tabar, P 2012, 'Democratic Transition and Sectarian Populism: The Case of Lebanon', *Contemporary Arab Affairs*, Vol. 5, No. 4, pp. 497–512.

Salem, P 1997, *Skirting Democracy: Lebanon's 1996 Elections and Beyond*, No. 203, MERIP Middle East Report, pp. 26–9.

——— 1998, 'Framing Post-War Lebanon: Perspectives on the Constitution and the Structure of Power', *Mediterranean Politics*, Vol. 3, No. 1, pp. 13–26.

——— 2012, *Can Lebanon Survive the Syrian Crisis?*, December, Carnegie Middle East Center, Carnegie Endowment for International Peace, Beirut, viewed on:

04-12-2013, available on: http://carnegieendowment.org/files/lebanon_syrian_
crisis.pdf.

Salhani, C 2004, *The Syria Accountability Act: Taking the Wrong Road to Damascus*,
No. 512, Cato Institute, Washington, viewed on: 15-10-2013, available on:
http://www.cato.org/sites/cato.org/files/pubs/pdf/pa512.pdf.

Salibi, K 1988, *A House of Many Mansions: The History of Lebanon Reconsidered*,
I.B.Tauris, London.

Salloukh, B 2005, *Syria and Lebanon: A Brotherhood Transformed*, No. 236, MERIP
Middle East Report Online, viewed on: 03-02-2012, available on: http://www.
merip.org/mer/mer236/syria-lebanon-brotherhood-transformed.

——— 2006, 'The Limits of Electoral Engineering in Divided Societies: Elections
in Postwar Lebanon', *Canadian Journal of Political Science*, Vol. 39, No. 3,
pp. 635–55.

——— 2008, 'The Art of the Impossible: The Foreign Policy of Lebanon', in
Korany, B & Dessouki, AEH (eds), *The Foreign Policies of Arab States: The
Challenge of Globalization*, The American University in Cairo Press, Cairo,
pp. 283–317.

——— 2009, 'Democracy in Lebanon: The Primacy of the Sectarian System', in
Brown, N & Shahin, EE-D (eds), *The Struggle for Democracy in the Middle East*,
Routledge, London & New York, pp. 134–50.

——— 2010, 'Remaking Lebanon After Syria: The Rise and Fall of Proxy
Authoritarianism', in Albrecht, H (ed.), *Contentious Politics in the Middle East:
Political Opposition under Authoritarianism*, University Press of Florida,
Gainesville, pp. 205–28.

Salman, T 2011, 'Fī Zaman Al-Ththawrāt Al-ʿArabiyya: Ḥal Lubanān 'Istithnā'',
Assafir, March 7, p. 1.

Samad, A-A 2009, 'Karami Yanām Milaʾa Juwfūnihī ʿan Shwārd Intikhabāt
Ṭarāblus', *Al-Akhbar*, February 28, viewed on: 06-03-2013, available on: http://
www.al-akhbar.com/node/91311.

Saouli, A 2006, 'Stability Under Late State Formation: The Case of Lebanon',
Cambridge Review of International Affairs, Vol. 19, No. 4, pp. 701–17.

Sartori, G 1976, *Parties and Party Systems: A Framework for Analysis*, Vol. 1,
Cambridge University Press, Cambridge & New York.

Schmitter, PC & Karl, TL 1991, 'What Democracy Is. and Is … Not', *Journal of
Democracy*, Vol. 2, No. 3, pp. 75–88.

Seaver, BM 2000, 'The Regional Sources of Power-Sharing Failure: The Case of
Lebanon ', *Political Science Quarterly*, Vol. 115, No. 2, pp. 247–71.

Sharaf, R 2008, "An "'Aṣal" Al-Tayyar Al-Waṭanī wa-ʿImadahū', *Al-Akhbar*,
July 3, viewed on: 21-01-2015, available on: http://www.al-akhbar.com/node/
113234.

——— 2010, 'Al-Ttarāṣ Al-ʿAunṣurī 'Inda Al-Ṭṭabaqa Al-Ssiyāsiyya: 'Istiʿāb
Al-Ḥāla Al-ʿAuwniyya', *Al-Akhbar*, July 27, viewed on: 28-02-2013, available
on: http://www.al-akhbar.com/node/48344.

Sirriyeh, H 1998, 'Triumph or Compromise: The Decline of Political Maronitism in
Lebanon After the Civil War', *Civil Wars*, Vol. 1, No. 4, pp. 56–68.

Sisk, TD 1996, *Power Sharing and International Mediation in Ethnic Conflicts*, Carnegie
Commission on Preventing Deadly Conflict and the United States Institute of
Peace, Washington.

————— 2008, 'Power Sharing After Civil Wars: Matching Problems to Solutions', in Darby, J & Ginty, RM (eds), *Contemporary Peacemaking: Conflict, Violence, and Peace Processes*, 2nd edn, Palgrave Macmillan, Basingstoke, pp. 195–209.

SLHC 1991, *Agreements and Accords After the Treaty*, Lebanon–Syria, Syrian Lebanese Higher Council, Damascus, viewed on: 23-03-2012, available on: http://www.syrleb.org/conference.asp?conftype=1&page=1.

Smith, A 1985, 'Ethnie and Nation in the Modern World', *Millennium – Journal of International Studies*, Vol. 14, No. 2, pp. 127–42.

Soffer, A 1986, 'Lebanon: Where Demography is the Core of Politics and Life', *Middle Eastern Studies*, Vol. 22, No. 2, pp. 197–205.

Spears, IS 2002, 'Africa: The Limits of Power-Sharing', *Journal of Democracy*, Vol. 13, No. 3, pp. 123–36.

Sriram, CL 2012, 'The Special Tribunal for Lebanon: Promoting Justice or Prolonging Conflict?', *Accord*, Vol. 24, pp. 49–51.

Suleiman, M 1967a, *Political Parties in Lebanon: The Challenge of a Fragmented Political Culture*, Cornell University Press, New York.

————— 1967b, 'The Role of Political Parties in a Confessional Democracy: The Lebanese Case', *The Western Political Quarterly*, Vol. 20, No. 3, pp. 682–93.

Ta'if Constitution 1989, *The Taif Agreement*, United Nations Official Website, viewed on: 23-01-2016, available on: https://www.un.int/lebanon/sites/www.un.int/files/Lebanon/the_taif_agreement_english_version_.pdf.

Taagepera, R 2002, 'Designing Electoral Rules and Waiting for an Electoral System to Evolve', in Reynolds, A (ed.), *The Architecture of Democracy*, Oxford University Press, Oxford, pp. 248–64.

The Daily Star 2006, 'Geagea Scoffs at Hizbullah's Claims of "Victory"', *The Daily Star*, September 25, viewed on: 06-12-2013, available on: http://www.dailystar.com.lb/News/Lebanon-News/2006/Sep-25/42588-geagea-scoffs-at-hizbullahs-claims-of-victory.ashx#axzz2mi066Ud2.

————— 2009, 'Berri: Lebanese Will Show Support for Resistance', *The Daily Star*, June 1, viewed on: 06-11-2013, available on: http://www.dailystar.com.lb/News/Lebanon-News/2009/Jun-01/55001-berri-lebanese-will-show-support-for-resistance.ashx#axzz2jsiDTTcy.

————— 2010, 'Berri: 'Sectarian Spirit' Will not be Eradicated Overnight', *The Daily Star*, April 20, viewed on: 05-12-2013, available on: http://www.dailystar.com.lb/News/Lebanon-News/2010/Apr-20/56590-berri-sectarian-spirit-will-not-be-eradicated-overnight.ashx#axzz2mc7JOB6H.

————— 2013a, 'Future Movement Says Hezbollah's Resistance is Against Them', *The Daily Star*, February 17, viewed on: 19-10-2013, available on: http://www.dailystar.com.lb/News/Politics/2013/Feb-17/206791-future-movement-says-hezbollahs-resistance-is-against-them.ashx#ixzz2iA0jTmxx.

————— 2013b, 'Geagea Defends LF, Says Orthodox Law Futureless', *The Daily Star*, May 15, viewed on: 03-12-2013, available on: http://www.dailystar.com.lb/News/Politics/2013/May-15/217215-geagea-defends-lf-says-orthodox-law-futureless.ashx#axzz2mPWuURsF.

Thompson, EV 2002, 'Will Syria Have to Withdraw from Lebanon?', *The Middle East Journal*, Vol. 56, No. 1, pp. 72–93.

Tilly, C 2007, *Democracy*, Cambridge University Press, Cambridge.

Traboulsi, F 2007, *A History of Modern Lebanon*, Pluto Press, London.

Tsebelis, G 1990, 'Elite Interaction and Constitution Building in Consociational Democracies', *Journal of Theoretical Politics*, Vol. 2, No. 5, pp. 5–29.

UNSC, 2004, *Resolution 1559* (2 September 2004), UN Doc S/RES/1559, United Nations Security Council, viewed on: 03-02-2013, available on: http://unscr. com/en/resolutions/doc/1559.

———, 2005a, *Resolution 1595* (7 April 2005), UN Doc S/RES/1595, United Nations Security Council, viewed on: 10-08-2013, available on: http://unscr. com/en/resolutions/doc/1595.

———, 2005b, *Resolution 1614* (29 July 2005), UN Doc S/RES/1614, United Nations Security Council, viewed on: 18-12-2013, available on: http://unscr.com/en/resolutions/doc/1614.

———, 2005c, *Resolution 1636* (31 October 2005), UN Doc S/RES/1636, United Nations Security Council, viewed on: 13-12-2013, available on: http://unscr. com/en/resolutions/doc/1636.

———, 2006a, *Resolution 1664* (29 March 2006), UN Doc S/RES/1664, United Nations Security Council, viewed on: 15-12-2013, available on: http://unscr. com/en/resolutions/doc/1664.

———, 2006b, *Resolution 1680* (17 May 2006), UN Doc S/RES/1680, United Nations Security Council, viewed on: 15-12-2013, available on: http:// unscr.com/en/resolutions/doc/1680.

———, 2006c, *Resolution 1686* (15 June 2006), UN Doc S/RES/1686, United Nations Security Council, viewed on: 13-12-2013, available on: http://unscr. com/en/resolutions/doc/1686.

———, 2006d, *Resolution 1701* (11 August 2006), UN Doc S/RES/1701, United Nations Security Council, viewed on: 10-09-2013, available on: http://unscr. com/en/resolutions/doc/1701.

USC, 2003, *Syria Accountability and Lebanese Sovereignty Restoration Act of 2003* (12 December 2003), PL 108-175, United States Congress, Government Printing Office, viewed on: 05-03-2013, available on: http://www.gpo.gov/fds ys/pkg/PLAW-108publ175/pdf/PLAW-108publ175.pdf.

Van Schendelen, MCPM 1985, 'Consociational Democracy: The Views of Arend Lijphart and Collected Criticisms', *Political Science Reviewer*, Vol. 15, No. 1, pp. 144–83.

Ware, A 1996, *Political Parties and Political Systems*, Oxford University Press, Oxford & New York.

Whitehead, L 2002, *Democratization: Theory and Experience*, Oxford University Press, Oxford.

Worth, RF 2009, 'Foreign Money Seeks to Buy Lebanese Votes', *The New York Times*, April 22, viewed on: 30-12-2013, available on: http://www.nytimes.com/2009/ 04/23/world/middleeast/23lebanon.html?pagewanted=all&_r=0.

Yacoubian, M 2006, *Syria's Role in Lebanon*, November, United States Institute of Peace, Washington, viewed on 25-09-2013, available on: http://www.usip.org/s ites/default/files/syria_lebanon.pdf.

Yadav, SP 2008, *Lebanon's Post-Doha Political Theater*, July 23, MERIP Middle East Report Online, viewed on: 19-01-2012, available on: http://www.merip.org/ mero/mero072308.

Younes, N 2013, *Naā'ib ʿAounī li-'Now': Al-Khuwaf min Tsunami Jadīd li-Aoun Sabbab Al-Ttamdīd*, Now Media News Website, June 1, viewed on: 05-11-2013, available   on: https://now.mmedia.me/lb/ar/nowspecialar/نائب-عوني-ل-now-الخوف-من-تسونامي-جديد-لعون-سبب-التمديد.

Zaatari, M & Zeineddine, M 2009, 'Rival Lebanese Camps Hold Massive Election Rallies', *The Daily Star*, May 25, viewed on: 02-01-2014, available on: http://www.dailystar.com.lb/News/Lebanon-News/2009/May-25/54423-rival-lebanese-camps-hold-massive-election-rallies.ashx#axzz2ogpySdCQ.

Zahar, M-J 2005, 'Power Sharing in Lebanon: Foreign Protectors, Domestic Peace, and Democratic Failure', in Roeder, PG & Rothchild, D (eds), *Sustainable Peace: Power and Democracy After Civil Wars*, Cornell University Press, Ithaca & London, pp. 219–40.

————— 2012a, 'Foreign Interventions, Power Sharing and the Dynamics of Conflict and Coexistence in Lebanon', in Knudsen, A & Kerr, M (eds), *Lebanon After the Cedar Revolution*, Hurst and Company Publishers, London, pp. 63–81.

————— 2012b, 'Internal Choice or External Fate? Recasting the Debate on Lebanon's Vulnerability', *Accord*, No. 24, pp. 55–6.

INDEX

7

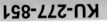

THE
REVENANT

ALSO BY MICHAEL PUNKE

Last Stand: George Bird Grinnell, the Battle to Save the Buffalo,
and the Birth of the New West

Fire and Brimstone: The North Butte Mining Disaster of 1917

THE
REVENANT

MICHAEL
PUNKE

THE BOROUGH PRESS

The Borough Press
An imprint of HarperCollins*Publishers*
1 London Bridge Street,
London SE1 9GF

First published in Great Britain by The Borough Press 2015

Originally published in 2002 by Carroll & Graf

Copyright © Michael Punke 2002

Map © Jeffrey L. Ward 2002

Michael Punke asserts the moral right to
be identified as the author of this work

A catalogue record for this book is
available from the British Library

978 0 00 752129 6

Printed and bound in Great Britain by
Clays Ltd, St Ives plc

MIX
Paper from
responsible sources
FSC
www.fsc.org
FSC® C007454

FSC™ is a non-profit international organisation established to promote
the responsible management of the world's forests. Products carrying the
FSC label are independendently certified to assure consumers that they come
from forests that are managed to meet the social, economic and
ecological needs of present and future generations,
and other controlled sources.

Find out more about HarperCollins and the environment at
www.harpercollins.co.uk/green

For my parents, Marilyn and Butch Punke

Avenge not yourselves, but rather give place unto wrath: for it is written, Vengeance is mine; I will repay, saith the Lord.

—ROM. 12:19

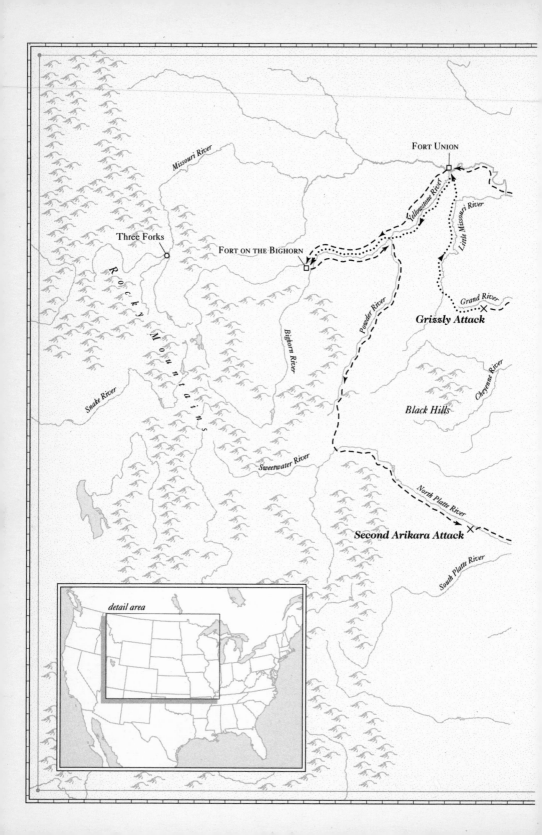

FORT UNION

Three Forks

FORT ON THE BIGHORN

Missouri River

Yellowstone River

Little Missouri River

R
o
c
k
y

M
o
u
n
t
a
i
n
s

Powder River

Bighorn River

Snake River

Grand River

Grizzly Attack

Cheyenne River

Black Hills

Sweetwater River

North Platte River

Second Arikara Attack

South Platte River

detail area

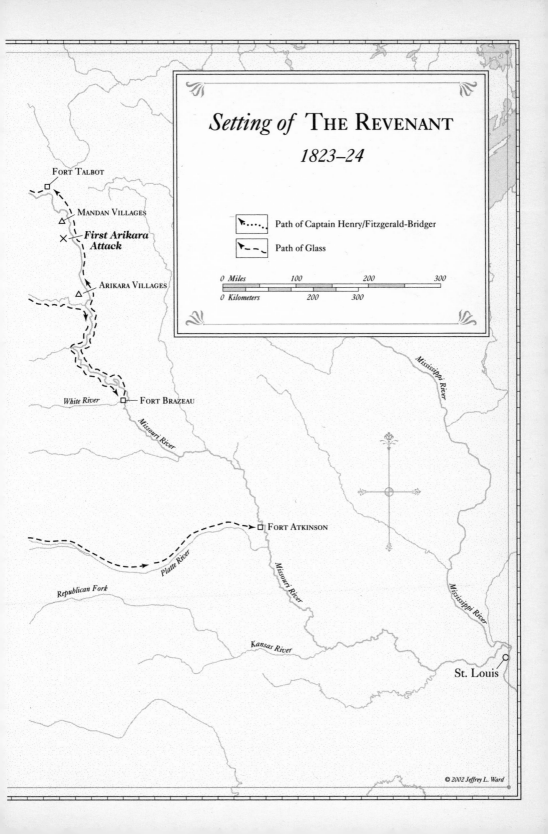

Setting of THE REVENANT
1823–24

FORT TALBOT

MANDAN VILLAGES

✕ — *First Arikara Attack*

ARIKARA VILLAGES

White River

FORT BRAZEAU

Missouri River

Mississippi River

FORT ATKINSON

Platte River

Republican Fork

Missouri River

Kansas River

Mississippi River

St. Louis

Path of Captain Henry/Fitzgerald-Bridger

Path of Glass

| 0 Miles | 100 | 200 | 300 |
| 0 Kilometers | 200 | 300 | |

© 2002 Jeffrey L. Ward

SEPTEMBER 1, 1823

THEY WERE ABANDONING HIM. The wounded man knew it when he looked at the boy, who looked down, then away, unwilling to hold his gaze.

For days, the boy had argued with the man in the wolf-skin hat. *Has it really been days?* The wounded man had battled his fever and pain, never certain whether conversations he heard were real, or merely by-products of the delirious wanderings in his mind.

He looked up at the soaring rock formation above the clearing. A lone, twisted pine had managed somehow to grow from the sheer face of the stone. He had stared at it many times, yet it had never appeared to him as it did at that moment, when its perpendicular lines seemed clearly to form a cross. He accepted for the first time that he would die there in that clearing by the spring.

The wounded man felt an odd detachment from the scene in which he played the central role. He wondered briefly what he would do in their position. If they stayed and the war party came up the creek, all of them would die. *Would I die for them . . . if they were certain to die anyway?*

"You sure they're coming up the creek?" The boy's voice cracked as he said it. He could effect a tenor most of the time, but his tone still broke at moments he could not control.

The man in the wolf skin stooped hurriedly by the small meat rack near the fire, stuffing strips of partially dried venison into his parfleche. "You want to stay and find out?"

The wounded man tried to speak. He felt again the piercing pain in his throat. Sound came forth, but he could not shape it into the one word he sought to articulate.

The man in the wolf skin ignored the sound as he continued to gather his few belongings, but the boy turned. "He's trying to say something."

The boy dropped on one knee next to the wounded man. Unable to speak, the man raised his working arm and pointed.

"He wants his rifle," said the boy. "He wants us to set him up with his rifle."

The man in the wolf skin covered the ground between them in quick, measured steps. He kicked the boy hard, square in the back. "Move, goddamn you!"

He strode quickly from the boy to the wounded man, who lay next to the meager pile of his possessions: a possibles bag, a knife in a beaded scabbard, a hatchet, a rifle, and a powder horn. As the wounded man watched helplessly, the man in the wolf skin stooped to pick up the possibles bag. He dug inside for the flint and steel, dropping them into the pocket on the front of his leather tunic. He grabbed the powder horn and slung it over his shoulder. The hatchet he tucked under his broad leather belt.

"What're you doing?" asked the boy.

The man stooped again, picked up the knife, and tossed it to the boy.

"Take that." The boy caught it, staring in horror at the scabbard in his hand. Only the rifle remained. The man in the wolf skin picked it up, checking quickly to ensure it was charged. "Sorry, old Glass. You ain't got much more use for any of this."

The boy appeared stunned. "We can't leave him without his kit." The man in the wolf skin looked up briefly, then disappeared into the woods.

The wounded man stared up at the boy, who stood there for a long moment with the knife—his knife. Finally, the boy raised his eyes. At first it appeared that he might say something. Instead, he spun around and fled into the pines.

The wounded man stared at the gap in the trees where they had disappeared. His rage was complete, consuming him as fire envelops the needles of a pine. He wanted nothing in the world except to place his hands around their necks and choke the life from them.

Instinctively he started to yell out, forgetting again that his throat produced no words, only pain. He raised himself on his left elbow. He could bend his right arm slightly, but it would support no weight. The movement sent agonizing bolts through his neck and back. He felt the strain of his skin against the crude sutures. He looked down at his leg, where the bloody remnants of an old shirt were tightly wrapped. He could not flex his thigh to make the leg work.

Marshaling his strength, he rolled heavily to his stomach. He felt the snap of a suture breaking and the warm wetness of new blood on his back. The pain diluted to nothing against the tide of his rage.

Hugh Glass began to crawl.

PART

ONE

PART
ONE

ONE

AUGUST 21, 1823

"MY KEELBOAT FROM ST. LOUIS is due here any day, Monsieur Ashley." The portly Frenchman explained it again in his patient but insistent tone. "I'll gladly sell the Rocky Mountain Fur Company the entire contents of the boat—but I can't sell you what I don't have."

William H. Ashley slammed his tin cup on the crude slats of the table. The carefully groomed gray of his beard did not conceal the tight clench of his jaw. For its part, the clenched jaw seemed unlikely to contain another outburst, as Ashley found himself confronting again the one thing he despised above all else—waiting.

The Frenchman, with the unlikely name of Kiowa Brazeau, watched Ashley with growing trepidation. Ashley's presence at Kiowa's remote trading post presented a rare opportunity, and Kiowa knew that the successful management of this relationship could lay a permanent foundation for his venture. Ashley was a prominent man in St. Louis business and politics, a man with both the vision to bring commerce to the West and the money to make it happen. "Other people's money," as Ashley had called it. Skittish money. Nervous money. Money that would flee easily from one speculative venture to the next.

Kiowa squinted behind his thick spectacles, and though his vision was not sharp, he had a keen eye for reading people. "If you will indulge me, Monsieur Ashley, perhaps I can offer one consolation while we await my boat."

Ashley offered no affirmative acknowledgment, but neither did he renew his tirade.

"I need to requisition more provisions from St. Louis," said Kiowa. "I'll send a courier downstream tomorrow by canoe. He can carry a dispatch from you to your syndicate. You can reassure them before rumors about Colonel Leavenworth's debacle take root."

Ashley sighed deeply and took a long sip of the sour ale, resigned, through lack of alternative, to endure this latest delay. Like it or not, the Frenchman's advice was sound. He needed to reassure his investors before news of the battle ran unchecked through the streets of St. Louis.

Kiowa sensed his opening and moved quickly to keep Ashley on a productive course. The Frenchman produced a quill, ink, and parchment, arranging them in front of Ashley and refilling the tin cup with ale. "I'll leave you to your work, monsieur," he said, happy for the opportunity to retreat.

By the dim light of a tallow candle, Ashley wrote deep into the night:

Fort Brazeau,
On the Missouri
August 21, 1823

James D. Pickens, Esquire
Pickens and Sons
St. Louis

Dear Mr. Pickens,
*   It is my unfortunate responsibility to inform you of the events*
of the past two weeks. By their nature these events must alter—
though not deter—our venture on the Upper Missouri.
*   As you probably know by now, the men of the Rocky Moun-*

tain Fur Company were attacked by the Arikara after trading in good faith for sixty horses. The Arikara attacked without provocation, killing 16 of our men, wounding a dozen, & stealing back the horses they had feigned to sell to us the day before.

In face of this attack, I was forced to retreat downstream, while at the same time requesting the aid of Colonel Leavenworth & the US Army in responding to this clear affront to the sovereign right of US citizens to traverse the Missouri unimpeded. I also requested the support of our own men, who joined me (led by Capt. Andrew Henry) at great peril, from their position at Fort Union.

By August 9th, we confronted the Arikara with a combined force of 700 men, including 200 of Leavenworth's regulars (with two howitzers) and forty men of the RMF Co. We also found allies (albeit temporary) in 400 Sioux warriors, whose enmity for the Arikara stems from historical grudge, the origin of which I do not know.

Suffice it to say that our assembled forces were more than ample to carry the field, punish the Arikara for their treachery, & reopen the Missouri for our venture. That such results did not occur we owe to the unsteady timber of Colonel Leavenworth.

The details of the inglorious encounter can await my return to St. Louis, but suffice it to say that the Colonel's repeated reluctance to engage in an inferior foe allowed the entire Arikara tribe to slip our grasp, the result being the effective closure of the Missouri between Fort Brazeau & the Mandan villages. Somewhere between here and there are 900 Arikara warriors, newly entrenched, no doubt, & with new motive to foil all attempts up the Missouri.

Colonel Leavenworth has returned to garrison at Fort Atkinson, where he no doubt will pass the winter in front of a warm hearth, carefully mulling his options. I do not intend to wait for him. Our venture, as you know, can ill-afford the loss of eight months.

Ashley stopped to read his text, unhappy with its dour tone. The letter reflected his anger, but did not convey his predominant emotion—a

bedrock optimism, an unwavering faith in his own ability to succeed. God had placed him in a garden of infinite bounty, a Land of
Goshen in which any man could prosper if only he had the courage
and the fortitude to try. Ashley's weaknesses, which he confessed
forthrightly, were simply barriers to be overcome by some creative
combination of his strengths. Ashley expected setbacks, but he would
not tolerate failure.

> *We must turn this misfortune to our benefit, press on while our
> competitors take pause. With the Missouri effectively closed, I have
> decided to send two groups West by alternate route. Captain Henry
> I have already dispatched up the Grand River. He will ascend the
> Grand as far as possible and make his way back to Fort Union.
> Jedidiah Smith will lead a second troop up the Platte, his target the
> waters of the Great Basin.*
>
> *You no doubt share my intense frustration at our delay. We must
> now move boldly to recapture lost time. I have instructed Henry and
> Smith that they shall not return to St. Louis with their harvest in
> the Spring. Rather, we shall go to them—rendezvous in the field
> to exchange their furs for fresh supplies. We can save four months
> this way, & repay at least some portion of our debt to the clock. Mean-
> while, I propose a new fur troop be raised in St. Louis & dispatched
> in the Spring, led by me personally.*

The remnants of the candle sputtered and spit foul black smoke.
Ashley looked up, suddenly aware of the hour, of his deep fatigue. He
dipped the quill and returned to his correspondence, writing firmly and
quickly now as he drew his report to its conclusion:

> *I urge you to communicate to our syndicate—in strongest
> possible terms—my complete confidence in the inevitable success
> of our endeavor. A great bounty has been laid by Providence be-*

fore us, & we must not fail to summon the courage to claim our
rightful share.
  Your Very Humble Servant,
  William H. Ashley

Two days later, August 16, 1823, Kiowa Brazeau's keelboat arrived from St. Louis. William Ashley provisioned his men and sent them west on the same day. The first rendezvous was set for the summer of 1824, the location to be communicated through couriers.

Without understanding fully the significance of his decisions, William H. Ashley had invented the system that would define the era.

TWO

AUGUST 23, 1823

ELEVEN MEN HUNKERED in the camp with no fire. The camp took advantage of a slight embankment on the Grand River, but the plain afforded little contour to conceal their position. A fire would have signaled their presence for miles, and stealth was the trappers' best ally against another attack. Most of the men used the last hour of daylight to clean rifles, repair moccasins, or eat. The boy had been asleep from the moment they stopped, a crumpled tangle of long limbs and ill-shod clothing.

The men fell into clusters of three or four, huddled against the bank or pressed against a rock or clump of sage, as if these minor protusions might offer protection.

The usual banter of camp had been dampened by the calamity on the Missouri, and then extinguished altogether by the second attack only three nights before. When they spoke at all they spoke in hushed and pensive tones, respectful of the comrades who lay dead in their trail, heedful of the dangers still before them.

"Do you think he suffered, Hugh? I can't get it out of my head that he was suffering away, all that time."

Hugh Glass looked up at the man, William Anderson, who had

posed the question. Glass thought for a while before he answered, "I don't think your brother suffered."

"He was the oldest. When we left Kentucky, our folks told *him* to look after *me*. Didn't say a word to me. Wouldn't have occurred to them."

"You did your best for your brother, Will. It's a hard truth, but he was dead when that ball hit him three days ago."

A new voice spoke from the shadows near the bank. "Wish we'd have buried him then, instead of dragging him for two days." The speaker perched on his haunches, and in the growing darkness his face showed little feature except a dark beard and a white scar. The scar started near the corner of his mouth and curved down and around like a fishhook. Its prominence was magnified by the fact that no hair grew on the tissue, cutting a permanent sneer through his beard. His right hand worked the stout blade of a skinning knife over a whetstone as he spoke, mixing his words with a slow, rasping scrape.

"Keep your mouth shut, Fitzgerald, or I swear on my brother's grave I'll rip out your bloody tongue."

"Your brother's grave? Not much of a grave now, was it?"

The men within earshot paid sudden attention, surprised at this conduct, even from Fitzgerald.

Fitzgerald felt the attention, and it encouraged him. "More just a pile of rocks. You think he's still in there, moldering away?" Fitzgerald paused for a moment, so that the only sound was the scraping of the blade on the stone. "I doubt it—speaking for myself." Again he waited, calibrating the effect of his words as he spoke them. "Course, could be the rocks kept the varmints off. But I think the coyotes are dragging little bits of him across . . ."

Anderson lunged at Fitzgerald with both hands extended.

Fitzgerald brought his leg up sharply as he rose to meet the attack, his shin catching Anderson full-force in the groin. The kick folded Anderson in two, as if some hidden cord drew his neck to his knees. Fitzgerald drove his knee into the helpless man's face and Anderson flipped backward.

Fitzgerald moved spryly for someone his size, pouncing to pin his knee against the chest of the gasping, bleeding man. He put the skinning knife to Anderson's throat. "You want to go join your brother?" Fitzgerald pressed the knife so that the blade drew a thin line of blood.

"Fitzgerald," Glass said in an even but authoritative tone. "That's enough."

Fitzgerald looked up. He contemplated an answer to Glass's challenge, while noting with satisfaction the ring of men that now surrounded him, witnesses to Anderson's pathetic position. Better to claim victory, he decided. He'd see to Glass another day. Fitzgerald removed the blade from Anderson's throat and rammed the knife into the beaded sheath on his belt. "Don't start things you can't finish, Anderson. Next time I'll finish it for you."

Captain Andrew Henry pushed his way through the circle of spectators. He grabbed Fitzgerald from behind and ripped him backward, pushing him hard into the embankment. "One more fight and you're out, Fitzgerald." Henry pointed beyond the perimeter of the camp to the distant horizon. "If you've got an extra store of piss you can go try making it on your own."

The captain looked around him at the rest of the men. "We'll cover forty miles tomorrow. You're wasting time if you're not asleep already. Now, who's taking first watch?" No one stepped forward. Henry's eyes came to rest on the boy, oblivious to the commotion. Henry took a handful of determined steps to the crumpled form. "Get up, Bridger."

The boy sprang up, wide-eyed as he grasped, bewildered, for his gun. The rusted trading musket had been an advance on his salary, along with a yellowed powder horn and a handful of flints.

"I want you a hundred yards downstream. Find a high spot along the bank. Pig, the same thing upstream. Fitzgerald, Anderson—you'll take the second watch."

Fitzgerald had stood watch the night before. For a moment it appeared he would protest the distribution of labor. He thought better of it, sulking instead to the edge of the camp. The boy, still disoriented, half stumbled across the rocks that spilled along the river's edge, disappearing into the cobalt blackness that encroached on the brigade.

The man they called "Pig" was born Phineous Gilmore on a dirt-poor farm in Kentucky. No mystery surrounded his nickname: he was enormous and he was filthy. Pig smelled so bad it confused people. When they encountered his reek, they looked around him for the source, so implausible did it seem that the odor could emanate from a human. Even the trappers, who placed no particular premium on cleanliness, did their best to keep Pig downwind. After hoisting himself slowly to his feet, Pig slung his rifle over his shoulder and ambled upstream.

Less than an hour passed before the daylight receded completely. Glass watched as Captain Henry returned from a nervous check of the sentries. He picked his way by moonlight among the sleeping men, and Glass realized that he and Henry were the only men awake. The captain chose the ground next to Glass, leaning against his rifle as he eased his large frame to the ground. Repose took the weight off his tired feet, but failed to relieve the pressure he felt most heavily.

"I want you and Black Harris to scout tomorrow," said Captain Henry. Glass looked up, disappointed that he could not respond to the beckoning call of sleep.

"Find something to shoot in late afternoon. We'll risk a fire." Henry lowered his voice, as if making a confession. "We're way behind, Hugh." Henry gave every indication that he intended to talk for a while. Glass reached for his rifle. If he couldn't sleep, he might as well tend his weapon. He had doused it in a river crossing that afternoon and wanted to apply fresh grease to the trigger works.

"Cold'll set in hard by early December," continued the captain. "We'll need two weeks to lay in a supply of meat. If we're not on the Yellowstone before October we'll have no fall hunt."

If Captain Henry was racked by internal doubt, his commanding physical presence betrayed no infirmity. The band of leather fringe on his deerskin tunic cut a swath across his broad shoulders and chest, remnants of his former profession as a lead miner in the Saint Genevieve district of Missouri. He was narrow at the waist, where a thick leather belt held a brace of pistols and a large knife. His breeches were doeskin to the knee, and from there down red wool. The captain's pants had been specially tailored in St. Louis and were a badge of his wilderness experience. Leather provided excellent protection, but wading made it heavy and cold. Wool, by contrast, dried quickly and retained heat even when wet.

If the brigade he led was motley, Henry at least drew satisfaction from the fact they called him "captain." In truth, of course, Henry knew the title was an artifice. His band of trappers had nothing to do with the military, and scant respect for any institution. Still, Henry was the only man among them to have trod and trapped the Three Forks. If title meant little, experience was the coin of the realm.

The captain paused, waiting for acknowledgment from Glass. Glass looked up from his rifle. It was a brief look, because he had unscrewed the elegantly scrolled guard that covered the rifle's twin triggers. He cupped the two screws carefully in his hand, afraid of dropping them in the dark.

The glance sufficed, enough to encourage Henry to continue. "Did I ever tell you about Drouillard?"

"No, Captain."

"You know who he was?"

"George Drouillard—Corps of Discovery?"

Henry nodded his head. "Lewis and Clark man, one of their best—a scout and a hunter. In 1809 he signed up with a group I led—he led, really—to the Three Forks. We had a hundred men, but Drouillard and Colter was the only ones who'd ever been there.

"We found beaver thick as mosquitoes. Barely had to trap 'em—could go out with a club. But we ran into trouble with the Blackfeet from the start. Five men killed before two weeks was up. We had to fort up, couldn't send out trapping parties.

"Drouillard holed up there with the rest of us for about a week before he said he was tired of sitting still. He went out the next day and came back a week later with twenty plews."

Glass paid the captain his full attention. Every citizen of St. Louis knew some version of Drouillard's story, but Glass had never heard a first-person account.

"He did that twice, went out and came back with a pack of plews. Last thing he said before he left the third time was, 'Third time's charmed.' He rode off and we heard two gunshots about half an hour later—one from his rifle and one from his pistol. Second shot must have been him shooting his horse, trying to make a barrier. That's where we found him behind his horse. There must have been twenty arrows between him and the horse. Blackfeet left the arrows in, wanted to send us a message. They hacked him up, too—cut off his head."

The captain paused again, scraping at the dirt in front of him with a pointed stick. "I keep thinking about him."

Glass searched for words of reassurance. Before he could say anything the captain asked, "How long do you figure this river's gonna keep running west?"

Glass stared intently, now, searching for the captain's eyes. "We'll start making better time, Captain. We can follow the Grand for the time being. We know the Yellowstone's north and west." In truth, Glass had developed significant doubts about the captain. Misfortune seemed to hang on him like day-before smoke.

"You're right." The captain said it and then he said it again, as if to convince himself. "Of course you're right."

Though his knowledge was born of calamity, Captain Henry knew as much about the geography of the Rockies as almost any man alive. Glass, though an experienced plainsman, had never set foot on the Upper Missouri. Yet Henry found something steady and reassuring in Glass's voice. Someone had told him that Glass had been a mariner in his youth. There was even a rumor that he'd been a prisoner of the pirate Jean Lafitte. Perhaps it was those years on the empty expanse of the high seas that left him comfortable on the featureless plain between St. Louis and the Rocky Mountains.

"We'll be lucky if the Blackfeet haven't wiped out the whole lot at Fort Union. The men I left there aren't exactly the cream of the crop." The captain continued now with his usual catalog of concerns. On and on into the night. Glass knew that it was enough just to listen. He looked up or grunted from time to time, but focused in the main on his rifle.

Glass's rifle was the one extravagance of his life, and when he rubbed grease into the spring mechanism of the hair trigger, he did so with the tender affection that other men might reserve for a wife or child. It was an Anstadt, a so-called Kentucky flintlock, made, like most of the great arms of the day, by German craftsmen in Pennsylvania. The octagonal barrel was inscribed at the base with the name of its maker, "Jacob Anstadt," and the place of its manufacture, "Kutztown, Penn." The barrel was short, only thirty-six inches. The classic Kentucky rifles were longer, some with barrels stretching fifty inches. Glass liked a shorter gun because shorter meant lighter, and lighter meant easier to carry. For those rare moments when he might be mounted, a shorter gun was easier to maneuver from the back of a horse. Besides, the expertly crafted rifling of the Anstadt made it deadly accurate, even without the longer barrel. A hair trigger enhanced its accuracy, allowing discharge with the lightest touch. With a full charge of 200 grains of black powder, the Anstadt could throw a .53 caliber ball nearly 200 yards.

His experiences on the western plains had taught Glass that the performance of his rifle could mean the difference between life and death. Of course, most men in the troop had reliable weapons. It was the Anstadt's elegant beauty that set his gun apart.

It was a beauty that other men noticed, asking, as they often did, if they might hold the rifle. The iron-hard walnut of the stock took an elegant curve at the wrist, but was thick enough to absorb the recoil of a heavy powder charge. The butt featured a patchbox on one side and a carved cheek piece on the other. The stock turned gracefully at the butt, so that it fit against the shoulder like an appendage of the shooter's own body. The stock was stained the deepest of browns, the last tone before black. From even a short distance, the grain of the wood was imperceptible, but on close examination, irregular lines seemed to swirl, animated beneath the hand-rubbed coats of varnish.

In a final indulgence, the metal fittings of the rifle were silver instead of the usual brass, adorning the gun at the butt-plate, the patchbox, the trigger guard, the triggers themselves, and the cupped fittings on the ends of the ramstaff. Many trappers pounded brass studs into their rifle stocks for decoration. Glass could not imagine such a gaudy disfigurement of his Anstadt.

Satisfied that his rifle's works were clear, Glass returned the trigger guard to its routed groove and replaced the two screws that held it. He poured fresh powder in the pan beneath the flint, ensuring that the gun was primed to fire.

He noticed suddenly that the camp had fallen still, and wondered vaguely when the captain had stopped talking. Glass looked toward the center of the camp. The captain lay sleeping, his body twitching fitfully. On the other side of Glass, closest to the camp's perimeter, Anderson lay against a chunk of driftwood. No sound rose above the reassuring flow of the river.

The sharp crack of a flintlock pierced the quiet. It came from downstream—from Jim Bridger, the boy. The sleeping men lurched in unison, fearful and confused as they scrambled for weapons and cover. A dark form hurtled toward the camp from downstream. Next to Glass, Anderson cocked and raised his rifle in a single motion. Glass raised the Anstadt. The hurtling form took shape, only forty yards from the camp. Anderson sighted down the barrel, hesitating an instant before pulling the trigger. At the same instant, Glass swung the Anstadt beneath Anderson's arms. The force knocked Anderson's barrel skyward as his powder ignited.

The hurtling form stopped cold at the explosion of the shot, the distance now close enough to perceive the wide eyes and heaving chest. It was Bridger. "I . . . I . . . I . . ." A panicked stammer paralyzed him.

"What happened, Bridger?" demanded the captain, peering beyond the boy into the darkness downstream. The trappers had fallen into a defensive semicircle with the embankment behind them. Most had assumed a firing position, perched on one knee, rifles at full cock.

"I'm sorry, Captain. I didn't mean to fire. I heard a sound, a crash in the brush. I stood up and I guess the hammer slipped. It just went off."

"More likely you fell asleep." Fitzgerald uncocked his rifle and rose from his knee. "Every buck for five miles is headed our way now."

Bridger started to speak, but searched in vain for the words to express the depth of his shame and regret. He stood there, open-mouthed, staring in horror at the men arrayed before him.

Glass stepped forward, pulling Bridger's smoothbore from his hands.

He cocked the musket and pulled the trigger, catching the hammer with his thumb before the flint struck the frisson. He repeated the action. "This is a poor excuse for a weapon, Captain. Give him a decent rifle and we'll have fewer problems on watch." A few of the men nodded their heads.

The Captain looked first at Glass, then at Bridger, and he said, "Anderson, Fitzgerald—it's your watch." The two men took their positions, one upstream and one down.

The sentries were redundant. No one slept in the few hours remaining before dawn.

THREE

AUGUST 24, 1823

HUGH GLASS STARED DOWN at the cloven tracks, the deep in-
dentions clear as newsprint in the soft mud. Two distinct sets began at
the river's edge, where the deer must have drunk, and then trailed into
the heavy cover of the willows. The persistent work of a beaver had
carved a trail, now trod by a variety of game. Dung lay piled next to
the tracks, and Glass stooped to touch the pea-sized pellets—still warm.

Glass looked west, where the sun still perched high above the plateau that formed the distant horizon. He guessed there were three hours
before sunset. Still early, but it would take the captain and the rest of
the men an hour to catch up. Besides, it was an ideal campsite. The river
folded gently against a long bar and gravel bank. Beyond the willows,
a stand of cottonwoods offered cover for their campfires and a supply
of firewood. The willows were ideal for smoke racks. Glass noticed plum
trees scattered among the willows, a lucky break. They could grind pemmican from the combined fruit and meat. He looked downriver. *Where's
Black Harris?*

In the hierarchy of challenges the trappers faced each day, obtaining food was the most immediate. Like other challenges, it involved a
complicated balancing of benefits and risks. They carried virtually no

food with them, especially since abandoning the flatboats on the Missouri and proceeding on foot up the Grand. A few men still had tea or sugar, but most were down to a bag of salt for preserving meat. Game was plentiful on this stretch of the Grand, and they could have dined on fresh meat each night. But harvesting game meant shooting, and the sound of a rifle carried for miles, revealing their position to any foe within earshot.

Since leaving the Missouri, the men had held closely to a pattern. Each day, two scouted ahead of the others. For the time being their path was fixed—they simply followed the Grand. The scouts' primary responsibilities were to avoid Indians, select a campsite, and find food. They shot fresh game every few days.

After shooting a deer or buffalo calf, the scouts prepared the camp for the evening. They bled the game, gathered wood, and set two or three small fires in narrow, rectangular pits. Smaller fires produced less smoke than a single conflagration, while also offering more surface for smoking meat and more sources of heat. If enemies did spot them at night, more fires gave the illusion of more men.

Once flames were burning, the scouts butchered their game, pulling choice cuts for immediate consumption and cutting thin strips with the rest. They constructed crude racks with green willow branches, rubbed the meat strips with a little salt and hung them just above the flames. It wasn't the type of jerky they would make in a permanent camp, which would keep for months. But the meat would keep for several days, enough to last until the next fresh game.

Glass stepped from the willows into a clearing, scanning for the deer he knew must be just ahead.

He saw the cubs before he saw the sow. There was a pair, and they tumbled toward him, bawling like playful dogs. The cubs had been dropped in the spring, and at five months weighed a hundred pounds each. They nipped at each other as they bore down on Glass, and for the briefest of instants the scene had a near comic quality. Transfixed by the whirling motion of the cubs, Glass had not raised his glance to the far end of the clearing, fifty yards away. Nor had he yet to calculate the certain implication of their presence.

Suddenly he knew. A hollowness seized his stomach half an instant before the first rumbling growl crossed the clearing. The cubs skidded to an immediate stop, not ten feet in front of Glass. Ignoring the cubs now, Glass peered toward the brush line across the clearing.

He heard her size before he saw it. Not just the crack of the thick underbrush that the sow moved aside like short grass, but the growl itself, a sound deep like thunder or a falling tree, a bass that could emanate only through connection with some great mass.

The growl crescendoed as she stepped into the clearing, black eyes staring at Glass, head low to the ground as she processed the foreign scent, a scent now mingling with that of her cubs. She faced him head-on, her body coiled and taut like the heavy spring on a buckboard. Glass marveled at the animal's utter muscularity, the thick stumps of her forelegs folding into massive shoulders, and above all the silvery hump that identified her as a grizzly.

Glass struggled to control his reaction as he processed his options. His reflex, of course, screamed at him to flee. Back through the willows. Into the river. Perhaps he could dive low and escape downstream. But the bear was already too close for that, barely a hundred feet in front of him. His eyes searched desperately for a cottonwood to climb; perhaps he could scramble out of reach, then shoot from above. No, the trees were behind the bear. Nor did the willows provide sufficient cover. His options dwindled to one: Stand and shoot. One chance to stop the grizzly with a .53 caliber ball from the Anstadt.

The grizzly charged, roaring with the focused hate of protective maternal rage. Reflex again nearly compelled Glass to turn and run. Yet the futility of flight was instantly apparent as the grizzly closed the ground between them with remarkable speed. Glass pulled the hammer to full-cock and raised the Anstadt, staring through the pronghorn sight in stunned horror that the animal could be, at the same time, enormous and lithe. He fought another instinct—to shoot immediately. Glass had seen grizzlies absorb half a dozen rifle balls without dying. He had one shot.

Glass struggled to sight on the bouncing target of the sow's head, unable to align a shot. At ten paces, the grizzly lifted herself to a standing position. She towered three feet over Glass as she pivoted for the raking swipe of her lethal claws. Point-blank, he aimed at the great bear's heart and pulled the trigger.

The flint sparked the Anstadt's pan, setting off the rifle and filling the air with the smoke and smell of exploding black powder. The grizzly roared as the ball entered her chest, but her attack did not slow. Glass dropped his rifle, useless now, and reached for the knife in the scabbard on his belt. The bear brought down her paw, and Glass felt the sickening sensation of the animal's six-inch claws dredging deep into the flesh of his upper arm, shoulder, and throat. The blow threw him to his back. The knife dropped, and he pushed furiously against the earth with his feet, futilely seeking the cover of the willows.

The grizzly dropped to all fours and was on him. Glass rolled into a ball, desperate to protect his face and chest. She bit into the back of his neck and lifted him off the ground, shaking him so hard that Glass wondered if his spine might snap. He felt the crunch of her teeth striking the bone of his shoulder blade. Claws raked repeatedly through the flesh of his back and scalp. He screamed in agony. She dropped him, then sank her teeth deep into his thigh and shook him again, lifting him and throwing him to the ground with such force that he lay stunned—conscious, but unable to resist any further.

He lay on his back staring up. The grizzly stood before him on her hind legs. Terror and pain receded, replaced by a horrified fascination at the towering animal. She let out a final roar, which registered in Glass's mind like an echo across a great distance. He was aware of enormous weight on top of him. The dank smell of her coat overwhelmed his other senses. *What was it?* His mind searched, then locked on the image of a yellow dog, licking a boy's face on the plank porch of a cabin.

The sunlit sky above him faded to black.

Black Harris heard the shot, just ahead around a bend in the river, and hoped that Glass had shot a deer. He moved forward quickly but quietly, aware that a rifle shot could mean many things. Harris began to trot when he heard the roar of the bear. Then he heard Glass scream.

At the willows, Harris found the tracks of both the deer and Glass. He peered into the path cut by a beaver, listening intently. No sound rose above the hushed trickle of the river. Harris pointed the rifle from his hip, his thumb on the hammer and his forefinger near the trigger. He glanced briefly at the pistol on his belt, assuring himself it was primed. He stepped into the willows, carefully placing each moccasin as he peered ahead. The bawling of the cubs broke the silence.

At the edge of the clearing Black Harris stopped to absorb the scene before him. An enormous grizzly lay sprawled on her belly, eyes open but dead. One cub stood on hind legs, pressing against the sow with its nose, futilely seeking to evoke some sign of life. The other cub rooted at something, tugging with its teeth. Harris realized suddenly it was a man's arm. *Glass.* He raised his rifle and shot the nearer of the two cubs. It fell limp. The sibling scampered for the cottonwoods and disappeared. Harris reloaded before walking forward.

Captain Henry and the men of the brigade heard the two shots and hurried upstream. The first shot didn't worry the captain, but the second one did. The first shot was expected—Glass or Harris bringing down game as they had planned the night before. Two shots closely spaced also would be normal. Two men hunting together might come upon more than one target, or the first shooter might miss. But several minutes separated the two shots. The captain hoped that the hunters were working apart. Perhaps the first shooter had flushed game to the second. Or perhaps they had been lucky enough to come across buffalo. Buffalo would sometimes stand, unfazed by the clap of a rifle, allowing a hunter to reload and casually pick a second target. "Keep tight, men. And check your arms."

For the third time in a hundred paces, Bridger checked the new rifle that Will Anderson had given to him. "My brother don't need this no more," was all he had said.

In the clearing, Black Harris looked down at the body of the bear. Only Glass's arm protruded from underneath. Harris glanced around before setting his rifle on the ground, tugging at the bear's foreleg in an attempt to move the carcass. Heaving, he pulled the animal far enough to see Glass's head, a bloody tangle of hair and flesh. *Jesus Christ!* He worked urgently, fighting against the fear of what he would find.

Harris moved to the opposite side of the bear, climbing across the animal to grab its foreleg, then tugging, his knees pressed against the grizzly's body for leverage. After several attempts, he managed to roll the front half of the bear so that the giant animal lay twisted at the mid-section. Then he pulled several times at the rear leg. He gave a final heave, and the bear tumbled heavily onto her back. Glass's body was free. On the sow's chest, Black Harris noticed the matted blood where Glass's shot had found its mark.

Black Harris knelt next to Glass, unsure of what to do. It was not through lack of experience with the wounded. He had removed arrows and bullets from three men, and twice had been shot himself.

But he had never seen human carnage like this, fresh in the wake of attack. Glass was shredded from head to foot. His scalp lay dangling to one side, and it took Harris an instant to recognize the components that made up his face. Worst was his throat. The grizzly's claws had cut three deep and distinct tracks, beginning at the shoulder and passing straight across his neck. Another inch and the claws would have severed Glass's jugular. As it was, they had laid open his throat, slicing through muscle and exposing his gullet. The claws had also cut the trachea, and Harris watched, horrified, as a large bubble formed in the blood that seeped from the wound. It was the first clear sign that Glass was alive.

Harris rolled Glass gently on his side to inspect his back. Nothing remained of his cotton shirt. Blood oozed from deep puncture wounds at his neck and shoulder. His right arm flopped unnaturally. From the middle of his back to his waist, the bear's raking claws left deep, parallel cuts. It reminded Harris of tree trunks he had seen where bears mark their territory, only these marks were etched in flesh instead of wood. On the back of Glass's thigh, blood seeped through his buckskin breeches.

Harris had no idea where to begin, and was almost relieved that the throat wound appeared so obviously mortal. He pulled Glass a few yards to a grassy, shaded spot and eased him to his back. Ignoring the bubbling throat, Harris focused on the head. Glass at least deserved the dignity of wearing his scalp. Harris poured water from his canteen, attempting to wash away as much of the dirt as possible. The skin was so loose that it was almost like replacing a fallen hat on a bald man. Harris pulled the scalp across Glass's skull, pressing the loose skin against his forehead and tucking it behind his ear. They could stitch it later if Glass lasted that long.

Harris heard a sound in the brush and drew his pistol. Captain Henry stepped into the clearing. The men filed grimly behind, eyes moving from Glass to the sow, from Harris to the dead cub.

The captain surveyed the clearing, oddly numb as his mind filtered the scene through the context of his own past. He shook his head and for a moment his eyes, normally sharp, seemed not to focus. "Is he dead?"

"Not yet. But he's tore to pieces. His windpipe's cut."

"Did he kill the sow?"

Harris nodded. "I found her dead on top of him. There's a ball in her heart."

"Not soon enough, eh." It was Fitzgerald.

The captain knelt next to Glass. With grimy fingers he poked at the throat wound, where bubbles continued to form with each breath. The breathing had grown more labored, and a tepid wheeze now rose and fell with Glass's chest.

"Somebody get me a clean strip of cloth and some water—and whiskey in case he wakes up."

Bridger stepped forward, rummaging through a small satchel from his back. He pulled a wool shirt from the bag, and handed it to Henry. "Here, Captain."

The captain paused, hesitant to take the boy's shirt. Then he grabbed it, tearing strips from the coarse cloth. He poured the contents of his canteen on Glass's throat. Blood washed away, quickly replaced by the wound's heavy seep. Glass began to sputter and cough. His eyes fluttered, then opened wide, panicky.

Glass's first sensation was that he was drowning. He coughed again as his body attempted to clear the blood from his throat and lungs. He focused briefly on Henry as the captain rolled him to his side. From his side, Glass was able to swallow two breaths before nausea overwhelmed him. He vomited, igniting excruciating pain in his throat. Instinctively, Glass reached to touch his neck. His right arm wouldn't function, but his left hand found the gaping wound. He was overcome with horror and panic at what his fingers discovered. His eyes became wild, searching for reassurance in the faces surrounding him. Instead he saw the opposite—awful affirmation of his fears.

Glass tried to speak, but his throat could muster no sound beyond an eerie wail. He struggled to rise on his elbows. Henry pinned him to the ground, pouring whiskey on his throat. A searing burn replaced all other pain. Glass convulsed a final time before again losing consciousness.

"We need to bind his wounds while he's down. Cut more strips, Bridger."

The boy began ripping long lengths from the shirt. The other men watched solemnly, standing like casket bearers at a funeral.

The captain looked up. "Rest of you get moving. Harris, scout a wide circle around us. Make sure those shots didn't draw attention our way. Someone get the fires going—make sure the wood's dry—we don't need a damn smoke signal. And get that sow butchered."

The men moved off and the captain turned again to Glass. He took a strip of cloth from Bridger and threaded it behind Glass's neck, tying it as tightly as he dared. He repeated the action with two more strips.

Blood soaked the cloth instantly. He wound another strip around Glass's head in a crude effort to hold his scalp in place. The head wounds also bled heavily, and the captain used water and the shirt to mop the blood pooling around Glass's eyes. He sent Bridger to refill the canteen from the river.

When Bridger returned, they again rolled Glass onto his side. Bridger held him, keeping his face from the ground, while Captain Henry inspected his back. Henry poured water on the puncture wounds from the bear's fangs. Though deep, they bled very little. The five parallel wounds from the bear's claws were a different story. Two in particular cut deep into Glass's back, exposing the muscle and bleeding heavily. Dirt mixed freely with the blood, and the captain again dumped water from the canteen. Without the dirt, the wounds seemed to bleed even more, so the captain left them alone. He cut two long strips from the shirt, worked them around Glass's body and tied them tightly. It didn't work. The strips did little to stop his back from bleeding.

The captain paused to think. "These deep wounds need to be stitched or he'll bleed to death."

"What about his throat?"

"I ought to sew that up too, but it's such a damn mess I don't know where to start." Henry dug into his possibles bag and pulled out coarse black thread and a heavy needle.

The captain's thick fingers were surprisingly nimble as he threaded the needle and tied an end knot. Bridger held the edges of the deepest wound together and watched, wide-eyed, as Henry pressed the needle into Glass's skin. He worked the needle from side to side, four stitches pulling the skin together in the center of the cut. He tied off the ends of the thick thread. Of the five claw wounds on Glass's back, two were deep enough to need stitches. For each wound, the captain made no effort to sew the entire length. Instead, he simply bound the middle together, but the bleeding slowed.

"Now let's look at his neck."

They rolled Glass onto his back. Despite the crude bandages, the throat continued to bubble and wheeze. Beneath the open skin Henry could see the bright white cartilage of the gullet and windpipe. He knew from the bubbles that the windpipe was cut or nicked, but he had no idea how to repair it. He held his hand over Glass's mouth, feeling for breath.

"What are you gonna do, Captain?"

The captain tied a new end knot in the thread on the needle. "He's still getting some air through his mouth. Best we can do is close up the skin, hope for the rest he can heal himself." At inchwide intervals, Henry sewed stitches to close Glass's throat. Bridger cleared a piece of ground in the shade of the willows and arranged Glass's bedroll. They laid him there as gently as they could.

The captain took his rifle and walked away from the clearing, back through the willows toward the river.

When he reached the water he set his rifle on the bank and removed his leather tunic. His hands were coated in sticky blood, and he reached into the stream to wash them. When some spots would not come clean, he scooped sand from the bank and scrubbed it against the stains. Finally he gave up, cupping his hands and pressing the icy stream water to his bearded face. Familiar doubt crept back. *It's happening again.*

It was no surprise when the green succumbed to the wilderness, but it came as a shock when the veterans fell victim. Like Drouillard, Glass had spent years on the frontier. He was a keel, steadying others through his quiet presence. And Henry knew that by morning he would be dead.

The captain thought back to his conversation with Glass the night before. *Was it only last night?* In 1809, Drouillard's death had been the beginning of the end. Henry's party abandoned the stockade in the Valley of the Three Forks and fled south. The move put them out of range of the Blackfeet, but did not protect them from the harshness of the Rockies themselves. The party endured savage cold, near starvation, and then robbery at the hands of the Crow. When they finally limped from the mountains in 1811, the viability of the fur trade remained an unsettled question.

More than a decade later, Henry again found himself leading trappers in pursuit of the Rockies' elusive wealth. In his mind Henry flipped through the pages of his own recent past: A week out of St. Louis, he lost a keelboat with $10,000 in trading goods. The Blackfeet killed two of his men near the Great Falls of the Missouri. He had rushed to Ashley's aid at the Arikara villages, participated in the debacle with Colonel Leavenworth, and then watched the Arikara close the Missouri. In a week of overland travel up the Grand, three of his men had been killed by Mandans, normally peaceful Indians who attacked by mistake in the night. Now Glass, his best man, lay mortally wounded after stumbling upon a bear. *What sin has plagued me with this curse?*

Back in the clearing, Bridger arranged a blanket over Glass and turned to look at the bear. Four men worked at butchering the animal. The choicest cuts—the liver, heart, tongue, loin, and ribs—were set aside for immediate consumption. The rest they cut into thin strips and rubbed with salt.

Bridger walked up to the great bear's paw and removed his knife from its scabbard. As Fitzgerald looked up from his butchering, Bridger began to cut the largest of the claws from the paw. He was shocked at its size—nearly six inches long and twice as thick as his thumb. It was razor sharp at the point and still bloody from the attack on Glass.

"Who says you get a claw, boy?"

"It ain't for me, Fitzgerald." Bridger took the claw and walked to Glass.

Glass's possibles bag lay next to him. Bridger opened it and dropped in the claw.

The men gorged for hours that night, their bodies craving the rich nutrients of the greasy meat. They knew it would be days before they ate fresh meat again, and they took advantage of the feast. Captain Henry posted two sentries. Despite the relative seclusion of the clearing, he worried about the fires.

Most of the men sat within reach of the flames, tending skewers of willow branches laden with meat. The captain and Bridger took turns checking on Glass. Twice his eyes were open, unfocused and glazed. They reflected the firelight, but seemed not to spark from within. Once he managed to swallow water in a painful convulsion.

They fed the fire in the long pits often enough to keep heat and smoke on the racks of drying meat. In the hour before dawn, Captain Henry checked on Glass and found him unconscious. His breathing had become labored, and he rasped as if each breath required the sum total of his strength.

Henry returned to the fire and found Black Harris there, gnawing on a rib. "Coulda been anyone, Captain—stepping on Old Ephraim like that. There's no accounting for bad luck."

Henry just shook his head. He knew about luck. For a while they sat in silence, as the first hint of another day was born in a barely perceptible glow on the eastern horizon. The captain gathered his rifle and powder horn. "I'll be back before the sun's up. When the men wake up, pick two to dig a grave."

An hour later the captain returned. The shallow beginnings of a grave had been dug, but apparently abandoned. He looked at Harris. "What's the hitch?"

"Well, Captain—for starters he ain't dead. Didn't seem right to keep digging with him laying there."

They waited all morning for Hugh Glass to die. He never gained consciousness. His skin was pallid from the loss of blood and his breathing remained labored. Still, his chest rose and fell, each breath stubbornly followed by another.

Captain Henry paced between the stream and the clearing, and by midmorning sent Black Harris to scout upstream. The sun stood directly overhead when Harris returned. He had seen no Indians, but a game trail on the opposite bank was covered with the tracks of men and horses. Two miles upstream Harris had found a deserted campsite. The captain could wait no more.

He ordered two men to cut saplings. With Glass's bedroll, they would fashion a litter.

"Why don't we make a travois, Captain? Use the mule to pull it?"

"Too rough to pull a travois by the river."

"Then let's move off the river."

"Just build the damn litter," said the captain. The river was the sole marker across unknown terrain. Henry had no intention of veering so much as an inch from its banks.

FOUR

AUGUST 28, 1823

ONE BY ONE the men reached the obstacle and stopped. The Grand River flowed directly into the steep face of a sandstone cliff, which forced it to turn. The waters swirled and pooled deeply against the wall before spreading widely toward the opposite shore. Bridger and Pig arrived last, bearing Glass between them. They eased the litter to the ground. Pig plopped heavily to his rump, panting, his shirt stained dark with sweat.

Each man looked up as he arrived, quickly appreciating the two choices for moving forward. One was to climb along the steep face of the cliff. It was possible, but only by using hands as well as feet. This was the path taken by Black Harris when he had passed two hours before them. They could see his tracks and the broken branch on the sagebrush that he had grabbed to pull himself up. It was obvious that neither the litter bearers nor the mule could make the climb.

The other option was to cross the river. The opposite bank was level and inviting, but the problem was getting there. The pool created by the embankment appeared at least five feet deep, and the current ran swift. Seam water toward the middle of the river marked the place where the stream shallowed. From there it was an easy wade to the other side.

A surefooted man might keep his feet in the deep water, holding his rifle and powder above his head; the less agile might fall, but could certainly swim the few yards to the shallower water.

Getting the mule in the river was no problem. So famous was the animal's love of water that the men called her "Duck." At the end of the day she would stand for hours in water up to her sagging belly. In fact, it was this odd predilection that kept the Mandans from stealing her along with the rest of their stock. While the other animals were grazing or sleeping along the shore, Duck was standing in shallow water on a sandbar. When the bandits tried to take her, she was firmly stuck in the mud. It ultimately took half the brigade to pull her out.

So the problem wasn't the mule. The problem, of course, was Glass.

It would be impossible to hold the litter above the water while crossing.

Captain Henry mulled his choices, cursing Harris for not leaving a sign to cross earlier. They had passed an easy ford a mile downstream. He hated to divide the men, even for a few hours, but it seemed silly to march them all back. "Fitzgerald, Anderson—it's your turn on the litter. Bernot—you and me will go back with 'em to the crossing we passed. Rest of you cross here and wait."

Fitzgerald glared at the captain, muttering under his breath. "You got something to say, Fitzgerald?"

"I signed on to be a trapper, Captain—not a goddamned mule."

"You'll take your turn like everybody else."

"And I'll tell you what everybody else is afraid to say to your face. We're all wondering if you intend to drag this corpse all the way to the Yellowstone."

"I intend to do the same with him that I'd do for you or any other man in this brigade."

"What you'll be doing for all of us is digging graves. How long do you figure we can parade through this valley before we stumble on some hunting party? Glass ain't the only man in this brigade."

"You ain't the only man either," said Anderson. "Fitzgerald don't speak for me, Captain—and I bet he don't speak for many others."

Anderson walked to the litter, placing his rifle next to Glass. "You gonna make me drag him?"

For three days they had carried Glass. The banks of the Grand alternated between sandbar and jumbled rock. Occasional stands of cottonwood gave way at the high water line to the graceful branches of willows, some reaching ten feet in height. Cut banks forced them to climb, giant scoops where erosion sliced away the earth as neatly as a cleaver. They maneuvered around the tangled debris left piled behind the spring flood—mounded stones, tangled branches, and even entire trees, their sun-bleached trunks as smooth as glass from the beating of water and stone. When the terrain became too rugged, they crossed the river to continue upstream, wet buckskins compounding the weight of their load.

The river was a highway on the plains, and Henry's men were not the only travelers on its banks. Tracks and abandoned campsites were numerous. Black Harris had twice seen small hunting parties. The distance had been too great to determine if they were Sioux or Arikara, though both tribes presented danger. The Arikara were certain enemies since the battle on the Missouri. The Sioux had been allies in that fight, but their current disposition was unknown. With only ten able men, the small party of trappers offered little deterrent to attack. At the same time, their weapons, traps, and even the mule were attractive targets. Ambush was a constant danger, with only the scouting skills of Black Harris and Captain Henry to steer them clear.

Territory to cross quickly, thought the captain. Instead, they plodded forward at the leaden pace of a funeral procession.

Glass slipped in and out of consciousness, though one state differed little from the other. He could occasionally take water, but the throat wounds made it impossible to swallow solid food. Twice the litter spilled, dumping Glass on the ground. The second spill broke two of the stitches in his throat. They stopped long enough for the captain to resuture the neck, red now with infection. No one bothered to inspect the other wounds. There was little they could do for them, anyway. Nor could Glass protest. His wounded throat rendered him mute, his only sound the pathetic wheeze of his breathing.

At the end of the third day they arrived at the confluence of a small creek with the Grand. A quarter mile up the creek, Black Harris found a spring, surrounded by a thick stand of pines. It was an ideal campsite. Henry dispatched Anderson and Harris to find game.

The spring itself was more seep than font, but its icy water filtered over mossy stones and collected in a clear pool. Captain Henry stooped to drink while he thought about the decision he had made.

In three days of carrying Glass, the captain estimated they had covered only forty miles. They should have covered twice that distance or more. While Henry believed they might be beyond Arikara territory, Black Harris found more signs each day of the Sioux.

Beyond his concerns about where they were, Henry fretted about where they needed to be. More than anything, he worried that they would arrive too late on the Yellowstone. Without a couple of weeks to lay in a supply of meat, the whole brigade would be at jeopardy. Late fall weather was as capricious as a deck of cards. They might find Indian summer, or the howling winds of an early blizzard.

Aside from their physical safety, Henry felt enormous pressure for commercial success. With luck, a few weeks of fall hunting, and some trading with the Indians, they might net enough fur to justify sending one or two men downriver.

The captain loved to imagine the effect of a fur-laden pirogue arriving in St. Louis on some bright February day. Stories of their successful establishment on the Yellowstone would headline the *Missouri Republican.* The press would bring new investors. Ashley could parley fresh capital into a new fur brigade by early spring. By late summer, Henry envisioned himself commanding a network of trappers up and down the Yellowstone. With enough men and trading goods, maybe he could even buy peace with the Blackfeet, and once again trap in the beaver-rich valleys of the Three Forks. By next winter it would take flatboats to carry the plews they would harvest.

But it all depended upon time. Being there first and in force. Henry felt the press of competition from every point on the compass.

From the north, the British North West Company had established forts as far south as the Mandan villages. The British also dominated the western coast, from which they now pushed inland along the Columbia and its tributaries. Rumors circulated that British trappers had penetrated as far as the Snake and the Green.

From the south, several groups spread northward from Taos and Santa Fe: the Columbia Fur Company, the French Fur Company, StoneBostwick and Company.

Most visible of all was the competition from the east, from St. Louis itself. In 1819, the U.S. Army began its "Yellowstone Expedition" with the express goal of enlarging the fur trade. Though extremely limited, the army's presence emboldened entrepreneurs already eager to pursue the fur trade. Manuel Lisa's Missouri Fur Company opened trade on the Platte. John Jacob Astor revived the remnants of his American Fur Company, driven from the Columbia by the British in the War of 1812, by establishing a new headquarters in St. Louis. All competed for limited sources of capital and men.

Henry glanced at Glass, lying on the litter in the shade of the pines.

He had never returned to the task of properly stitching Glass's scalp. It still lay haphazardly atop his head, purple-black around the edges where dried blood now held it in place, a grotesque crown on a shattered body. The captain felt anew the polarizing mix of sympathy and anger, resentment and guilt.

He could not blame Glass for the grizzly attack. The bear was simply a hazard in their path, one of many. When the troop left St. Louis, Henry knew that men would die. Glass's wounded body merely underscored the precipice that each of them walked every day. Henry considered Glass his best man, the best mix of seasoning, skills, and disposition. The others, with the possible exception of Black Harris, he viewed as subordinates. They were younger, dumber, weaker, less experienced. But Captain Henry saw Glass as a peer. If it could happen to Glass, it could happen to anyone; it could happen to him. The captain turned from the dying man.

He knew that leadership required him to make tough decisions for the good of the brigade. He knew that the frontier respected—required—independence and self-sufficiency above all else. There were no entitlements west of St. Louis. Yet the fierce individuals who comprised his frontier community were bound together by the tight weave of collective responsibility. Though no law was written, there was a crude rule of law, adherence to a covenant that transcended their selfish interests. It was biblical in its depth, and its importance grew with each step into wilderness. When the need arose, a man extended a helping hand to his friends, to his partners, to strangers. In so doing, each knew that his own survival might one day depend upon the reaching grasp of another.

The utility of his code seemed diminished as the captain struggled to apply it to Glass. *Haven't I done my best for him?* Tending his wounds, portaging him, waiting respectfully so that he might at least have a civilized burial. Through Henry's decisions, they had subordinated their collective needs to the needs of one man. It was the right thing to do, but it could not be sustained. Not here.

The captain had thought of abandoning Glass outright. In fact, so great was Glass's suffering that Henry wondered briefly whether they should put a bullet in his head, bring his misery to an end. He quickly dismissed any notion of killing Glass, but he wondered if he could somehow communicate with the wounded man, make him understand that he could no longer risk the entire brigade. They could find him shelter, leave him with a fire, weapons, and provisions. If his condition improved, he could join them on the Missouri. Knowing Glass, he suspected this was what the man would ask for if he could speak for himself. Surely he wouldn't jeopardize the lives of the other men.

Yet Captain Henry couldn't bring himself to leave the wounded man behind. There had been no coherent conversation with Glass since the bear attack, so ascertaining his wishes was impossible. Absent such clear guidance, he would make no assumptions. He was the leader, and Glass was his responsibility.

But so are the other men. So was Ashley's investment. So was his family back in St. Louis, a family that had waited more than a decade for the commercial success that seemed always as distant as the mountains themselves.

That night the men of the brigade gathered around the three small fire pits. They had fresh meat to smoke, a buffalo calf, and the shelter of the pines gave them added confidence in building fires. The late August evening cooled quickly after sunset: not cold, but a reminder that a change of season lurked just over the horizon.

The captain stood to address the men, a formality that foreshadowed the seriousness of what he would say. "We need to make better time. I need two volunteers to stay with Glass. Stay with him here until he dies, give him a proper burial, then catch up. The Rocky Mountain Fur Company will pay $70 for the risk of staying back."

A pine knot burst from one of the fires, catapulting sparks into the clear night sky. Otherwise the camp fell silent as the men pondered the situation and the offer. It was eerie to contemplate Glass's death, however certain. A Frenchman named Jean Bernot crossed himself. Most of the others simply stared at the fire.

No one said anything for a long time. They all thought about the money. Seventy dollars was more than a third of their wage for the entire year. Viewed through the cold prism of economics, Glass would surely die soon. Seventy dollars to sit in a clearing for a few days, then a week of tough marching to catch up with the brigade. Of course they all knew there was a real risk in staying back. Ten men were little deterrent from attack. Two men were none. If a war party happened upon them . . . Seventy dollars bought you nothing if you were dead.

"I'll stay with him, Captain." The other men turned, surprised that the volunteer was Fitzgerald.

Captain Henry was unsure how to react, so suspicious was he of Fitzgerald's motive.

Fitzgerald read the hesitation. "I ain't doing it for love, Captain. I'm doing it for money, pure and simple. Pick somebody else if you want somebody to mother him."

Captain Henry looked around the loose circle of men. "Who else'll stay?" Black Harris threw a small stick on the fire. "I will, Captain." Glass had been a friend to Harris, and the idea of leaving him with Fitzgerald didn't sit right.

None of the men liked Fitzgerald. Glass deserved better.

The captain shook his head. "You can't stay, Harris."

"What do you mean I can't stay?"

"You can't stay. I know you were his friend, so I'm sorry. But I need you to scout."

Another long silence followed. Most of the men stared blankly into the fire. One by one they arrived at the same uncomfortable conclusion: It wasn't worth it. The money wasn't worth it. Ultimately, Glass wasn't worth it. Not that they didn't respect him, like him even. Some, like Anderson, felt an additional debt, a sense of obligation for gratuitous acts of past kindness. It would be different, thought Anderson, if the captain were asking them to defend Glass's life—but that was not the task at hand. The task at hand was waiting for Glass to die, then burying him. It wasn't worth it.

Henry began to wonder if he would have to entrust the job to Fitzgerald alone, when suddenly Jim Bridger rose clumsily to his feet. "I'll stay."

Fitzgerald snorted sarcastically. "Jesus, Captain, you can't leave me to do this with some pork-eating boy! If it's Bridger that stays you better pay me double for tending to two."

The words jabbed at Bridger like punches. He felt his blood rise in embarrassment and anger. "I promise you, Captain—I'll pull my weight."

This was not the outcome the captain had expected. A part of him felt that leaving Glass with Bridger and Fitzgerald differed little from abandonment. Bridger was barely more than a boy. In his year with the Rocky Mountain Fur Company, he had proved himself to be honest and capable, but he was no counterweight to Fitzgerald. Fitzgerald was a mercenary. But then, thought the captain, wasn't that the essence of the course he had chosen? Wasn't he simply buying proxies, purchasing a substitute for their collective responsibility? For his own responsibility? What else could he do? There was no better choice.

"All right, then," said the captain. "Rest of us leave at dawn."

FIVE

AUGUST 30, 1823

IT WAS THE EVENING of the second day since the departure of Captain Henry and the brigade. Fitzgerald had dispatched the boy to gather wood, leaving himself and Glass alone in the camp. Glass lay near one of the small fires. Fitzgerald ignored him.

A rock formation crowned the steep slope above the clearing. Massive boulders stood in a rocky stack, as if titanic hands had piled them one on top of the other and then pressed.

From a crack between two of the great stones grew a lone, twisted pine.

The tree was a sibling to the lodgepole pines that the local tribes used to frame their teepees, but the seed of its origin had been lifted high above the fertile soil of the forest below. A sparrow had pried it from a pine cone decades before, carrying it to a lofty height above the clearing. The sparrow lost the seed to a crevice between the rocks. There was soil in the crevice, and a timely rain for germination. The rocks drew heat in the daytime, compensating in part for the exposure of the outcropping. There was no straight path to sunlight, so the pine grew sideways before it grew upward, worming its way from the crevice before turning toward the sky. A few gnarled branches extended from the warped trunk, each capped with a scruffy tuft of needles. The lodge-poles below grew straight as arrows, some towering sixty feet above the floor of the forest. But none grew higher than the twisted pine on top of the rock.

Since the captain and the brigade left, Fitzgerald's strategy was simple: lay in a supply of jerked meat so they were ready to move fast when Glass died; in the meantime, stay away from their camp as much as possible.

Though they were off the main river, Fitzgerald had little confidence in their position on the creek. The little stream led straight to the clearing. The charred remains of campfires made it clear that others had availed themselves of the sheltered spring. In fact, Fitzgerald feared that the clearing was a well-known campsite. Even if it were not, the tracks of the brigade and the mule led clearly from the river. A hunting or war party couldn't help but find them if they came up the near bank of the Grand.

Fitzgerald looked bitterly at Glass. Out of morbid curiosity, he had examined Glass's wounds on the day the rest of the troop left. The sutures in the wounded man's throat had held since the litter spilled, but the entire area was red with infection. The puncture wounds on his leg and arm seemed to be healing, but the deep slashes on his back were inflamed. Luckily for him, Glass spent most of his time unconscious. *When will the bastard die?*

It was a twisted path that brought John Fitzgerald to the frontier, a path that began with his flight from New Orleans in 1815, the day after he stabbed a prostitute to death in a drunken rage.

Fitzgerald grew up in New Orleans, the son of a Scottish sailor and a Cajun merchant's daughter. His father put in port once a year during the ten years of marriage before his ship went down in the Caribbean. On each call to New Orleans he left his fertile wife with the seed of a new addition to the family. Three months after learning of her husband's death, Fitzgerald's mother married the elderly owner of a sundry shop, an action she viewed as essential to support her family. Her pragmatic decision served most of her children well. Eight survived to adulthood. The two eldest sons took over the sundry shop when the old man died. Most of the other boys found honest work and the girls married respectably. John got lost somewhere in the middle.

From an early age, Fitzgerald demonstrated both a reflex toward and a skill for engaging in violence. He was quick to resolve disputes with a punch or a kick, and was thrown out of school at the age of ten for stabbing a classmate in the leg with a pencil. Fitzgerald had no interest in the hard labor of following his father to sea, but he mixed eagerly in the seedy chaos of a port town. His fighting skills were tested and honed on the docks where he spent his teenage days. At seventeen, a boatman slashed his face in a barroom brawl. The incident left him with a fishhook scar and a new respect for cutlery. He became fascinated with knives, acquiring a collection of daggers and scalpers in a wide range of sizes and shapes.

At the age of twenty, Fitzgerald fell in love with a young whore at a dockside saloon, a French girl named Dominique Perreau. Despite the financial underpinnings of their relationship, the full implications of Dominique's métier apparently did not register with Fitzgerald. When he walked in on Dominique plying her trade with the fat captain of a keelboat, the young man fell into a rage. He stabbed them both before fleeing into the streets. He stole eighty-four dollars from his brothers' store and hired passage on a boat headed north up the Mississippi.

For five years he made his living in and around the taverns of Memphis. He tended bar in exchange for room, board, and a small salary at an establishment known, with pretensions that exceeded its grasp, as the Golden Lion. His official capacity as barkeep gave him something he had not possessed in New Orleans—a license to engage in violence. He removed disorderly patrons with a relish that startled even the rough-cut clientele of the saloon. Twice he nearly beat men to death.

Fitzgerald possessed some of the mathematical skills that made his brothers successful storekeepers, and he applied his native intelligence toward gambling. For a while he was content to squander his paltry stipend from the bar. Over time he was drawn to higher stakes. These new games required more money to play, and Fitzgerald found no shortage of lenders.

Not long after borrowing two hundred dollars from the owner of a rival tavern, Fitzgerald hit it big. He won a thousand dollars on a single hand of queens over tens, and spent the next week in a celebratory debauch. The payoff infused him with a false confidence in his gambling skills and a ravenous hunger for more. He quit his work at the Golden Lion and sought to make his living at cards. His luck veered sharply south, and a month later he owed two thousand dollars to a loan shark named Geoffrey Robinson. He dodged Robinson for several weeks before two henchmen caught him and broke his arm. They gave him a week to pay the balance due.

In desperation, Fitzgerald found a second lender, a German named Hans Bangemann, to pay off the first. With the two thousand dollars in his hands, however, Fitzgerald had an epiphany: He would flee Memphis and start someplace new. The next morning he took passage on another boat north. He landed in St. Louis late in the month of February 1822.

After a month in the new city, Fitzgerald learned that two men had been asking at pubs about the whereabouts of a "gambler with a scar on his face." In the small world of Memphis moneylenders, it had not taken long for Geoffrey Robinson and Hans Bangemann to discover the full measure of Fitzgerald's treachery. For one hundred dollars each, they hired a pair of henchmen to find Fitzgerald, kill him, and recover as much of their loans as possible. They harbored little hope of getting their money back, but they did want Fitzgerald dead. They had reputations to uphold, and word was spread of their plan through the network of Memphis taverns.

Fitzgerald was trapped. St. Louis was the northernmost outpost of civilization on the Mississippi. He was afraid to go south, where trouble awaited him in New Orleans and Memphis. That day Fitzgerald overheard a group of pub patrons talking excitedly about a newspaper ad in the *Missouri Republican*. He picked up the paper to read for himself:

> To enterprising young men. The subscriber wishes to engage one hundred young men to ascend the Missouri river to its source, there to be employed for one, two, or three years. For particulars enquire of Captain Henry, near the lead mines in the country of Washington, who will ascend with, and command, the party.

Fitzgerald made a rash decision. With the paltry remnants of the money he had stolen from Hans Bangemann, he bought a weathered leather tunic, moccasins, and a rifle. The next day he presented himself to Captain Henry and requested a spot with the fur brigade. Henry was suspicious of Fitzgerald from the beginning, but pickings were slim. The captain needed a hundred men and Fitzgerald looked fit. If he'd been in a few knife fights, so much the better. A month later Fitzgerald was on a keelboat headed north up the Missouri River.

Although he fully intended to desert the Rocky Mountain Fur Company when the opportunity presented itself, Fitzgerald took to life on the frontier. He found that his skill with knives extended to other weapons. Fitzgerald had none of the tracking skills of the real woodsmen in the brigade, but he was an excellent shot. With a sniper's patience, he had killed two Arikara during the recent siege on the Missouri. Many of Henry's men had been terrified in their fights with various Indians. Fitzgerald found them exhilarating, even titillating.

Fitzgerald glanced at Glass, his eyes falling on the Anstadt lying next to the wounded man. He looked around to make sure that Bridger wasn't returning, then picked up the rifle. He pulled it to his shoulder and sighted down the barrel. He loved how the gun fit snug against his body, how the wide pronghorn sites found targets quickly, how the lightness of the weapon let him hold a steady bead. He swung from target to target, up and down, until the sights came to rest on Glass.

Once again Fitzgerald thought about how the Anstadt soon would be his. They hadn't talked about it with the captain, but who deserved the rifle more than the man who stayed behind? Certainly his claim was better than Bridger's. All the trappers admired Glass's gun. Seventy dollars was paltry pay for the risk they were taking—Fitzgerald was there for the Anstadt. Such a weapon should not be wasted on a boy. Besides, Bridger was happy enough to get William Anderson's rifle. Throw him some other crumb—Glass's knife, perhaps.

Fitzgerald mulled the plan he had formed since he volunteered to stay with Glass, a plan that seemed more compelling with each passing hour. *What difference does a day make to Glass?* On the other hand, Fitzgerald knew exactly the difference a day meant to his own prospects for survival.

Fitzgerald set the Anstadt down. A bloody shirt lay next to Glass's head. *Push it against his face for a few minutes—we could be on our way in the morning.* He looked again at the rifle, its dark brown striking against the orange hue of fallen pine needles. He reached for the shirt.

"Did he wake up?" Bridger stood behind him, his arms full of firewood. Fitzgerald startled, fumbling for an instant. "Christ, boy! Sneak up on me again like that and I swear to God I'll cut you down!"

Bridger dropped the wood and walked over to Glass. "I was thinking maybe we ought to try giving him some broth."

"Why, that's mighty kind of you, Bridger. Pour a little broth down that throat and maybe he'll last a week instead of dying tomorrow! Will that make you sleep better? What do you think, that if you give him a little soup he's going to get up and walk away from here?"

Bridger was quiet for a minute, then said, "You act like you want him to die."

"Of course I want him to die! Look at him. *He* wants to die!" Fitzgerald paused for effect. "You ever go to school, Bridger?" Fitzgerald knew the answer to his question.

The boy shook his head.

"Well, let me give you a little lesson in arithmetic. Captain Henry and the rest are probably making around thirty miles a day now that they're not dragging Glass. Let's figure we'll be faster—say we make forty. Do you know what's forty minus thirty, Bridger?" The boy stared blankly.

"I'll tell you what it is. It's ten." Fitzgerald held up the fingers of both hands in a mocking gesture. "This many, boy. Whatever their head start is—we only make up ten miles a day once we take after them. They're already a hundred miles ahead of us. That's ten days on our own, Bridger. And that assumes he dies today and we find them straight away. Ten days for a Sioux hunting party to stumble on us. Don't you get it? Every day we sit here is another three days we're on our own. You'll look worse than Glass when the Sioux are finished with you, boy. You ever see a man who got scalped?"

Bridger said nothing, though he had seen a man scalped. He was there near the Great Falls when Captain Henry brought the two dead trappers back to camp, butchered by Blackfeet. Bridger vividly remembered the bodies. The captain had tied them belly down to a single pack mule. When he cut them loose, they fell stiffly to the ground. The trappers had gathered round them, mesmerized as they contemplated the mutilated corpses of the men they had seen that morning at the campfire. And it wasn't just their scalps that were missing. Their noses and ears had been hacked away, and their eyes gouged out. Bridger remembered how, without noses, the heads looked more like skulls than faces. The men were naked, and their privates were gone, too. There was a stark tan line at their necks and wrists. Above the line their skin was as tough and brown as saddle leather, but the rest of their bodies was as white as lace. It looked funny, almost. It was the type of thing that one of the men would have joked about, if it hadn't been so horrible. Of course nobody laughed. Bridger always thought about it when he washed himself—how underneath, they all had this lacy white skin, weak as a baby.

Bridger struggled, desperately wanting to challenge Fitzgerald, but wholly incapable of articulating a rebuttal. Not for lack of words, this time, but rather for lack of reasons. It was easy to condemn Fitzgerald's motivation—he said himself it was money. But what, he wondered, was his own motivation? It wasn't money. The numbers all jumbled together, and his regular salary was already more wealth than he had ever seen. Bridger liked to believe that his motive was loyalty, fidelity to a fellow member of the brigade. He certainly respected Glass. Glass had been kind, watching out for him in small ways, schooling him, defending him against embarrassments. Bridger acknowledged a debt to Glass, but how far did it extend?

The boy remembered the surprise and admiration in the eyes of the men when he had volunteered to stay with Glass. What a contrast to the anger and contempt of that terrible night on sentry duty. He remembered how the captain had patted him on the shoulder when the brigade departed, and how the simple gesture had filled him with a sense of affiliation, as if for the first time he deserved his place among the men. Wasn't that why he was there in the clearing—to salve his wounded pride? Not to take care of another man, but to take care of himself? Wasn't he just like Fitzgerald, profiting from another man's misfortune? Say what you would about Fitzgerald, at least he was honest about why he stayed.

SIX

AUGUST 31, 1823

ALONE IN THE CAMP on the morning of the third day, Bridger spent several hours repairing his moccasins, both of which had developed holes in the course of their travels. As a consequence, his feet were scraped and bruised, and the boy appreciated the opportunity for the repair work. He cut leather from a rawhide left when the brigade departed, used an awl to punch holes around the edge, and replaced the soles with the new hide on bottom. The stitching was irregular but tight.

As he examined his handiwork his eyes fell on Glass. Flies buzzed around his wounds and Bridger noticed that Glass's lips were cracked and parched. The boy questioned again whether he stood on any higher moral plane than Fitzgerald. Bridger filled his large tin cup with cold water from the spring and put it to Glass's mouth. The wetness triggered an unconscious reaction, and Glass began to drink.

Bridger was disappointed when Glass finished. It was good to feel useful. The boy stared at Glass. Fitzgerald was right, of course. There was no question that Glass would die. *But shouldn't I do my best for him? At least provide comfort in his final hours?*

Bridger's mother could tease a healing property from anything that grew. He wished many times that he had paid more attention when she had returned from the woods, her basket filled with flowers, leaves, and bark. He did know a few basics, and on the edge of the clearing he found what he was looking for, a pine tree with its sticky gum oozing like molasses. He used his rusty skinning knife to scrape off the gum, working until his blade was smeared with a good quantity. He walked back to Glass and knelt next to him. The boy focused first on the leg and arm wounds, the deep punctures from the grizzly's fangs. While the surrounding areas remained black-and-blue, the skin itself appeared to be repairing. Bridger used his finger to apply the gum, filling the wounds and smearing the surrounding skin.

Next he rolled Glass to his side in order to examine his back. The crude sutures had snapped when the litter spilled, and there were signs of more recent bleeding. Still, it wasn't blood that gave Glass's back its crimson sheen. It was infection. The five parallel cuts extended almost the entire length of his back. There was yellow pus in the center of the cuts, and the edges practically glowed fiery red. The odor reminded Bridger of sour milk. Unsure what to do, he simply smeared the entire area with pine gum, returning twice to the trees to gather more.

Bridger turned last to the neck wounds. The captain's sutures remained in place, though to the boy they seemed merely to conceal the carnage beneath the skin. The wheezing rumble continued from Glass's unconscious breathing, like the loose rattle of broken parts in a machine. Bridger walked again into the pines, this time looking for a tree with loose bark. He found one and used his knife to pry loose the outer skin. The tender inner bark he gathered in his hat.

Bridger filled his cup again with water at the spring and set it in the coals of the fire. When it boiled, he added the pine bark, mashing the mixture with the pommel of his knife. He worked until the consistency was thick and smooth as mud. He waited for the poultice to cool slightly, then applied it to Glass's throat, packing the mixture against the slashes and spreading it outward toward his shoulder. Next Bridger walked to his small pack, pulling out the remnants of his spare shirt.

He used the cloth to cover the poultice, lifting Glass's head to tie a knot firmly behind the man's neck.

Bridger let the wounded man's head return gently to the ground, surprised to find himself staring into Glass's open eyes. They burned with an intensity and lucidity that juxtaposed oddly against his broken body. Bridger stared back, searching to discern the message that Glass clearly intended to convey. *What is he saying?*

Glass stared at the boy for a minute before allowing his eyes to fall closed. In his fleeting moments of consciousness, Glass felt a heightened sensitivity, as if suddenly made aware of the secret workings of his body. The boy's efforts provided topical relief. The slight stinging of the pine gum had a medicinal quality, and the heat from the poultice created a steeping comfort at his throat. At the same time, Glass sensed that his body was marshaling itself for another, decisive battle. Not at the surface, but deep within.

By the time Fitzgerald returned to camp, the shadows of late afternoon had stretched into the fading glow of early evening. He carried a doe over his shoulder. He had field-dressed the animal, slitting her neck and removing the entrails. He let the deer fall next to one of the fires. She landed in an unnatural pile, so different from her grace in life.

Fitzgerald stared at the fresh dressings on Glass's wounds. His face tensed. "You're wasting your time with him." He paused. "I wouldn't give a tinker's damn, except you're wasting my time too."

Bridger ignored the comment, though he felt the blood rise in his face. "How old are you, boy?"

"Twenty."

"You lying piece of horseshit. You can't even talk without squeaking. I bet you never seen a tit that wasn't your ma's."

The boy looked away, hating Fitzgerald for his bloodhound ability to sense weakness.

Fitzgerald absorbed Bridger's discomfort like the nourishment of raw meat. He laughed. "What! You never been with a woman? I'm right, aren't I, boy? What's the matter, Bridger—you didn't have two bucks for a whore before we left St. Louis?"

Fitzgerald eased his large frame to the ground, sitting down to better enjoy himself. "Maybe you don't like girls? You a bugger, boy? Maybe I need to sleep on my back, keep you from rutting at me in the night." Still Bridger said nothing.

"Or maybe you got no pecker at all."

Without thinking, Bridger jumped to his feet, grabbed his rifle, cocked it, and pointed the long barrel at Fitzgerald's head. "You son of a bitch, Fitzgerald! Say another word and I'll blow your damn head off!"

Fitzgerald sat stunned, staring at the dark muzzle of the rifle barrel. For a long moment he sat like that, just staring at the muzzle. Then his dark eyes moved slowly up to Bridger's, a smile creeping to join the scar on his face. "Well, good for you, Bridger. Maybe you don't squat when you piss, after all."

He snorted at his joke, pulled out his knife, and set to butchering the deer.

In the quiet of the camp, Bridger became aware of the heavy sound of his own breathing, and could feel the rapid beat of his heart. He lowered the gun and set the butt on the ground, then lowered himself. He felt suddenly tired, and pulled his blanket around his shoulders.

After several minutes, Fitzgerald said, "Hey, boy."

Bridger looked over, but said nothing in acknowledgment.

Fitzgerald casually wiped the back of a bloody hand against his nose.

"That new gun of yours won't fire without a flint."

Bridger looked down at his rifle. The flint was missing from the lock.

The blood rose again in his face, though this time he hated himself as much as Fitzgerald. Fitzgerald laughed quietly and continued his skillful work with the long knife.

In truth, Jim Bridger was nineteen that year, with a slight build that made him look younger still. The year of his birth, 1804, coincided with the launch of the Lewis and Clark expedition, and it was the excitement generated by their return that led Jim's father to venture west from Virginia in 1812.

The Bridger family settled on a small farm at Six-Mile-Prairie near St. Louis. For a boy of eight, the voyage west was a grand adventure of bumpy roads, hunting for supper, and sleeping beneath a canopy of open sky. In the new farm, Jim found a forty-acre playground of meadows, woods, and creeks. Their first week on the new property, Jim discovered a small spring. He remembered vividly his excitement as he led his father to the hidden seep, and his pride when they built the springhouse. Among many trades, Jim's father dabbled in surveying. Jim often tagged along, further fixing a taste for exploration.

Bridger's childhood ended abruptly at the age of thirteen, when his mother, father, and older brother all died of fever in the space of a single month. The boy found himself suddenly responsible for both himself and a younger sister. An elderly aunt came to tend for his sister, but the financial burden for the family fell upon Jim. He took a job with the owner of a ferry.

The Mississippi of Bridger's boyhood teemed with traffic. From the south, manufactured supplies moved upriver to the booming St. Louis, while downstream flowed the raw resources of the frontier. Bridger heard stories about the great city of New Orleans and the foreign ports beyond. He met the wild boatmen who pushed their craft upstream through sheer strength of body and will. He talked to teamsters who portaged products from Lexington and Terre Haute. He saw the future of the river in the form of belching steamboats, churning against the current.

Yet it wasn't the Mississippi River that captured Jim Bridger's imagination—it was the Missouri. A mere six miles from his ferry the two great rivers joined as one, the wild waters of the frontier pouring into the bromide current of the everyday. It was the confluence of old and new, known and unknown, civilization and wilderness. Bridger lived for the rare moments when the fur traders and voyageurs tied their sleek

Mackinaws at the ferry landing, sometimes even camping for the night. He marveled at their tales of savage Indians, teeming game, forever plains, and soaring mountains.

The frontier for Bridger became an aching presence that he could feel, but could not define, a magnetic force pulling him inexorably toward something that he had heard about, but never seen. A preacher on a swaybacked mule rode Bridger's ferry one day. He asked Bridger if he knew God's mission for him in life. Without pause Bridger answered, "Go to the Rockies." The preacher was elated, urging the boy to consider missionary work with the savages. Bridger had no interest in bringing Jesus to the Indians, but the conversation stuck with him. The boy came to believe that going west was more than just a fancy for someplace new. He came to see it as a part of his soul, a missing piece that could only be made whole on some far-off mountain or plain.

Against this backdrop of an imagined future, Bridger poled the sluggish ferry. To and fro, back and forth, motion without progression, never venturing so much as a mile beyond the fixed points of the two landings. It was the polar opposite of the life he imagined for himself, a life of wandering and exploration through country unknown, a life in which he never once retraced his steps.

After a year on the ferry, Bridger made a desperate and ill-thought effort to make some progress westward, apprenticing himself to a blacksmith in St. Louis. The blacksmith treated him well, and even provided a modest stipend to send to his sister and aunt. But the terms of apprenticeship were clear—five years of servitude.

If the new job did not put him in the wilderness, at least St. Louis talked of little else. For half a decade Bridger soaked in frontier lore. When the plainsmen came to shoe their horses or repair their traps, Bridger overcame his reserve to ask about their travels. Where had they been? What had they seen? The boy heard tales of a naked John Colter, outracing a hundred Blackfeet intent on taking his scalp. Like everyone in St. Louis, he came to know details of successful traders like Manuel Lisa and the Chouteau brothers. Most exciting to Bridger were occasional glimpses of his heroes in the flesh. Once a month, Captain Andrew Henry visited the blacksmith to shoe his horse. Bridger made sure to volunteer for the work, if only for the chance that he might exchange a few words with the captain. His brief encounters with Henry were like a reaffirmation of faith, a tangible manifestation of something that otherwise might exist only as fable and tale.

The term of Bridger's apprenticeship ran to his eighteenth birthday, on March 17, 1822. To coincide with the Ides of March, a local actors' brigade played a rendition of Shakespeare's *Julius Caesar.* Bridger paid two bits for a seat. The long play made little sense. The men looked silly in full-length gowns, and for a long time Bridger was unsure whether the actors were speaking English. He enjoyed the spectacle, though, and after a while began to develop a feel for the rhythm of the stilted language. A handsome actor with a bellowing voice spoke a line that would stick with Bridger for the rest of his life:

> *There is a tide in the affairs of men,*
> *Which, taken at the flood, leads on to fortune . . .*

Three days later, the blacksmith told Bridger about a notice in the *Missouri Republican:* "To Enterprising Young Men . . ." Bridger knew his tide had come in.

The next morning Bridger awoke to find Fitzgerald bent over Glass, his hand pressed against the forehead of the wounded man.

"What're you doing, Fitzgerald?"

"How long's he had this fever?"

Bridger moved quickly to Glass and felt his skin. It was steamy with heat and perspiration. "I checked him last night and he seemed all right."

"Well, he's not all right now. It's the death sweats. The son of a bitch is finally going under."

Bridger stood there, unsure whether to feel upset or relieved. Glass began to shiver and shake. There seemed little chance that Fitzgerald was wrong.

"Listen, boy—we got to be ready to move. I'm going to scout up the Grand. You take the berries and get that meat pounded into pemmican."

"What about Glass?"

"What about him, boy? You become a doctor while we've been camping here? There's nothing we can do now."

"We can do what we're supposed to be doing—wait with him and bury him when he dies. That was our deal with the captain."

"Scrape out a grave if it'll make you feel better! Hell, build him a goddamn altar! But if I come back here and that meat's not ready, I'll whip on you till you're worse off than him!" Fitzgerald grabbed his rifle and disappeared down the creek.

The day was typical of early September, sunny and crisp in the morning, hot by afternoon. The terrain flattened where the creek met the river, its trickling waters spreading wide across a sandbar before joining the rushing current of the Grand. Fitzgerald's eyes were drawn downward to the scattered tracks of the fur brigade, still apparent after four days. He glanced upriver, where an eagle perched like a sentry on the bare branch of a dead tree. Something startled the bird. It opened its wings, and with two powerful flaps lifted itself from its perch. Carving a neat pivot on the tip of its wing, the bird turned and flew upriver.

The screaming whinny of a horse cut the morning air. Fitzgerald spun around. The morning sun sat directly on the river, its piercing rays merging with water to form a dancing sea of light. Squinting against the glare, Fitzgerald could discern the silhouettes of mounted Indians. He dropped to the ground. *Did they see me?* He lay on the ground for an instant, his breath arriving in staccato spurts. He snaked toward the only cover available, a scrubby stand of willows. Listening intently, he heard again the whinny of the horse—but not the churning pound of charging horses. He checked to ensure his rifle and pistol were charged, removed his wolf-skin hat, and lifted his head to peer through the willows.

There were five Indians at a distance of about two hundred yards on the opposite bank of the Grand. Four of the riders formed a loose semicircle around the fifth, who quirted a balking pinto. Two of the Indians laughed, and all of them seemed transfixed by the struggle with the horse.

One of the Indians wore a full headdress of eagle feathers. Fitzgerald was close enough to see clearly a bear-claw necklace around his chest and the otter pelts that wrapped his braids. Three of the Indians carried guns; the other two bows. There was no war paint on the men or the horses, and Fitzgerald guessed they were hunting. He wasn't sure of the tribe, although his working assumption was that any Indians in the area would view the trappers with hostility. Fitzgerald calculated that they were just beyond rifle range. That would change quickly if they charged. If they came, he would have one shot with the rifle and one with the pistol. He might be able to reload his rifle once if the river slowed them down. *Three shots at five targets.* He didn't like the odds.

Belly to the ground, Fitzgerald wormed his way toward the cover of the higher willows near the creek. He crawled through the middle of the brigade's old tracks, cursing the markings that so clearly betrayed their position. He turned again when he reached the thicker willows, relieved that the Indians remained preoccupied with the stubborn pinto. Still, they would arrive at the confluence of the creek with the river in a matter of instants. They would notice the creek, and then they would notice the tracks. *The goddamn tracks!* Pointing like an arrow up the creek.

Fitzgerald worked his way from the willows to the pines. He pivoted to take one final look at the hunting party. The skittish pinto had settled, and all five Indians now continued up the river. *We have to leave now.* Fitzgerald ran up the creek the short distance to the camp.

Bridger was pounding venison against a stone when Fitzgerald burst into the clearing. "There's five bucks coming up the Grand!" Fitzgerald began wildly stuffing his few possessions into his pack. He looked up suddenly, his eyes focused in intensity and fear, then anger. "Move, boy! They'll be on our tracks any minute!"

Bridger stuffed meat into his parfleche. Next he threw his pack and possibles bag over his shoulders, then turned to grab his rifle, leaning against a tree next to Glass's Anstadt. *Glass.* The full implications of flight struck the boy like a sudden, sobering slap. He looked down at the wounded man.

For the first time that morning, Glass's eyes were open. As Bridger stared down, the eyes initially had the glassy, uncomprehending gaze of one awakening from deep sleep. The longer Glass stared, the more his eyes seemed to focus. Once focused, it was clear that the eyes stared back with complete lucidity, clear that Glass, like Bridger, had calculated the full meaning of the Indians on the river.

Every pore in Bridger's body seemed to pound with the intensity of the moment, yet to Bridger it seemed that Glass's eyes conveyed a serene calmness. *Understanding? Forgiveness? Or is that just what I want to believe?* As the boy stared at Glass, guilt seized him like clenched fangs. *What does Glass think? What will the captain think?*

"You sure they're coming up the creek?" Bridger's voice cracked as he said it. He hated the lack of control, the demonstrable weakness in a moment demanding strength.

"Do you want to stay and find out?" Fitzgerald moved to the fire, grabbing the remaining meat from the drying racks.

Bridger looked again at Glass. The wounded man worked his parched lips, struggling to form words through a throat rendered mute. "He's trying to say something." The boy knelt, struggling to understand. Glass slowly raised his hand and pointed a shaking finger. *He wants the Anstadt.* "He wants his rifle. He wants us to set him up with his rifle."

The boy felt the blunt pain of a forceful kick against his back and found himself lying facedown on the ground. He struggled to his hands and knees, looking up at Fitzgerald. The rage on Fitzgerald's face seemed to merge with the distorted features of the wolf-skin hat. "Move, goddamn you!"

Bridger scrambled to his feet, wide-eyed and startled. He watched as Fitzgerald walked to Glass, who lay on his back with his few possessions piled next to him: a possibles bag, a knife in a beaded scabbard, a hatchet, the Anstadt, and a powder horn.

Fitzgerald stooped to pick up Glass's possibles bag. He dug inside for the flint and steel, dropping them into the pocket on the front of his leather tunic. He grabbed the powder horn and slung it over his shoulder. The hatchet he tucked under his broad leather belt.

Bridger stared, uncomprehending. "What are you doing?"

Fitzgerald stooped again, picked up Glass's knife, and tossed it to Bridger. "Take that." Bridger caught it, staring in horror at the scabbard in his hand. Only the rifle remained. Fitzgerald picked it up, checking quickly to ensure it was charged. "Sorry, old Glass. You ain't got much more use for any of this."

Bridger was stunned. "We can't leave him without his kit."

The man in the wolf skin looked up briefly, then disappeared into the woods.

Bridger looked down at the knife in his hand. He looked at Glass, whose eyes glared directly into him, animated suddenly like coals beneath a bellows. Bridger felt paralyzed. Conflicting emotions fought inside of him, struggling to dictate his action, until one emotion came suddenly and overwhelmingly to prevail: He was afraid.

The boy turned and ran into the woods.

SEVEN

SEPTEMBER 2, 1823—MORNING

THERE WAS DAYLIGHT. Glass could tell that much without moving, but otherwise he had no idea of the time. He lay where he collapsed the day before. His rage had carried him to the edge of the clearing, but his fever stopped him there.

The bear had carved away at Glass from the outside and now the fever carved away from within. It felt to Glass as if he had been hollowed out. He shivered uncontrollably, yearning for the seeping warmth of a fire. Looking around the campsite, he saw that no smoke rose from the charred remains of the fire pits. No fire, no warmth.

He wondered if he could at least scoot back to his tattered blanket, and made a tentative effort to move. When he summoned his strength, the reply that issued back from his body was like a faint echo across a wide chasm.

The movement irritated something deep in his chest. He felt a cough coming on and tensed his stomach muscles to suppress it. The muscles were sore from numerous earlier battles, and despite his effort, the cough burst forth. Glass grimaced at the pain, like the extraction of a deep-set fishhook. It felt like his innards were being ripped out through his throat.

When the pain of coughing receded, he focused again on the blanket.

I have to get warm. It took all his strength to lift his head. The blanket lay about twenty feet away. He rolled from his side to his stomach, maneuvering his left arm out in front of his body. Glass bent his left leg, then straightened it to push. Between his one good arm and his one good leg, he push-dragged himself across the clearing. The twenty feet felt like twenty miles, and three times he stopped to rest. Each breath drew like a rasp through his throat, and he felt again the dull throbbing in his cleaved back. He stretched to grab the blanket when it came within reach. He pulled it around his shoulders, embracing the weighty warmth of the Hudson Bay wool. Then he passed out.

Through the long morning, Glass's body fought against the infection of his wounds. He slipped between consciousness, unconsciousness, and a confusing state in between, aware of his surroundings like random pages of a book, scattered glimpses of a story with no continuity to bind them. When conscious, he wished desperately to sleep again, if only to gain respite from the pain. Yet each interlude of sleep came with a haunting precursor—the terrifying thought that he might never wake again. *Is this what it's like to die?*

Glass had no idea how long he had been lying there when the snake appeared. He watched with a mixture of terror and fascination as it slid almost casually from the woods into the clearing. There was an element of caution; the snake paused on the open ground of the clearing, its tongue slithering in and out to test the air. On the whole, though, this was a predator in its element, in confident pursuit of prey. The snake began to move again, the slow serpentine motion accelerating suddenly to propel it with surprising speed. It went straight for him.

Glass wanted to roll away, but there was something inevitable about the way the snake moved. Some part of Glass remembered an admonishment to hold still in the presence of a snake. He froze, as much from hypnosis as from choice. The snake moved to within a few feet of his face and stopped. Glass stared, trying to mimic the serpent's unblinking stare. He was no match. The snake's black eyes were as unforgiving as the plague. He watched, mesmerized, as the snake wrapped itself slowly into a perfect coil, its entire body made for the sole purpose of launching forward in attack. The tongue moved in and out, testing, probing. From the midst of the coil, the snake's tail began quivering back and forth, the rattle like a metronome marking the brief moments before death. The first strike came so quickly that Glass had no time to recoil. He stared down in horror as the rattler's head shot forward, jaws distended to reveal fangs dripping with poison. The fangs sunk into Glass's forearm. He screamed in pain as the venom coursed into his body. He shook his arm but the fangs held on, the snake's body flailing with Glass's arm through the air. Finally the snake dropped, its long body perpendicular to Glass's torso. Before Glass could roll away, the snake rewound itself and struck again. Glass couldn't scream this time. The serpent had buried its fangs in his throat.

Glass opened his eyes. The sun stood directly above him, the only angle from which it could throw light onto the floor of the clearing. He rolled gingerly to his side to avoid the glare. Ten feet away, a six-foot rattlesnake lay fully extended. An hour before it had swallowed a cottontail kit. Now a large lump distorted the snake's proportions as the rabbit worked its way slowly down the serpent's digestive tract.

Panicked, Glass looked down at his arm. There were no fang marks.

Gingerly, he touched his neck, half expecting to find a serpent attached. Nothing. Relief flooded over him as he realized the snake—or at least the snake bites—were the imagined horror of a nightmare. He looked again at the snake, torpid, as its body worked to digest its prey.

He moved his hand from his throat to his face. He felt the thick coat of salty wetness from heavy sweat, yet his skin was cool. The fever had broken. *Water!* His body screamed at him to drink. He dragged himself to the spring. His shredded throat still permitted only the smallest of sips. Even these caused pain, although the icy water felt like tonic, replenishing and cleansing him from within.

———————

Hugh Glass's remarkable life began unremarkably as the firstborn son of Victoria and William Glass, an English bricklayer in Philadelphia. Philadelphia was growing rapidly at the turn of the century, and builders found no shortage of work. William Glass never became wealthy, but he comfortably supported five children. With a bricklayer's eye, William viewed his responsibility to his children as the laying of a foundation. He considered his provision for their formal education as the crowning achievement of his life.

When Hugh demonstrated considerable academic aptitude, William urged him to consider a career in the law. Hugh, though, had no interest in the white wigs and musty books of lawyers. He did have a passion— geography.

The Rawsthorne & Sons Shipping Company kept an office on the same street as the Glass family. In the foyer of their building they displayed a large globe, one of the few in Philadelphia. On his way home from school each day, Hugh stopped in the office, spinning the globe on its axis, his fingers exploring the oceans and mountains of the world. Colorful maps adorned the office walls, sketching the major shipping routes of the day. The thin lines traversed broad oceans, connecting Philadelphia to the great ports of the world. Hugh liked to imagine the places and people at the ends of those thin lines: from Boston to Barcelona, from Constantinople to Cathay.

Willing to allow his son some rein, William encouraged Hugh to consider a career in cartography. But to Hugh, the mere drawing of maps seemed too passive. The source of Hugh's fascination lay not in the abstract representation of places, but rather in the places themselves, and above all the vast masses marked terra incognita. The cartographers of the day populated these unknown spaces with etchings of the most fanciful and terrifying monsters. Hugh wondered if such beasts could truly exist, or if they were mere fabrications of the mapmaker's pen. He asked his father, who told him, "No one knows." His father's intent was to frighten Hugh toward more practical pursuits. The tactic failed. At the age of thirteen, Hugh announced his intention to become the captain of a ship.

In 1802, Hugh turned sixteen, and William, afraid the boy might run off to sea, relented to the wishes of his son. William knew the Dutch captain of a Rawsthorne & Sons frigate, and asked that Hugh be taken aboard as a cabin boy. The captain, Jozias van Aartzen, had no children of his own. He took his responsibility for Hugh seriously, and for a decade worked to school him in the ways of the sea. By the time the captain died in 1812, Hugh had risen to the rank of first mate.

The War of 1812 interrupted Rawsthorne & Sons' traditional trade with Great Britain. The company quickly diversified into a dangerous but lucrative new business—blockade running. Hugh spent the war years dodging British warships as his speedy frigate transported rum and sugar between the Caribbean and embattled American ports. When the war ended in 1815, Rawsthorne & Sons maintained its Caribbean business, and Hugh became the captain of a small freighter.

Hugh Glass had just turned thirty-one the summer he met Elizabeth van Aartzen, the nineteen-year-old niece of the captain who had mentored him. Rawsthorne & Sons sponsored a Fourth of July celebration, complete with line dancing and Cuban rum. The style of dance did not lend itself to conversation, but it did result in dozens of brief, twirling, thrilling exchanges. Glass sensed something unique about Elizabeth, something confident and challenging. He found himself taken completely.

He called on her the next day, then whenever he docked in Philadelphia. She was traveled and educated, talking easily of far-off peoples and places. They could speak an abbreviated language, each able to complete the other's thoughts. They laughed easily at each other's stories. Time away from Philadelphia became torture, as Glass remembered her eyes in the sparkle of the morning sun, her pale skin in the light of the moon on a sail.

On a bright May day in 1818, Glass returned to Philadelphia with a tiny velvet bag in the breast pocket of his uniform. Inside was a gleaming pearl on a delicate, golden chain. He gave it to Elizabeth and asked her to marry. They planned a wedding for the summer.

Glass left a week later for Cuba. He found himself stuck in the port of Havana, awaiting the resolution of a local dispute over the tardy delivery of a hundred barrels of rum. After a month in Havana, another Rawsthorne & Sons ship arrived. It carried a letter from his mother with the news that his father had died. She implored him to return to Philadelphia immediately.

Hugh knew that the dispute over the rum might well take months to resolve. In that time he could travel to Philadelphia, settle his father's estate, and return to Cuba. If the legal proceedings in Havana proceeded more quickly, his first mate could pilot the ship back to Philadelphia. Glass booked passage on *Bonita Morena,* a Spanish merchant bound that week for Baltimore.

As it turned out, the Spanish merchant would never sail past the ramparts of Fort McHenry. And Glass would never again see Philadelphia. A day's sail from Havana there appeared on the horizon a ship with no flag. *Bonita Morena*'s captain attempted to flee, but his sluggish boat was no match for the speedy pirate cutter. The cutter came abreast of the merchant and fired five cannons loaded with grape. With five of his sailors dead on the decks, the captain took down his sails.

The captain expected his surrender to result in quarter. It did not.

Twenty pirates boarded *Bonita Morena.* The leader, a mulatto with a golden tooth and a golden chain, approached the captain who was standing formally on the quarterdeck.

The mulatto pulled a pistol from his belt and shot the captain point-blank in the head. The crew and passengers stood shocked, awaiting their fates. Hugh Glass stood among them, looking at the buccaneers and their ship. They spoke a jumbled mix of Creole, French, and English. Glass suspected, correctly, that they were Baratarians—foot soldiers in the growing syndicate of the pirate Jean Lafitte.

Jean Lafitte had plagued the Caribbean for years before the War of 1812. The Americans paid little attention, since his targets were primarily British. In 1814, Lafitte discovered a sanctioned avenue for his hatred of England. Major-General Sir Edward Pakenham and six thousand veterans of Waterloo laid siege to New Orleans. In command of the American army, General Andrew Jackson found himself outnumbered five to one. When Lafitte offered the services of his Baratarians, Jackson did not ask for references. Lafitte and his men fought valiantly in the Battle of New Orleans. In the heady wake of the American victory, Jackson recommended a full pardon of Lafitte's earlier crimes, which President Madison quickly granted.

Lafitte had no intention of abandoning his chosen profession, but he had learned the value of sovereign sponsorship. Mexico was at war with Spain. Lafitte established a settlement he called Campeche on the island of Galveston and offered his services to Mexico City. The Mexicans commissioned Lafitte and his small navy, authorizing the attack of any Spanish ship. Lafitte, in turn, won a license to plunder.

The brutal reality of this arrangement now played out before Hugh Glass's eyes. When two crew members stepped forward to aid the mortally wounded captain, they too were shot. The three women onboard, including an ancient widow, were carried to the cutter, where a leering crew welcomed them aboard. While one band of pirates went belowdecks to inspect the cargo, another group began a more systematic appraisal of the crew and passengers. Two elderly men and one obese banker were stripped of their possessions and pushed into the sea.

The mulatto spoke Spanish as well as French. He stood before the captured crew, explaining their options. Any man willing to renounce Spain could join the service of Jean Lafitte. Any man unwilling could join their captain. The dozen remaining sailors chose Lafitte. Half were taken to the cutter, half left to join a pirate crew on the *Bonita Morena*.

Though Glass spoke barely a word of Spanish, he understood the gist of the mulatto's ultimatum. When the mulatto approached him, pistol in hand, Glass pointed to himself and said one word in French: *"Marin."* Sailor.

The mulatto stared at him in silent appraisal. An amused smirk appeared at the corner of his mouth, and he said, *"Ah bon? Okay, monsieur le marin, hissez le foc."* Hoist the jib.

Glass desperately rummaged the corners of his rudimentary French. He had no idea of the meaning of *hissez le foc.* In context though, he understood quite clearly the high stakes connected with passing the mulatto's test. Assuming that the challenge involved his bona fides as a sailor, he strode confidently to the fore of the ship, reaching for the jib line that would set the ship into the wind.

"Bien fait, monsieur le marin," said the mulatto. It was August of 1819.

Hugh Glass had become a pirate.

Glass looked again at the gap in the woods where Fitzgerald and Bridger had fled. His jaw set as he thought about what they had done, and he felt again the visceral desire to strike out in pursuit. This time though, he also felt the weakness of his body. For the first time since the bear attack, his mind was clear. With clarity came an alarming assessment of his situation.

It was with considerable trepidation that Glass began an examination of his wounds. He used his left hand to trace the edges of his scalp. He'd caught a blurry glimpse of his face in the pooled waters of the spring, and he could see that the bear had nearly scalped him. Never a vain man, his appearance struck him as particularly irrelevant in his current state of affairs. If he survived, he supposed that his scars might even afford him a certain measure of respect among his peers.

What did concern him was his throat. Unable to see the throat wound except in the watery reflection of the spring, he could only probe gingerly with his fingers. Bridger's poultice had fallen off in his short crawl the day before. Glass touched the sutures and appreciated Captain Henry's rudimentary surgical skills. He had a vague memory of the captain working over him in the moments after the attack, although the details and chronology remained murky.

By craning his neck downward he could see the claw marks that extended from his shoulder to his throat. The bear had raked deeply through the muscles of his chest and upper arm. Bridger's pine tar had sealed the wounds. They looked relatively healthy, though a sharp muscular pain kept him from lifting his right arm. The pine tar made him think of Bridger. He remembered that the boy had tended his wounds. Still, it wasn't the image of Bridger nursing him that stuck in his mind. Instead, he saw Bridger looking back from the edge of the clearing, the stolen knife in his hand.

He looked at the snake and thought, *God, what I'd give for my knife.* The rattler had yet to move. He suppressed further thoughts about Fitzgerald and Bridger. *Not now.*

Glass looked down at his right leg. Bridger's tar smeared the puncture wounds in his upper thigh. Those wounds also looked relatively healthy. Cautiously, he straightened the leg. It was stiff as a corpse. He tested the leg by rolling slightly to shift his weight, then pushing down. Excruciating pain radiated outward from the wounds. Clearly, the leg would bear no weight.

Last of all, Glass used his left arm to explore the deep slashes on his back. His probing fingers counted the five parallel cuts. He touched the sticky mess of pine tar, suture, and scab. When he looked at his hand, there was fresh blood too. The cuts began on his butt and got deeper as they rose up his back. The deepest part of the wounds lay between his shoulder blades, where his hand could not reach.

Having completed his self-examination, Glass arrived at several dispassionate conclusions: He was defenseless. If Indians or animals discovered him, he could muster no resistance. He could not stay in the clearing. He wasn't sure how many days he had been in the camp, but he knew that the sheltered spring must be well known to any Indians in the area. Glass had no idea why he had not been discovered the day before, but he knew his luck could not last much longer.

Despite the risk of Indians, Glass had no intention of veering from the Grand. It was a known source for water, food, and orientation. There was, however, one critical question: Upstream or down? As much as Glass might want to embark in immediate pursuit of his betrayers, he knew that to do so would be folly. He was alone with no weapons in hostile country. He was weak from fever and hunger. He couldn't walk.

It pained him to consider retreat, even temporary retreat, but Glass knew there was no real option. The trading post of Fort Brazeau lay 350 miles downstream at the confluence of the White River and the Missouri. If he could make it there, he could reprovision himself, then begin his pursuit in earnest.

Three hundred and fifty miles. A healthy man in good weather could cover that ground in two weeks. *How far can I crawl in a day?* He had no idea, but he did not intend to sit in one place. His arm and leg did not appear inflamed, and Glass assumed they would mend with time. He would crawl until his body could support a crutch. If he only made three miles a day, so be it. Better to have those three miles behind him than ahead. Besides, moving would increase his odds of finding food.

The mulatto and his captured Spanish ship sailed west for Galveston Bay and Lafitte's pirate colony at Campeche. They attacked another Spanish merchantman a hundred miles south of New Orleans, luring their prey into cannon range under the guise of the *Bonita Morena*'s Spanish flag. Once aboard this newest victim, the *Castellana,* the buccaneers again conducted their brutal triage. This time the urgency was greater, since the cannon barrage had ripped open the *Castellana* below the waterline. She was sinking.

The pirates' luck ran flush. The *Castellana* was bound from Seville to New Orleans with a cargo of small arms. If they could remove the guns from the ship before it sank, they would turn an enormous profit. Lafitte would be pleased.

The settlement of Texas had begun in earnest by 1819, and Jean Lafitte's pirate enclave on Galveston Island worked diligently to supply it. Towns sprouted from the Rio Grande to the Sabine, and all of them needed provisions. Lafitte's particular method of obtaining his wares cut out the middleman. In fact, it cut up the middleman. With this competitive advantage over more conventional traders, Campeche thrived, becoming a magnet for all manner of smugglers, slavers, picaroons, and anyone else seeking a tolerant environment for illicit trade. The ambiguous status of Texas helped to shelter the Campeche pirates from intervention by outside powers. Mexico benefited from the attacks on Spanish ships, and Spain was too weak to challenge them. For a while, the United States was willing to look the other way. After all, Lafitte left American ships alone, and he was a hero of the Battle of New Orleans to boot.

Though not physically shackled, Hugh Glass found himself thoroughly imprisoned by Jean Lafitte's criminal enterprise. Onboard ship, any form of mutiny would result in his death. His participation in various attacks on Spanish merchantmen left no doubt about the pirates' perspective on dissent. Glass managed to avoid spilling blood by his own hand; his other actions he justified by the doctrine of necessity.

Nor did Glass's time ashore in Campeche offer any reasonable opportunity for escape. Lafitte reigned supreme on the island. Across the bay on the Texas mainland, the dominant inhabitants were the Karankawa Indians, notorious for cannibalism. Beyond the territory of the Karankawa lay the Tonkawas, the Comanches, the Kiowas, and the Osage. None were hospitable to whites, though they were less inclined to eat them. The scattered pockets of civilization still included a large number of Spaniards, likely to hang as a pirate anyone who walked up from the coast. Mexican banditos and vigilante Texicans added final spice to the mainland mix.

Ultimately, there were limits on the civilized world's willingness to tolerate a thriving pirate state. Most significantly, the United States decided to improve its relations with Spain. This diplomatic endeavor was made more difficult by the constant harassment of Spanish ships, often in U.S. territorial waters. In November 1820, President Madison sent Lieutenant Larry Kearney, the *USS Enterprise,* and a fleet of American warships to Campeche. Lieutenant Kearney presented Lafitte with a succinct choice: Leave the island or be blown to pieces.

Jean Lafitte may have been a swashbuckler, but he was also a pragmatist. He loaded his ships with as much plunder as could be carried, set Campeche ablaze, and sailed away with his buccaneer fleet, never again to be glimpsed by history.

Hugh Glass stood in the chaotic streets of Campeche that November night and made an abrupt decision about the course of his future. He had no intention of joining the fleeing band of pirates. Glass had come to view the sea, which he once embraced as synonymous with freedom, as no more than the confining parameters of small ships. He resolved to turn a new direction.

The crimson glow of fire cast Campeche's last night in apocalyptic splendor. Men swarmed through the scattered buildings, grabbing for anything of value. Liquor, never in short supply on the island, flowed with particular abandon. Disputes over plunder found quick resolution through gunfire, filling the town with the staccato explosions of small arms. Wild rumors spread that the American fleet was about to shell the town. Men fought wildly to clamber aboard departing ships, whose crews used swords and pistols to fight off unwanted passengers.

As Glass wondered where to go, he ran headlong into a man named Alexander Greenstock. Like Glass, Greenstock was a prisoner, impressed into duty when his ship had been captured. Glass had served with him on a recent foray into the Gulf. "I know about a skiff on the South Shore," said Greenstock. "I'm taking it to the mainland." Among the contending poor options, the risks on the mainland seemed least bad. Glass and Greenstock picked their way through the town. Before them on a narrow road, three heavily armed men sat atop a horse-drawn cart, stacked precariously with barrels and crates. One man whipped the horse, while two others stood guard from the top of their loot. The cart hit a stone and a crate tumbled to the ground with a crash. The men ignored it, racing to catch their ship.

The top of the crate read "Kutztown, Pennsylvania." Inside were newly crafted rifles from the gunsmith shop of Joseph Anstadt. Glass and Greenstock each grabbed a gun, incredulous at their luck. They scavenged through the few buildings that hadn't been reduced to ashes, eventually finding ball, powder, and a few trinkets for trading.

It took them most of the night to row around the east end of the island and across Galveston Bay. The water caught the dancing light from the burning colony, making it appear as if the whole bay was ablaze. They could see clearly the hulking profiles of the American fleet and the fleeing ships of Lafitte. When they were a hundred yards from the mainland shore, a great explosion erupted from the island. Glass and Greenstock looked back to see mushrooming flames bellow forth from Maison Rouge, the residence and armory of Jean Lafitte. They rowed across the final few yards of the bay and jumped into the shallow surf. Glass waded ashore, leaving the sea behind him forever.

With no plan or destination, the two men picked their way slowly down the Texas coast. They set their course based more on that which they sought to avoid than on that which they sought to find. They worried constantly about the Karankawa. On the beach they felt exposed, but thick cane jungles and swampy bayous discouraged turning inland. They worried about Spanish troops and they worried about the American fleet.

After walking seven days, the tiny outpost of Nacogdoches appeared in the distance. News of the American raid on Campeche no doubt had spread. They guessed that the locals would view anyone approaching from Galveston as a runaway pirate, likely to be hanged on sight. Glass knew that Nacogdoches was the trailhead for the Spanish enclave of San Fernando de Bexar. They decided to avoid the village and cut inland. Away from the coast, they hoped, there would be less awareness of the events at Campeche.

Their hopes were misguided. They arrived at San Fernando de Bexar after six days and were promptly arrested by the Spanish. After a week in a stifling jail cell, the two men were brought before Major Juan Palacio del Valle Lersundi, the local magistrate.

Major Palacio gazed at them wearily. He was a disillusioned soldier, a would-be conquistador who instead found himself the administrator of a dusty backwater at the tail end of a war that he knew Spain would lose. As Major Palacio looked at the two men before him, he knew that the safest course would be to order them hanged. Wandering up from the coast with only their rifles and the clothes on their backs, he assumed they were pirates or spies, although both claimed to have been captured by Lafitte while traveling on Spanish ships.

But Major Palacio was not in a hanging mood. The week before, he had sentenced to death a young Spanish soldier for falling asleep while on sentry duty, the proscribed punishment for the infraction. The hanging had left him deeply depressed, and he had spent the better part of the past week in confession with the local *padre*. He stared at the two prisoners and listened to their story. Was it the truth? How could he know for sure, and not knowing, by what authority could he take their lives?

Major Palacio offered Glass and Greenstock a deal. They were free to leave San Fernando de Bexar on one condition—that they traveled north. If they traveled south, Palacio feared that other Spanish troops would pick them up. The last thing he needed was a reprimand for pardoning pirates.

The men knew little about Texas, but Glass found himself suddenly exhilarated, about to embark without compass into the interior of the continent.

And so they made their way north and east, assuming at some point they would collide with the great Mississippi. In more than a thousand miles of wandering, Glass and Greenstock managed to survive on the open plain of Texas. Game was plentiful, including thousands of wild cattle, so food was rarely a problem. The danger came from successive territories of hostile Indians. Having survived their traipse through the territory of the Karankawa, they succeeded in avoiding the Comanches, the Kiowas, the Tonkawas, and the Osage.

Their luck ran out on the banks of the Arkansas River. They had just shot a buffalo calf and were preparing to butcher it. Twenty mounted Loup Pawnees heard the shot and came thundering over the crest of a rolling butte. The treeless plain offered no cover, not even rocks. Without horses, they stood no chance. Foolishly, Greenstock raised his weapon and fired, shooting the horse from one of the charging braves. An instant later he lay dead, three arrows protruding from his chest. A single arrow struck Glass in the thigh.

Glass didn't even raise his rifle, staring in detached fascination as nineteen horses barreled toward him. He saw the flash of paint on the chest of the lead horse and black hair against the blue sky, but he barely felt the round stone of the coup stick that crashed against his skull.

Glass awoke in the Pawnee village. His head throbbed and he was tied at the neck to a post driven into the ground. They had bound his wrists and ankles, though he could move his hands. A crowd of children stood around him, chattering excitedly when he opened his eyes.

An ancient chief with stiffly spiked hair approached him, staring down at the strange man before him, one of the few white men he had ever seen. The chief, named Kicking Bull, said something that Glass could not understand, though the assembled Pawnee began whooping and howling in obvious delight. Glass lay on the edge of a great circle in the middle of the village. As his blurry vision began to focus, he noticed a carefully prepared pyre in the center of the circle and quickly surmised the source of the Pawnee glee. An old woman yelled at the children. They ran off as the Pawnee dispersed to prepare for the ceremonial conflagration.

Glass was left alone to assess his situation. Twin images of the camp floated before his eyes, merging only if he squinted or closed one eye. Looking down at his leg, he saw that the Pawnee had done him the favor of plucking out the arrow. It had not penetrated deeply, but the wound would certainly slow him down if he tried to flee. In short, he could barely see and he could barely walk, let alone run.

He patted the pocket in the front of his shirt, relieved that a small container of cinnabar paint had not fallen out. The cinnabar was one of the few trading goods he had grabbed in his escape from Campeche. Rolling to his side to conceal his actions, he pulled out the container, opened it, and spit into the powder, mixing it with his finger. Next he spread the paint on his face, careful to cover every inch of exposed skin from his forehead to the top of his shirt. He also smeared a large quantity of the thick paint into the palm of his hand. He recapped the small jar and buried it in the sandy soil beneath him. Finally finished, he rolled onto his stomach, resting his head on the crook of his arm so that his face remained hidden.

He stayed in that position until they came for him, listening to the excited preparations for his execution. Night fell, though an enormous fire illuminated the circle in the center of the Pawnee camp.

Glass was never really sure whether he intended his act as some type of symbolic final gesture, or whether he actually hoped for the effect which in fact occurred. He had heard that most savages were superstitious. In any event, the effect was dramatic, and, as it turned out, saved his life.

Two Pawnee braves and Chief Kicking Bull came to carry him to the pyre. When they found him, facedown, they read it as a sign of fear. Kicking Bull cut the bindings to the post, while the two braves each reached for a shoulder to pull him upright. Ignoring the pain in his thigh, Glass sprang to his feet, facing the chief, the braves, and the assembled tribe.

The collected Pawnee tribe stood in front of him, openmouthed in shock. Glass's entire face was blood red, as if his skin had been stripped away. The whites of his eyes caught the light of the fire and shone like a fall moon. Most of the Indians had never seen a white man, so his full beard added to the impression of a demonic animal. Glass slapped one of the braves with his open hand, leaving a vermillion hand print etched on his chest. The tribe let out a collective gasp.

For a long moment there was complete silence. Glass stared at the Pawnee and the stunned Pawnee stared back. Somewhat surprised at the success of his tactic, Glass wondered what he should do next. He panicked at the thought that one of the Indians might suddenly regain his composure. Glass decided to begin shouting, and unable to think of anything else to say, he launched into a screaming recitation of the Lord's Prayer: "Our Father, Who art in Heaven, hallowed be Thy Name . . ."

Chief Kicking Bull stared in complete confusion. He had seen a few whites before, but this man appeared to be some type of medicine man or devil. Now the man's strange chant appeared to be putting the entire tribe under some type of spell.

Glass ranted on: "For Thine is the Kingdom, and the Power, and the Glory, forever. Amen."

Finally the white man stopped yelling. He stood there, panting like a spent horse. Chief Kicking Bull looked around him. His people looked back and forth between the chief and the crazy devil man. Chief Kicking Bull could feel the tribe's blame. What had he brought upon them? It was time for a new course of action.

He walked slowly up to Glass, stopping directly in front of him. The chief reached around his neck, removing a necklace from which dangled a pair of hawk's feet. He placed the necklace around Glass's neck, staring questioningly into the devil man's eyes.

Glass looked into the circle before him. At its center, near the pyre, stood a row of four-low chairs made from woven willows. Clearly, these were the front-row seats to the spectacle that was to have been his ritual burning. He limped to one of the seats and sat down. Chief Kicking Bull said something, and two women scrambled to fetch food and water. Then he said something to the brave with the vermillion hand print on his chest. The brave darted off, returning with the Anstadt, which he placed on the ground next to Glass.

Glass spent almost a year with the Loup Pawnee on the plains between the Arkansas and Platte Rivers. After overcoming his initial reti-
cence, Kicking Bull adopted the white man like a son. What Glass had
not learned about wilderness survival in his trek from Campeche, he
learned from the Pawnee that year.

By 1821, scattered white men had begun to travel the plains between
the Platte and the Arkansas. In the summer of that year, Glass was hunting with a party of ten Pawnee when they came across two white men
with a wagon. Telling his Pawnee friends to stay behind, Glass rode
slowly forward. The men were federal agents dispatched by William
Clark, United States Superintendent of Indian Affairs. Clark invited
the chiefs of all the surrounding tribes to St. Louis. To demonstrate the
government's good faith, the wagon was loaded with gifts—blankets,
sewing needles, knives, cast iron pots.

Three weeks later, Glass arrived in St. Louis in the company of Kicking Bull.

St. Louis lay at the frontier of the two forces tugging at Glass. From
the east he felt anew the powerful pull of his ties to the civilized world—to
Elizabeth and to his family, to his profession and to his past. From the
west he felt the tantalizing lure of terra incognita, of freedom unmatched,
of fresh beginnings. Glass posted three letters to Philadelphia: to Elizabeth, to his mother, and to Rawsthorne & Sons. He took a clerical job
with the Mississippi Shipping Company and waited for replies.

It took more than six months. In early March 1822, a letter arrived
from his brother. Their mother had died, he wrote, following their
father after barely a month.

There was more. "It is also my sad duty to tell you that your dear
Elizabeth has died. She contracted a fever last January, and, though she
struggled, she did not recover." Glass collapsed into a chair. The blood
drained from his face and he wondered if he would be sick. He read
on: "I hope it will give you comfort to know that she was laid to rest
near Mother. You should also know that her fidelity to you never wa-
vered, even when we all believed that you had perished."

On March 20th, Glass arrived at the offices of the Mississippi Shipping Company to find a group of men huddled around an advertisement in the *Missouri Republican*. William Ashley was raising a fur brigade, bound for the upper Missouri.

A week later, a letter arrived from Rawsthorne & Sons, offering Glass a new commission as the captain of a cutter on the Philadelphia to Liverpool run. On the evening of April 14th, he read the offer one last time, then threw it on the fire, watching as the flames devoured this last tangible link to his former life.

The next morning, Hugh Glass embarked with Captain Henry and the men of the Rocky Mountain Fur Company. At thirty-six, Glass no longer considered himself a young man. And unlike young men, Glass did not consider himself as someone with nothing to lose. His decision to go west was not rash or forced, but as fully deliberate as any choice in his life. At the same time, he could not explain or articulate his reasons. It was something that he felt more than understood.

In a letter to his brother he wrote, "I am drawn to this endeavor as I have never before been drawn to anything in my life. I am sure that I am right to do this, though I cannot tell you precisely why."

EIGHT

GLASS TOOK ANOTHER LONG LOOK at the rattlesnake, still lying torpid in the all-consuming state of digesting its prey. The snake hadn't moved an inch since Glass had been conscious. *Food.* His thirst quenched at the seeping spring, Glass became suddenly aware of a profound and gnawing hunger. He had no idea how long it had been since he had eaten, but his hands trembled from the lack of subsistence. When he lifted his head, the clearing spun a slow circle around him.

Glass crawled cautiously toward the snake, the imagery of his horrific dream still vivid. He moved to within six feet, stopping to pick up a walnut-size rock. With his left hand, he rolled the rock, which skipped toward the snake, bumping its body. The snake didn't move. Glass picked up a fist-size rock and crawled within reach. Too late, the snake made a sluggish move toward cover. Glass smashed the rock on its head, beating the serpent repeatedly until he was certain it was dead.

Having killed the rattlesnake, Glass's next challenge was to gut it out.

He looked around the camp. His possibles bag lay near the edge of the clearing. He crawled to it, emptying its remaining contents on the ground: a few rifle patches, a razor, two hawk's feet on a beaded necklace, and the six-inch claw of a grizzly bear. Glass picked up the claw, fixating on the thick coat of dried blood at its tip. He returned it to the bag, wondering how it got there. He picked up the patches, thinking that he might use them for tinder, bitter anew that they would not serve their intended purpose. The razor was the one true find. Its blade was too fragile to make of a weapon, but it could serve a number of useful purposes. Most immediately, he could use it to skin the snake. He dropped the razor into the possibles bag, slung the bag over his shoulder, and crawled back to the snake.

Already flies buzzed around the snake's bloody head. Glass was more respectful. He had once seen a severed snake head implant itself on the nose of a fatally curious dog. Remembering the unfortunate dog, he laid a long stick across the snake's head and pressed down on it with his left leg. He couldn't lift his right arm without setting off intense pain in his shoulder, but the hand functioned normally. He used it to work the razor, sawing the blade to sever the head. He used the stick to flip the head toward the edge of the clearing.

He sliced down the belly beginning at the neck. The razor dulled quickly, reducing its effectiveness with each inch. He managed to cut the length of the snake, nearly five feet to the vent. With the snake laid open he pulled out the entrails, throwing them aside. Beginning again at the neck, he used the razor to peel the scaly skin away from the muscle. The meat now glistened before him, irresistible in the face of his hunger.

He bit into the snake, ripping into the raw flesh as if it were an ear of corn. Finally a piece tore free. He gnawed at the springy meat, though his teeth did little to break it down. Oblivious to anything but his hunger, he made the mistake of swallowing. The large chunk of raw meat felt like a stone as it passed through his wounded throat. The pain made him gag. He coughed, and for an instant he thought the chunk of meat might choke him. Finally it passed down his gullet.

He learned his lesson. He spent the rest of the daylight hours carving small bits of meat with the razor, pounding them between two rocks to break down the fibrous flesh, and then mixing each bite with a mouthful of spring water. It was an arduous way to eat, and Glass still felt hungry when he reached the tail. It was worrisome, since he doubted that his next meal would be delivered to him so easily.

In the last moments of daylight he examined the rattles at the tip of the tail. There were ten, one added in each year of the snake's life. Glass had never seen a snake with ten rattles. *A long time, ten years.* Glass thought about the snake, surviving, thriving for a decade on the strength of its brutal attributes. And then a single mistake, a moment of exposure in an environment without tolerance, dead and devoured almost before its blood ceased to pump. He cut the rattles from the remains of the snake and fingered them like a rosary. After a while he dropped them into his possibles bag. When he looked at them, he wanted to remember.

It was dark. Glass pulled his blanket around him, hunched his back, and fell asleep.

He awoke thirsty and hungry from a fitful sleep. Every wound ached. *Three hundred and fifty miles to Fort Kiowa.* He knew he couldn't allow himself to think about it, not in its totality. *A mile at a time.* He set the Grand as his first goal. He'd been unconscious when the brigade veered off the main river up the spring creek, but from Bridger and Fitzgerald's discussions he assumed it lay near.

Glass pulled the Hudson Bay blanket from his shoulders. With the razor, he cut three long strips from the wool cloth. He wrapped the first around his left knee—his good knee. He would need a pad if he was going to crawl. The other two strips he wrapped around his palms, leaving the fingers free. He rolled up the rest of the blanket and looped the long strap of the possibles bag around both ends. He checked to make sure the bag was tied firmly shut, then situated the bag and blanket across his back. The strap he wore around both shoulders, leaving his hands free.

Glass took a long drink from the creek and began to crawl. Actually, it wasn't a crawl so much as a scooting sort of drag. He could use his right arm for balance, but it would not support his weight. His right leg he could only string along behind him. He had worked to loosen the muscles by bending and straightening the leg, but it remained as rigid as a flagpole.

He fell into the best rhythm he could manage. With his right hand as a sort of outrigger, he kept his weight on his left side, leaning forward on his left arm, pulling up his left knee, then dragging his stiff right leg behind him. Over and over, yard after yard. He stopped several times to adjust the blanket and the possibles bag. His hurky-jerk motion kept loosening the ties of his pack. Eventually he found the right series of knots to keep the bundle in place.

For a while the wool strips on his knee and palms worked fairly well, though they required frequent adjustment. He had failed to consider the effect of dragging his right leg. His moccasin provided protection to the lower part of his foot, but did not cover his ankle. Within a hundred yards he had developed an abrasion, and stopped to cut a strip of blanket for the area in contact with the ground.

It took him almost two hours to crawl down the creek to the Grand.

By the time he arrived at the river, his legs and arms ached from the awkward, unaccustomed motion. He stared down at the old tracks of the brigade and wondered by what providence the Indians had not seen them.

Though he would never see it, the explanation lay clearly on the opposite bank. Had he crossed the river, he would have found the enormous prints of a bear spread throughout a patch of serviceberries. Just as clear were the tracks of the five Indian ponies. In an irony that Glass would never appreciate, it was a grizzly bear that saved him from the Indians. Like Fitzgerald, the bear had discovered the berry patch near the Grand. The animal was gorging itself when the five Arikara warriors rode up the river. In fact it was the scent of the bear that had made the pinto skittish. Confused by the sight and smell of five mounted Indians, the bear lumbered into the brush. The hunters charged after it, never to notice the tracks on the opposite bank.

Once Glass emerged from the protective shelter of the pines, the horizon broadened in a landscape broken only by rolling buttes and scattered clumps of cottonwoods. Thick willows along the river impeded his ability to crawl forward, but did little to block the penetrating heat of the late morning sun. He felt the rivulets of sweat across his back and chest and the sting of salt when it seeped into his wounds. He took one last drink from the cool spring creek. He gazed upriver between swallows, giving one last consideration to the idea of direct pursuit. *Not yet.*

The frustrating necessity of delay was like water on the hot iron of his determination—hardening it, making it unmalleable. He vowed to survive, if for no other reason than to visit vengeance on the men who betrayed him.

Glass crawled for three more hours that day. He guessed he had covered two miles. The Grand's banks varied, with alternating stretches of sand, grass, and rock. Had he been able to stand, there were frequent stretches of shallow water, and Glass could have crossed the river frequently to take advantage of the easiest terrain.

But crossing was not an option for Glass, whose crawling relegated him to the north bank. The rocks created particular difficulty. By the time he stopped, the woolen pads were in tatters. The wool succeeded in keeping abrasions from forming, but it could not stop the bruising. His knee and his palms were black-and-blue, tender to the touch. The muscle in his left arm began to cramp, and once again he felt the quivering weakness from a lack of food. As he anticipated, no easy source of meat fell into his path. For the time being, his subsistence would have to come from plants.

From his time with the Pawnee, Glass possessed a broad familiarity with the plants of the plains. Cattails grew in plentiful clumps wherever the terrain flattened to create marshy backwaters, their furry brown heads capping slender green stalks as high as four feet. Glass used a stave to dig up the root stalks, peeled away the outer skin, and ate the tender shoots. While cattails grew thickly in the marsh, so too did mosquitoes. They buzzed incessantly around the exposed skin on his head, neck, and arms. He ignored them for a while as he dug hungrily among the cat-tails. Eventually, he gnawed the edge off his hunger, or at least fed his hunger sufficiently that he worried more about the stinging bites of the mosquitoes. He crawled another hundred yards down the river. There was no escaping the mosquitoes at that hour, but their numbers diminished away from the stagnant water of the marsh.

For three days he crawled down the Grand River. Cattails contin-ued to be plentiful, and Glass found a variety of other plants that he knew to be edible—onions, dandelions, even willow leaves. Twice he happened upon berries, stopping each time to gorge himself, picking until his fingers were purple from the juice.

Yet he did not find what his body craved. It had been twelve days since the attack by the grizzly. Before he was abandoned, Glass had swal-lowed a few sips of broth on a couple occasions. Otherwise, the rattler had been his only real food. Berries and roots might sustain him for a few days. To heal, though, to regain his feet, Glass knew he needed the rich nourishment that only meat could provide. The snake had been a bit of random luck, unlikely to be repeated.

Still, he thought, there was no luck at all in standing still. The next morning he would crawl forward again. If luck wouldn't find him, he would do his best to make his own.

NINE

SEPTEMBER 8, 1823

HE SMELLED THE BUFFALO CARCASS before he saw it. He heard it too. Or at least he heard the clouds of flies that swirled around the heaping mass of hide and bone. Sinews held the skeleton mostly intact, although scavengers had picked it clean of any meat. The massive, bushy head and swooping black horns lent the animal its only measure of dignity, though this too had been undermined by the birds that had picked away the eyes.

Looking at the beast, Glass felt no revulsion, only disappointment that others had beaten him to this potential source of nourishment. A variety of tracks surrounded the area. Glass guessed that the carcass was four or five days old. He stared at the pile of bones. For an instant he imagined his own skeleton—scattered across the bleak ground on some forgotten corner of prairie, his flesh eaten away, carrion for the magpies and coyotes. He thought about a line from Scripture, "dust to dust." *Is this what it means?*

His thoughts turned quickly to more practical considerations. He had seen starving Indians boil hides into a gluey, edible mass. He would willingly have attempted the same, except he had no vessel to contain boiling water. He had another thought. The carcass lay next to a head-sized rock. He picked it up with his left hand and threw it clumsily against the line of smaller ribs. One of the bones snapped, and Glass reached for one of the pieces. The marrow he sought was dry. *I need a thicker bone.*

One of the buffalo's forelegs lay apart from the rest, bare bone down to the hoof. He laid it against a flat stone and began to beat on it with the other rock. Finally a crack appeared, and then the bone broke.

He was right—the thicker bone still contained the greenish marrow. In hindsight, he should have known not to eat it by the smell, but his hunger robbed him of reason. He ignored the bitter taste, sucking the liquid from the bone, then digging for more with the piece of broken rib. *Better to take the risk than to die of starvation.* At least the marrow was easy to swallow. Frenzied by the idea of food, by the very mechanics of eating, he spent the better part of an hour breaking bones and scraping their contents.

About then the first cramp hit. It began as a hollow aching deep inside his bowels. He felt suddenly incapable of supporting his own weight and rolled to his side. The pressure in his head became so intense that Glass was aware of the very fissures in his skull. He began to sweat profusely. Like sunlight through glass, the pain in his abdomen became quickly more focused, burning. Nausea rose in his stomach like a great and inevitable tide. He began to retch, the indignity of the convulsions secondary to the excruciating pain as the bile passed his wounded throat.

For two hours he lay there. His stomach emptied quickly but did not cease to convulse. Between bouts of retching he was perfectly still, as if through lack of motion he could hide from the sickness and pain.

When the first round of sickness was over, he crawled away from the carcass, eager now to escape the sickeningly sweet smell. The motion reignited both the pain in his head and the nausea in his stomach. Thirty yards from the buffalo he crawled into a thick stand of willows, curled onto his side, and lapsed into a state that resembled unconsciousness more than sleep.

For a day and a night his body purged itself of the rancid marrow. The focused pain of his wounds from the grizzly now combined with a diffuse and permeating weakness. Glass came to visualize his strength as the sand in an hourglass. Minute by minute he felt his vitality ebbing away. Like an hourglass, he knew, a moment would arrive when the last grain of sand would tumble down the aperture, leaving the upper chamber void.

He could not shake the image of the buffalo skeleton, of the mighty beast, stripped of its flesh, rotting away on the prairie.

On the morning of the second day after the buffalo, Glass awoke hungry, ravenously hungry. He took it as a sign that the poison had passed from his system. He had tried to continue his laborious crawl downriver, in part because he still hoped to stumble across some other source of food, but more because he sensed the significance of stopping. In two days, he estimated that he had covered no more than a quarter mile. Glass knew that the sickness had cost him more than time and distance. It had sapped him of strength, eaten away at whatever tiny reservoir remained to him.

Without meat in the next few days, Glass assumed that he would die.

His experience with the buffalo carcass and its aftermath would keep him away from anything not freshly killed, no matter how desperate he grew. His first thought was to make a spear, or to kill a cottontail with a stone. But the pain in his right shoulder kept him from raising his arm, let alone thrusting it hard enough to generate a lethal throw. With his left hand, he lacked the accuracy to hit anything.

So hunting was out. That left trapping. With cordage and a knife to carve triggers, Glass knew a variety of ways to trap small game with snares. Lacking even those basics, he decided to try deadfalls. A deadfall was a simple device—a large rock leaning precariously on a stick, rigged to collapse when some unwary prey tripped a trigger.

The willows along the Grand were zigzagged with game trails. Tracks dotted the moist sand near the river. In the tall grass he saw the swirling depressions where deer had bedded down for the night. Glass considered it unlikely that he could trap a deer with a deadfall. For one thing, he doubted he could hoist a rock or tree of sufficient heft. He decided to set his sights on rabbits, which he encountered continuously along the river.

Glass looked for trails near the thick cover preferred by rabbits. He found a cottonwood downed recently by beaver, its leaf-covered branches creating a giant web of obstacles and hiding places. The trails leading to and from the tree were littered with pea-sized scat.

Near the river Glass found three suitable stones: flat enough to provide a broad surface for crushing when the trap was tripped; heavy enough to provide lethal force. The stones he selected were the size of a powder keg and weighed about thirty pounds each. With his crippled arm and leg, it took nearly an hour to push them, one by one, up the bank to the tree.

Next Glass searched for the three sticks he needed to support the deadfalls. The downed cottonwood provided an array of choices. He selected three branches about an inch in diameter and broke them off at a span about the length of his arm. Next he broke the three sticks in two. Snapping the first stick sent a jarring pain through his shoulder and back, so the next two he leaned against the cottonwood and broke with one of his rocks.

When he was finished he had a stick, broken in two, for each trap. Reassembled at the break, the broken stick would support, albeit precariously, the weight of the leaning rock. Where the two pieces of the support stick came together, Glass would wedge a baited trigger stick. When the trigger stick was bumped or tugged, the support stick would collapse like a buckling knee, dropping the lethal weight on the unsuspecting target.

For the trigger sticks, Glass selected three slender willows, cut to a length of about sixteen inches. He had noticed dandelion leaves near the river, and he gathered a large handful to bait the traps, jabbing a number of the tender leaves on each trigger stick.

A narrow trail covered with droppings led into the thickest part of the downed cottonwood. Glass selected this location for the first dead-fall and began to assemble the components.

The difficulty with a deadfall lay in striking a balance between stability and fragility. Stability kept the trap from collapsing on its own, though too much would prevent it from collapsing at all; fragility allowed the trap to collapse easily when tripped by its prey, though too much would cause it to collapse on its own. Striking this balance required strength and coordination, and Glass's wounds robbed him of both. His right arm could not support the weight of the rock, so he perched it clumsily against his right leg. Meanwhile, he struggled with his left hand to hold the two pieces of the support stick with the trigger stick wedged in between. Again and again the entire structure collapsed. Twice he decided that he had set the trap too firmly, and knocked it down himself.

After nearly an hour, he finally struck a proper balance point. He found two more suitable locations on the trails near the cottonwood and set the other deadfalls, then retreated away from the cottonwood toward the river.

Glass found a sheltered spot against a cut bank. When he could no longer stand the pangs of hunger, he ate the bitter roots from the dandelions he had plucked for the traps. He drank from the river to wash the taste from his mouth and lay down to sleep. Rabbits were most active at night. He would check the deadfalls in the morning.

Sharp pain in his throat awakened Glass before dawn. The first light of the new day seeped like blood into the eastern horizon. Glass shifted his position in an unsuccessful effort to relieve the pain in his shoulder. As the pain eased he became aware of the chill in the early morning air. He hunched his shoulders and pulled his shredded blanket tightly around his neck. He lay there uncomfortably for an hour, waiting for sufficient light to check the traps.

The bitter taste still lingered in his mouth as he crawled toward the downed cottonwood. He was vaguely aware of the rotten stench of skunk. Both of these sensations evaporated as he imagined a rabbit roasting on a spit above a crackling fire. The nourishment of flesh; he could smell it, taste it.

From fifty yards, Glass could see all three deadfalls. One stood un-moved, but the other two had been tripped—their rocks lay flat on the ground, the support sticks collapsed. Glass could feel his pulse pound-ing in his throat as he crawled hurriedly forward.

Ten feet from the first trap, he noticed the multitude of new tracks on the narrow game trail, the scattered piles of fresh scat. His breath grew short as he peered around the backside of the rock—nothing pro-truded. He lifted the rock, still hopeful. The trap was empty. His heart sank in disappointment. *Did I set it too finely? Did it collapse on its own?* He crawled rapidly to the other rock. Nothing protruded from the front. He strained to see around to the blind side of the trap.

He saw a flash of black and white and heard a hiss, barely percep-tible.

Pain registered before his mind could grasp what had happened. The deadfall had pinned a skunk by its foreleg, but the animal's capacity to spew forth a noxious spray was very much alive. It felt as if burning lamp oil had been poured into his eyes. He rolled backward in a futile effort to avoid more of the vapor. Completely blind, he half crawled, half rolled toward the river.

He crashed into a deep pool by the bank, desperately seeking to wash away the searing spray. With his face under water, Glass attempted to open his eyes, but the burning was too intense. It took twenty minutes before he could see again, and then only by squinting painfully through bloodred, watery slits. Finally Glass crawled to the bank. The nauseat-ing reek of the skunk's scent clung to his skin and clothing like frost on a windowpane. He had once watched a dog roll in the dirt for a week, trying to rid itself of skunk. Like the dog, he knew the stink would ride him for days.

As the burning in his eyes slowly subsided, Glass took a quick in-ventory of his wounds. He touched his neck and looked at his fingers. There was no blood, though the internal pain continued when he swallowed or inhaled deeply. He realized that he hadn't tried to speak for several days. Tentatively, he opened his mouth and forced air over his voice box. The action produced sharp pain and a pathetic, squeaking whine. He wondered if he would ever be able to speak normally.

By craning his neck, he could see the parallel cuts that ran from his throat to his shoulder. Bridger's pine tar still coated the area. His entire shoulder ached, but the cuts appeared to be healing. The puncture wounds on his thigh also looked relatively healthy, although his leg still would not support the weight of his body. From touching his scalp he could imagine that it looked horrible, but it no longer bled and it caused no pain.

Aside from his throat, the area that most concerned him was his back. He lacked the agility to inspect the wounds with his hands, and unable to see them, his mind conjured horrible images. He felt strange sensations that he assumed were the repeated breaking of scabs. He knew that Captain Henry had tied sutures, and he occasionally felt scratching from the loose ends of thread.

More than anything he felt the corrosive void of hunger.

He lay on the sandy bank, exhausted and utterly demoralized by this latest turn of events. A clump of yellow flowers stood atop a slender green stalk. The stalk looked like wild onion, but Glass knew better. It was Death Camas. *Is it Providence? Has this been placed here for me?* Glass wondered how the poison would work. Would he drift off peacefully into a never-ending sleep? Or would his body contort in an agonizing death? How different could it be from his current state? At least there would be certainty that the end was coming.

As he lay on the riverbank in the early moments of dawn, a fat doe emerged from the willows on the opposite shore. She looked cautiously left and right before stepping forward, haltingly, to drink from the river. She was barely thirty yards away, an easy shot with his rifle. *The Anstadt.*

For the first time that day, he thought about the men who abandoned him. His rage grew as he stared at the doe. Abandonment seemed too benign to describe their treachery. Abandonment was a passive act—running away or leaving something behind. If his keepers had done no more than abandon him, he would at this moment be sighting down the barrel of his gun, about to shoot the deer. He would be using his knife to butcher the animal, and sparking his flint against steel to start a fire and cook it. He looked down at himself, wet from head to toe, wounded, reeking from the skunk, the bitter taste of roots still in his mouth.

What Fitzgerald and Bridger had done was much more than abandonment, much worse. These were not mere passersby on the road to Jericho, looking away and crossing to the other side. Glass felt no entitlement to a Samaritan's care, but he did at least expect that his keepers do no harm.

Fitzgerald and Bridger had acted deliberately, robbed him of the few possessions he might have used to save himself. And in stealing from him this opportunity, they had killed him. Murdered him, as surely as a knife in the heart or a bullet in the brain. Murdered him, except he would not die. Would not die, he vowed, because he would live to kill his killers.

Hugh Glass pushed himself up and continued his crawl down the banks of the Grand.

Glass studied the contour of the land in his immediate vicinity. Fifty yards away, a gentle swale led down on three sides to a broad, dry gully. Sage and low grasses provided moderate cover. The swale reminded him suddenly of the gently rolling hills along the Arkansas River. He remembered a trap he had once seen set by Pawnee children. For the children, it had been a game. For Glass, the exercise was now deadly serious.

He crawled slowly to the bottom of the swale, stopping at the point that seemed like the natural hub. He found a sharp-edged rock and began to dig in the hard-packed, sandy soil.

He dug a pit with a four-inch diameter to the depth of his bicep.

Beginning halfway down, he widened the hole so that it was shaped like a wine bottle with the neck at the top. Glass spread the dirt from the hole to conceal the evidence of recent digging. Breathing heavily from the exertion, he stopped to rest.

Next Glass went in search of a large, flat rock. He found one about forty feet from the hole. He also found three small rocks, which he placed in a triangular pattern around the hole. The flat rock he set on top like a roof over the hole, with a space underneath creating the illusion of a place to hide.

Glass used a branch to camouflage the area around the trap, then crawled slowly away from the hole. In several spots he saw tiny, telltale droppings—a good sign. Fifty yards from the hole he stopped. His knee and palms were raw from crawling. His thigh ached from the motion, and again he felt the awful cracking sensation as the scabbing on his back began to bleed. Stopping provided temporary relief to his wounds, but it also made him aware of his profound fatigue, a low-grade ache that emanated from deep within, then circulated outward. Glass fought the urge to close his eyes and succumb to the beckoning sleep. He knew he could not regain his strength unless he ate.

Glass forced himself into a crawling position. Paying careful attention to his distance, he moved in a wide circle with the pit he had dug as the center point. It took him thirty minutes to complete a circuit. Again his body pleaded with him to stop and rest, but he knew that stopping now would undermine the effectiveness of his trap. He kept crawling, spiraling inward toward the pit in ever-smaller circles. When he encountered a thick clump of brush, he would stop to shake it. Anything inside his circles was driven slowly toward the hidden pit.

An hour later, Glass arrived at his hole. He removed the flat rock from the top and listened. He had seen a Pawnee boy reach his hand into a similar trap and pull it out, screaming, with a rattlesnake attached. The boy's error left a strong impression. He looked around for a suitable branch. He found a long one with a flat end and pounded it several times into the hole.

Having assured himself that anything in his trap was dead, he reached into the hole. One by one, he pulled out four dead mice and two ground squirrels. There was no glory in this method of hunting, but Glass was elated with the results.

The swale provided some measure of concealment, and Glass decided to risk a fire, cursing the lack of his flint and steel. He knew it was possible to create a flame by rubbing two sticks together, but he had never started a fire that way. He suspected that the method, if it worked at all, would take forever.

What he needed was a bow and spindle—a crude machine for making fire. The machine had three parts: a flat piece of wood with a hole where a spindle stick was planted, a round spindle stick about three-quarters of an inch thick and eight inches long, and a bow—like a cellist's—to twirl the spindle.

Glass searched the gully to find the parts. It wasn't hard to locate a flat piece of driftwood and two sticks for the spindle and the bow. *String for the bow.* He had no cord. *The strap on my bag.* He pulled out the razor and sliced the strap from his bag, then tied it to the ends of the stick. Next he used the razor to carve away the edges for a hole in the flat piece of driftwood, careful to make it slightly bigger than the spindle stick.

With the bow and spindle assembled, Glass gathered tinder and fuel.

From his possibles bag, he removed the ball patches, ripping them to fray the edges. He also had saved cattail cotton. He piled the tinder loosely in a shallow pit, then added dry grass. To the few pieces of dry wood in the area he added buffalo dung, bone dry from long weeks in the sun.

With the makings of the fire in place, Glass grabbed the components of the bow and spindle. He filled the hole in the flat piece of wood with tinder, set the spindle stick in the hole, and looped the bowstring around it. He held the spindle stick against the palm of his right hand, still protected by the woolen pad he used to crawl. With his left hand he worked the bow. The back-and-forth motion spun the spindle in the hole on the flat driftwood, creating friction and heat.

The fault in his machine became immediately apparent as he spun the spindle with the bow stick. One end of the spindle rubbed in the hole on the flat driftwood—the end where he wanted to create the fire. The other end, though, spun against the flesh of his hand. Glass remembered that the Pawnee used a palm-size piece of wood to hold the top end of the spindle. He searched again to find the right piece of wood. He located an appropriate chunk and used the razor to carve away a hole for the top of the spindle stick.

He was clumsy with his left hand, and it took several attempts to find the right rhythm, moving the bow in a steady motion without losing his grip on the spindle stick. Soon, though, he had the spindle twirling smoothly. After several minutes, smoke began to rise from the hole. Suddenly the tinder burst into flames. He grabbed cattail cotton and set it to the lick of flame, protecting it with a cupped hand. When the cotton caught fire, he transferred the flame to the tinder in the small pit. He felt the wind whip across his back, and panicked for an instant that it would extinguish the flame, but the tinder caught, then the dry grass. In a few minutes he was feeding the buffalo chips into a small blaze.

There wasn't much meat left by the time he skinned the tiny rodents and removed their entrails. Still, it was fresh. If his trapping technique was time-consuming, at least it had the benefit of simplicity.

Glass was still ravenous as he picked at the tiny rib cage of the last rodent. He resolved to stop earlier the next day. Perhaps dig pits in two locations. The thought of slower progress irritated him. How long could he avoid Arikara on the banks of the well-traveled Grand? *Don't do that. Don't look too far ahead. The goal each day is tomorrow morning.*

With his dinner cooked, the fire no longer merited its risk. He covered it with sand and went to sleep.

TEN

SEPTEMBER 15, 1823

TWIN BUTTES FRAMED THE VALLEY in front of Glass, forcing the Grand River through a narrow channel between. Glass remembered the buttes from the trip upriver with Captain Henry. As he crawled farther east along the Grand, distinctive features became increasingly rare. Even the cottonwoods seemed to have been swallowed by the sea of prairie grass.

Henry and the fur brigade had camped near the buttes, and Glass intended to stop in the same spot, hoping that something useful might have been left behind. In any event, he remembered that the high bank near the buttes made good shelter. Great stacks of black thunderheads sat ominously on the western horizon. The storm would be overhead in a couple of hours, and he wanted to dig in before it hit.

Glass crawled along the river to the campsite. A ring of blackened stones marked a recent fire. He remembered that the fur brigade had camped with no fire, and wondered who had followed behind them. He stopped, removed the possibles bag and blanket from his back, and took a long drink from the river. Behind him, the cut bank created the shelter he remembered. He scanned up and down the river, watchful for signs of Indians, disappointed that the vegetation looked sparse. He felt the familiar rumble of hunger, and wondered if there was enough cover to dig an effective mouse pit. *Is it worth the effort?* He weighed the benefits of shelter against the benefits of food. Rodents had sustained him now for a week. Still, Glass knew he was treading water—not drowning, but making no progress toward a safer shore.

A light breeze heralded the approaching clouds, cool across the sweat on his back. Glass turned from the river and crawled up the high bank to check on the storm.

What lay beyond the rim of the bank took his breath away. Thousands of buffalo grazed in the vale below the butte, blackening the plain for a solid mile. A great bull stood sentry no more than fifty yards in front of him. The animal stood close to seven feet at the hump. The shaggy shawl of tawny fur on top of its black body accentuated the powerful head and shoulders, making the horns seem almost redundant. The bull snorted and sniffed at the air, frustrated by the swirling breeze. Behind the bull, a cow wallowed on her back, lifting a cloud of dust. A dozen other cows and calves grazed obliviously nearby.

Glass had glimpsed his first buffalo on the Texas plains. Since then he had seen them, in herds great and herds small, on a hundred different occasions. Yet the sight of the animals never failed to fill him with awe, awe for their infinite numbers, awe for the prairie that sustained them.

A hundred yards downstream from Glass, a pack of eight wolves also watched the great bull and the outliers he guarded. The alpha male sat on his haunches near a clump of sage. All afternoon he had waited patiently for the moment that just arrived, the moment when a gap emerged between the outliers and the rest of the herd. A gap. A fatal weakness. The big wolf raised himself suddenly to all fours.

The alpha male stood tall but narrow. His legs seemed ungainly, knobby and somehow oddly proportioned to his coal-black body. His two pups wrestled playfully near the river. Some of the wolves lay sleeping, placid as barnyard hounds. Taken together, the animals seemed more like pets than predators, though they all perked to life at the sudden movement from the big male.

It wasn't until the wolves began to move that their lethal strength became obvious. The strength was not derivative of muscularity or grace. Rather it flowed from a single-minded intelligence that made their movements deliberate, relentless. The individual animals converged into a lethal unit, cohering in the collective strength of the pack.

The alpha male trotted toward the gap between the outliers and the herd, breaking into a full run after a few yards. The pack fanned out behind him with a precision and unity of purpose that struck Glass as almost military. The pack poured into the gap. Even the pups seemed to grasp the purpose of their enterprise. Buffalo on the edge of the main herd retreated, pushing their calves in front of them before turning outward, shoulder to shoulder in a line against the wolves. The gap widened with the movement of the main herd, stranding the bull and a dozen other buffalo outside its perimeter.

The great bull charged, catching one wolf with its horn and tossing the yelping animal twenty feet. The wolves snarled and growled, snapping with brutal fangs at exposed flanks. Most of the outliers broke for the main herd, realizing instinctively that their safety lay in numbers.

The alpha male nipped at the tender haunch of a calf. Confused, the calf broke away from the herd, toward the steep bank by the river. Collectively aware of the deadly error, the pack fell instantly behind its prey. Bawling as it ran, the calf dashed wildly ahead. It tumbled over the bank, snapping its leg in the fall. The calf struggled to regain its feet. Its broken leg dangled in an odd direction and then collapsed completely when the calf tried to plant it. The calf fell to the ground and the pack was on it. Fangs planted themselves in every part of its body. The alpha male sunk its teeth into the tender throat and ripped.

The calf's last stand took place no more than seventy-five yards down the bank from Glass. He watched with a mixture of fascination and fear, glad that his vantage point lay downwind. The pack focused its complete attention on the calf. The alpha male and his mate ate first, their bloody snouts buried in the soft underbelly. They let the pups eat, but not the others. Occasionally another wolf would slink up to the fallen prey, only to be sent scrambling by a snap or snarl from the big black male.

Glass stared at the calf and the wolves, his mind turning quickly. The calf had been dropped in the spring. After a summer of fattening on the prairie, it weighed close to a hundred and fifty pounds. *A hundred and fifty pounds of fresh meat.* After two weeks of catching his food by the mouthful, Glass could scarcely imagine such bounty. Initially, Glass had hoped that the pack might leave enough for him to scavenge. As he continued to watch, though, the bounty diminished at an alarming rate. Satiated, the alpha male and his mate eventually wandered casually away from the carcass with a severed hind quarter in tow for the pups. The four other wolves fell on the carcass.

In growing desperation, Glass considered the options. If he waited too long, he doubted whether anything would be left. He weighed the prospect of continuing to live off mice and roots. Even if he could find enough to sustain himself, the task took too much time. He doubted he had covered thirty miles since beginning his crawl. At his current pace, he would be lucky to reach Fort Kiowa before cold set in. And of course, every day of exposure on the river was another day for Indians to stumble upon him.

He desperately needed the certain strength that the buffalo meat would give him. He did not know by what Providence the calf had been placed in his path. *This is my chance.* If he wanted his share of the calf, he would have to fight for it. And he needed to do it now.

He scanned the area for the makings of some weapon. Nothing presented itself beyond rocks, driftwood, and sage. *A club?* He wondered for a moment if he could beat back the wolves. It seemed implausible. He couldn't swing hard enough to inflict much of a blow. And from his knees, he forfeited any advantage of height. *Sage.* He remembered the brief but impressive flames created by dry sage branches. *A torch?*

Seeing no other option, he scurried around him for the makings of a fire. The spring floods had tossed the trunk of a large cottonwood against the cut bank, creating a natural windbreak. Glass scooped a shallow pit in the sand next to the trunk.

He took out his bow and spindle, grateful that he at least had the means for quickly creating a flame. From the possibles bag he removed the last of the patches and a large clump of cattail cotton. Glass looked downriver at the wolf pack, still ripping at the calf. *Damn it!*

He looked around him for fuel. The river had left little of the cottonwood beyond the trunk. He found a clump of dead sage and snapped off five large branches, piling them next to the fire pit.

Glass set the bow and spindle in the sheltered pit, carefully placing the tinder. He began to work the bow, slowly at first, then faster as he found his rhythm. In a few minutes he had a low fire burning in the pit by the cottonwood.

He looked downriver toward the wolves. The alpha male, his mate, and their two pups huddled together about twenty yards beyond the calf. Having taken first dibs at the calf, they now were content to gnaw casually at the tasty marrow of the hindquarter. Glass hoped they would stay out of the coming battle. That left four wolves on the carcass itself.

The Loup Pawnee, as their name implied, revered the wolf for its strength and above all for its cunning. Glass had been with Pawnee hunting parties that shot wolves; their hides were an important part of many ceremonies. But he had never done anything like what he prepared to do at that moment: crawl into a pack of wolves and challenge them for food, armed only with a torch of sage.

The five sage branches twisted like giant, arthritic hands. Smaller twigs extended from the main branches at frequent intervals, most of them covered with spindly strands of bark and brittle, blue-green leaves. He grabbed one of the branches and set it to the fire. It caught immediately, a foot-high flame soon roaring from its top. *It's burning too fast.* Glass wondered if the flame would last the distance between him and the wolves, let alone provide a weapon in whatever struggle that lay before him. He decided to hedge his bet. Rather than lighting all of the sage now, he would carry most of the branches unlit, backup ammunition to be added to the torch as needed.

Glass looked again at the wolves. They suddenly seemed larger. He hesitated for an instant. No turning back, he decided. *This is my chance.* With the burning sage branch in one hand and the four backup branches in the other, Glass crawled down the bank toward the wolves. At fifty yards, the alpha male and his mate looked up from the hindquarter to stare at this strange animal approaching the buffalo calf. They viewed Glass as a curiosity, not a challenge. After all, they had eaten their fill.

At twenty yards, the wind shifted and the four animals on the carcass caught scent of the smoke. They all turned. Glass stopped, face-to-face now with four wolves. From a distance, it was easy to see the wolves as mere dogs. Up close, they bore no relation to their domestic cousins. A white wolf showed its bloody teeth and took a half step toward Glass, a deep growl pouring from its throat. It lowered its shoulder, a move that seemed somehow both defensive and offensive at the same time.

The white wolf fought conflicting instincts—one defensive of its prey, the other afraid of fire. A second wolf, this one missing most of one ear, fell in beside the first. The other two continued to rip at the buffalo carcass, appreciative, it seemed, of the exclusive attention to the calf. The burning branch in Glass's right hand began to flicker. The white wolf took another step toward Glass, who remembered suddenly the sickening sensation of the bear's teeth, ripping at his flesh. *What have I done?*

Suddenly there was a flash of bright light, a brief pause, and then the deep bass of thunder rolling down the valley. A raindrop struck Glass's face and wind whipped at the flame. He felt a sickening churn in his stomach. *God no—not now!* He had to act quickly. The white wolf was poised to attack. *Could they really smell fear?* He had to do the unexpected. He had to attack them.

He grabbed the four sage branches from his right hand and added them to the burning branch in his left. Flames leapt up, hungrily swallowing the dry fuel. It took both hands now to hold the branches together, which meant he could no longer use his left hand for balance. Excruciating pain extended outward from his wounded right thigh as weight shifted to his leg, and he almost fell. He managed to stay upright as he lurched, hobbling forward on his knees in his best approximation of a charge. He let loose the loudest sound he could muster, which came out as a sort of eerie wail. Forward he moved, swinging the burning torch like a fiery sword.

He thrust the torch toward the wolf with one ear. Flames singed the animal's face and it jumped backward with a yelp. The white wolf leapt at Glass's flank, sinking its teeth into his shoulder. Glass pivoted, craning his neck to keep the wolf off his throat. Only a few inches separated Glass's face from the wolf's, and he could smell the animal's bloody breath. Glass struggled again to keep his balance. He swung his arms around to bring the flames in contact with the wolf, burning the animal's belly and groin. The wolf released its grip on his shoulder, retreating a step.

Glass heard a snarl behind him and ducked instinctively. The one-eared wolf came tumbling over his head, missing his strike at Glass's neck, but knocking Glass to his side. He groaned at the impact of the fall, which reignited pain in his back, throat, and shoulder. The bundled torch hit the ground, spilling on the sandy soil. Glass grasped at the branches, desperate to pick them up before they extinguished. At the same time, he struggled to regain the upright position on his knees.

The two wolves circled slowly, waiting for their moment, more cautious now that they had tasted the flame. *I can't let them get behind me.* Lightning struck again, followed rapidly this time by the boom of thunder. The storm was nearly over him. Rain would pour down at any minute. *There's no time.* Even without the rain, the flames on the torch were burning low.

The white wolf and the wolf with one ear closed. They too seemed to sense that the battle was nearing its climax. Glass feigned at them with the torch. They slowed, but did not retreat. Glass had worked himself into a position only a few feet from the calf. The two wolves feeding on the carcass succeeded in tearing off a hindquarter, and retreated from the commotion of the battling wolves and the strange creature with the fire. For the first time, Glass noticed the clumps of dry sage around the carcass. *Would they burn?*

Eyes fixed on the two wolves, Glass set his torch to the sage. There had been no rain for weeks. The brush was dry as tinder and caught fire easily. In an instant, flames rose two feet above the sage next to the carcass. Glass lit two other clumps. Soon, the carcass lay in the middle of three burning bushes. Like Moses, Glass planted himself with his knees on the carcass, waving the remnants of his torch. Lightning struck and thunder boomed. Wind whipped the flames around the brush. Rain fell now, though not yet enough to douse the sage.

The effect was impressive. The white wolf and the wolf with one ear looked around. The alpha male, his mate, and the pups loped across the prairie. With full bellies and a breaking storm, they headed for the shelter of their nearby den. The two other wolves from the carcass also followed, struggling to pull the calf's hindquarter across the prairie.

The white wolf crouched, poised, it seemed, to attack again. But suddenly the wolf with one ear turned and ran after the pack. The white wolf stopped to contemplate the changing odds. He knew well his place in the pack: Others led and he followed. Others picked out the game to be killed, he helped to run it down. Others ate first, he contented himself with the remainder. The wolf had never seen an animal like the one that appeared today, but he understood precisely where it fit in the pecking order. Another clap of thunder erupted overhead, and the rain began to pour down. The white wolf took one last look at the buffalo, the man, and the smoking sage, then he turned and loped after the others.

Glass watched the wolves disappear above the rim of the cut bank. Around him, smoke rose as the rain doused the sage. Another minute and he would be defenseless. He marveled at his fortune as he glanced quickly at the bite on his shoulder. Blood trickled from two puncture wounds, but they were not deep.

The calf lay in the grotesque throes of its failed efforts to escape the wolves. Brutally efficient fangs had ripped the carcass open. Fresh blood pooled beneath the open throat, an eerily brilliant crimson against the muted tans of the sand in the gully. The wolves had focused their attention on the rich entrails that Glass himself craved. He rolled the calf from its side to its back, noting with brief disappointment that nothing remained of the liver. Gone too were the gallbladder, the lungs, and the heart. But a small bit of intestine hung from the animal. Glass removed the razor from his possibles bag, followed the snaking organ into the body cavity with his left hand, and cut a two-foot length at the stomach. Barely able to control himself at the immediacy of food, he put the cut end to his mouth and guzzled.

If the wolf pack had availed itself of the choicer organs, it also had done Glass the favor of nearly skinning its prey. Glass moved to the throat, where with the aid of the razor he could pull back the supple skin. The calf was well fed. Delicate white fat clung to the muscle of its plump neck. The trappers called this fat "fleece" and considered it a delicacy. He cut chunks and stuffed them into his mouth, barely chewing before he swallowed. Each swallow revived the excruciating fire in his throat, but hunger trumped the pain. He gorged himself in the pouring rain, arriving finally at some minimal threshold that allowed him to consider other dangers.

Glass climbed again to the rim of the cut bank, scanning the horizon in all directions. Scattered clumps of buffalo grazed obliviously, but there was no sign of wolf or Indian. The rain and thunder had ended, blowing past as rapidly as they appeared. Angled rays of afternoon sunlight succeeded in breaking through the great thunderheads, streaming forth in iridescent rays extending from heaven to earth.

Glass settled back to consider his fortune. The wolves had taken their share, but an enormous resource lay below him. Glass suffered no illusions about his situation. But he would not starve.

Glass camped for three days on the cut bank next to the calf. For the first few hours he didn't even set a fire, gorging uncontrollably on thin slices of the gloriously fresh meat. Finally he paused long enough to start a low blaze for roasting and drying, concealing the flames as much as possible by setting them near to the bank.

He built racks from the green branches of a nearby stand of willows. Hour after hour he carved away at the carcass with the dull razor, hanging meat on the racks while he steadily fed the fires. In three days he dried fifteen pounds of jerky, enough to sustain him for two weeks if need be. Longer if he could supplement along the way.

The wolves did leave one choice cut—the tongue. He relished this delicacy like a king. The ribs and remaining leg bones he roasted on the fire one by one, cracking them for their rich, fresh marrow.

Glass removed the hide with the dull razor. A task that should have taken minutes took hours, an interval during which he thought bitterly about the two men who stole his knife. He had neither the time nor the tools to work the fur properly, but he did cut a crude parfleche before the skin dried into stiff rawhide. He needed the bag to carry the jerky.

On the third day, Glass went searching for a long branch to use as a crutch. In the fight with the wolves, he had been surprised at the weight that his wounded leg could support. He had exercised the leg over the past two days, stretching and testing it. With the aid of a crutch, Glass believed he could now walk upright, a prospect he relished after three weeks of crawling like a gimpy dog. He found a cottonwood branch of the appropriate length and shape. He cut a long strip from the Hudson Bay blanket, wrapping it around the top of the crutch as a pad.

The blanket had been reduced, strip by strip, to a piece of cloth no more than one foot wide by two feet long. Glass used the razor to cut an opening in the middle of the cloth, large enough so that he could poke his head through. The resulting garment wasn't big enough to call a capote, but at least it would cover his shoulders and keep the parfleche from digging against his skin.

There was a chill in the air again on that last night by the buttes. The last shreds of the slaughtered calf hung drying on the racks above the crimson coals. The fire cast a comforting glow on his camp, a tiny oasis of light amid the black of the moonless plain. Glass sucked the marrow from the last of the ribs. As he tossed the bone on the fire, he realized suddenly that he was not hungry. He savored the seeping warmth of the fire, a luxury he would not enjoy again in the foreseeable future.

Three days of food had worked to repair his wounded body. He bent his right leg to test it. The muscles were tight and sore, but functional. His shoulder too had improved. Strength had not returned to his arm, but some flexibility had. It still scared him to touch his throat. The remnants of the stitches protruded, although the skin had fused. He wondered if he should attempt to cut them away with the razor, but had been afraid to try. Aside from his effort to yell at the wolves, he had not tested his voice for days. He would not do so now. His voice had little to do with his survival in the coming weeks. If it were changed, so be it. He did appreciate the fact that he now could swallow with less pain.

Glass knew that the buffalo calf had turned his fortune. Still, it was easy to temper the assessment of where he stood. He had lived to fight another day. But he was alone and without weapons. Between him and Fort Brazeau lay three hundred miles of open prairie. Two Indian tribes—one possibly hostile and the other certainly so—followed the same river that he depended on to navigate the open space. And of course, as Glass knew painfully well, Indians were not the only hazard before him.

He knew he should sleep. With the new crutch, he hoped to make ten or even fifteen miles the next day. Still, something drew him to linger in the fleeting moment of contentment—sated, rested, and warm.

Glass reached into the possibles bag and pulled out the bear claw.

He turned it slowly in the low light of the fire, fascinated again at the dried blood on the tip—his blood, he now realized. He began to carve at the thick base of the claw with the razor, etching a narrow groove that he carefully worked to deepen. From his bag he also removed the hawk's-feet necklace. He wrapped the string of the necklace around the groove he had carved at the base of the claw, tying it into a tight knot. Finally, he tied the ends behind his neck.

He liked the idea that the claw that inflicted his wounds now hung, inanimate, around his neck. *Lucky charm,* he thought, then fell asleep.

ELEVEN

SEPTEMBER 16, 1823

GODDAMN IT! JOHN FITZGERALD STOOD staring at the river in front of him, or more accurately, at the bend in the river.

Jim Bridger walked up beside him. "What's it doing, turning east?" Without warning, Fitzgerald backhanded the boy across the mouth. Bridger sprawled backward, landing on his backside with a stunned look on his face. "What'd you do that for?"

"You think I can't see that the river turns east? When I need you to scout, I'll ask you! Otherwise, keep your eyes open and your goddamned mouth shut!"

Bridger was right, of course. For more than a hundred miles, the river they followed had run predominantly north, the exact bearing they sought to follow. Fitzgerald wasn't even sure of the river's name, but he knew that everything flowed eventually into the Missouri. If the river had continued its northern course, Fitzgerald believed it might intersect within a day's march of Fort Union. Fitzgerald even held out some hope that they were actually on the Yellowstone, though Bridger maintained that they were too far east.

In any event, Fitzgerald had hoped to stick to the river until they hit the Missouri. In truth, he had no instinct for the geography of the vast wasteland before him. There had been little feature to the land since they struck out from the headwaters of the Upper Grand. The horizon stretched out for miles in front of them, a sea of muted grass and swelling hills, each exactly like the last.

Sticking to the river made for straightforward navigation, and it assured an easy supply of water. Still, Fitzgerald had no desire to turn east—the new direction of the river for as far as their eyes could see. Time remained their enemy. The longer they wandered separate from Henry and the brigade, the greater the odds for calamity.

They stood there for several minutes while Fitzgerald stared and stewed.

Finally Bridger took a deep breath and said, "We should cut northwest."

Fitzgerald started to rebuke him, except that he was utterly at a loss about what to do. He pointed to the dry grassland that stretched to the horizon. "I suppose you know where to find water out there?"

"Nope. But we don't need much in this weather." Bridger sensed Fitzgerald's indecision, and felt a corresponding increase in the strength of his own opinion. Unlike Fitzgerald, he *did* have an instinct across open country. He always had, an internal compass that seemed to shepherd him in unmarked terrain. "I think we're no more than two days from the Missouri—and maybe that close to the Fort."

Fitzgerald fought back the urge to strike Bridger again. In fact, he thought again about killing the boy. He would have done it back on the Grand, had he not felt dependent upon the extra rifle. Two shooters weren't many, but two were better than one alone.

"Listen, boy. You and I need to reach a little understanding before we join up with the others." Bridger had anticipated this conversation ever since they abandoned Glass. He looked down, already ashamed of what he knew was coming.

"We did our best for old Glass, stayed with him longer than most would've. Seventy dollars isn't enough to get scalped by the Rees," Fitzgerald said, using the short name for the Arikara.

Bridger said nothing, so Fitzgerald continued. "Glass was dead from the minute that grizzly finished with him. Only thing we didn't do was bury him." Still Bridger looked away. Fitzgerald's anger began to rise again.

"You know what, Bridger? I don't give a tinker's damn what you think about what we did. But I'll tell you this—you spill your guts and I'll carve your throat from ear to ear."

TWELVE

SEPTEMBER 17, 1823

CAPTAIN ANDREW HENRY did not pause to appreciate the raw splendor of the valley spread before him. From his vantage point on a high bluff above the confluence of the Missouri and Yellowstone rivers, Henry and his seven companions commanded a vast horizon demarcated by a blunt plateau. In front of the plateau flowed gentle buttes, spilling like flaxen waves between the steep bench and the Missouri. Though the near bank had been stripped of its timber, thick cottonwoods still held the far bank, fighting against autumn for temporary possession of their greenery.

Nor did Henry stop to contemplate the philosophical significance of two rivers joining. He did not imagine the high mountain meadows where the waters began their journey as pure as liquid diamond. He did not even linger to appreciate the practical import of the fort's location, neatly collecting commerce from two great highways of water.

Captain Henry's thoughts concerned not what he did see, but rather what he did not: He did not see horses. He saw the scattered motion of men and the smoke of a large fire, but not a single horse. *Not even a damn mule.* He fired his rifle into the air, as much in frustration as in greeting. The men in the camp stopped their activities, searching for the source of the shot. Two guns answered in return. Henry and his seven men trudged down the valley toward Fort Union.

It had been eight weeks since Henry left Fort Union, rushing to Ashley's aid at the Arikara village. Henry left two instructions behind: Trap the surrounding streams and guard the horses at all costs. Captain Henry's luck, it appeared, would never change.

Pig lifted his rifle from his right shoulder, where it seemed to have augured a permanent indentation in his flesh. He started to move the heavy gun to his left shoulder, but there the strap of his possibles bag had worn its own abrasion. He finally resigned himself to simply carrying the gun in front of him, a decision that reminded him of the aching pain in his arms.

Pig thought of the comfortable straw tick in back of the cooper's shop in St. Louis, and he arrived once again at the conclusion that joining Captain Henry had been a horrible mistake.

In the first twenty years of his life, Pig had never once walked more than two miles. In the past six weeks, not a single day had passed when he had walked fewer than twenty miles, and often the men covered thirty or even more. Two days earlier, Pig had worn through the bottoms of his third pair of moccasins. Gaping holes admitted frosty dew in the morning. Rocks cut jagged scrapes. Worst of all, he stepped squarely on a prickly pear cactus. He had failed in repeated efforts to pick out the tines with his skinning knife, and now a festering toe made him wince with every step.

Not to mention the fact that he had never been hungrier in his life.

He longed for the simple pleasure of dunking a biscuit in gravy, or sinking his teeth into a fat chicken leg. He remembered fondly the heaping tin plate of food provided thrice daily by the cooper's wife. Now his breakfast consisted of cold jerky—and not much of that. They barely stopped for lunch, which also consisted of cold jerky. With the captain skittish about gunshots, even dinners consisted primarily of cold jerky. And on the occasions when they did have fresh game, Pig struggled to eat it, hacking at slabs of wild game or wrestling to break bones for their marrow. Food on the frontier required so damn much work. The effort it took to eat left him famished.

Pig questioned his decision to go west with each rumble of his stomach, with every painful step. The riches of the frontier remained as elusive as ever. Pig had not set a beaver trap for six months. As they walked into the camp, horses were not the only thing absent. *Where are the pelts?* A few beaver plews hung on willow frames against the timber walls of the fort, along with a mishmash of buffalo, elk, and wolf. But this was hardly the bonanza to which they had hoped to return.

A man named Stubby Bill stepped forward and started to extend his hand to Henry in greeting.

Henry ignored the hand. "Where the hell are the horses?"

Stubby Bill's hand hung there for a moment, lonely and uncomfortable.

Finally he let it drop. "Blackfeet stole 'em, Captain."

"You ever hear of posting a guard?"

"We posted guards, Captain, but they came out of nowhere and stampeded the herd."

"You go after them?"

Stubby Bill shook his head slowly. "We ain't done so well against the Blackfeet." It was a subtle reminder, but also effective. Captain Henry sighed deeply. "How many horses left?"

"Seven . . . well, five and two mules. Murphy's got all of them with a trapping party on Beaver Creek."

"Doesn't look like there's been much trapping going on."

"We've been at it, Captain, but everything near the Fort is trapped out. Without more horses we can't cover any ground."

Jim Bridger lay curled beneath a threadbare blanket. There would be heavy frost on the ground in the morning, and the boy felt the damp chill as it seeped into the deepest marrow of his bones. They slept again with no fire. In fits and starts, his discomfort surrendered to his fatigue and he slept.

In his dream he stood near the edge of a great chasm. The sky was the purple-black of late evening. Darkness prevailed, but enough light remained to illuminate objects in a faint glow. The apparition appeared at first as the vaguest of shapes, still distant. It approached him slowly, inevitably. Its contours took form as it drew closer, a twisted and limping body. Bridger wanted to flee, but the chasm behind him made escape impossible.

At ten paces he could see the horrible face. It was unnatural, its features distorted like a mask. Scars crisscrossed the cheeks and forehead. The nose and ears were placed haphazardly, with no relation to balance or symmetry. The face was framed by a tangled mane and beard, furthering the impression that the being before him was something no longer human.

As the specter moved closer still, its eyes began to burn, locked onto Bridger in a hateful gaze he could not break.

The specter raised its arm in a reaper's arc and drove a knife deep into Bridger's chest. The knife cleaved his sternum cleanly, shocking the boy with the piercing strength of the blow. The boy staggered backward, caught a final glimpse of the burning eyes, and fell.

He stared at the knife in his chest as the chasm swallowed him. He recognized with little surprise the silver cap on the pommel. It was Glass's knife. In some ways it was a relief to die, he thought, easier than living with his guilt.

Bridger felt a sharp thud in his ribs. He opened his eyes with a start to find Fitzgerald standing above him. "Time to move, boy."

THIRTEEN

OCTOBER 5, 1823

THE BURNT REMAINS OF THE Arikara village reminded Hugh
Glass of skeletons. It was eerie to walk among them. This place that
teemed so recently with the vibrant life of five hundred families now
sat dead as a graveyard, a blackened monument on the high bluff above
the Missouri.

The village lay eight miles north of the confluence with the Grand,
while Fort Brazeau lay seventy miles south. Glass had two reasons for
the diversion up the Missouri. He had run out of jerky from the buffalo calf and found himself once again reliant upon roots and berries.
Glass remembered the flush cornfields surrounding the Arikara villages
and hoped to scavenge from them.

He also knew that the village would provide the makings of a raft.

With a raft, he could float lazily downstream to Fort Brazeau. As
he walked slowly through the village, he realized there would be no
problem finding building materials. Between the huts and the palisades,
there were thousands of suitable logs.

Glass stopped to peer into a big lodge near the center of the village,
clearly some type of communal building. He saw a flash of motion in
the dark interior. He stumbled back a step, his heart racing. He stopped,

peering into the lodge as his eyes adjusted to the light. No longer need-ing the crutch, he had sharpened the end of the cottonwood branch to make a crude spear. He held it in a ready position.

A small dog, a pup, whimpered in the middle of the lodge. Relieved and excited at the prospect of fresh meat, Glass took a slow step for-ward. He turned the spear to bring the blunt end forward. If he could lure the dog closer, a quick whack would smash the animal's skull. *No need to damage the meat.* Sensing the danger, the dog bolted toward dark recesses at the back of the open room.

Glass moved quickly in pursuit, stopping in shock when the dog jumped into the arms of an ancient squaw. The old woman huddled on a pallet, curled into a tight ball on a tattered blanket. She held the puppy like a baby. With her face buried against the animal, only her white hair was visible in the shadows. She cried out and began to wail hysterically. After a few moments, the wailing took on a pattern, a fright-ening and foreboding chant. *Her death chant?*

The arms and shoulders gripping the little dog were nothing more than leathery old skin hung loosely on bone. As Glass's eyes adjusted, he saw the waste and filth scattered about her. A large earthen pot con-tained water, but there was no sign of food. *Why hasn't she gathered corn?* Glass had gathered a few ears as he walked into the village. The Sioux and the deer had taken most of the crop, but certainly remnants re-mained. *Is she lame?*

He reached into his parfleche and pulled out an ear of corn. He shucked it and bent down to offer it to the old woman. Glass held out the corn for a long time as the woman continued her wailing chant. After a while the puppy sniffed at the corn, then began to lick it. Glass reached out and touched the old woman on the head, gently stroking the white hair. Finally the woman stopped chanting and turned her face toward the light that streamed in from the door.

Glass gasped. Her eyes were perfectly white, completely blind. Now Glass understood why the old woman had been left behind when the Arikara fled in the middle of the night.

Glass took the old woman's hand and gently wrapped it round the corn. She mumbled something that he could not understand and pushed the corn to her mouth. Glass saw that she had no teeth, pressing the raw corn between her gums. The sweet juice seemed to awaken her hunger, and she gnawed ineffectively at the cob. *She needs broth.*

He looked around the hut. A rusty kettle sat next to the fire pit in the center of the room. He looked at the water in the large earthen pot. It was brackish and sediment floated on the surface. He picked up the pot and carried it outside. He dumped the water and refilled it from a small creek that flowed through the village.

Glass spotted another dog by the creek, and this one he did not spare.

Soon he had a fire burning in the center of the hut. Part of the dog he roasted on a spit over the fire and part he boiled in the kettle. He threw corn into the pot with the dog meat and continued his search through the village. Fire had not affected many of the earthen huts, and Glass was pleased to find several lengths of cordage for a raft. He also found a tin cup and a ladle made from a buffalo horn.

When he returned to the big lodge he found the blind old woman as he had left her, still sucking at the cob of corn. He walked to the kettle and filled the tin cup with broth, setting it next to her on the pallet. The pup, unsettled at the smell of his brethren roasting on the fire, huddled at the woman's feet. The woman could smell the meat too. She grasped the cup and gulped the broth the first moment the temperature would allow. Glass filled the cup again, this time adding tiny bits of meat that he cut with the razor. He filled the cup three times before the old woman stopped eating and fell asleep. He adjusted the blanket to cover her bony shoulders.

Glass moved to the fire and began to eat the roasted dog. The Pawnee considered dog a delicacy, harvesting an occasional canine the way white men butchered a spring pig. Glass certainly preferred buffalo, but in his present state, dog would do just fine. He pulled corn from the pot and ate that too, saving the broth and the boiled meat for the squaw.

He had eaten for about an hour when the old woman cried out. Glass moved quickly to her side. She said something over and over. *"He tuwe he . . . He tuwe he . . ."* She spoke this time not in the fearful tone of her death chant, but in a quiet voice, a voice seeking urgently to communicate an important thought. The words meant nothing to Glass. Not knowing what else to do, he took the woman's hand. She squeezed it weakly and pulled it to her cheek. They sat like that for a while. Her blind eyes closed and she drifted off to sleep.

In the morning she was dead.

Glass spent the better part of the morning building a crude pyre overlooking the Missouri. When it was finished, he returned to the big hut and wrapped the old woman in her blanket. He carried her to the pyre, the dog trailing pitifully behind them in an odd cortege. Like his wounded leg, Glass's shoulder had healed nicely in the weeks since the battle with the wolves. Still, he winced as he hoisted the body up on the pyre. He felt the familiar, disconcerting twinges along his spine. His back continued to worry him. With luck, he would be at Fort Brazeau in a few days. Someone there could tend to him properly.

He stood for a moment at the pyre, old conventions calling from a distant past. He wondered for a moment what words had been spoken at his mother's funeral, what words had been spoken for Elizabeth. He pictured a mound of fresh-turned earth next to an open grave. The notion of burial had always struck him as stifling and cold. He liked the Indian way better, setting the bodies up high, as if passing them to the heavens.

The dog growled suddenly and Glass whipped around. Four mounted Indians rode slowly toward him from the village at a distance of only seventy yards. From their clothing and hair, Glass recognized them immediately as Sioux. He panicked for an instant, calculating the distance to the thick trees of the bluff. He thought back to his first encounter with the Pawnee, and decided to hold his ground.

It had been little more than a month since the trappers and the Sioux had been allies in the siege against the Arikara. Glass remembered that the Sioux had quit the fight in disgust over Colonel Leavenworth's tactics, a sentiment shared by the men of the Rocky Mountain Fur Company. *Do remnants of that alliance still stand?* So he stood there, affecting as much confidence as he could muster, and watched the Indians approach.

They were young; three were barely more than teens. The fourth was slightly older, perhaps in his mid-twenties. The younger braves approached warily, weapons ready, as if moving toward a strange animal. The older Sioux rode a half-length ahead of the others. He carried a London fusil, but he held the gun casually, the barrel resting across the neck of an enormous buckskin stallion. A brand etched the animal's haunch, "U.S." *One of Leavenworth's.* In another setting, Glass might have found humor in the colonel's misfortune.

The older Sioux reined his horse five feet in front of Glass, studying him from head to foot. Then the Sioux looked beyond him to the pyre. He struggled to understand the relationship between this mangled, filthy white man and the dead Arikara squaw. From a distance they had watched him struggle to place her body on the scaffolding. It made no sense.

The Indian swung his leg across the big stallion and slipped easily to the ground. He walked up to Glass, his dark eyes penetrating. Glass felt his stomach roil, though he met the gaze unflinchingly.

The Indian accomplished effortlessly what Glass was compelled to pretend—an air of complete confidence. His name was Yellow Horse. He was tall, over six feet, with square shoulders and perfect posture that accentuated a powerful neck and chest. In his tightly braided hair he wore three eagle feathers, notched to signify enemies killed in battle. Two decorative bands ran down the doeskin tunic on his chest. Glass noticed the intricacy of the work, hundreds of interwoven porcupine quills dyed brilliantly in vermillion and indigo.

As the two men stood face-to-face, the Indian reached out, slowly extending his hand to Glass's necklace, examining the enormous bear claw as he turned it in his fingers. He let the claw drop, his eyes moving to trace the scars around Glass's skull and throat. The Indian nudged

Glass's shoulder to turn him, examining the wounds beneath his tattered shirt. He said something to the other three as he looked at Glass's back. Glass heard the other braves dismount and approach, then talk excitedly as they pushed and probed at his back. *What's happening?*

The source of the Indians' fascination was the deep, parallel wounds extending the length of Glass's back. The Indians had seen many wounds, but never this. The deep gashes were animated. They were crawling with maggots.

One of the Indians managed to pinch a twisting white worm between his fingers. He held it for Glass to see. Glass cried out in horror, tearing at the remnants of his shirt, reaching ineffectively toward the wounds he could not touch, and then falling to his hands and knees, retching at the sickening thought of this hideous invasion.

They put Glass on a horse behind one of the young braves and rode away from the Arikara village. The old woman's dog started to follow behind the horses. One of the Indians stopped, dismounted, and coaxed the dog close. With the dull side of a tomahawk, he bashed the dog's skull, grabbed the animal by the hind legs, and rode to catch the others.

The Sioux camp lay just south of the Grand. The arrival of the four braves with a white man sparked immediate excitement, and scores of Indians trailed behind them like a parade as they rode through the teepees.

Yellow Horse led the procession to a low teepee set away from the camp. Wild designs covered the teepee: lightning bolts spewing from black clouds, buffalo arranged geometrically around a sun, vaguely human figures dancing around a fire. Yellow Horse called out a greeting, and after a few moments, an ancient, gnarled Indian emerged from a flap on the teepee. He squinted in the bright sun, although even without squinting, his eyes were barely visible beneath deep wrinkles. Black paint covered the upper half of his face, and he had tied a dead, withered raven behind his right ear. He was naked from the chest up despite the chill of the October day, and below the waist he wore only a loincloth. The skin hanging loosely from his sunken chest was painted in alternating stripes of black and red.

Yellow Horse dismounted, and signaled Glass to do the same. Glass stepped down stiffly, his wounds aching anew from the unaccustomed bouncing of the ride. Yellow Horse told the medicine man about the strange white man they found in the remains of the Arikara village, how they had watched as he set loose the spirit of the old squaw. He told the medicine man that the white man had shown no fear as they approached him, though he had no weapons but a sharpened stick. He told about the bear-claw necklace and the wounds on the man's throat and back.

The medicine man said nothing during Yellow Horse's long explanation, though his eyes peered intently through the furrowed mask of his face. The assembled Indians huddled close to listen, a murmur rising at the description of the maggots in the wounded back.

When Yellow Horse finished, the medicine man stepped up to Glass.

The top of the shrunken man's head barely rose to Glass's chin, which put the old Sioux at a perfect angle to examine the bear claw. He poked at the tip with his thumb, as if to verify its authenticity. His palsied hands trembled slightly as they reached to touch the pinkish scars extending from Glass's right shoulder to his throat.

Finally he turned Glass around to examine his back. He reached up to the collar of the threadbare shirt and ripped. The cloth offered little resistance. The Indians pushed close to see for themselves what Yellow Horse had described. They broke instantly into excited chatter in the strange language. Glass again felt his stomach turn at the thought of the spectacle that sparked such fervor.

The medicine man said something and the Indians fell instantly silent.

He turned and disappeared behind the flap on his teepee. When he emerged a few minutes later, his arms were full of assorted gourds and beaded bags. He returned to Glass and motioned him to lie facedown on the ground. Next to Glass, he spread out a beautiful white pelt. On the pelt he laid out an array of medicines. Glass had no idea what the vessels contained. *I don't care.* Only one thing mattered. *Get them off me.*

The medicine man said something to one of the young braves, who ran off, returning in a few minutes with a black pot full of water. Meanwhile, the medicine man sniffed at the largest of the gourds, adding ingredients from the assortment of bags. He broke into a low chant as he worked, the only sound to rise above the respectful silence of the villagers.

The principal ingredient of the big gourd was buffalo urine, taken from the bladder of a large bull in a hunt the past summer. To the urine he added alder root and gunpowder. The resulting astringent was as potent as turpentine.

The medicine man handed Glass a short stick, six inches in length. It took a moment before Glass understood its purpose. He took a deep breath and placed the stick between his teeth.

Glass braced himself and the medicine man poured.

The astringent ignited the most intense pain that Glass had ever felt, like molten iron in a mold of human flesh. At first the pain was specific, as the liquid seeped into each of the five cuts, inch by excruciating inch. Soon though, the pointed fire spread into a broader wave of agony, pulsating with the rapid beat of his heart. Glass sunk his teeth into the soft wood of the stick. He tried to imagine the cathartic effect of the treatment, but he could not transcend the immediacy of the pain.

The astringent had the desired effect on the maggots. Dozens of the wriggling white forms struggled to the surface. After a few minutes, the medicine man used a large ladle of water to wash the worms and the burning liquid from Glass's back. Glass panted as the pain slowly receded. He had just begun to catch his breath when the medicine man poured again from the big gourd.

The medicine man applied four doses of the astringent. When he had washed the final traces away, he packed the wounds in a steaming poultice of pine and larch. Yellow Horse helped Glass into the medicine man's teepee. A squaw brought freshly cooked venison. He ignored his stinging back long enough to gorge himself, then laid down on a buffalo robe and fell into a deep sleep.

He passed in and out of sleep for almost two straight days. In his moments of wakefulness, he found next to him a replenished supply of food and water. The medicine man tended his back, twice changing the poultice. After the jolting pain of the astringent, the humid warmth of the poultice was like the soothing touch of a maternal hand.

The first light of early morning lit the teepee in a faint glow when Glass awoke on the morning of the third day, the silence broken only by the occasional rustling of horses and the cooing of mourning doves. The medicine man lay sleeping, a buffalo robe pulled over his bony chest. Next to Glass lay a pile of neatly folded, buckskin clothing—breeches, beaded moccasins, and a simple doeskin tunic. He raised himself slowly and dressed.

The Pawnee considered the Sioux their mortal enemies. Glass had even fought against a band of Sioux hunters in a small skirmish during his days on the Kansas plains. He had a new perception now. How could he be anything but appreciative for the Samaritan actions of Yellow Horse and the medicine man? The medicine man stirred, raising himself to a sitting position when he saw Glass. He said something that Glass could not understand.

Yellow Horse showed up a few minutes later. He seemed pleased that Glass was up and about. The two Indians examined his back and seemed to speak approvingly at what they found. When they finished, Glass pointed to his back, raised his eyebrows questioningly to ask, "Does it look okay?" Yellow Horse pursed his lips and nodded his head.

They met later that day in Yellow Horse's teepee. Through a hodgepodge of sign language and drawings in the sand, Glass attempted to communicate where he came from and where he wanted to go. Yellow Horse seemed to understand "Fort Brazeau," which Glass confirmed when the Indian drew a map showing the precise placement of the fort at the confluence of the Missouri with the White River. Glass nodded his head furiously. Yellow Horse said something to the braves assembled in the teepee. Glass could not understand, and went to sleep that night wondering if he should simply strike out on his own.

He awoke the next morning to the sound of horses outside the medicine man's teepee. When he emerged, he found Yellow Horse and the three young braves from the Arikara village. They were mounted, and one of the braves held the bridle of a riderless pinto.

Yellow Horse said something and pointed to the pinto. The sun had just crested the horizon as they began the ride south toward Fort Brazeau.

FOURTEEN

OCTOBER 6, 1823

JIM BRIDGER'S SENSE OF DIRECTION did not fail him. He had been right when he urged Fitzgerald to cut overland and away from the eastern turn of the Little Missouri River. The western horizon swallowed the last sliver of sun when the two men fired a rifle shot to signal their approach to Fort Union. Captain Henry sent out a rider to greet them.

The men of the Rocky Mountain Fur Company treated Fitzgerald's and Bridger's entry into the fort with somber respect. Fitzgerald bore Glass's rifle like the proud ensign of their fallen comrade. Jean Poutrine crossed himself as the Anstadt paraded past, and a few of the men removed their hats. Inevitable or not, the men found it unsettling to confront Glass's death.

They gathered in the bunkhouse to hear Fitzgerald's account. Bridger had to marvel at his skill, at the subtlety and deftness with which he lied. "Not much to tell," said Fitzgerald. "We all knew where it was going. I won't pretend to have been his friend, but I respect a man who fights like he fought.

"We buried him deep . . . covered him with enough rock to keep him protected. Truth is, Captain, I wanted to get moving right away—but

Bridger said we ought to make a cross for the grave." Bridger looked up, horrified at this last bit of embellishment. Twenty admiring faces stared back at him, a few nodding in solemn approval. *God—not respect!* What he had craved was now his, and it was more than he could bear. Whatever the consequences, he had to purge the awful burden of their lie—his lie.

He felt Fitzgerald's icy stare from the corner of his eye. *I don't care.* He opened his mouth to speak, but before he could find the right words, Captain Henry said, "I knew you'd pull your weight, Bridger." More approving nods from the men of the brigade. *What have I done?* He cast his eyes to the ground.

FIFTEEN

OCTOBER 9, 1823

FORT BRAZEAU'S CLAIM TO THE appellation of "fort" was tenuous at best. Perhaps the motivation for the name had been vanity—a desire to institutionalize a family name. Or perhaps the hope had been to deter attack through sheer force of nomenclature. Either way, the name exceeded its grasp.

Fort Brazeau consisted of a single log cabin, a crude dock, and a hitching post. The cabin's narrow slits for shooting represented the only evidence that any consideration had been given to the martial aspects of the building, and they did more to impede light than arrows.

Scattered teepees spotted the clearing around the fort, a few pitched temporarily by Indians visiting to trade, a few pitched permanently by resident Yankton Sioux drunks. Anyone traveling on the river put in for the night. They usually camped under the stars, although for two bits the prosperous could share space on a straw tick in the cabin.

Inside, the cabin was part sundry shop and part saloon. Dimly lit, the main sensations were olfactory: day-old smoke, the greasy musk of fresh hides, open barrels of salted codfish. Barring drunken conversation, the primary sounds came from the constant buzz of flies and occasional buzz of snoring from a sleeping loft among the rafters.

The fort's namesake, Kiowa Brazeau, peered at the five approaching riders through thick spectacles that made his eyes appear unnaturally large. It was with considerable relief that he made out the face of Yellow Horse. Kiowa had worried about the disposition of the Sioux.

William Ashley had just spent the better part of a month at Fort Brazeau, planning the future of his Rocky Mountain Fur Company in the wake of the debacle at the Arikara villages. The Sioux had been allies with the whites in the battle against the Arikara. Or, more accurately, the Sioux had been allies until they had grown weary of Colonel Leavenworth's listless tactics. Halfway through Leavenworth's siege, the Sioux abruptly departed (though not before stealing horses from both Ashley and the U.S. Army). Ashley viewed the Sioux desertion as treachery. Kiowa harbored quiet sympathy for the attitude of the Sioux, though he saw no need to offend the founder of the Rocky Mountain Fur Company. After all, Ashley and his men had been Kiowa's best customers ever, purchasing virtually his entire inventory of supplies.

Ultimately, though, Fort Brazeau's meager economy depended on trade with the local tribes. The Sioux took on added significance since the dramatic change in relations with the Arikara. Kiowa worried that the Sioux's disdain for Leavenworth might extend to him and his trading post. The arrival of Yellow Horse and three other Sioux braves was a good sign, particularly when it became clear that they were delivering a white man who had apparently been in their care.

A small crowd of resident Indians and transiting voyageurs gathered to greet the newcomers. They stared in particular at the white man with the horrible scars on his face and scalp. Brazeau spoke to Yellow Horse in fluent Sioux, and Yellow Horse explained what he knew of the white man. Glass became the uncomfortable focus of dozens of gazing eyes. Those who spoke Sioux listened to Yellow Horse's description of finding Glass, alone with no weapons, grievously wounded by a bear. The rest were left to wonder, though it was obvious that the white man had a story to tell.

Kiowa listened to Yellow Horse's story before addressing himself to the white man. "Who are you?" The white man seemed to struggle with his words. Thinking he did not understand, Brazeau switched to French:

"*Qui êtes-vous?*"

Glass swallowed and gently cleared his throat. He remembered Kiowa from the Rocky Mountain Fur Company's brief layover on its way upriver. Kiowa obviously didn't remember him. It occurred to Glass that his appearance had changed significantly, although he still had not had a good glimpse of his own face since the attack. "Hugh Glass." It pained him to speak, and his voice came out as a kind of pitiful, screeching whine. "Ashley man."

"You just missed Monsieur Ashley. He sent Jed Stuart west with fifteen men, then headed back to St. Louis to raise another brigade." Kiowa waited a minute, thinking that if he paused the wounded man might offer more information.

When the man showed no signs of saying anything further, a one-eyed Scotsman gave voice to the group's impatience. In a dim-witted brogue he asked, "What happened to you?"

Glass spoke slowly and with as much economy as possible. "Grizzly attacked me on the Upper Grand." He hated the pathetic whine of his voice, but he continued. "Captain Henry left me with two men." He paused again, placing his hand to comfort his wounded throat. "They ran off and stole my kit."

"Sioux bring you all the way here?" asked the Scot.

Seeing the pain in Glass's face, Kiowa answered for him. "Yellow Horse found him alone at the Arikara villages. Correct me if I'm wrong, Monsieur Glass, but I'll wager you made it down the Grand on your own."

Glass nodded.

The one-eyed Scotsman started to ask another question, but Kiowa cut him off. "Monsieur Glass can save his tale for later. I'd say he deserves a chance to eat and sleep." The eyeglasses lent Kiowa's face an intelligent and avuncular air. He grabbed Glass by the shoulder and led him into the cabin. Inside, he placed Glass at a long table and said something in

Sioux to his wife. She produced a heaping plate of stew from a giant, cast iron pot. Glass inhaled the food, then two more large helpings.

Kiowa sat across the table from him, watching patiently through the dim light and shooing away the gawkers.

As he finished eating, Glass turned to Kiowa with a sudden thought. "I can't pay."

"I didn't expect that you'd be carrying a lot of cash. An Ashley man can draw credit at my fort." Glass nodded his head in acknowledgment. Kiowa continued, "I can equip you and get you on the next boat to St. Louis."

Glass shook his head violently. "I'm not going to St. Louis." Kiowa was taken aback. "Well, just where do you plan on going?"

"Fort Union."

"Fort Union! It's October! Even if you make it past the Rees to the Mandan villages, it'll be December by the time you get there. And that's still three hundred miles from Fort Union. You going to walk up the Missouri in the middle of winter?"

Glass didn't answer. His throat hurt. Besides, he wasn't looking for permission. He took a sip of water from a large tin cup, thanked Kiowa for the food, and started to climb the rickety ladder to the sleeping loft. He stopped part way, climbed back down and walked outside.

Glass found Yellow Horse camped away from the Fort on the banks of the White River. He and the other Sioux had tended their horses, done a little trading, and would leave in the morning. Yellow Horse avoided the fort as much as possible. Kiowa and his Sioux wife had always treated him honestly, but the whole establishment depressed him. He felt disdain and even shame for the filthy Indians who camped around the fort, prostituting their wives and daughters for the next drink of whiskey. There was something to fear in an evil that could make men leave their old lives behind and live in such disgrace.

Beyond Fort Brazeau's effect on the resident Indians, other aspects of the post left him profoundly disquieted. He marveled at the intricacy and quality of the goods produced by the whites, from their guns

and axes to their fine cloth and needles. Yet he also felt a lurking trepidation about a people who could make such things, harnessing powers that he did not understand. And what about the stories of the whites'
great villages in the East, villages with people as numerous as the buffalo. He doubted these stories could be true, though each year the trickle
of traders increased. Now came the fight with the Arikara and the soldiers. True, it was the Arikara that the whites sought to punish, a tribe
for which he himself held no goodwill. And true, the white soldiers had
been cowards and fools. He struggled to understand his unease. Taken
bit by bit, none of his forebodings seemed overwhelming. Yet Yellow
Horse sensed that these scattered strands came together somehow,
braided in a warning that he could not yet fully perceive.

Yellow Horse stood when Glass walked into the camp, a low fire
illuminating their faces. Glass had thought about trying to pay the Sioux
for their care, but something told him that Yellow Horse would take
offense. He thought about some small gift—a pigtail of tobacco or a
knife. Such trifles seemed inadequate expressions of his gratitude.
Instead he walked up to Yellow Horse, removed his bear-claw necklace, and placed it around the Indian's neck.

Yellow Horse stared at him for a moment. Glass stared back, nodded
his head, then turned and walked back toward the cabin.

When Glass climbed again to the sleeping loft, he found two voyageurs already asleep on the large straw tick. In a corner under the eaves,
a ratty hide had been spread in the cramped space. Glass eased himself
down and found sleep almost instantly.

A loud conversation in French woke Glass the next morning, rising to the loft from the open room below. Jolly laughter interspersed
the discussion, and Glass noticed he was alone in the loft. He lay there
for a while, enjoying the luxury of shelter and warmth. He rolled from
his stomach to his back.

The medicine man's brutal treatment had worked. If his back was
not yet fully healed, the wounds at least had been purged of their vile
infection. He stretched his limbs one by one, as if examining the

complex components of a newly purchased machine. His leg could bear the full weight of his body, although he still walked with a pronounced limp. And though his strength had not returned, his arm and shoulder could function normally. He assumed that the recoil of a rifle would cause sharp pain, but he was confident in his ability to handle a gun.

A *gun*. He appreciated Kiowa's willingness to equip him. What he wanted, though, was *his* gun. His gun and a reckoning from the men who stole it. Reaching Fort Brazeau seemed markedly anticlimactic. True, it was a milestone. Yet for Glass the fort did not mark a finish line to cross with elation, but rather a starting line to cross with resolve. With new equipment and his increasingly healthy body, he now had advantages that he had lacked in the past six weeks. Still, his goal lay far away.

As he lay on his back in the loft, he noticed a bucket of water on a table. The door opened below and a cracked mirror on the wall caught the morning light. Glass rose from the floor and walked slowly to the mirror.

He wasn't exactly shocked at the image staring back at him. He expected to look different. Still, it was strange finally to see the wounds that for weeks he could only imagine. Three parallel claw marks cut deep lines through the heavy beard on his cheek. They reminded Glass of war paint. No wonder the Sioux had been respectful. Pinkish scar tissue ringed his scalp line, and several gashes marked the top of his head. Where hair did grow, he noticed that gray now mixed with the brown he knew before—particularly in his beard. He paid particular attention to his throat. Again, parallel swaths marked the path of the claws. Knobby scars marked the points where the sutures had been tied.

Glass lifted his doeskin blouse in an effort to look at his back, but the dark mirror showed little more than the outline of the long wounds. The mental image of the maggots still haunted him. Glass left the mirror and climbed down from the loft.

A dozen men gathered in the room below, crowding the long table and spilling beyond. The conversation stopped as Glass descended the ladder from the loft.

Kiowa greeted him, switching easily to English. The Frenchman's facility with language was an asset for a trader amid the frontier Babel.

"Good morning, Monsieur Glass. We were just talking about you." Glass nodded his head in acknowledgment but said nothing.

"You're in luck," continued Kiowa. "I may have found you a ride upriver." Glass's interest was immediate.

"Meet Antoine Langevin." A short man with a long mustache stood up formally from the table, reaching to shake Glass's hand. Glass was surprised by the power of the small man's grip.

"Langevin arrived last night from upriver. Like you, Monsieur Glass, he arrived with something of a story to tell. Monsieur Langevin came all the way from the Mandan villages. He tells me that our wandering tribe, the Arikara, has established a new village on land only a mile south of the Mandans."

Langevin said something in French that Glass did not understand. "I'm getting to that, Langevin," said Kiowa, irritated at the interruption.

"I thought our friend might appreciate a bit of historical context." Kiowa continued with his explanation. "As you can imagine, our friends the Mandans are nervous that their new neighbors are bringing trouble with them. As a condition of occupying Mandan territory, the Mandans have exacted a promise that the Arikara will cease their attacks on whites."

Kiowa removed his spectacles, wiping the lenses with his long shirt-tail before returning them to the perch on his ruddy nose. "Which brings me to my own circumstances. My little fort depends on river traffic. I need trappers and traders like yourself moving up and down the Missouri. I appreciated the lengthy visit by Monsieur Ashley and his men, but this fighting with the Arikara will drive me out of business.

"I've asked Langevin to lead a deputation up the Missouri. They'll take gifts and reestablish ties with the Arikara. If they succeed, we'll send word to St. Louis that the Missouri is open for business.

"There's room for six men and supplies on Langevin's *bâtard*. This is Toussaint Charbonneau." Kiowa pointed to another man at the table.

Glass knew the name, and stared with interest at the husband of Sacagewea. "Toussaint translated for Lewis and Clark. He speaks Mandan, Arikara, and anything else you might need on the way."

"And I speak English," said Charbonneau, which sounded like, *end ah speak eegleesh.* Kiowa's English was almost without accent, but Charbonneau's carried the thick melody of his native tongue. Glass reached for Charbonneau's hand.

Kiowa continued with the introductions. "This is Andrew MacDonald." He pointed to the one-eyed Scot from the day before. Glass noticed that in addition to the missing eye, the Scot was missing a significant portion from the tip of his nose. "There's a good chance he's the dumbest man I ever met," said Kiowa. "But he can paddle all day without stopping. We call him 'Professeur.'" Professeur cocked his head to bring Kiowa within range of his good eye, which squinted in dim recognition at the mention of his name, although the irony clearly eluded him.

"Finally—there is Dominique Cattoire." Kiowa pointed to a voyageur smoking a thin clay pipe. Dominique rose, shook Glass's hand and said, *"Enchanté."*

"Dominique's brother is Louis Cattoire, king of the *putains.* He's going too, if we pry him and his *andouille* out of the whore's tent. We call Louis 'La Vierge.'" The men around the table laughed.

"Which brings me to you. They're rowing upriver, so they need to travel light. "They need a hunter to provide meat for the camp. I suspect you are pretty good at finding food. Probably even better once we get you a rifle."

Glass nodded his head in response.

"There's another reason our deputation can use an extra rifle," continued Kiowa. "Dominique heard rumors that an Arikara chief named Elk's Tongue has broken away from the main tribe. He's leading a small band of warriors and their families somewhere between Mandan and the Grand. We don't know where they're at, but he's vowed to avenge the attack on the Ree village.

Glass thought about the blackened remnants of the Arikara village and nodded in response.

"Are you in?"

Part of Glass did not want the encumbrance of fellow travelers. His plan had been to make his way up the Missouri alone, on foot. He intended to leave that day, and hated the idea of waiting. Still, he recognized the opportunity. Numbers meant safety, if the men were any good. The men of Kiowa's deputation seemed seasoned, and Glass knew there were no finer boatmen than the scrappy voyageurs. He also knew that his body was still healing, and his progress would be slow if he walked. Paddling the *bâtard* upstream would be slow too. But riding while the others paddled would give him another month to mend.

Glass put his hand to his throat. "I'm in."

Langevin said something to Kiowa in French. Kiowa listened and then turned to Glass. "Langevin says he needs today to make repairs to the *bâtard*. You'll leave tomorrow at dawn. Eat some food and then let's get you provisioned."

Kiowa kept his wares along a wall at the far end of the cabin. A plank over two empty barrels served as the counter. Glass focused first on a long arm. There were five weapons to choose from. Three were rusted northwest muskets of ancient vintage, clearly meant for trade with the Indians. Between the two rifles, the choice at first seemed obvious. One was a classic Kentucky long rifle, beautifully crafted with a burnished walnut finish. The other was a weathered Model 1803 U.S. Infantry rifle whose stock had been broken and repaired with rawhide. Glass picked up the two rifles and carried them outside, accompanied by Kiowa. Glass had an important decision to make, and he wanted to examine the weapons in full light.

Kiowa looked on expectantly as Glass examined the long Kentucky rifle. "That's a beautiful weapon," said Kiowa. "The Germans can't cook for shit but they know how to make a gun."

Glass agreed. He had always admired the elegant lines of Kentucky rifles. But there were two problems. First, Glass noticed with disappointment the rifle's small caliber, which he correctly gauged as .32. Second, the gun's great length made it heavy to carry and cumbersome to load. This was an ideal gun for a gentleman farmer, squirrel hunting in Virginia. Glass needed something different.

He handed the Kentucky rifle to Kiowa and picked up the Model 1803, the same gun carried by many of the soldiers in Lewis and Clark's Corps of Discovery. Glass first examined the repair work on the broken stock. Wet rawhide had been tightly stitched around the break, then allowed to dry. The rawhide had hardened and shrunk as it dried, creating a rock-sturdy cast. The stock was ugly, but it felt solid. Next Glass examined the lock and trigger works. There was fresh grease and no sign of rust. He ran his hand slowly down the half stock, then continued the length of the short barrel. He put his finger into the fat hole of the muzzle, noting approvingly the heft of its .53 caliber.

"You like the big gun, eh?" Glass nodded in reply.

"A big gun is good," said Kiowa. "Give it a try." Kiowa smiled wryly. "Gun like that, you could kill a bear!"

Kiowa handed Glass a powder horn and a measure. Glass poured a full charge of 200 grains and dumped it into the muzzle. Kiowa handed him a big .53 ball and a greased patch from his vest pocket. Glass wrapped the ball in the patch and tapped it into the muzzle. He pulled out the ramrod and set the ball firmly in the breech. He poured powder in the pan and pulled the hammer to full cock, searching for a target.

Fifty yards away a squirrel sat placidly in the crotch of a big cottonwood.

Glass sighted on the squirrel and pulled the trigger. The briefest of instants separated the ignition in the pan and the primary explosion deep in the barrel. Smoke filled the air, momentarily obscuring the target from sight. Glass winced at the stiff punch of the recoil against his shoulder.

As the smoke cleared, Kiowa ambled slowly to the foot of the cottonwood. He stooped to pick up the tattered remains of the squirrel, which now consisted of very little beyond a bushy tail. He walked back to Glass and tossed the tail at Glass's feet. "I think that gun is not so good for squirrels."

This time Glass smiled back. "I'll take it."

They returned to the cabin and Glass picked out the rest of his supplies. He chose a .53 pistol to complement the rifle. A ball mold, lead, powder, and flints. A tomahawk and a large skinning knife. A thick leather belt to hold his weapons. Two red cotton shirts to wear beneath the doeskin tunic. A large Hudson's Bay capote. A wool cap and mittens. Five pounds of salt and three pigtails of tobacco. Needle and thread. Cordage. To carry his newfound bounty, he picked a fringed leather possibles bag with intricate quill beading. He noticed that the voyageurs all wore small sacks at the waist for their pipe and tobacco. He took one of those too, a handy spot for his new flint and steel.

When Glass finished, he felt rich as a king. After six weeks with nothing but the clothes on his back, Glass felt immensely prepared for whatever battles lay before him. Kiowa calculated the bill, which totaled one hundred twenty-five dollars. Glass wrote a note to William Ashley:

> *October 10, 1823*
> *Dear Mr. Ashley:*
> *My kit was stolen by two men of our brigade with whom I will settle my own account. Mr. Brazeau has extended me credit against the name of the Rocky Mountain Fur Co. I have taken the liberty of advancing the attached goods against my pay. I intend to recover my property and I pledge to repay my debt to you.*
> *Your most obedient servant,*
> *Hugh Glass*

"I'll send your letter with the invoice," said Kiowa.

Glass ate a hearty dinner that evening with Kiowa and four of his five new companions. The fifth, Louis "La Vierge" Cattoire, had yet to emerge from the whore's tent. His brother Dominique reported that La Vierge had alternated between bouts of inebriation and fornication since the moment of their arrival at Fort Brazeau. Except when it directly involved Glass, the voyageurs did most of their talking in French. Glass recognized scattered words and phrases from his time on Campeche, though not enough to follow the conversation.

"Make sure your brother's ready in the morning," said Langevin. "I need his paddle."

"He'll be ready."

"And remember the task at hand," said Kiowa. "Don't be laying up with the Mandans all winter. I need confirmation that the Arikara won't attack traders on the river. If I haven't heard from you by New Year's, I can't get word to St. Louis in time to effect planning for the spring."

"I know my job," said Langevin. "I'll get you the information you need."

"Speaking of information"—Kiowa switched seamlessly from French to English—"we'd all like to know exactly what happened to you, Monsieur Glass." At this, even the dim eye of Professeur flickered with interest.

Glass looked around the table. "There's not much to tell." Kiowa translated as Glass spoke, and the voyageurs laughed when they heard what Glass had said.

Kiowa laughed too, then said: "With all due respect, *mon ami,* your face tells a story by itself—but we'd like to hear the particulars."

Settling in for what they expected to be an entertaining tale, the voyageurs packed fresh tobacco into their long pipes. Kiowa removed an ornate silver snuffbox from his vest pocket and put a pinch to his nose.

Glass put his hand to his throat, still embarrassed by his whining voice.

"Big grizzly attacked me on the Grand. Captain Henry left John Fitzgerald and Jim Bridger behind to bury me when I died. They robbed me instead. I aim to recover what's mine and see justice done."

Glass finished. Kiowa translated. A long silence followed, pregnant with expectation.

Finally Professeur asked in this thick brogue, "Ain't he gonna tell us anymore?"

"No offense, monsieur," said Toussaint Charbonneau, "but you're not much of a *raconteur*."

Glass stared back, but offered no further detail.

Kiowa spoke up. "It's your business if you want to keep the details of your fight with the bear, but I won't let you leave without telling me about the Grand."

Kiowa understood early in his career that his trade dealt not only in goods, but also in information. People came to his trading post not just for the things they could buy, but also for the things they could learn. Kiowa's fort sat at the confluence of the Missouri and the White River, so the White he knew well. So too the Cheyenne River to his north. He had learned what he could about the Grand from a number of Indians, but details remained sparse.

Kiowa said something in Sioux to his wife, who retrieved for him a well-worn book which they both handled as if it were the family Bible. The book wore a long title on its tattered cover. Kiowa adjusted his spectacles and read the title aloud: *"History of the Expedition . . ."*

Glass finished it: ". . . *Under the Command of Captains Lewis and Clark."* Kiowa looked up excitedly. *"Ah bon!* Our wounded traveler is a man of letters!"

Glass too was excited, forgetting for a while the pain of speaking.

"Edited by Paul Allen. Published in Philadelphia, 1814."

"Then you're also familiar with Captain Clark's map?"

Glass nodded. He remembered well the electricity that accompanied the long-awaited publication of the memoirs and map. Like the maps that shaped his boyhood dreams, Glass first saw *History of the Expedition* in the Philadelphia offices of Rawsthorne & Sons.

Kiowa set the book on its spine and it fell open to Clark's map, entitled *"A Map of Lewis and Clark's Track, Across the Western Portion of North America From the Mississippi to the Pacific Ocean."* To prepare for their expedition, Clark had trained intensively in cartography and its tools. His map was the marvel of its day, surpassing in detail and accuracy anything produced before it. The map showed clearly the major tributaries feeding the Missouri from St. Louis to the Three Forks.

Though the map portrayed accurately the rivers that flowed into the Missouri, detail usually ended near the point of confluence. Little was known about the course and source of these streams. There were a few exceptions: By 1814, the map could incorporate discoveries in the Yellowstone Basin by Drouillard and Colter. It showed the trace of Zebulon Pike through the southern Rockies. Kiowa had sketched in the Platte, including a rough estimate of its north and south forks. And on the Yellowstone, Manuel Lisa's abandoned fort was marked at the mouth of the Bighorn.

Glass pored eagerly over the document. What interested him was not Clark's map itself, which he knew well from his long hours at Rawsthorne & Sons and his more recent studies in St. Louis. What interested Glass were the details added by Kiowa, the penciled etchings of a decade's accreted knowledge.

The recurrent theme was water, and the names told the stories of the places. Some memorialized fights—War Creek, Lance Creek, Bear in the Lodge Creek. Others described the local flora and fauna—Antelope Creek, Beaver Creek, Pine Creek, the Rosebud. Some detailed the character of water itself—Deep Creek, Rapid Creek, the Platte, Sulphur Creek, Sweet Water. A few hinted at something more mystical—Medicine Lodge Creek, Castle Creek, Keya Paha.

Kiowa peppered Glass with questions. How many days had they walked up the Grand before striking the upper fork? Where did creeks flow into the river? What landmarks distinguished the path? What signs of beaver and other game? How much wood? How far to the Twin Buttes? What signs of Indians? Which tribes? Kiowa used a sharp pencil to sketch in the new details.

Glass took as well as gave. Though the rough map was etched in his memory, the details assumed new urgency as he contemplated traversing the land alone. How many miles from the Mandan villages to Fort Union? What were the principal tributaries above Mandan, and how many miles between them? What was the terrain? When did the Missouri freeze over? Where could he save time by cutting across the bends in the river? Glass copied key portions of Clark's map for his own future reference. He focused on the expanse between the Mandan villages and Fort Union, tracing both the Yellowstone and the Missouri rivers for several hundred miles above Fort Union.

The others drifted away from the table as Kiowa and Glass continued into the night, the dim oil lamp casting wild shadows on the log walls. Hungry at the rare opportunity for intelligent conversation, Kiowa would not release Glass from his grasp. Kiowa marveled at Glass's tale of walking from the Gulf of Mexico to St. Louis. He brought out fresh paper and made Glass draw a crude map of the Texas and Kansas plains.

"A man like you could do well at my post. Travelers are hungry for the type of information you possess."

Glass shook his head.

"Truly, *mon ami*. Why don't you lay up for the winter? I'll hire you on."

Kiowa would gladly have paid, just for the company.

Glass shook his head again, more firmly this time. "I have my own affairs to attend."

"Bit of a silly venture, isn't it? For a man of your skills? Traipsing across Louisiana in the dead of winter. Chase down your betrayers in the spring, if you're still inclined."

The warmth of the earlier conversation seemed to drain from the room, as if a door had been opened on a frigid winter day. Glass's eyes flashed and Kiowa regretted immediately his comment.

"It's not an issue on which I asked your counsel."

"No, monsieur. No, it was not."

There remained barely two hours before sunlight when Glass, exhausted, finally climbed up the ladder to the loft. Still, the anticipation of debarkation allowed him little sleep.

———

Glass awoke to a potpourri of shouted obscenities. One of the speakers was a man, screaming in French. Glass did not understand the individual words, but context made their general meaning clear.

The speaker was "La Vierge" Cattoire, having just been rudely roused from the depths of a drunken slumber by his brother Dominique. Weary of his sibling's antics and unable to awaken him with the standard kick in the ribs, Dominique tried another tactic: He made water on his brother's face. It was this act of considerable disrespect that triggered the rantings from La Vierge. Dominique's actions also angered the squaw with whom La Vierge had spent the night. She tolerated many forms of indecency in her teepee. Some she even encouraged. But Dominique's indiscriminate pissing had soiled her best blanket, and that made her mad. She yelled with the piercing screech of an offended magpie.

By the time Glass emerged from the cabin, the yelling match had degenerated into a fistfight. Like an ancient Greek wrestler, La Vierge stood facing his brother without a stitch of clothing. La Vierge had the advantage of size over his elder brother, but he bore the disadvantage of three consecutive days of heavy drinking, not to mention a rather abrupt and distasteful awakening. His vision had not cleared and his balance was off, though these handicaps did not temper his willingness to engage. Familiar with La Vierge's fighting style, Dominique stood firm, waiting for the inevitable attack. With a guttural roar, La Vierge lowered his head and barreled forward.

La Vierge put the full momentum of his charge behind the looping swing he aimed at his brother's head. Had he connected, he might well have planted Dominique's nose in the back of his brain. As it was, Dominique parried casually to the side.

Missing his target completely, La Vierge's swing threw him completely off balance. Dominique kicked him hard across the back of his knees, sweeping his feet from under him. La Vierge landed square on his back, knocking the wind from his lungs. He writhed pathetically for a moment, gasping for air. As soon as he could breathe again, he resumed his swearing and struggled for his feet. Dominique kicked him hard in the solar plexus, returning La Vierge to his quest for air.

"I told you to be ready, you miserable pinhead! We leave in half an hour." To underscore his point, Dominique kicked La Vierge in the mouth, splitting his upper and lower lips.

The fight over, the assembled crowd broke up. Glass walked down to the river. Langevin's *bâtard* floated at the dock, the swift current of the Missouri tugging against its mooring rope. As its name implied, the *bâtard* lay between the normal sizes of voyageur cargo canoes. Though smaller than the big *canots de maître,* the *bâtard* was sizable, almost thirty feet in length.

With the downstream current of the Missouri to propel them, Langevin and Professeur had been able to steer the *bâtard* by themselves, along with a full load of furs obtained in trade with the Mandans. Fully loaded, the *bâtard* would have required ten men to paddle upstream. Langevin's cargo would be light—a few gifts to bestow upon the Mandan and Arikara. Still, with only four men to paddle, their progress would be arduous.

Toussaint Charbonneau sat atop a barrel on the dock, casually eating an apple, while Professeur loaded the canoe under Langevin's supervision. To distribute the weight of their cargo, they laid two long poles on the floor of the canoe from bow to stern. On these poles Professeur placed the cargo, neatly arranged in four small bales. Professeur appeared to speak no French (at times, the Scotsman appeared to speak no English). Langevin compensated for Professeur's lack of comprehension by speaking more loudly. The increased volume aided Professeur very little, though Langevin's constant gesticulating provided a wealth of clues.

Professeur's blind eye contributed to his dim appearance. He lost the eye in a Montreal saloon, when a notorious brawler named "Oyster Joe" nearly shucked it from the Scotsman's skull. Professeur had managed to pop the eye back in place, but it no longer functioned. The unblinking orb was fixed permanently at a skewed angle, as if watching for an attack from his flank. Professeur had never gotten around to making a patch.

There was little fanfare to their departure. Dominique and La Vierge arrived at the dock, each with a rifle and a small bag of possessions. La Vierge squinted at the glare of the morning sun on the river. Mud caked his long hair, and blood from the split lips painted his chin and the front of his blouse. Still, he hopped spryly into bowsman's position at the front of the *bâtard,* and a glint filled his eyes that had nothing to do with the angle of the sun. Dominique took the position of the steersman in the stern. La Vierge said something and both brothers laughed.

Langevin and Professeur sat next to each other in the wide middle of the canoe, each paddling to one side. One cargo bale sat before them, one behind. Charbonneau and Glass arranged themselves around the cargo, with Charbonneau toward the bow and Glass toward the stern.

The four voyageurs picked up their paddles, bringing the bow into the swift current. They dug deep and the *bâtard* moved upstream.

La Vierge began to sing as he paddled, and the voyageurs joined in:

Le laboureur aime sa charrue,
Le chasseur son fusil, son chien;
Le musicien aime sa musique;
Moi, mon canot—c'est mon bien!
His cart is beloved of the ploughman,
The hunter loves his gun, his hound;
The musician is a music lover;
To my canoe I'm bound!

"Bon voyage, mes amis!" yelled Kiowa. "Don't lay up with the Mandans!" Glass turned to look behind him. He stared for a moment at Kiowa Brazeau, standing and waving from the dock at his little fort. Then Glass turned to look upriver and did not look back.

It was October 11, 1823. For more than a month he had moved away from his quarry. A strategic retreat—but retreat none the less. Beginning today, Glass resolved to retreat no more.

PART
TWO

SIXTEEN

NOVEMBER 29, 1823

FOUR PADDLES HIT THE WATER in perfect unison. The slender blades cut the surface, pushed to a depth of eighteen inches, then dug hard. The *bâtard* slogged forward with the stroke, bucking against the heavy flow of the current. When the stroke ended, the paddles lifted from the water. For an instant it appeared that the river would steal back their progress, but before it could rob them completely, the paddles hit the water again.

A paper-thin layer of ice had covered the still water when they embarked at dawn. Now, a few hours later, Glass leaned back against a thwart, basking appreciatively in the midmorning sun and enjoying the nostalgic, buoyant sensation of floating on water.

On their first day out of Fort Brazeau, Glass actually tried to handle a paddle. After all, he reasoned, he was a sailor by training. The voyageurs laughed when he picked up the oar, strengthening his determination. His folly became obvious immediately. The voyageurs paddled at the remarkable rate of sixty strokes a minute, regular as a fine Swiss watch. Glass could not have kept pace even if his shoulder had been fully healed. He flailed at the water for several minutes before something soft and wet hit him in the back of the head. He turned to see

Dominique, a mocking grin filling his face. "For you, Mr. Pork Eater!" *For yew, meeSTER pork eeTAIR!* For the rest of their voyage, Glass manned not a paddle but an enormous sponge, constantly bailing water as it pooled on the bottom of the canoe.

It was a full-time job, since the *bâtard* leaked steadily. The canoe reminded Glass of a floating quilt. Its patchwork skin of birch bark was sewn together with *wattope,* the fine root of a pine tree. The seams were sealed with pine tar, reapplied constantly as leaks appeared. As birch had become more difficult to find, the voyageurs were forced to use other materials in their patching and plugging. Rawhide had been employed in several spots, stitched on and then slathered in gum. Glass was amazed at the fragility of the craft. A stiff kick would easily puncture the skin, and one of La Vierge's main tasks as steersman was the avoidance of lethal, floating debris. At least they benefited from the relatively docile flow of the fall season. The spring floods could send entire trees crashing downstream.

There was an upside to the *bâtard*'s shortcomings. If the vessel was frail, it was also light, an important consideration as they labored against the current. Glass came quickly to understand the odd affection of voyageurs for their craft. It was a marriage of sorts, a partnership between the men who propelled the boat and the boat that propelled the men. Each relied upon the other. The voyageurs spent half their time complaining bitterly about the manifold ails of the craft, and half their time nursing them tenderly.

They took great pride in the appearance of the *bâtard,* dressing it in jaunty plumes and bright paint. On the high prow they had painted a stag's head, its antlers tilted challengingly toward the flowing water. (On the stern, La Vierge had painted the animal's ass.)

"Good landing up ahead," said La Vierge from his vantage point on the prow.

Langevin peered upriver, where a gentle current brushed lightly against a sandy bank; then he glanced up to judge the position of the sun. "Okay, I'd say that's a pipe. *Allumez.*"

So vaunted was the pipe in voyageur culture that they used it to measure distance. A "pipe" stood for the typical interval between their short breaks for smoking. On a downstream run, a pipe might represent ten miles; on flat water, five; but on the tough pull up the Missouri, they felt lucky to make two.

Their days fell quickly into a pattern. They ate breakfast in the purple-blue glow before dawn, fueling their bodies with leftover game and fried dough, chasing away the morning chill with tin cups of scalding hot tea. They were on the water as soon as the light allowed them to see, eager to squeeze motion from every hour of the day. They made five or six pipes a day. Around noon they stopped long enough to eat jerky and a handful of dried apples, but they didn't cook again until supper. They put ashore with the setting sun after a dozen hours on the water. Glass usually had an hour or so of dimming light to find game. The men waited with anticipation for the single shot that signaled his success. Rarely did he return to camp without meat.

La Vierge jumped into the knee-deep water near the bank, careful to keep the *bâtard*'s fragile bottom from scraping against the sand. He waded ashore, securing the cordelle to a large piece of driftwood. Langevin, Professeur, and Dominique jumped out next, rifles in hand, scanning the tree line. Glass and Professeur covered the others from the canoe as they waded ashore, then followed. The day before, Glass found an abandoned campsite, including the stone rings of ten teepees. They had no way of knowing if it was Elk Tongue's band, but the discovery put them on edge.

The men pulled pipes and tobacco from the *sacs au feu* at their waists, passing a flame from a tiny fire set by Dominique. The two brothers sat on their butts in the sand. In their positions as bowsman and steersman, Dominique and La Vierge stood to paddle. As a consequence, they sat to smoke. The others stood, happy for the opportunity to stretch the kinks from their legs.

The colder weather settled into Glass's wounds the way a storm creeps its way up a mountain valley. He awoke each morning stiff and sore, his condition made worse by the long hours at his cramped perch in the *bâtard*. Glass took full advantage of the break, pacing up and down the sandbar to coax circulation through his aching limbs.

He regarded his travel companions as he walked back toward them. The voyageurs were remarkably similar in dress, almost, thought Glass, as if they all had been issued a formal uniform. They wore red woolen caps with sides that could be turned down to cover their ears and a tassel trailing off the top. (La Vierge dressed his cap with a jaunty ostrich feather.) For shirts they wore long cotton blouses in white, red, or navy, tucked in at the waist. Each voyageur tied a parti-colored sash around his waist, its ends left to dangle down one leg or the other. Over the sash hung the *sac au feu,* keeping their pipes and a few other essentials close at hand. They wore doeskin breeches, supple enough to allow the comfortable folding of legs in a canoe. Below each knee they tied a bandanna, adding more dandy dash to their attire. On their feet they wore moccasins with no socks.

With the exception of Charbonneau, who was gloomy as January rain, the voyageurs approached each waking moment with an infallibly cloudless optimism. They laughed at the slimmest opportunity. They showed little tolerance for silence, filling the day with unceasing and passionate discussion of women, water, and wild Indians. They fired constant insults back and forth. Indeed, to pass up an opportunity for a good joke was viewed as a character flaw, a sign of weakness. Glass wished he understood more French, if only for the entertainment value of following the banter that kept them all so jolly.

In the rare moments when conversation lagged, someone would break out in zestful song, an instant cue for the others to join in. What they lacked in musical ability, they compensated in unbridled enthusiasm. All in all, thought Glass, an agreeable way of life.

During this break, Langevin interrupted their brief rest with a rare moment of seriousness. "We need to start setting a sentry at night," he said. "Two men each night, half shifts."

Charbonneau blew a long stream of smoke from his lungs. "I told you at Fort Brazeau—I translate. I don't stand watch."

"Well, I'm not pulling extra watch so he can sleep," stated La Vierge flatly.

"Me either," said Dominique.

Even Professeur looked distressed.

They all looked to Langevin expectantly, but he refused to allow the dispute to intrude on his enjoyment of the pipe. When he finished, he simply stood and said, "*Allons-y*. We're wasting daylight."

Five days later they arrived at the confluence of the river and a small creek. The crystal water of the stream discolored quickly when it mixed with the muddy flow of the Missouri. Langevin stared at the stream, wondering what to do.

"Let's camp, Langevin," said Charbonneau. "I'm sick of drinking mud."

"I hate to agree with him," said La Vierge, "but Charbonneau's right. All this bad water is giving me the shits."

Langevin too liked the prospect of clear drinking water. What bothered him was the location of the stream—on the western bank of the Missouri. He assumed that Elk Tongue's band was west of the river. Since Glass found the recent Indian campsite, the deputation had hung scrupulously to the eastern bank, especially when deciding where to stop for the night. Langevin looked west, where the horizon swallowed the last crimson sliver of sun. He looked east, but there were no landings before the next bend in the river. "Okay. We don't have much choice."

They paddled to the bank. Professeur and La Vierge unloaded the packs, and with the canoe empty, the voyageurs carried it ashore. There they flipped the boat on its side, creating a rough shelter that opened toward the river.

Glass waded ashore, nervously scanning the landing. The sandbar ran a hundred yards downstream to natural jetty-mounded boulders overgrown with thick willows and brush. Driftwood and other debris caught behind the jetty, obstructing the river and forcing it away from the gentle bank. Beyond the sandbar, more willows led to a stand of cottonwoods, increasingly rare as they paddled north.

"I'm hungry," said Charbonneau. "Get us some good supper, Mr. Hunter."

Geet US some goood suPEUR, MeeSTER HunTEUR.

"No hunting tonight," said Glass. Charbonneau started to object, but Glass cut him off. "We've got plenty of jerky. You can go a night without fresh meat, Charbonneau."

"He's right," agreed Langevin.

So they ate jerky along with fried mush, cooked in an iron skillet over a low fire. The fire drew them close. A bitter wind had diminished with the setting sun, but they could see their breath. The clear sky meant a cold night and a hard frost by morning.

Langevin, Dominique, and La Vierge lit their clay pipes and sat back to enjoy a smoke. Glass had not smoked since the grizzly attack; the burning sensation hurt his throat. Professeur scraped mush from the skillet. Charbonneau had walked away from the camp a half hour before.

Dominique sang quietly to himself, as if daydreaming out loud:

I have culled that lovely rosebud,
I have culled that lovely rosebud,
I have culled petal by petal,
Filled my apron with its scent . . .

"It's a good thing you can sing about it, brother," remarked La Vierge. "I bet you haven't culled any rosebuds for a year. They ought to call *you* the Virgin."

"Better to go thirsty than to drink out of every mud hole on the Missouri."

"Such a man of standards. So discriminating."

"I don't see a need to apologize for having standards. Unlike you, for example, I am quite fond of women with teeth."

"I'm not asking them to chew my food."

"You'd lay down with a pig if it wore a calico skirt."

"Well, I guess that makes you the pride of the Cattoire family. I'm sure Maman would be very proud to know that you only sleep with the fancy whores in St. Louis."

"Maman, no. Papa—maybe." They both laughed loudly, then solemnly crossed themselves.

"Keep your voices down," hissed Langevin. "You know how sound carries on the water."

"Why are you so cross tonight, Langevin?" asked La Vierge. "It's bad enough putting up with Charbonneau. I've had more fun at funerals."

"We'll be having a funeral if you two keep yelling."

La Vierge refused to let Langevin spoil a good conversation. "Do you know that squaw back at Fort Kiowa had *three* nipples."

"What good are three nipples?" asked Dominique.

"Your problem is that you lack imagination."

"Imagination, eh? If you had a little bit less imagination maybe it wouldn't hurt so bad when you piss."

La Vierge pondered a reply, but in truth, he had grown weary of conversation with his brother. Langevin clearly was not in a talking mood. Charbonneau was off in the woods. He looked at Professeur, with whom he'd never known anyone to have a conversation.

Finally La Vierge looked at Glass. It occurred to him suddenly that they had not really spoken with Glass since leaving Fort Kiowa. There had been scattered exchanges, most concerning Glass's success in putting fresh game in their pot. But no real conversation, certainly none of the ambling forays on which La Vierge liked to embark.

La Vierge felt suddenly guilty for his lack of social graces. He knew little about Glass beyond the fact that he had come up short in a scrape with a bear. More importantly, thought La Vierge, Glass knew little about *him*—and he must certainly want to know more. Besides, it was a good opportunity to practice his English, a language in which La Vierge considered himself an accomplished speaker.

"Hey, Pork Eater." When Glass looked up he asked, "From where do you come?"

The question—and the sudden use of English—took Glass by surprise.

He cleared his throat. "Philadelphia."

La Vierge nodded his head, waiting for a reciprocal inquiry from Glass.

None came.

Finally La Vierge said, "My brother and I, we are from Contrecoeur." Glass nodded his head, but said nothing. Clearly, decided La Vierge, this American would need to be coaxed along.

"You know how it is that we all come to be voyageurs?" *Yew NO how eet EES zat wi all come to bee voyaGEURS?*

Glass shook his head no. Dominique rolled his eyes, recognizing the prelude to his brother's tired stories.

"Contrecoeur is on the great St. Lawrence River. There was a time, a hundred years ago, when all the men in our village were poor farmers. All day they worked in the fields, but the dirt was bad, the weather too cold—they never made a good crop.

"One day a beautiful maiden named Isabelle was working in a field by the river. Suddenly from the water came a stallion—big and strong, black like coal. He stood in the river, staring at the girl. And she was very afraid. The stallion, he sees that she is about to run away, so he kicks at the water—and a trout goes flying to the girl. It lands there in the dirt at her feet. . . ." La Vierge couldn't find the English word he wanted, so he made a flip-flop motion with his hands.

"Isabelle, she sees this *petit cadeau,* and she is very happy. She picks it up and she takes to her family for dinner. She tells her papa and her brothers about this horse, but they think she is making a joke. They laugh and they tell her to get more fish from her new friend.

"Isabelle goes back to the field, and each day now she sees the black stallion again. Each day he comes a little closer, and each day he gives to her a gift. One day an apple, one day some flowers. Each day she tells her family about this horse who comes from the river. And each day they laugh at her story.

"Finally there comes a day when the stallion walks all the way up to Isabelle. She climbs on his back, and the stallion runs to the river. They disappear into the current—and they are never seen again."

The fire cast dancing shadows behind La Vierge as he spoke. And the rush of the river was like a hissing affirmation of his tale.

"That night, when Isabelle doesn't come home, her father and her brothers go looking for her in the fields. They find the tracks of Isabelle and they find the tracks of the stallion. They see that Isabelle has mounted the horse, and they see that the horse has run into the river. They search up and down the river, but they cannot find the girl.

"The next day, all the men of the village take to their canoes and join the search. And they take a vow—they will abandon their farms and stay on the river until they find the poor Isabelle. But they never find her. And so you see, Monsieur Glass, since that day we are voyageurs. Still this day we keep up the search for the poor Isabelle."

"Where's Charbonneau?" asked Langevin.

"Where's Charbonneau!" retorted La Vierge. "I tell you the story of a lost maiden and you're thinking about a lost old man?"

Langevin said nothing in reply. "He's *malade comme un chien,*" said La Vierge with a smile. "I'll call to him—make sure he's safe." He cupped his hand to his mouth and yelled into the willows. "Don't worry, Charbonneau—we're sending out Professeur to help you wipe your ass!"

Touissaint Charbonneau sat on his haunches, his naked ass pointing discreetly toward a bush. He had been in that position for some time. Long enough, in fact, that he had begun to develop a cramp in his thigh.

He hadn't been right since Fort Brazeau. No doubt he'd been poisoned by Kiowa's shitty food. He could hear La Vierge taunting him from the camp. He was starting to hate that bastard. A twig snapped.

Charbonneau bolted upright. One hand reached for his pistol and the other tugged at his deerskin trousers. Neither hand accomplished its task. The pistol slipped to the dark ground. His pants slipped to his ankles. When he lurched again for the pistol, his pants tripped him. He sprawled on the ground, scraping his knee on a large rock. He grunted in pain while from the corner of his eye he watched a large elk lope through the timber.

"Merde!" Charbonneau returned to his business, grimacing at the sharp new pain in his leg.

By the time he made his way back to camp, Charbonneau's normal pique had been ratcheted up a notch. He stared at Professeur, who sat reclining against a large log. The big Scot wore a beard of mush.

"It's disgusting the way he eats," said Charbonneau.

La Vierge looked up from his pipe. "I don't know, Charbonneau. The way the fire lights up the porridge on his chin—it kind of reminds me of the Northern Lights." Langevin and Dominique laughed, which further irritated Charbonneau. Professeur continued to chew, oblivious to the humor at his expense.

Charbonneau spoke again in French: "Hey, you idiot Scot bastard, do you understand a word of what I'm saying?" Professeur continued to work on the mush, placid as a cow with its cud.

Charbonneau smiled thinly. He appreciated the opportunity for such wholly naked cattiness. "What happened to his eye, anyway?"

No one jumped at the opportunity for conversation with Charbonneau.

Finally Langevin said, "Poked out in a brawl in Montreal."

"It looks like all hell. Makes me nervous, having the damn thing staring at me all day."

"Blind eye can't stare," said La Vierge. He had come to like Professeur, or at least to appreciate the Scot's ability with a paddle. Whatever he thought of Professeur, he was certain that he did not like Charbonneau. The old man's grousing commentary had grown stale by the first bend in the river.

"Well, it sure seems to stare," insisted Charbonneau. "Always looks like he's peeking around the corner. Never blinks, either. I don't see how the damn thing doesn't dry up."

"What if it could see—it's not like you're much to look at, Charbonneau," said La Vierge.

"He could at least put a patch over it. I'm tempted to tack one on there myself."

"Why don't you? Be nice if you had something to do."

"I'm not your damned *engagé!*" hissed Charbonneau. "You'll be glad I'm along when the Arikara come looking for your flea-bit scalp!" The translator had worked himself into a frothy lather, spittle forming in the corner of his mouth as he talked. "I was blazing trails with Lewis and Clark when you were still messing your pants."

"Jesus Christ, old man! If I hear one more of your damned Lewis and Clark stories, I swear I'm going to put a bullet in my brain—or better yet, your brain! Everyone would appreciate that."

"*Ça suffit!*" Langevin finally interjected. "Enough! I'd put you both out of *my* misery if I didn't need you!"

Charbonneau gave a triumphant sneer.

"But you listen, Charbonneau," said Langevin. "There's none of us that wears just one hat. We're too few. You'll take your turn with the dirty work just like everyone else. And you can start with the second watch tonight."

It was La Vierge's turn to sneer. Charbonneau stalked away from the fire, muttering something about the bitterroot as he laid out his bedroll under the *bâtard*.

"Who says he gets the *bâtard* tonight?" complained La Vierge. Langevin started to say something, but Dominique beat him to the punch. "Let it go."

SEVENTEEN

DECEMBER 5, 1823

PROFESSEUR WOKE THE NEXT MORNING to two urgent sensations: He was cold, and he needed to piss. His thick wool blanket failed to cover his ankles, not even when he curled his long frame and lay on his side. He lifted his head so that his good eye could see, and found that frost had settled on the blanket in the night.

The first hint of a new day glowed faintly beneath the eastern horizon, but a bright half-moon still dominated the sky. All the men but Charbonneau lay sleeping, radiating like spokes around the last embers of the fire.

Professeur stood slowly, his legs stiff from the cold. At least the wind had died down. He threw a log on the fire and walked toward the willows. He had taken a dozen steps when he nearly tripped on a body. It was Charbonneau.

Professeur's first thought was that Charbonneau was dead, killed on his watch. He started to yell an alarm when Charbonneu bolted upright, fumbling for his rifle, eyes wide as he struggled to orient himself. *Asleep on watch,* thought Professeur. *Langevin won't like that.* Professeur's pressing need became more urgent, and he hurried past Charbonneau toward the willows.

Like many of the things he encountered each day, Professeur was confused by what happened next. He felt an odd sensation and looked down to find the shaft of an arrow protruding from his stomach. For a moment he wondered if La Vierge had played some kind of joke. Then a second arrow appeared, then a third. Professeur stared in horrified fascination at the feathers on the slender shafts. Suddenly he could not feel his legs and he realized he was falling backward. He heard his body make heavy contact with the frozen ground. In the brief moments before he died, he wondered, *Why doesn't it hurt?*

Charbonneau turned at the sound of Professeur falling. The big Scot lay flat on his back with three arrows in his chest. Charbonneau heard a hissing sound and felt a burning sensation as an arrow grazed his shoulder. *"Merde!"* He dropped instinctively to the ground and scanned the dark willows for the shooter. The move saved his life. Forty yards away, the flash of guns erupted in the inky predawn light.

For an instant, the shots revealed the positions of their attackers. Charbonneau guessed that there were eight guns at least, plus a number of Indians with bows. He cocked his rifle, drew a bead on the nearest target and fired. A dark form slumped. More arrows flew out of the willows. He spun around and broke for the camp, twenty yards behind him.

Charbonneau's expletive woke the camp. The Arikara volley ignited chaos. Musket balls and arrows rained into the half-sleeping men like iron hailstones. Langevin cried out as a bullet ricocheted off his short rib. Dominique felt a shot rip the muscle of his calf. Glass opened his eyes in time to watch an arrow bury itself in the sand, five inches in front of his face.

The men scrambled for the paltry cover of the beached canoe as two Arikara braves broke from the willows. They hurtled toward the camp, their piercing war cries filling the air. Glass and La Vierge paused long enough to aim their rifles. They fired almost in sync at a range of no more than a dozen yards. With no time to coordinate or even to think, they had both aimed at the same target—a large Arikara with a buffalo horn helmet. He crashed to the ground as both shots penetrated his chest. The other brave ran full force toward La Vierge, the arc of his battle-ax descending toward the voyageur's head. La Vierge brought his rifle up with both hands to block the blow.

The Indian's ax locked with the barrel of La Vierge's rifle, the force knocking both of them to the ground. The Arikara found his feet first. His back to Glass, he raised the ax to strike at La Vierge again. Glass used both hands to drive his rifle butt into the back of the Indian's head. He felt the sickening sensation of breaking bone as the metal butt-plate connected. Stunned, the Arikara dropped to his knees in front of La Vierge, who by this time had scrambled to his feet. La Vierge swung his rifle like a club, catching the Indian full force across the side of his skull. The brave toppled sideways, and Glass and La Vierge tumbled behind the canoe.

Dominique raised himself long enough to fire toward the willows.

Langevin handed Glass his rifle, the other hand pressed against the bullet hole on his side. "You shoot—I'll load."

Glass raised to fire, finding and hitting his target with cool precision.

"How bad are you hit?" he asked Langevin.

"Not bad. *Òu se trouve Professeur?*"

"Dead by the willows," said Charbonneau matter-of-factly as he rose to fire.

Shots continued to pour from the willows as they hunkered behind the canoe. The report of the guns mixed with the sound of the bullets and arrows smashing through the thin skin of the *bâtard*.

"You son of a bitch, Charbonneau!" screamed La Vierge. "You fell asleep, didn't you?" Charbonneau ignored him, focused instead on pouring powder into the muzzle of his rifle.

"It doesn't matter now!" said Dominique. "Let's get the damn canoe in the water and get out of here!"

"Listen to me!" ordered Langevin. "Charbonneau, La Vierge, Dominique—the three of you carry the boat to the water. Take another shot first, then reload your rifle and lay it here." He pointed to the ground between him and Glass. "Glass and I will cover you with a last round of shots, then join you. Cover us from the boat with your pistols."

Glass understood most of what Langevin had said from context. He looked around the tense faces. No one had a better idea. They had to get off the beach. La Vierge popped above the lip of the canoe to fire his rifle, followed by Dominique and Charbonneau. Glass raised himself to take another shot as the others reloaded. By exposing themselves they prompted heavier fire from the Arikara. Bullet-size holes kept punching through the birch bark, but the voyageurs managed—at least for the moment—to deter an all-out rush.

Dominique tossed two paddles on the stack with the rifles. "Make sure you bring these!"

La Vierge threw his rifle between Glass and Langevin and braced himself against the middle thwart of the *bâtard*. "Let's go!" Charbonneau slid to the front of the canoe, Dominique to the rear.

Langevin shouted, "On my count! *Un, deux, trois!*" They lifted the *bâtard* above their heads in a single motion and made for the water, ten yards away. They heard excited shouts and the firing again intensified. Arikara warriors began emerging from concealed positions.

Glass and Dominique aimed their shots. With the canoe gone, the only cover came from pressing flat against the ground. They were only about fifty yards from the willows. Glass could see clearly the boyish face of an Arikara, squinting as he drew a short bow. Glass fired and the boy pitched backward. He reached for Dominique's rifle. Langevin's gun exploded next to him as Glass pulled the hammer of Dominique's to full cock. Glass found another target and squeezed the trigger. There was a spark in the pan, but the main charge failed to ignite. "Damn it!"

Langevin reached for Charbonneau's rifle while Glass refilled the pan on Dominique's. Langevin started to fire, but Glass put his hand on his shoulder. "Hold one shot!" They scooped up the rifles and paddles and broke for the river.

Ahead of Glass and Langevin, the three men with the *bâtard* covered the short distance to the river. In their haste to escape, they practically threw the canoe into the water. Charbonneau crashed into the river behind it and scrambled to climb in. "You're tipping it!" yelled La Vierge. Charbonneau's weight on the edge of the craft rocked it wildly—but it stayed upright. He flipped his legs over the lip and flattened himself on the floor of the boat, already taking on water from the seeping bullet holes. Charbonneau's momentum pushed the *bâtard* away from the shoreline. The current caught the stern and spun the boat around, propelling the craft away from shore. The long cordelle trailed behind it like a snake. The brothers saw Charbonneau's eyes, peering above the gunwale. Mini-geysers from bullets erupted in the water around them.

"Grab the rope!" shouted Dominique. Both brothers dove for the line, desperate to keep the canoe from floating away. La Vierge caught the cordelle in both hands, struggling to gain his feet in the thigh-deep water. He pulled back with all his strength as the slack disappeared from the line. Dominique slogged heavily through the water to come to his aid. His foot crashed hard into a submerged rock. He grunted in pain as the current swept his feet from beneath him. He found himself completely submerged. He recovered and stood up, two yards from La Vierge.

"I can't hold it!" yelled La Vierge. Dominique started to reach for the taut line, when suddenly La Vierge let go. Dominique watched in horror as the cordelle skidded across the water, trailing after the drifting *bâtard*. He started to swim after it when he noticed the stunned look on La Vierge's face.

"Dominique . . ." stammered La Vierge, "I think I'm shot." Dominique sloshed to his brother's side. Blood streamed into the river from a gaping hole in his upper back.

Glass and Langevin reached the river at the same moment that the bullet crashed into La Vierge. They watched in horror as he recoiled at the impact of the shot, dropping the cordelle. For a moment they thought that Dominique could grab the line, but he ignored it, turning instead to his brother.

"Get the boat!" barked Langevin.

Dominique paid no attention. In frustration Langevin screamed, "Charbonneau!"

"I can't stop it!" yelled Charbonneau. In an instant the boat was fifty feet from shore. With no paddle, it was true that Charbonneau could do nothing to slow the boat. It was certainly true that he had no intention of trying.

Glass turned to Langevin. Langevin started to say something when a musket ball buried itself in the back of his head. He was dead before his body hit the water. Glass looked back at the willows. At least a dozen Arikara poured toward the shoreline. Gripping a rifle in each hand, Glass dove toward Dominique and La Vierge. They had to swim for it.

Dominique supported La Vierge, struggling to keep his brother's head above the water. Looking at La Vierge, Glass could not tell for sure if he was alive or dead. Distraught and nearly hysterical, Dominique yelled something incomprehensible in French.

"Swim for it!" yelled Glass. He grabbed Dominique by the collar and pulled him deeper into the river, losing his grip on one of the rifles in the process. The current caught the three men and dragged them downstream. Bullets continued to rain into the water, and Glass looked back to see the Arikara lining the shoreline.

Glass struggled to keep one hand gripped on La Vierge and one hand gripped on the remaining rifle while kicking furiously to stay afloat. Dominique kicked too, and they managed to clear the jetty. La Vierge's face kept bobbing beneath the water. Both men battled to keep the wounded man afloat. Dominique started to yell something, which was drowned out when a rapid swamped his own face. The same rapid nearly caused Glass to lose his grip on his rifle. Dominique began to kick toward the shoreline.

"Not yet!" Glass implored. "Further downstream!" Dominique ignored him. His feet brushed the bottom in chest-deep water, and he flailed toward the shallows. Glass looked behind them. The rocks of the jetty created a significant barrier on land. The shoreline below the jetty consisted of a high-cut bank. Still, it wouldn't take the Arikara more than a few minutes to maneuver their way around it.

"We're too close!" yelled Glass. Again Dominique ignored him. Glass contemplated swimming on alone, but instead helped Dominique drag La Vierge ashore. They lay him on his back, reclined against the steep curve of the bank. His eyes flickered open, but when he coughed, blood spit forth from his mouth. Glass rolled him to his side to inspect the wound.

The bullet had entered La Vierge's back below his left shoulder blade.

Glass saw no way that it could have missed his heart. Dominique came silently to the same conclusion. Glass checked the rifle. For the moment, the wet charge rendered it useless. He looked at his belt. The hatchet still hung in its place, but his pistol was lost. Glass looked at Dominique. *What do you want to do?*

They heard a soft sound and turned to see La Vierge, the faintest smile at the corner of his mouth. His lips began to move, and Dominique took his brother's hand and held his ear close to understand. In a faint whisper, La Vierge was singing:

Tu es mon compagnon de voyage. . . .

Dominique recognized instantly the familiar song, though never before had it seemed so completely despondent. His eyes welled with tears, and he sang along in a gentle voice:

Tu es mon compagnon de voyage.
Je veux mourir dans mon canot.
Sur le tombeau, près du rivage,
Vous renverserez mon canot.

You are my voyageur companion.
I'll gladly die in my canoe.
And on the grave beside the canyon,
You'll overturn my canoe.

Glass looked toward the jetty, seventy-five yards upriver. Two Arikara appeared on the rocks. They pointed guns and began to yell.

Glass put his hand on Dominique's shoulder. He started to say, "They're coming," but the report of two rifles said it for him. The bullets thudded against the bank.

"Dominique, we can't stay here."

"I won't leave him," he said in his thick accent.

"Then we've all got to try the river again."

"No." Dominique shook his head emphatically. "We can't swim with him."

Glass looked again toward the jetty. The Arikara swarmed over now. *There's no time!*

"Dominique." Glass's tone was urgent now. "If we stay here, we'll all die." More guns cracked.

For an excruciating moment, Dominique said nothing, gently stroking his brother's ashen cheek. La Vierge stared peacefully ahead, a dim light glinting in his eyes. Finally Dominique turned to Glass. "I won't leave him." More guns.

Glass fought a collision of instincts. He needed time, time to think through his action, time to justify it—but there was none. Rifle in hand, he dove into the river.

Dominique heard a whining sound and felt a bullet bury itself in his shoulder. He thought about the horrible stories he had heard of Indian mutilations. He looked down at La Vierge. "I won't let them cut us up." He grabbed his brother under the arms and dragged him into the river. Another bullet crashed into his back. "Don't worry, little brother," he whispered, leaning back into the current's welcoming arms. "It's all downstream from here."

EIGHTEEN

DECEMBER 6, 1823

GLASS SQUATTED NAKED next to the small fire, as close to the flame as he could bear. He cupped his hands to capture the heat. He held them close, waiting until the last instant before he was certain his skin would blister, then pressed the hot flesh against his shoulders or thighs. The heat seeped in for a moment, but failed to penetrate the chill instilled in him by the icy waters of the Missouri.

His clothing hung on crude racks around three sides of the fire. The buckskins remained soggy, though he noted with relief that his cotton shirt was mostly dry.

He had floated nearly a mile downstream before climbing out into the thickest stand of brush he could find. He burrowed into the center of the bramble on a trail cut by rabbits, hopeful that no larger animal would follow. Within the tangle of willows and driftwood, he found himself once again taking somber inventory of his wounds and his possessions.

By comparison to the recent past, Glass felt considerable relief. He had a number of bruises and abrasions from the fight on the banks and the flight down the river. He even discovered a wound on his arm where it appeared that a bullet had grazed him. His old wounds ached in the cold, but did not appear otherwise aggravated. Except for the possibility that he would freeze to death, a possibility that seemed very real, he had managed to survive the Arikara attack. For an instant he saw again the image of Dominique and La Vierge, huddled on the cut bank. He pushed the thought from his mind.

As for his possessions, the most significant loss was his pistol. His rifle was soaked but serviceable. He had his knife and his possibles bag with flint and steel. He had his hatchet, which he used to shave kindling into a shallow pit. He hoped his powder was dry. He uncapped his powder horn and poured a dab on the ground. He set a flame to it from the fire and the powder ignited with a smell like rotten eggs.

His satchel was gone, with his spare shirt, blanket, and mittens. The satchel also contained his hand-sketched map, carefully marking the tributaries and landmarks of the upper Missouri. It mattered little since he remembered them by heart. Relatively speaking, he felt well equipped.

Though still damp, he decided to put on his cotton shirt. At least the weight of the cloth helped take the chill off his aching shoulder. Glass tended the fire for the rest of the day. He worried about the smoke it created, but he worried more about catching his death of cold. He tended his rifle to take his mind off the chill, drying it completely and applying grease from a small container in his possibles bag. By nighttime his clothing and rifle were ready.

He considered moving only at night. Somewhere nearby lurked the same Arikara that attacked the camp. He hated just sitting there, even if his position was well concealed. But there was no moon to light a path along the rough bank of the Missouri. He had no choice but to wait until morning.

As daylight faded, Glass took the clothes from the willow rack and dressed himself. Next he scooped a shallow, square pit near the fire. He used two sticks to remove scorching-hot stones from a ring around the flames, arranged them in the pit, then covered them with a thin layer of dirt. He added as much wood to the fire as he dared, then lay down on top of the seething stones. Between the mostly dry buckskins, the stones, the fire, and sheer exhaustion, he crossed a minimal threshold for warmth that permitted his body to sleep.

For two days Glass crept up the Missouri. For a while he wrestled with the question of whether he had inherited responsibility for Langevin's mission with the Arikara. He finally decided that he had not. Glass's commitment to Brazeau had been to provide game for the deputation, a task he had dutifully performed. He had no idea whether Elk Tongue's band represented the intentions of the other Arikara. It mattered little. The ambush underscored the vulnerability of slogging upriver by boat. Even if he received assurances from some faction of the Arikara, he had no intention of returning to Fort Brazeau. His own business was more pressing.

Glass guessed, correctly, that the Mandan village lay nearby. Though the Mandan were known as peaceful, he worried about the effect of their new alliance with the Arikara. *Would the Arikara be present in the Mandan village? How might the attack on the voyageurs have been portrayed?* Glass saw no reason to find out. He knew that a small trading post called Fort Talbot lay ten miles up the Missouri from the Mandan village. He decided to skirt the Mandans altogether, aiming instead for Fort Talbot. The few supplies he wanted, a blanket and a pair of mittens, he could find at the fort.

On the evening of the second day after the attack, Glass decided that he could no longer avoid the risk of hunting. He was ravenous, and a hide would also give him something to trade. He found fresh elk tracks near the river and followed them through a grove of cottonwoods into a large clearing, flanking the river for half a mile. A small stream parceled the clearing in two. Grazing near the stream, Glass could see a large bull along with two cows and three fat calves. Glass worked his way slowly through the clearing. He was almost within range when something spooked the elk. All six stood staring in the direction of Glass.

Glass started to shoot when he realized that the elk weren't looking at him—they were looking behind him.

Glass looked over his shoulder to find three mounted Indians emerging from the cottonwoods, a quarter mile back. Even at that distance, Glass could make out the spiked hairstyle worn by Arikara braves. He could see the Indians pointing as they kicked their horses and galloped toward him.

He desperately looked around him for any source of cover. The closest trees stood more than two hundred yards in front of him. He would never cover the ground in time. Nor could he make it to the river—he was cut off. He could stand and shoot, but even if he hit his target, he could never reload in time to hit all three riders, probably not even two. In desperation he ran for the distant trees, ignoring the pain that shot up his leg.

Glass had barely covered thirty yards when he pulled up in dread— another mounted Indian stepped from the cover of the cottonwoods in *front* of him. He looked back. The charging Arikara had covered half the distance between them. He looked again toward the new rider—now aiming down the barrel of his gun. The new rider fired. Glass winced in anticipation of the shot, but it flew high over his head. He turned back toward the Arikara. One of their horses was down! The Indian in front of him had shot at the other three! Now the shooter galloped toward him, as Glass realized he was Mandan.

Glass had no idea why, but the Mandan appeared to be coming to his aid. Glass spun to face his attackers. The two remaining Arikara had closed to within a hundred and fifty yards. Glass cocked his rifle and aimed. At first he tried to line his sights on one of the riders, but both Arikara hunched low behind their ponies' heads. He moved his aim to one of the horses, picking the hollow spot just below the neck.

He squeezed the trigger and the rifle spit forth his shot. The horse screamed and its legs seemed to fold in front of it. Dust flew as it ploughed to an abrupt stop, its rider flying over the dead animal's head.

Glass heard the pounding of hooves and looked up at the Mandan, who motioned him to jump on the horse. He leapt up, looking back to see the remaining Arikara rider rein his mount, firing a shot that missed. The Mandan kicked his horse and they broke for the trees. He turned the horse when they reached the cottonwoods. Both men dismounted to reload their rifles.

"Rees," said the Indian, pointing in their direction. "No good."

Glass nodded as he rammed a new charge home.

"Mandan," said the Indian, pointing to himself. "Good friendly." Glass aimed at the Arikara, but the sole remaining rider had retreated out of range. The two mountless Indians flanked him on either side. The loss of two horses had stolen their appetite for pursuit.

The Mandan called himself Mandeh-Pahchu. He had been tracking the elk when he had stumbled across Glass and the Arikara. Mandeh-Pahchu had a good idea where the scarred white man came from. Only the day before, the translator Charbonneau had arrived in the Mandan village. Well known to the Mandans from his time with Lewis and Clark, Charbonneau related the story of the Arikara attack on the voyageurs. Mato-Tope, a Mandan chief, had been furious with Elk Tongue and his renegade band. Like the trader Kiowa Brazeau, Chief Mato-Tope wanted the Missouri open for business. Though he understood Elk Tongue's anger, clearly the voyageurs meant no harm. In fact, according to Charbonneau, they had come bearing gifts and an offer of peace.

Mato-Tope had feared exactly this type of incident when the Arikara came seeking a new home. The Mandan relied increasingly on commerce with the white man. There had been no traffic from the south since Leavenworth's attack on the Arikara. Now word of this newest incident would keep the river closed.

Word of Chief Mato-Tope's anger spread quickly through the Mandan village. The young Mandeh-Pahchu saw the rescue of Glass as an opportunity to gain favor with the chief. Mato-Tope had a beautiful daughter for whose affection Mandeh-Pahchu had been competing.

He pictured himself parading through the village with his new trophy, delivering the white man to Mato-Tope, the entire village looking on as he recounted his tale. The white man, though, seemed to suspect the detour. He doggedly repeated a single phrase: "Fort Talbot."

From his vantage point on the back of his horse, Glass regarded Mandeh-Pahchu with keen interest. Though he had heard many stories, he had never seen a Mandan in the flesh. The young brave wore his hair like a crown—a preening mane to which he obviously devoted considerable attention. A long ponytail wrapped in strips of rabbit skin trailed down his back. On the top of his head his hair hung loose, flowing like water over the sides, plastered down with grease and cut bluntly at the jaw line. In the center of his forehead a forelock had also been greased and combed. There were other gaudy adornments. Large pewter earrings tugged at three gaping holes where his right ear had been pierced. A choker of white beads contrasted sharply against the copper skin of his neck.

Reluctantly, Mandeh-Pahchu decided to take the white man to Fort Talbot. It was close, barely three hours' ride. Besides, perhaps he could learn something at the fort. There had been rumors of an incident with the Arikara at Fort Talbot. Perhaps the fort would want to pass a message to Mato-Tope. It was a big responsibility, passing messages. Between the story about the white man and the important message he would no doubt be carrying, Mato-Tope would be pleased. His daughter could not help but be impressed.

It was almost midnight when the onyx profile of Fort Talbot loomed up suddenly against the featureless night. The fort cast no light onto the plain, and Glass was surprised to find himself only a hundred yards from the log ramparts.

They saw a flash of fire and at the same instant heard the sharp crack of a rifle from the fort. A musket ball whined inches above their heads.

The horse jumped and Mandeh-Pahchu struggled to control it. Glass mustered his voice, calling out angrily, "Hold your fire! We're friendly!"

A voice answered suspiciously from the blockhouse. "Who are you?"

Glass saw a glimmer of light off the barrel of a rifle and the dark form of a man's head and shoulders.

"I'm Hugh Glass with the Rocky Mountain Fur Company." He wished that he could still project strength with his voice. As it was, he could barely make himself heard across even this short distance.

"Who's the savage?"

"He's a Mandan—he just saved me from three Arikara warriors." The man on the tower yelled something and Glass heard fragments of a conversation. Three more men with rifles appeared on the blockhouse. Glass heard noise behind the heavy gate. A small wicket opened and they felt themselves again under scrutiny. From the wicket a gruff new voice demanded, "Ride up where we can see you better."

Mandeh-Pahchu nudged the horse forward, reining in front of the gate. Glass dismounted and said, "Any particular reason you're so trigger-happy?"

The gruff voice said, "My partner was murdered by Rees in front of this gate last week."

"Well, neither one of us is Arikara."

"Wouldn't know that, sneaking around in the dark."

In contrast to Fort Brazeau, Fort Talbot felt like a place under siege. Its log walls rose twelve feet around a rectangular perimeter, perhaps a hundred feet on the long sides and no more than seventy on the short ones. Two crude blockhouses stood on diagonally opposite corners, built so that their innermost corner touched the outermost corner of the fort. From this abutted position they commanded all four walls. One of the blockhouses—the one above them—had a crude roof, evidently built to protect a large-bore swivel gun from the elements. The other had the beginnings of a roof that had never been completed. A rough corral backed up to the fort on one side, though no stock grazed within.

Glass waited while the eyes behind the wicket continued their scrutiny. "What's your business?" asked the gruff voice.

"I'm bound for Fort Union. I need a few provisions."

"Well we ain't got much to provide."

"I don't need food or powder. Just a blanket and mittens and I'll be on my way."

"Don't appear that you've got much to trade."

"I can sign a draft for a generous price on behalf of William Ashley. The Rocky Mountain Fur Company will be sending a party down-river in the spring. They'll make good on the draft." There followed a long pause. Glass added, "And they'll look favorably on a post that gives aid to one of their men."

Another pause, then the wicket closed. They heard the movement of a heavy timber and the gate began to yawn on its hinge. The gruff voice attached itself to a runt of a man who appeared to be in charge. He stood there with a rifle and two pistols at his belt. "Just you. No red niggers in my fort."

Glass looked at Mandeh-Pahchu, wondering how much the Man-dan understood. Glass started to say something, then stopped, proceed-ing inside as the gate slammed closed behind him.

Two ramshackle structures stood inside the walls. From one of them, the faint glow of light seeped through the greased hides that served as windows. The other building was dark and Glass assumed they used it for storage. The rear walls of the buildings served as the back wall of the fort. Their fronts faced a tiny courtyard, dominated by the stench of dung. The source of the odor stood hitched to a post—two mangy mules, presumably the only animals that the Arikara had been unable to steal. In addition to the animals, the courtyard held a large machine for pressing pelts, an anvil on a cottonwood stump, and a teetering pile of firewood. Five men stood inside, soon joined by the man from the blockhouse. The dim light illuminated Glass's scarred face, and Glass felt their curious stares.

"Come inside if you want."

Glass followed the men into the lit structure, crowding into a cramped room configured as a bunkhouse. A smoky fire burned in a crude clay fireplace against the back wall. The only redeeming quality of the sour-smelling room was its warmth, a heat generated as much by the proximity of other men as by the fire.

The runty man started to say something more when his body contorted in a deep, wet cough. A similar cough appeared to afflict most of the men, and Glass feared the source. When the runty man finally stopped hacking, he said again, "We ain't got any food to spare."

"I told you I don't need your food," said Glass. "Let's settle on the price of a blanket and mittens and I'll be gone." Glass pointed to a table in the corner. "Throw in that skinning knife."

The runty man puffed his chest as if offended. "We ain't meaning to be stingy, mister. But the Rees got us holed up in here. Stole all our stock. Last week, five braves come riding up to the gate like they want to trade. We open the gate and they start shooting. Killed my partner in cold blood."

Glass said nothing, so the man continued. "We haven't been able to get out to hunt or cut wood. So you'll understand if we're frugal with our supplies." He kept looking at Glass for affirmation, but Glass offered none.

Finally Glass said, "Shooting at a white man and a Mandan won't fix your problem with the Rees."

The shooter spoke up, a filthy man with no front teeth: "All I seen was some Indian slinking around in the middle of the night. How was I to know you're riding double?"

"You might make a habit of being able to see your target before you shoot."

The runty man spoke again. "I'll tell my men when to shoot, mister. The Rees and the Mandans ain't never looked no different to me. Besides, they're forting up together now. One big thieving tribe. I'd rather shoot the wrong one than trust the wrong one."

Words began to spill from the runty man like water from a broken dam, and he pointed a bony finger as he spoke. "I built this fort with my own hands—and I got a license to trade here from the governor of Missouri. We ain't ever leaving and we'll shoot anything red that falls in our sights. I don't care if we have to kill every damn one of those murdering, thieving bastards."

"Who exactly do you plan on trading with?" asked Glass.

"We'll make our way, mister. This is prime property. The army'll come up here before long and set these savages straight. There'll be plenty of white men trading up and down this river—you said it yourself."

Glass stepped into the night and the gate slammed behind him. He exhaled deeply, watching as his breath condensed in the cold night air, then drifted away on the hint of a frozen breeze. He saw Mandeh-Pahchu on his horse by the river. The Indian turned at the sound of the gate and rode forward.

Glass took the new skinning knife and cut a slit in the blanket, poking his head through and wearing it as a capote. He put his hands into the furry mittens, staring at the Mandan and wondering what to say. What was there to say, really? *I have my own business to attend.* He couldn't right every wrong in his path.

Finally he handed the skinning knife to Mandeh-Pahchu. "Thank you," said Glass. The Mandan looked at the knife and then looked at Glass, searching his eyes. Then he watched as Glass turned and walked away, up the Missouri and into the night.

NINETEEN

DECEMBER 8, 1823

JOHN FITZGERALD WALKED to his sentry post, just down the river from Fort Union. Pig stood there, his heaving chest sending great clouds of his breath into the frigid night air. "My watch," said Fitzgerald, practically friendly in his tone.

"Since when are you so cheery about standing watch?" asked Pig, then ambled toward camp, looking forward to the four hours of sleep before breakfast.

Fitzgerald cut a thick plug of tobacco. The rich flavor filled his mouth and calmed his nerves. He waited a long time before he spit. The night air bit at his lungs when he breathed, but Fitzgerald didn't mind the cold. The cold was a function of a perfectly clear sky—and Fitzgerald needed a clear sky. A three-quarter moon cast bright light on the river. Enough light, he hoped, to steer a clear channel.

Half an hour after the change of guard, Fitzgerald walked to the thick willows where he had cached his plunder: a pack of beaver pelts to trade downstream, twenty pounds of jerky in a jute sack, three horns of powder, a hundred lead balls, a small cooking pot, two wool blankets, and, of course, the Anstadt. He piled the supplies next to the water's edge, then turned upstream to get the canoe.

As he crept along the riverbank he wondered if Captain Henry would bother sending anyone after him. *Stupid bastard.* Fitzgerald had never met a man more likely to catch the tail end of a lightning bolt. Under Henry's star-crossed leadership, the men of the Rocky Mountain Fur Company never stood more than a short step from calamity. *It's a wonder we're not all dead.* They were down to three horses, which limited the reach of their trapping parties to a few local waters, long since played out. Henry's numerous efforts to trade with the local tribes for new mounts (or, in many cases, to buy back their own stolen mounts) met with uniform failure. Finding food each day for thirty men had become a problem. The hunting parties had not seen buffalo for weeks, and their primary subsistence now consisted of stringy antelope.

The final straw came the week before, when Fitzgerald heard a whispered rumor from Stubby Bill. "Captain's thinking about moving us up the Yellowstone—occupy what's left of Lisa's old fort on the Big Horn." In 1807, a cagey trader named Manuel Lisa established a trading post at the junction of the Yellowstone and Big Horn rivers. Lisa named the structure Fort Manuel, and used it as a base for trade and exploration of both rivers. Lisa maintained particularly good relations with the Crow and the Flathead, who used the guns they bought from Lisa to wage war on the Blackfeet. The Blackfeet, in turn, became bitter enemies of the whites.

Encouraged by his modest commercial success, in 1809 Lisa founded the St. Louis Missouri Fur Company. One of the new venture's investors was Andrew Henry. Henry led a party of a hundred trappers on his ill-fated venture to the Three Forks. On his way up the Yellowstone, Henry had stopped at Fort Manuel. He remembered the strategic location, ample game, and timber. Henry knew that Fort Manuel had been abandoned for more than a dozen years, but he hoped to salvage the beginnings of a new post.

Fitzgerald did not know the distance to the Big Horn, but he knew it lay in the opposite direction from where he wanted to go. While frontier life had been more agreeable than he expected when he fled

St. Louis, he had long since grown weary of the bad food, the cold, and the general discomfort of forting up with thirty smelly men. Not to mention the considerable chance of getting killed. He missed the taste of cheap whiskey and the smell of cheap perfume. And, with seventy dollars in gold coins—the bounty for tending Glass—he thought constantly about gambling. After a year and a half, things should have quieted down for him in St. Louis—perhaps even farther south. He intended to find out.

Two dugout canoes lay upside down on the long beach below the fort.

Fitzgerald had examined them thoroughly a few days before, determined that the smaller of the two was better made. Besides, though the downstream current would carry him, he needed a vessel small enough to manage on his own. He quietly flipped the canoe, set its two paddles inside, and pulled it across the sandbar to the water's edge.

Now the other. In planning his desertion, Fitzgerald had worried about how to immobilize the second canoe. He considered boring a hole through the log skin before arriving at a more straightforward solution. He returned to the second canoe, reaching underneath to grab its paddles. *Canoe's no good without a paddle.*

Fitzgerald pushed his canoe into the water, jumped aboard, and paddled twice to set the boat in the current. The water grabbed the canoe and propelled it downstream. He stopped after a few minutes to pick up his stolen provisions, then put the boat in the current again. In a matter of minutes Fort Union disappeared behind him.

Captain Henry sat alone in the musty confines of his quarters, the only private room at Fort Union. Beyond privacy, a rare commodity at the fort, there was little to commend the space. The only heat and light came from an open doorway to the adjoining room. Henry sat in the cold and dark, wondering what to do.

Fitzgerald himself was no great loss. Henry had distrusted the man since the first day in St. Louis. They could do without the canoe—it wasn't as if he'd stolen their remaining horses. The loss of a fur pack was maddening, but hardly fatal.

The loss was not the man who was gone, but rather its effect on the men who stayed. Fitzgerald's desertion was a statement—a statement loud and clear—of the other men's unspoken thoughts: The Rocky Mountain Fur Company was a failure. *He* was a failure. *Now what?*

Henry heard the latch open on the bunkhouse door. Short, heavy footsteps scuffed across the dirt floor toward his quarters, then Stubby Bill stood in the doorway.

"Murphy and the trapping party's coming in," reported Stubby.

"They got any plews?"

"No, Captain."

"None at all?"

"No, Captain. Well, you see, Captain—it's a little worse than just that."

"Well?"

"They ain't got no horses, either."

Captain Henry took a moment to absorb the news.

"Anything else?"

Stubby thought a minute and then said, "Yes, Captain. Anderson is dead."

The captain said nothing further. Stubby waited until the silence made him uncomfortable, then he left.

Captain Henry sat there for a few more minutes in the cold darkness before making his decision. They would abandon Fort Union.

TWENTY

DECEMBER 15, 1823

THE HOLLOW FORMED a near perfect bowl on the floor of the plains. On three sides, low hills rose to shelter the depression from the relentless winds of more open ground. The hollow funneled moisture toward its center, where a stand of hawthorn trees stood vigil. The combination of the hills and the trees created considerable shelter.

The little hollow stood barely fifty yards from the Missouri. Hugh Glass sat cross-legged beside a small fire, the flames tickling at the lean carcass of a rabbit suspended on a willow spit.

As he waited for the rabbit to roast, Glass became suddenly aware of the sound of the river. It was an odd thing to notice, he thought. He had clung to the river for weeks. Yet suddenly he heard the waters with the acute sensitivity of new discovery. He turned from the fire to stare at the river. It struck him as strange that the smooth flow of water would create any sound at all. Or that the wind would, for that matter. It occurred to him that it wasn't so much the water or the wind that accounted for the noise, but rather the objects in their path. He turned back to the fire.

Glass felt the familiar soreness in his leg and adjusted his position. His wounds posed constant reminders that, while he was healing, he was not healed. The cold accentuated the ache in both his leg and his shoulder. He assumed now that his voice would never return to normal. And of course his face gave permanent notice of his encounter on the Grand. It wasn't all bad, though. His back no longer caused him pain. Nor did it hurt to eat, something he appreciated as he inhaled the scent of the roasting meat.

Glass had shot the rabbit a few minutes earlier in the fading light of the day. He'd seen no sign of Indians for a week, and when the fat cottontail loped across his path, the prospect of such a tasty dinner had been too much to pass up.

A quarter mile upriver from Glass, John Fitzgerald had been watching for a spot to put ashore when he heard the nearby crack of the rifle. *Shit!* He paddled quickly toward shore to slow his forward drift. He bobbed in an eddy, back-paddling, as he peered through the dimming light to identify the source of the shot.

Too far north for Arikara. Assiniboine? Fitzgerald wished he could see better. The flicker of a campfire appeared a few minutes later. He could make out the buckskin form of a man, but could discern no detail. He assumed it was an Indian. Certainly no white man had business this far north, not in December, anyway. *Are there more than one?* Daylight faded rapidly.

Fitzgerald weighed the options. He sure as hell couldn't stay where he was. If he put ashore for the night, it seemed likely that the shooter would discover him in the morning. He thought about creeping up and killing the shooter, except he still wasn't sure whether he faced one man or many. Finally he decided to attempt slipping past. He would wait for the cover of nightfall and hope the distraction of the fire would keep the shooter's eye—and any others—off the water. Meanwhile, the full moon would provide enough light to steer.

Fitzgerald waited almost an hour, quietly pulling the prow of the dugout onto the soft sandbar. The western horizon swallowed the final remnants of daylight, sharpening the glow of the campfire. The shooter's silhouette hunched above the fire, and Fitzgerald assumed that he must be busy tending his dinner. *Now.* Fitzgerald checked the Anstadt and his two pistols, setting them within easy reach. Then he pulled the dugout off the bank and jumped aboard. He paddled twice to push the boat into the current. After that he used the paddle as a rudder, gently placing it on one side or the other. As much as he could, he let the boat drift.

Hugh Glass tugged at the rabbit's hindquarter. The joint was loose, and with a twist he tore off the leg. He sunk his teeth into the succulent meat.

Fitzgerald tried to steer as far away from the shoreline as possible, but the current ran practically beside it. The fire approached now with dizzying speed. Fitzgerald tried to watch the river while simultaneously peering at the back of the man by the fire. He could make out a capote made from a Hudson's Bay blanket—and what looked like a wool hat. *A wool hat? A white man?* Fitzgerald looked back toward the water. A giant boulder loomed suddenly from the dark water of the river—barely ten feet in front of him!

Fitzgerald thrust his paddle deep into the river, pulling as hard as he could. He lifted the paddle at the end of the stroke and pushed it against the rock. The dugout turned—but not enough. Its side scraped the rock with a rasping grate. Fitzgerald paddled with all his strength. *No point holding back now.*

Glass heard a splash followed by a long scrape. He reached instinctively for his rifle, then turned toward the Missouri, moving quickly away from the light of the fire. He crept rapidly toward the river, his eyes adjusting from the glare of the firelight.

He scanned the water for the source of the sound. He heard the splash of a paddle and could just make out a canoe at a distance of a hundred yards. He raised his rifle, cocking the hammer and sighting on the dark form of a man with a paddle. His finger moved inside the trigger guard. . . . He stopped.

Glass saw little point in shooting. Whoever it was, the boatman appeared intent on avoiding contact. In any event, he was headed rapidly in the opposite direction. Whatever his intention, the fleeing boatman appeared to pose little threat to Glass.

Onboard the dugout, Fitzgerald paddled hard until he rounded a bend in the river, a quarter mile from the campfire. He let the dugout drift for almost a mile before guiding the boat to the opposite bank and searching for a suitable landing.

Finally he pulled the dugout from the water and flipped it, spreading his bedroll underneath. He chewed on a piece of jerky while he contemplated again the figure by the fire. *Damn strange spot for a white man in December.*

Fitzgerald carefully lay the rifle and his two pistols beside him before curling beneath his blanket. The bright moon flooded his campsite with pale light. The Anstadt caught the light and held it, the silver fittings gleaming like mirrors in the sun.

Captain Henry finally caught a stretch of good luck. So many good things happened with such rapid succession that he barely knew what to make of it.

For starters, the skies shone blue as indigo for two straight weeks. With the good weather, the brigade covered the two hundred miles between Fort Union and the Big Horn River in six days.

When they arrived, the abandoned fort stood almost as Henry remembered it. The condition of the post far exceeded his expectations. The years of abandonment had worn on the structure, but most of the timber remained solid. The find would save them weeks of hard labor, cutting and hauling logs.

Henry's experience with the local tribes (at least initially) presented another stark contrast to his dismal fortune at Fort Union. He dispatched a party led by Allistair Murphy and showered gifts on his new neighbors, primarily bands of Flathead and Crow. In his relations with the

local Indians, Henry discovered that he was the beneficiary of his predecessor's diplomacy. Both tribes seemed relatively happy at the re-
settlement of the post. At least they were willing to trade.

The Crow, in particular, were flush with horses. Murphy traded for
seventy-two of the animals. Streams spilled off the nearby Big Horn
Mountains, and Captain Henry set out a plan for the aggressive deployment of his newly mobile trappers.

For two weeks, Henry kept checking his back, as if misfortune must
be stalking him from behind. He allowed himself the smallest bit of
optimism. *Maybe my luck has changed?* It had not.

Hugh Glass stood before the remnants of Fort Union. The gate itself lay
flat on the ground, its hinge carried off when Captain Henry abandoned
the post. The indignities of the failed venture continued inside. All of the
metal hinges had been removed, salvaged, Glass assumed, for use at
their next destination. Logs had been torn from the palisades, apparently used as firewood by the boorish visitors who followed Henry's
departure. One of the bunkhouses had a blackened wall from what
appeared to be a halfhearted attempt to fire the fort. Dozens of horse
tracks had churned the snow in the yard.

I'm chasing a mirage. How many days had he walked—crawled
toward this moment? He thought back to the clearing by the spring
on the Grand River. *What month was that? August? What is it now?
December?*

Glass climbed the crude ladder to the blockhouse, scanning the
whole valley from the top. A quarter mile away he saw the rusty smudge
of a dozen antelope, pawing through the snow to nibble at sage. A big
"V" of geese, wings locked to land, settled on the river. Otherwise there
were no signs of life. *Where are they?*

He camped for two nights in the fort, unable to simply walk away
from the destination he had so long pursued. Yet he knew his true aim
was not a place, but two people—two people and two final, vengeful acts.

———

Glass followed the Yellowstone from Fort Union. He could only guess at Henry's path, but he doubted that the captain would risk a repeat of his failure on the Upper Missouri. That left the Yellowstone.

He had followed the Yellowstone for five days when he crested a high bench above the river. He stopped, awestruck.

Fusing heaven to earth, the Big Horn Mountains stood before him. A few clouds swirled around the highest peaks, furthering the illusion of a wall reaching forever upward. His eyes watered from the glare of the sun against snow, but he could not look away. Nothing in Glass's twenty years on the plains had prepared him for such mountains.

Captain Henry had spoken often of the enormity of the Rockies, but Glass assumed his stories were infused with the standard dose of campfire embellishment. In actuality, Glass thought, Henry's portrait had been woefully inadequate. Henry was a straightforward man, and his descriptions focused on the mountains as obstacles, barriers to be surmounted in the drive to connect a stream of commerce between east and west. Missing entirely from Henry's description had been any hint of the devout strength that flowed into Glass at the sight of the massive peaks.

Of course he understood Henry's more practical reaction. The terrain of the river valleys was difficult enough. Glass could scarcely imagine the effort required to portage furs over mountains such as those before him now.

His awe of the mountains grew in the days that followed, as the Yellowstone River led him nearer and nearer. Their great mass was a marker, a benchmark fixed against time itself. Others might feel disquiet at the notion of something so much larger than themselves. But for Glass, there was a sense of sacrament that flowed from the mountains like a font, an immortality that made his quotidian pains seem inconsequential.

And so he walked, day after day, toward the mountains at the end of the plain.

Fitzgerald stood outside the crude stockade, enduring the interrogation of the runty, coughing man on the rampart above the gate.

Fitzgerald had practiced the lie during his long days in the canoe. "I'm carrying a message to St. Louis for Captain Henry of the Rocky Mountain Fur Company."

"Rocky Mountain Fur Company?" The runty man snorted. "We just saw another of yours headed the other direction—bad-mannered fellow riding double with a redskin. In fact, if you're from his company, you can make good on his draft."

Fitzgerald felt his stomach contract and his breath drew suddenly short. *The white man on the river!* He struggled to keep his voice calm, nonchalant. "I must have missed him on the river. What was his name?"

"Don't even recall his name. We gave him a couple of things and he left."

"What'd he look like?"

"Well, I do remember that. Scars all over his face, like he'd been chewed on by a wild animal."

Glass! Alive! Goddamn him!

Fitzgerald traded two plews for jerky, eager to get back on the water.

No longer content to drift with the current, he paddled to propel the dugout forward. Forward and away. Glass might be headed in the opposite direction, thought Fitzgerald, but he harbored no doubt about the old bastard's intent.

TWENTY-ONE

DECEMBER 31, 1823

SNOW BEGAN FALLING about halfway through the day. The storm clouds approached casually, obscuring the sun so gradually that Henry and his men took little notice.

They had no reason to be concerned. Their refurbished fort stood complete, ready to withstand whatever challenges the elements might present. Besides, Captain Henry had declared the day a celebration. Then he had broken out a surprise that resulted in delirious excitement among his men—alcohol.

Henry was a failure at many things, but he understood the power of incentives. Henry's brew was made from yeast and serviceberries, buried for a month in a barrel to allow fermentation. The resulting concoction tasted like acid. None of the men could drink it without wincing in pain, and none of them passed up the opportunity. The liquid resulted in a profound and almost immediate state of drunkenness.

Henry had a second bonus for his men. He was a decent fiddle player, and for the first time in months, his mood lifted sufficiently to pick up his battered instrument. The shrieking fiddle combined with drunken laughter to create a foundation of jovial chaos in the crowded bunkhouse.

A good part of the merriment centered around Pig, whose obese carcass lay sprawled in front of the fireplace. Pig's capacity for alcohol, it turned out, did not match his girth.

"Looks like he's dead," said Black Harris, kicking him squarely in the belly. Harris's foot disappeared momentarily in the squishy fat around Pig's midsection, but otherwise the kick evoked no response.

"Well if he's dead . . ." said Patrick Robinson, a quiet man who most of the trappers had never heard speak before the application of Henry's moonshine, "we owe him a decent burial."

"Too cold," said another trapper. "But we could make him a proper shroud!" This idea evoked great enthusiasm among the men. Two blankets were produced, along with a needle and heavy thread. Robinson, an able tailor, began the task of tightly sewing the shroud around Pig's great mass. Black Harris delivered a moving sermon, and one by one the men took turns with eulogies.

"He was a good man and a God-fearing man," said one speaker. "We return him to you, oh Lord, in his virgin state . . . never once having been touched by soap."

"If you can manage the lift," said another, "we beseech you to hoist him up to the Great Beyond."

A loud argument diverted attention from Pig's funeral. Allistair Murphy and Stubby Bill had a difference of opinion over who between them was the finer shot with a pistol. Murphy challenged Stubby Bill to a duel, a notion that Captain Henry quickly quashed. However, he did authorize a shooting match.

At first Stubby Bill suggested that they each shoot a tin cup from the other's head. Even in his drunken state, however, it occurred to him that such a contest might create a dangerous mixture of motivations. As a compromise, they ultimately decided to shoot a tin cup from *Pig's* head. Both Murphy and Stubby Bill considered Pig a friend, so both would have the appropriate incentive for marksmanship. They propped Pig's shroud-encased body in a sitting position against the wall, then placed a cup on his head.

The men cleared a path down the center of the long bunkhouse, with the shooters at one end and Pig at the other. Captain Henry hid a musket ball in one hand; Murphy picked correctly and elected to shoot second. Stubby Bill removed the pistol from his belt, carefully checking the powder in the pan. He adjusted his weight from foot to foot, ultimately situating himself sideways to his target. He bent his shooting arm to form a perfect right angle with the pistol pointing to the roof. His thumb reached up and cocked the pistol with a dramatic snap, the only sound in the tense cabin. After several pendulous moments in this position, he lowered the pistol to its firing position in a slow, graceful arc.

Then he hesitated. The impact of an errant shot became suddenly palpable at the vision—through his pistol sights—of Pig's lumpy mass. Stubby Bill liked Pig. Quite a lot, actually. *This is a bad idea.* He felt a bead of sweat trickle down his short spine. His peripheral vision made him newly aware of the men crowded on either side of him. His breathing became labored, causing his shooting arm to heave up and down. The pistol seemed suddenly heavy. He held his breath to stop the swaying, but then the lack of air made him light-headed and dizzy. *Don't miss now.*

Finally he hoped for the best and squeezed the trigger, closing his eyes with the flash of the powder. The ball crashed into the log wall behind Pig, a full twelve inches above the cup on the fat man's shrouded head. The spectators erupted in laughter. "Nice shot, Stubby!"

Murphy stepped forward. "You think too much." In a single, liquid motion, he drew, aimed, and fired. The shot exploded and the bullet ripped into the base of the tin cup on Pig's head. The cup slammed against the wall before clamoring to the floor next to Pig.

If neither shot killed Pig, the second at least succeeded in rousing him.

The lumpy shroud began a series of wild contortions. The men cheered the shot, then doubled over in unbridled glee at the sight of the writhing shroud. The long blade of a knife thrust suddenly out from the inside of the blanket, hacking open a narrow slit. Two hands appeared, ripping open the shroud. Next emerged Pig's fleshy face, blinking at the light. More laughter and taunts. "Like watching a calf get born!"

The gunfire had sprinkled their celebration with fitting punctuation, and soon all the men began firing their weapons into the ceiling. Black powder smoke filled the room along with hearty cries of "Happy New Year!"

"Hey, Captain," said Murphy. "We ought to fire off the cannon!" Henry had no objection, if for no other reason than to remove the trappers from the bunkhouse before they destroyed it. Clamoring loudly, the men of the Rocky Mountain Fur Company opened the door, stepped into the dark night, and stumbled en masse for the blockade.

They were surprised at the intensity of the storm. The light dusting of the afternoon had degenerated into a full-bore blizzard, swirling winds driving heavy snow. Ten inches or more had accumulated, deeper still where drifts had formed. Had they been cogent, the men would have appreciated the good fortune that held the storm at bay while they constructed shelter. Instead, they focused entirely on the cannon.

The four-pound howitzer was really more of a giant shotgun than cannon, designed not for the ramparts of a fort, but for the bow of a keelboat. It was mounted on a swivel in the corner of the blockhouse, which allowed it to command two of the fort's walls. The iron tube measured barely three feet, with three trunnions for reinforcement (insufficient, as it would turn out).

A big man named Paul Hawker fancied himself the resident cannoneer. He even claimed to have been an artilleryman in the War of 1812. Most of the men doubted this claim, though they admitted that Hawker sounded authoritative when he barked out the drill for loading. Hawker and two other men scrambled up the ladder to the blockhouse. The rest stayed below, content to watch from the relative shelter of the parade ground.

"Cannoneers to your posts!" shouted Hawker. Hawker may have known the drill, but his subordinates clearly did not. They stared blankly, waiting for a civilian explanation of their responsibilities. Under his breath, Hawker pointed to one and said, "You grab the powder and some wadding." Pointing to the other he said, "You go light the lanyard from the fire." Returning to his military bearing, he then shouted, "Commence firing. . . . Load!"

Under Hawker's direction, the man with the powder poured thirty drams into a measure, kept in the blockhouse for that purpose. Hawker tipped the brass muzzle of the cannon toward the sky and they dumped in the powder. Next they inserted a fist-size wad of old cloth and used a ramstaff to seat the charge firmly in the breech of the gun.

While they waited for the return of the lanyard, Hawker unwrapped an oilcloth that held the primers—three-inch sections of goose quill, packed with gunpowder and sealed at both ends with a dab of wax. One of these primers he placed in the small vent hole at the breech of the cannon. When the burning lanyard was set to the quill, it melted the wax and ignited the powder in the quill, which in turn set off the main charge in the breech.

The man with the burning lanyard now made his way up the ladder.

The lanyard was a long stick with a hole in the end. A thick piece of rope, treated with saltpeter to make it burn, threaded the hole. Hawker blew on the ember at the tip of the lanyard, the fiery glow casting an ominous red on his face. With the pomp of a West Point cadet, he screamed, "READY!"

The men below looked up at the blockhouse in eager anticipation of a colossal blast. Though he himself held the lanyard, Hawker yelled "FIRE!" and set the spark to the primer.

The ember on the lanyard melted quickly through the wax. The primer sparked with a hiss and then "pop." Compared with the stupendous explosion they expected, the cannon's bark seemed barely louder than the clap of two hands.

"What the hell was that?" came a cry from the yard, along with a sprinkling of catcalls and mocking laughter. "Why don't you just bang on a pot!"

Hawker stared at his cannon, horrified that this moment of testicular exhibition had wilted so prominently. This had to be rectified. "Just warming it up!" he yelled down. Then, urgently, "Cannoneers to your posts!"

His two cannoneers looked at Hawker dubiously now, suddenly mindful of the exposure of their own reputations.

"Move, you idiots!" hissed Hawker. "Triple the charge!" More powder would help. Then again, maybe the problem had been too little wadding. More stuffing, reasoned Hawker, would create more resistance—and a louder explosion. *I'll give them a blast.*

They poured the triple charge down the muzzle. *What to use for wadding?* Hawker ripped off his leather tunic and rammed it down the tube of the cannon. *More.* Hawker looked at his assistant. "Give me your tunics," he said to his crew.

The men stared back, clearly alarmed. "It's cold, Hawker."

"Give me your damn tunics!"

The men reluctantly complied, and Hawker added these new garments to the wadding. The jeering continued as Hawker worked furiously to reload the big gun. By the time he finished, the entire length of the cannon had been filled with buckskin, tightly packed.

"Ready!" yelled Hawker, reaching again for the burning lanyard.

"FIRE!" He set the spark to the primer and the cannon exploded. Actually exploded. The buckskins did indeed create additional resistance—so much so that the weapon blew itself into a thousand, glorious bits.

For a brilliant moment, the fire of the blast lit the night sky, then an enormous cloud of acrid smoke hid the blockhouse from view. The men ducked as shrapnel from the explosion ripped into the log walls of the fort and sunk hissing into the snow. The explosion knocked both of Hawker's crewmen over the edge of the blockhouse and into the yard below. One broke an arm in the fall; the other two ribs. Both might have died had they not managed to land in a deep snowdrift.

As the driving wind cleared the smoke from the blockhouse, all eyes turned upward, searching for their brave artilleryman. No one said anything for a moment, until the captain called out, "Hawker!"

Another long moment passed. The swirling winds pushed the smoke away from the blockhouse. They saw a hand reach over the edge of the rampart. A second hand appeared—and then Hawker's head. His face was black as coal from the blast. His hat had been blown from his head, and blood trickled from both ears. Even with his hands on the blockhouse he tottered from side to side. Most of the men expected him to pitch forward and die. Instead he yelled, "Happy New Year, you dirty sons of bitches!"

A great roar of approval filled the night.

Hugh Glass stumbled in the drift, surprised that the snow could already be so deep. He wore no mitten on his shooting hand, so the fall thrust his bare flesh into the snow. The icy sting made him wince. He pushed his hand under his capote to dry it. The snow had begun as scattered flurries, hardly enough to justify forting up. Glass now realized his mistake.

He looked around, trying to gauge the remaining daylight. The storm drew the horizon in close, as the high mountains in the background disappeared altogether. He could make out a thin ridge line of sandstone and the occasional pine sentinel. Otherwise, even the foothills seemed to fuse with the white-gray formless clouds of the sky. Glass was glad for the sure path of the Yellowstone River. *An hour before sunset?* Glass pulled the mitten from his possibles bag and placed it on his stiff, damp hand. *Nothing to shoot at in this weather anyway.*

It had been five days since Glass struck out from Fort Union. He knew now that Henry and his men had come this way; the path of thirty men was not difficult to follow. From the maps he had studied, Glass remembered Manuel Lisa's abandoned trading post on the Big Horn. *Surely Henry would go no farther—not in this season.* He had a rough idea of the distances. But how much ground had he covered? Glass could only guess.

The temperature dropped precipitously with the arrival of the storm, but it was the wind that worried Glass. The wind seemed to animate the cold, endowing it with an ability to penetrate every seam of his clothing. He felt it first as a biting sting on the exposed flesh of his nose and ears. Wind forced water from the corners of his eyes and his running nose created moisture, compounding the chill. As he trudged through the deepening snow, the sharp bite faded slowly into an aching numbness, leaving once agile fingers as lumps of dysfunctional flesh. He needed to seek shelter while he could still find fuel—and while his fingers could still work the flint and steel.

The opposite bank rose steeply from the river. It would have provided some cover, but there was no way to ford the river. The terrain along his side of the river was featureless and flat, making no concessions to the driving wind. He saw a stand of a dozen cottonwoods about a mile away, barely perceptible through the blowing snow and the growing darkness. *Why did I wait?*

It took twenty minutes to cover the distance. In places the whipping wind had cleared the ground down to the dirt, but in others the drifts rose to his knees. Snow filled his moccasins and he cursed himself for not having fashioned gaiters. His deerskin breeches became wet from the snow and then froze solid, stiff shells encasing his lower legs. By the time he reached the cottonwoods he could no longer feel his toes.

The storm intensified as he scanned the tree stand for the best shelter. The wind seemed to blow from every direction at once, making it difficult to pick a spot. He settled on a downed cottonwood. The upturned roots spread out in a perpendicular arc from the thick base of the trunk, creating a windbreak in two directions. *If only the wind would stop blowing from all four.*

He set down his rifle and immediately began to gather fuel. He found plenty of wood. The problem was tinder. Several inches of snow covered the ground. When he dug beneath it, the leaves were damp and unsuitable. He tried to snap small branches from the cottonwood, but it was still green. Glass scoured the clearing. Daylight seemed to pour away, and he realized with growing concern that it was later than he had thought. By the time he gathered what he needed, he was working in near total darkness.

Glass piled his fuel next to the downed tree, then dug furiously to create a sheltered depression for the fire. He removed his mittens to handle the tinder, but his frozen fingers barely functioned. He cupped his hands against his mouth and blew into them. His breath created a brief tingle of warmth which faded instantly against the onslaught of frigid air. He felt a new blast of bitter wind on his back and neck, penetrating to his skin and then, it seemed, deeper still. *Is the wind shifting?* He paused for an instant, wondering whether he should move to the other side of the cottonwood. The wind receded, and he decided to stay put.

He spread his tinder in the shallow depression, then dug into his *sac au feu* for the flint and steel. On his first attempt to strike the steel, his flint nicked the knuckle on his thumb. The sting extended all the way up his arm like the vibration of a tuning fork. He tried to ignore the pain as he struck again at the steel. Finally a spark landed in the tinder and began to burn. He dropped over the tiny flame, sheltering it with his body while blowing, desperate to breathe his own life into the fire. Suddenly he felt a great swirling rush of wind and his face filled with sand and smoke from the depression. He coughed and rubbed at his eyes and when he could open them, the flame was gone. *Damn it!*

He pounded the flint against the steel. Sparks showered down, but too much of the tinder had already burned. The backs of his hands ached from the exposure. His fingers, meanwhile, had lost all sensation. *Use the powder.*

He arranged the remaining tinder as best he could, this time adding larger pieces of wood. From his horn he poured gunpowder, cursing as it gushed into the depression. He situated his body again to block as much wind as possible, then struck at the steel with his flint.

A flash arose from the depression, burning his hands and singeing his face. He barely noticed the pain, so desperate was he to nurture the flames that now jumped up and down with the swirling wind. He crouched over the fire, spreading his capote to create a greater windbreak. Most of the tinder already had disappeared, but he saw with relief that some of the larger chunks were burning. He added more fuel, and in a few minutes was confident that the fire would continue to burn on its own.

He had just settled back against the downed tree when another great blast of wind nearly extinguished his fire. Again he threw himself over the flames, spreading his capote to block the wind while he blew against the glowing embers. Sheltered again, the flames sprang back to life.

Glass stayed in that position, hunched over the fire with his arms spread wide to hold the capote, for almost half an hour. Snow piled around him, several more inches in the short time he guarded the flames. He could feel the weight of the drifting snow where the capote dragged the ground. He felt something else, and his stomach sank at the realization. *It's shifted.* The wind beat against his back, no longer swirling, but with constant, relentless pressure. The cottonwood provided no shelter. Worse still, it caught the wind and turned it—back against him and into the fire.

He fought against a growing sense of panic, a vicious circle of conflicting fears. The starting point was clear—without a fire he would freeze to death. At the same time, he could not continue to hold his current position, stooped over the flames, arms spread wide, the blizzard beating at his back. He was exhausted, and the storm could easily rage for hours or even days. He needed shelter, however crude. The wind's direction now seemed consistent enough to bet on the other side of the tree. It couldn't be worse, but Glass doubted he could move without losing the fire. Could he start another fire from scratch? In the dark? With no tinder? He saw no choice but to try.

He set upon a plan. He would rush to the other side of the downed cottonwood, scoop a new depression for the fire, then seek to transfer the flames.

No sense waiting. He grabbed his rifle and as much of his fuel as he could carry. The wind seemed to sense the presence of a new target, blasting him with renewed fury. He ducked his head and waded around the giant roots, cursing as he felt more snow pour into his moccasins.

The opposite side did seem better sheltered from the wind, though the snow was piled just as deep. He dropped his rifle and wood and began to scoop. It took five minutes to scrape an area large enough for a fire. He rushed back to the other side, retracing his footprints in the snow. The clouds made it almost completely dark, and he hoped for the glow of his fire as he came around the base of the tree. *No light—no fire.*

The only sign of his fire was a faint depression in a mound of drifted snow. Glass dug down, foolishly hoping that somehow an ember might have survived. He found nothing, though the heat from the fire had turned the snow into a slushy mix. It soaked his woolen mittens. He felt the frigid chill of moisture on his hands, then an odd mixture of pains that seemed to burn and freeze, all at the same time.

He retreated quickly to the more sheltered side of the tree. The wind seemed to have settled on a course, but also intensified. His face ached and his hands again lost all dexterity. He ignored his feet, which was easy since he felt no sensation below his ankles. With the more consistent direction of the wind, the cottonwood at least created a windbreak. The temperature continued to drop, though, and without a fire, Glass again thought he would die.

There was no time to hunt for tinder, even if there had been enough light to see. He decided to cut kindling with his hatchet, then hope that another shot of gunpowder would be enough to start the blaze. For an instant he worried about conserving his powder. *Least of my problems.* He drove the hatchet into the end of a short log to seat the blade, then pounded up and down to split the wood.

The sound of his own work almost obscured another sound—a dull clap like distant thunder. He froze, his neck craning in search of the source. *A rifle shot? No—too big.* Glass had heard thunder before during snowstorms, but never in temperatures this cold.

He waited several minutes, listening intently. No sound competed with the screaming winds, and Glass became aware again of the excruciating pain in his hands. To wander in the storm on some quest for a strange sound seemed like folly. *Start the damn fire.* He planted the hatchet's blade in the top of another log.

When he had cut a sufficient amount, Glass arranged the kindling in a pile and reached for his powder horn. It scared him how little powder remained. As he poured he wondered if he should conserve some powder for a second attempt. He fumbled, barely able to calibrate the actions of his frozen hands. *No—this is it.* He emptied the powder horn, then reached again for his flint and steel.

He raised his flint to strike the steel, but before he could do so, an enormous roar rolled down the valley of the Yellowstone. This time he knew. The unmistakable blast of a cannon. *Henry!*

Glass stood, reaching for his rifle. The winds again found a target and pounded with a vigor that nearly staggered him. He began to wade through the deep snow toward the Yellowstone. *Hope I'm on the right side of the river.*

Captain Henry was outraged at the loss of the cannon. Though the weapon had little utility in actual combat, its deterrent value was significant. Besides, a real fort had a cannon, and Henry wanted one for his.

With the notable exception of the captain, the loss of the cannon had not dampened spirits at the fort's New Year's celebration. To the contrary, the great explosion seemed to boost the level of revelry. The blizzard drove the men back inside, but the cramped bunkhouse pulsed with a relentless cacophony of unbridled chaos.

Then the cabin door blasted suddenly open—completely open—as if some great external force had built up outside before blowing the portal inward. The elements came in with the open door, frigid fingers grabbing at the men inside, ripping them from the snug comfort of the shelter and fire.

"Close the door, you bloody idiot!" yelled Stubby Bill without looking at the door. Then they all did look. The wind shrieked outside. Snow swirled around the looming presence in the doorway, making it appear to be part of the storm, disgorged in their midst like some rogue element of the wilderness itself.

Jim Bridger stared in horror at the specter. Driven snow was plastered against every surface of its body, encasing it in frozen white. On its face, ice clung to a haggard beard and hung down like crystal daggers from the folded brow of a wool cap. The apparition might have been carved wholly of winter—had not the crimson streaks of raking scars dominated its face, had not its eyes burned as fiery as molten lead. Bridger watched as the eyes scanned the interior of the cabin, deliberate and searching.

Stunned silence filled the room as the men struggled to comprehend the vision before them. Unlike the others, Bridger understood instantly. In his mind he had seen this vision before. His guilt swelled up, churning like a paddle wheel in his stomach. He wanted desperately to flee. *How do you escape something that comes from inside?* The revenant, he knew, searched for him.

Several instants passed before Black Harris finally said, "Jesus Christ. It's Hugh Glass."

Glass scanned the stunned faces before him. Disappointment flashed briefly as he failed to locate Fitzgerald among the men—but he did find Bridger. Their eyes would have met, except Bridger turned away. *Just like before.* He noticed the familiar knife that Bridger now wore at his waist. Glass lifted his rifle and cocked it.

The desire to shoot Bridger down nearly overwhelmed him. Having crawled toward this moment for a hundred days, the prospect of vengeance was now immediate, the power to consummate requiring no more than the gentle squeeze of a trigger. Yet a mere bullet seemed too intangible to express his rage, an abstraction at a moment craving the satisfaction of flesh against flesh. Like a starving man set before a feast, he could pause briefly to enjoy the last moment of an aching hunger about to be sated. Glass lowered the rifle and leaned it against the wall.

He walked slowly toward Bridger, the other men clearing a path as he approached. "Where's my knife, Bridger?" Glass stood directly before him. Bridger turned his head to look up at Glass. He felt the familiar disconnect between his desire to explain and his inability to do so.

"Stand up," said Glass. Bridger stood.

Glass's first punch struck him full force in the face. Bridger offered no resistance. He saw the punch coming but did not turn his head or even wince. Glass could feel the cartilage snap in Bridger's nose, saw the torrent of blood set loose. He had imagined the satisfaction of this moment a thousand times, and now it had arrived. He was glad he hadn't shot him—glad that he hadn't robbed himself of the full carnal pleasure of revenge.

Glass's second blow caught Bridger under the chin, knocking him backward against the log wall of the cabin. Again Glass wallowed in the raw satisfaction of the contact. The wall kept Bridger from falling, holding him upright.

Glass closed in tight now, erupting in a spasm of punches against Bridger's face. When the blood became so thick that his punches began to slide off ineffectively, he shifted his blows to Bridger's stomach. Bridger crumpled as he lost his wind, finally falling to the floor. Glass began to kick him, and Bridger could not, or would not fight back. Bridger too had seen the approach of this day. It was his reckoning, and he felt no entitlement to resist.

Finally Pig stepped forward. Even through the haze of alcohol, Pig had pieced together the full implications of the violent event unfolding before him. Clearly, Bridger and Fitzgerald had lied about their time with Glass. Still, it seemed wrong to let Glass walk in and kill their friend and comrade. Pig reached to grab Glass from behind.

But someone grabbed him. Pig turned to find Captain Henry. Pig appealed to the captain: "You gonna let him kill Bridger?"

"I'm not gonna do anything," said the Captain. Pig started to protest further, but Henry cut him off. "This is for Glass to decide."

Glass delivered another brutal kick. Though he tried to contain it, Bridger groaned at the impact of the blow. Glass stood above the crumpled form at his feet, panting at the sheer exertion of the beating he had inflicted. He felt his heart pound in his temple as his eyes came to rest again on the knife in Bridger's belt. In his mind he saw Bridger standing at the edge of the clearing on that day—catching the knife that Fitzgerald had thrown to him. *My knife.* He reached down and pulled the long blade from its sheath. The grip of the molded pommel was like the embrace of a familiar hand. He thought of the times he had needed that knife and his hate spiked again. *The moment's arrived.*

How long had he nourished himself with the prospect of this moment?

And now it had arrived, a vengeance more perfect than even his imagination had conjured. He turned the blade in his hand, felt its weight, prepared to drive it home.

He looked down at Bridger, and something unexpected began to happen. The perfection of the moment began to evaporate. Bridger looked back at Glass, and in his eyes, Glass saw not malice, but fear; not resistance, but resignation. *Fight back, damn you!* One twitch of opposition to justify the final strike.

It never came. Glass continued to grip the knife, staring at the boy. *A boy!* As Glass looked down at him, new images suddenly competed with his memory of the stolen knife. He remembered the boy tending his wounds, arguing with Fitzgerald. He saw other images too, like the ashen face of La Vierge on the cut bank of the Missouri.

Glass's breathing began to slow. His temple ceased to pulsate in sync with his heart. He looked around the room, as if suddenly aware of the ring of men surrounding him. He stared for a long time at the knife in his hand, then slipped it in his belt. Turning from the boy, Glass realized he was cold and walked toward the fire, extending his bloodied hands to the warmth of the crackling flames.

TWENTY-TWO

FEBRUARY 27, 1824

A STEAMSHIP NAMED *DOLLEY MADISON* had arrived in St. Louis the week before. It carried a cargo of goods from Cuba, including sugar, rum, and cigars. William H. Ashley loved cigars, and he wondered briefly why the fat Cuban perched on his lip was failing to impart its usual pleasure. Of course he knew the reason. When he walked each day to the riverfront, he didn't go in search of steamships bearing trifles from the Caribbean. No, he went in ravenous anticipation of a fur-laden pirogue from the far west. *Where are they?* There had been no word from Andrew Henry or Jedediah Smith in five months. *Five months!*

Ashley paced the length of his cavernous office at the Rocky Mountain Fur Company. He hadn't been able to sit still all day. He stopped again in front of the enormous map on the wall. The map was ornate, or at least it had been. Ashley had punctured it with more pins than a tailor's dummy, and used a fat pencil to scratch the location of rivers, streams, trading posts, and other assorted landmarks.

His eyes traced the path up the Missouri and he tried again to fight off the sensation of impending ruin. He paused, staring at a spot on the river just west of St. Louis, where one of his flatboats had sunk with ten thousand dollars' worth of supplies. He paused at the pin marking the Arikara villages, where sixteen of his men had been murdered and robbed, and where even the power of the U.S. Army had been unable to clear a path for his venture. He paused at a bend in the Missouri above the Mandan villages, where two years before Henry had lost a herd of seventy horses to the Assiniboine. He followed the Missouri past Fort Union to the Great Falls, where an attack by the Blackfeet had later sent Henry retreating down the river.

He looked down at a letter in his hand, the latest inquiry from one of his investors. The letter demanded an update on the "status of the venture on the Missouri." *I have no idea.* And, of course, every penny of Ashley's own fortune rode with Andrew Henry and Jedediah Smith.

Ashley felt an overwhelming desire to act, to strike out, to do something, *to do anything*—yet there was nothing more he could do. He already had managed to secure a loan for a new keelboat and provisions. The keelboat floated at a dock on the river and his provisions sat stacked in a warehouse. His recruitment for a new fur brigade was oversubscribed. He'd spent weeks culling forty men from a hundred who applied. In April he would personally lead his men up the Missouri. *More than a month away!*

And where would he go? When Ashley dispatched Henry and Smith last August, their loose understanding was to rendezvous in the field—location to be determined through messengers. *Messengers!*

His eyes returned to the map. He used his finger to trace the scrawled line that represented the Grand River. He remembered drawing that line, and how he had guessed at the course of the river. *Was I right?* Did the Grand provide a direct line toward Fort Union? Or did it veer in some other direction? How long had it taken Henry and his men to reach the fort? Long enough, it appeared, that they had not been able to conduct a fall hunt. *Are they even alive?*

Captain Andrew Henry, Hugh Glass, and Black Harris sat next to the dying coals of the fire in the bunkhouse of the fort on the Big Horn. Henry stood and walked outside the cabin, returning with an armful of wood. He set a log on the coals and the three men watched as flames reached eagerly for the fresh fuel.

"I need a messenger to go back to St. Louis," said Henry. "I should have sent one before, but I wanted to wait till we were set up on the Big Horn."

Glass seized immediately at the opportunity. "I'll go, Captain." Fitzgerald and the Anstadt were somewhere down the Missouri. Besides, a month in Henry's company had been more than sufficient to remind Glass of the cloudy weather that the captain could not shake.

"Good. I'll give you three men and horses. I assume you agree that we ought to stay off the Missouri?"

Glass nodded. "I think we ought to try the Powder down to the Platte. Then it's a straight shot to Fort Atkinson."

"Why not the Grand?"

"More chance of Rees on the Grand. Besides, if we're lucky we might bump into Jed Smith on the Powder."

The next day, Pig heard from a trapper named Red Archibald that Hugh Glass was returning to St. Louis, carrying a message to William H. Ashley from the captain. He immediately sought out Captain Henry and volunteered to go along. As much as he feared a journey away from the relative comfort of the fort, the prospect of staying was worse. Pig was not cut out for life as a trapper and he knew it. He thought about his former life as a cooper's apprentice. He missed his old life and its rudimentary comforts more than he imagined possible.

Red was going too. And a friend of his, a bow-legged Englishman named William Chapman. Red and Chapman had been plotting to desert when the rumor spread about messengers to St. Louis. Captain Henry was even paying a bounty to the volunteers. Accompanying Glass would save them the trouble of sneaking off. They could leave early and get paid for the privilege. Chapman and Red could scarcely believe their good fortune. "You remember the saloon at Fort Atkinson?" asked Red.

Chapman laughed. He remembered it well, the last taste of decent whiskey on their way up the Missouri.

John Fitzgerald heard none of the bawdy din in the saloon at Fort Atkinson. He was too focused on his cards, picking them up, one by one as they were dealt, from the stained felt top of the table: Ace . . . *Maybe my luck is changing* . . . Five . . . Seven . . . Four . . . then—

Ace. *Yes.* He looked around the table. The smarmy lieutenant with the big pile of coins threw three cards on the table and said, "I'll take three and bet five dollars."

The sutler threw down all of his cards. "I'm out."

A strapping boatman threw down a single card and pushed five dollars to the center of the table.

Fitzgerald threw down three cards as he calculated his competition.

The boatman was an idiot, presumably drawing for a straight or a flush. The lieutenant was probably holding a pair, but not a pair that could beat his aces. "I'll see your five and I'll raise you five."

"See me five and raise me five with what?" asked the lieutenant. Fitzgerald felt the blood rise in his face, felt the familiar pounding at his temple. He was down one hundred dollars—every penny from the pelts he had sold that afternoon to the sutler. He turned to the sutler. "Okay, old man—I'll sell you the second half of that pack of beaver. Same price—five bucks a plew."

A poor cards player, the sutler was a cagey trader. "Price has gone down since this afternoon. I'll give you three dollars a plew."

"You son of a bitch!" hissed Fitzgerald.

"Call me whatever you like," replied the sutler. "But that's my price."

Fitzgerald took another look at the pompous lieutenant, then nodded to the sutler. The sutler counted sixty dollars from a leather purse, stacking the coins in front of Fitzgerald. Fitzgerald pushed ten dollars to the center of the table.

The dealer threw a card to the boatman and three each to Fitzgerald and the lieutenant. Fitzgerald picked them up. *Seven . . . Jack . . . Three . . . Goddamn it!* He struggled to keep his face impassive. He looked up to see the lieutenant staring at him, the slightest hint of a smile at the corner of his mouth.

You bastard. Fitzgerald pushed the rest of his money to the center of the table. "Raise you fifty dollars."

The boatman whistled and threw his cards on the table.

The lieutenant's eyes traveled across the mound of money in the center of the table and came to rest on Fitzgerald. "That's a lot of money Mr. . . . what was it—Fitzpatrick?"

Fitzgerald fought to control himself "Fitz*gerald*."

"Fitz*gerald*—yes, sorry."

Fitzgerald gauged the lieutenant. *He'll fold. He hasn't got the nerve.* The lieutenant held his cards in one hand and drummed his fingers with the others. He pursed his lips, making his long mustache droop even further. It irritated Fitzgerald, especially the way that he stared.

"I'll see your fifty and call," said the lieutenant.

Fitzgerald felt his stomach sink. His jaw tensed as he turned over the pair of aces.

"Pair of aces," said the lieutenant. "Well, that would have beat my pair."

He threw down a pair of threes. "Except I got another one." He tossed another three on the table. "I believe you're done for the evening, Mr. Fitz-whatever—unless the good sutler will buy your little canoe." The lieutenant reached for the mound of money in the center of the table.

Fitzgerald pulled the skinning knife from his belt and slammed it into the back of the lieutenant's hand. The lieutenant screamed as the knife pinned his hand to the table. Fitzgerald grabbed a whiskey bottle and shattered it on the pitiful lieutenant's head. He was poised to ram the jagged neck of the bottle into the lieutenant's throat when two soldiers grabbed him from behind, wrestling him to the ground.

Fitzgerald spent the night in the guardhouse. In the morning he found himself in shackles, standing before a major in a mess hall dressed up to look like a court of law.

The major talked for a long time in a stilted verse and cadence that made little sense to Fitzgerald. The lieutenant was there, his hand in a bloody bandage. The major interrogated the lieutenant for half an hour, then did the same thing with the sutler, the boatman, and three other witnesses from the bar. Fitzgerald found the whole proceeding curious, since he had no intention of denying that he'd stabbed the lieutenant.

After an hour the major told Fitzgerald to approach "the bench," which Fitzgerald assumed was the rather ordinary desk behind which the major had ensconced himself.

The major said, "This martial court finds you guilty of assault. You may choose between two sentences—five years imprisonment or three years enlistment in the United States Army." One quarter of Fort Atkinson's men had deserted that year. The major took full advantage of opportunities to replenish his troops.

For Fitzgerald, the decision was simple. He'd seen the guardhouse. No doubt he could break out eventually, but enlistment presented a far easier path.

Later that day John Fitzgerald raised his right hand and swore an oath of allegiance to the Constitution of the United States of America as a new private in the Sixth Regiment of the U.S. Army. Until such time as he could desert, Fort Atkinson would be his home.

Hugh Glass was tying a pack on a horse when he saw Jim Bridger walking toward him across the yard. Before now, the boy had avoided him scrupulously. This time both his walk and his gaze were unwavering. Glass stopped his work and watched the boy approach.

When Bridger reached Glass he stopped. "I want you to know that I'm sorry for what I did." He paused for a moment before adding, "I wanted you to know that before you left."

Glass started to respond, then stopped. He had wondered if the boy would approach him. He had even thought about what he would say, rehearsed in his mind a lengthy lecture. Yet as he looked now at the boy, the particulars of his prepared speech eluded him. He felt something unexpected, a strange mixture of pity and respect.

Finally Glass said simply, "Follow your own lead, Bridger." Then he turned back to the horse.

An hour later, Hugh Glass and his three companions rode out of the fort on the Big Horn, bound for the Powder and the Platte.

TWENTY-THREE

MARCH 6, 1824

ONLY THE TOPS OF the highest buttes held a grip on the few rays of sunlight. As Glass watched, even those were extinguished. It was an interlude that he held as sacred as Sabbath, the brief segue between the light of day and the dark of night. The retreating sun drew with it the harshness of the plain. Howling winds ebbed, replaced by an utter stillness that seemed impossible for a vista so grand. The colors too were transformed. Stark daytime hues blended and blurred, softened by a gentle wash of ever darkening purples and blues.

It was a moment for reflection in a space so vast it could only be divine.

And if Glass believed in a god, surely it resided in this great western expanse. Not a physical presence, but an idea, something beyond man's ability to comprehend, something larger.

The darkness deepened and Glass watched as the stars emerged, dim at first, later bright as lighthouse beacons. It had been a long time since he studied the stars, though the lessons of the old Dutch sea captain remained fixed in his mind: "Know the stars and you'll always have a compass." Glass picked out Ursa Major, followed its guide to the North

212 · MICHAEL PUNKE

Star. He searched for Orion, dominant on the eastern horizon. Orion, the hunter, his vengeful sword poised to strike.

Red interrupted the silence. "You get the late watch, Pig." Red kept a careful tally of the distribution of chores.

Pig needed no reminder. He pulled his blanket tightly over his head and closed his eyes.

They camped in a dry ravine that night, a ravine that cut the plain like a giant wound. Water had formed it, but not the gentle, nourishing rains of other places. Water came to the high plain in the torrential flood of spring runoff or as the violent spawn of a summer storm. Unaccustomed to moisture, the ground could not absorb it. The water's effect was not to nourish, but to destroy.

Pig was certain that he had just fallen asleep when he felt the persistent prodding of Red's foot. "You're up," said Red. Pig grunted, hoisting his body to a sitting position before working his way to his feet. The splash of the Milky Way was like a white river across the midnight sky. Pig looked up briefly, his only thought that the clear sky made it colder. He wrapped his blanket around his shoulders, picked up his rifle, and walked down the ravine.

Two Shoshone watched the changing of the guard from behind a clump of sagebrush. They were boys, Little Bear and Rabbit, twelve-year-olds on a quest not for glory but for meat. But it was glory that now stood before them in the form of five horses. The boys imagined themselves galloping into their village. They imagined the bonfires and feast that would celebrate them. They imagined the stories they would tell of their cunning and bravery. They could scarcely believe their good fortune as they stared into the ravine, though the nearness of the opportunity filled them with fear as much as excitement.

They waited until the last hour before dawn, hoping the guard's attentiveness would fade as the night wore on. It did. They could hear the man snoring as they crept from the sage. They let the horses see them and smell them as they crept up the ravine. The animals stood tense but quiet, ears perked as they watched the deliberate approach.

When the boys finally reached the horses, Little Bear slowly extended his arms, stroking the long neck of the nearest animal and whispering soothingly. Rabbit followed Little Bear's lead. They patted the horses for several minutes, gaining the animals' confidence before Little Bear pulled his knife and went to work on the hobbles that bound each animal's front legs together.

The boys had cut the hobbles from four of the five horses when they heard the sentry stir. They froze, each prepared to jump on a horse and gallop off. They stared at the dark hulk of the guard and he seemed to settle again. Rabbit motioned urgently to Little Bear—*Let's go!* Little Bear shook his head resolutely, pointing to the fifth horse. He walked to the animal and stooped to cut the hobble. His knife had grown dull, and it took an agonizing length of time to saw slowly through the twisted rawhide. In growing frustration and nervousness, Little Bear gave a hard tug at the knife. The rawhide snapped and his arm jerked backward. His elbow bashed into the horse's shin, eliciting a loud whinny from the animal in protest.

The sound jolted Pig from his sleep. He struggled to his feet, eyes wide and rifle cocked as he rushed toward the horses. Pig pulled up suddenly as a dark form appeared directly in front of him. He skidded to a halt, surprised to be confronted by a boy. The boy, Rabbit, looked about as menacing as his namesake, all wide eyes and spindly limbs. One of those limbs held a knife, though; another a length of rope. Pig struggled to know what to do. His job was to defend the horses, but even with the knife, the mere boy before him seemed a good measure short of threatening. Finally, Pig simply pointed his rifle and yelled, "Stop!"

Little Bear stared in horror at the scene before him. He had never seen a white man before that evening, and this one did not even appear to be human. He was enormous, with a chest like a bear and a face covered in fiery hair. The giant approached Rabbit, yelling wildly and pointing his gun. Without thinking, Little Bear rushed at the monster, burying his knife in its chest.

Pig saw a blur from his side before he felt the knife. He stood there, stunned. Little Bear and Rabbit stood there too, still terrified at the creature before them. Pig's legs felt suddenly weak and he dropped to his knees. Instinct told him to squeeze the trigger of his gun. It exploded, the bullet launching harmlessly toward the stars.

Rabbit managed to grab a horse by the mane, pulling himself to the animal's back. He yelled at Little Bear, who took one last look at the dying monster before leaping behind his friend. They had no control of the horse, which almost bucked them before all five animals galloped down the ravine.

Glass and the others arrived just in time to watch their horses disappear into the night. Pig still stood on his knees, his hands clutched to his chest. He fell to his side.

Glass bent over Pig, prying his hands away from the wound. He pulled back Pig's shirt. The three men stared grimly at the dark slit directly over his heart.

Pig looked up at Glass, his eyes a terrible mixture of pleading and fear.

"Fix me up, Glass."

Glass picked up Pig's massive hand and held it tightly. "I don't think I can, Pig."

Pig coughed. His big body gave a mighty shudder, like the ponderous moment before a great tree falls. Glass felt the hand go limp.

The giant man gave one final sigh and died there beneath the bright stars of the plain.

TWENTY-FOUR

MARCH 7, 1824

HUGH GLASS STABBED AT THE ground with his knife. It penetrated an inch at most; below that the frozen earth remained unpersuaded by the blade. Glass chipped away for almost an hour before Red observed, "You can't dig a grave in ground like that."

Glass sat back, his legs folded beneath him, panting from the exertion of the dig. "I'd make more progress if you pitched in."

"I'll pitch in—but I don't see much use in chipping away at ice." Chapman looked up from an antelope rib long enough to add, "Pig's gonna take a big hole."

"We could build him one of those scaffolds like they bury the Indians on," offered Red.

Chapman snorted. "What are you gonna build it with, sagebrush?"

Red looked around him, as if newly aware of the treeless plain. "Besides," continued Chapman, "Pig's too big for us to lift up on a scaffold."

"What if we just covered him with a big mound of rocks?" This idea had merit, and they spent half an hour scouring the area for stones. In the end, though, they managed to locate only a dozen or so. Most of those had to be extricated from the same frozen soil that prevented the digging of the grave.

"These are hardly enough to cover his head," said Chapman.

"Well," said Red. "If we covered up his head at least the magpies won't pick at his face."

Red and Chapman were surprised when Glass turned suddenly and walked away from the camp.

"Now where's he going?" asked Red. "Hey!" he shouted at Glass's back. "Where you going?"

Glass ignored them as he walked toward a small mesa, a quarter mile away.

"Hope those Shoshone don't come back while he's gone."

Chapman nodded his head in agreement. "Let's get a fire going and cook some more of the antelope."

Glass returned about an hour later. "There's an outcropping in the base of that mesa," he said. "It's big enough to hold Pig."

"In a cave?" said Red.

Chapman thought about it for a minute. "Well, I guess it's kinda like a crypt."

Glass looked at the two men and said, "It's the best we can do. Put out the fire and let's get on with it."

There was no dignified way to move Pig. There were no materials to build a litter and he was too heavy to carry. In the end, they put him facedown on a blanket and dragged him toward the mesa. Two men took turns with Pig while the third carried the four rifles. They did their best, with mixed results, to steer around the cactus and yucca that littered the ground. Twice Pig dropped to the ground, his rigid body landing in a plaintive, ungainly lump.

It took more than half an hour to reach the mesa. They rolled Pig on his back and covered him with the blanket while they gathered stones, now abundant, to seal the makeshift crypt. Sandstone formed the outcropping. It hung over a space about five feet in length and two feet in height. Glass used the butt of Pig's rifle to clear out the space inside. Some type of animal had nested in there, though there was no sign of recent occupation.

They piled up a great mound of loose sandstone, more than they needed, hesitant, it seemed, to move on to the final stage. Finally Glass threw a stone on the pile and said, "That's enough." He walked over to Pig's body and the other men helped him pull the dead man to the opening of the makeshift crypt. They lay him there, all of them staring.

The task of saying something fell to Glass. He removed his hat and the other men quickly followed suit, as if embarrassed at needing a prompt. Glass tried to clear his throat. He searched for the words to the verse about the "valley of death," but he couldn't remember enough to make it appropriate. In the end, the best he could come up with was the Lord's Prayer. He recited it in the strongest voice he could muster. It had been a long time since either Red or Chapman had said a prayer, but they mumbled along whenever a phrase evoked some distant memory.

When they were done, Glass said, "We'll take turns carrying his rifle."

Next he reached down and took the knife from Pig's belt. "Red, you look like you could use his knife. Chapman, you can have his powder horn."

Chapman accepted the horn solemnly. Red turned the knife in his hand. With a short smile and a brief flash of eagerness he said, "It's a pretty good blade."

Glass reached down and removed the small pouch that Pig wore around his throat. He dumped the contents onto the ground. A flint and steel tumbled out, along with several musket balls, patches—and a delicate pewter bracelet. It struck Glass as an odd possession for the giant man. *What story connected the dainty trinket to Pig? A dead mother? A sweetheart left behind?* They would never know, and the finality of the mystery filled Glass with melancholy thoughts of his own souvenirs.

Glass picked out the flint and steel, the balls and patches, transferring the items to his own possibles bag.

Sunlight gleamed off the bracelet. Red reached for it, but Glass caught his wrist.

Red's eyes flashed defensively. "He don't need that."

"You don't need it, either." Glass returned the bracelet to Pig's pouch, then lifted Pig's massive head to replace the pouch round his neck.

It took another hour to finish their work. They had to bend Pig's legs to make him fit. There was barely enough space between Pig and the walls of the outcropping to pull the blanket over his body. Glass did his best to tuck the fabric tightly over the dead man's face. They piled the rocks to seal the crypt as best they could. Glass placed the last stone, gathered his rifle, and walked away. Red and Chapman stared for a moment at the stone wall they had built, then scampered after Glass.

They walked down the Powder River along the face of the mountains for two more days, until the river took a sharp turn west. They found a creek heading south and followed that until it petered out, swallowed in the alkali flats of the most wretched land they had crossed. They kept heading south toward a low mountain shaped flat on top like a table. In front of the mountain ran the wide, shallow water of the North Platte River.

The day after they reached the Platte a big wind picked up and the temperature began a rapid plunge. By late morning close clouds filled the air with big, puffy flakes. Glass's memory of the blizzard on the Yellowstone remained vivid, and this time he vowed to take no chances. They stopped at the next stand of cottonwoods. Red and Chapman built a crude but solid lean-to while Glass shot and dressed a deer.

By late afternoon a full-fledged blizzard raged down the North Platte valley. The great cottonwoods creaked at the strain of the howling wind and wet snow piled up rapidly all around them, but their shelter held firm. They wrapped themselves in blankets and kept an enormous fire burning in front of the lean-to. Heat seeped from the great mound of crimson embers that accumulated as the night wore on. They roasted venison on the fire and the hot food warmed them from within. The wind began to subside about an hour before dawn, and by sunrise the storm had blown past. The sun rose on a world so uniformly white that it forced them to squint against its brilliant reflection.

Glass scouted downstream while Red and Chapman broke camp. Glass struggled to walk through the snow. A thin crust on the surface supported each step for an instant, but then his foot would break through and sink to the ground below. Some of the drifts measured more than three feet high. He guessed that the March sun would melt it all within a day or two, but in the meantime the snow would cripple their progress on foot. Glass cursed again the loss of their horses. He wondered whether they should wait, use the time to lay in a supply of jerky. A good supply of meat would relieve the need for daily foraging. And, of course, the faster they moved the better. A number of tribes considered the Platte their hunting ground—the Shoshone, the Cheyenne, the Pawnee, the Arapaho, the Sioux. Some of these Indians might be friendly, though Pig's death certainly underscored the hazards.

Glass crested a butte and stopped dead in his tracks. A hundred yards in front of him, a small herd of fifty or so buffalo huddled together, holding a protective, circular formation from their own recent battle with the storm. The lead bull spotted him immediately. The animal pivoted into the herd and the great mass of animals began to move. *They're going to stampede.*

Glass dropped to his knee and brought his rifle to his shoulder. He aimed at a fat cow and fired. He saw the cow stagger at the shot, but she held her feet. *Not enough powder at this range.* He doubled the charge, reloading in ten seconds. He sighted again on the cow and pulled the trigger. The cow pitched into the snow.

He scanned the horizon as he jammed the ramrod down the barrel.

When he looked back at the herd, Glass was surprised that they hadn't stampeded out of range—and yet every animal seemed in flailing motion. He watched a bull struggling at the front of the herd. The bull lunged forward, sinking to his chest in the deep, wet snow. *They can barely move.*

Glass wondered if he should shoot another cow or calf, but quickly decided that they had more than enough meat. *Too bad,* he thought. *I could shoot a dozen if I wanted.*

Then an idea struck him, and he wondered why he hadn't thought of it before. He moved to within forty yards of the herd, aimed at the biggest bull he could find and fired. He reloaded and quickly shot another bull. Suddenly two shots rang out behind him. A calf fell into the snow and he turned to see Chapman and Red. "Yee-haw!" yelled Red.

"Just the bulls!" yelled Glass.

Red and Chapman moved up beside him, eagerly reloading. "Why?" asked Chapman. "The calves is better eating."

"It's the hides I'm after," said Glass. "We're making a bullboat."

Five minutes later eleven bulls lay dead in the little vale. It was more than they needed, but Red and Chapman were caught in a frenzy once the shooting started. Glass pushed his ramrod hard to reload. The flurry of shooting had fouled his barrel. Only when the charge was seated and the pan primed did he approach the closest bull. "Chapman, get up on that ridgeline and take a look around. That's a lot of noise we just made. Red, start putting that new knife to use."

Glass approached the closest bull. In his glazed eye shone the last dim spark of vitality as its lifeblood pooled around him on the snow. Glass walked from the bull to the cow. He pulled out his knife and cut her throat. This is the one they would eat and he wanted to be sure she was properly bled. "Come over here, Red. It's easier if we skin them together." They rolled the cow on her side and Glass made a deep cut the length of the belly. Red used his hands to pull the hide back while Glass cut it away from the carcass. They laid the hide fur-side down while they carved out the best cuts: the tongue, the liver, the hump, and the loins. They threw the meat on the hide and then went to work on the bulls.

Chapman returned and Glass set him to work, too. "We need to cut as big a square as we can out of each hide, so don't be hacking away."

His arms already red to the shoulder, Red looked up from the great carcass beneath him. Shooting the buffalo had been exhilarating; skinning them was just a big damn mess. "Why don't we just make a raft?" he complained. "There's plenty of timber along the river."

"Platte's too shallow—especially this time of year." Aside from the abundance of building materials, the great benefit of the bullboat was its draft—barely nine inches. The mountain runoff that would flood the banks was still months away. In early spring the Platte hardly trickled.

Around noon Glass sent Red back to camp to set fires for jerking meat.

Behind him Red dragged the cow's hide across the snow, piled high with choice cuts. They took the tongues from the bulls, but otherwise worried only about the hides. "Roast up that liver and a couple of those tongues for tonight," yelled Chapman.

Skinning the bulls was the first of many steps. With each hide, Glass and Chapman worked to cut the largest square possible—they needed uniform edges. Their knives dulled quickly against the thick winter fur, forcing them to stop frequently and sharpen their blades. When they finished it took three trips to drag the hides back to camp. A new moon danced merrily on the North Platte by the time they laid out the last skin in a clearing near the camp.

To his credit, Red had worked diligently. Three low fires burned in rectangular pits. All the meat had been cut into thin slices and hung over willow racks. Red had been gorging himself all afternoon, and the smell of the roasting meat was overwhelming. Glass and Chapman stuffed mouthful after mouthful of the succulent meat. They ate for hours, contented not only by the abundant food, but also by the absence of wind and cold. It seemed incredible that they had huddled in a blizzard the night before.

"You ever make a bullboat?" asked Red at one point.

Glass nodded. "Pawnee use them on the Arkansas. Takes a while, but there's not much to it—frame of branches wrapped in skin—like a big bowl."

"I don't see how they float."

"The hides stretch tight as drums when they dry. You just caulk up the seams every morning."

It took a week to build the bullboats. Glass opted for two smaller boats rather than one large one. All of them could fit into one in a pinch. The smaller craft were also lighter and could float easily in any water deeper than a foot.

They spent the first day cutting sinews from the buffalo carcasses and building the frames. They used large cottonwood branches for the gunwales, bent in the shape of a ring. From the gunwales they worked their way down with progressively narrower rings. Between the rings they braided vertical supports with stout willow branches, tying the joints with sinew.

Working the hides took the longest. They used six per boat. Stitching the skins together was tedious work. They used their knife tips to auger holes, then sewed the skins tightly together with the sinew. When they finished, they had two giant squares, each consisting of four hides laid out two-by-two.

In the center of each rectangle they placed their wooden frames. They pulled the hides over the gunwale with the fur toward the inside of the boat. They trimmed the excess, then used sinew to stitch around the top. When they were finished, they set the boats upside down to dry.

Caulk required another trip to the dead buffalo in the vale. "Jesus it stinks," said Red. Sunny weather since the blizzard had melted the snow and set the carcasses to rot. Magpies and crows swarmed over the plentiful meat, and Glass worried that the circling carrion eaters would signal their presence. Not much they could do about it, except finish the boats and leave.

They cut tallow from the buffalo and used their hatchets to hack off slices from the hooves. Back at the camp they combined the reeking mixture with water and ash, melting it together slowly over coals into a sticky, liquid mass. Their cooking pot was small, so it took two days to prepare the dozen batches necessary to render the quantity they required.

They applied the caulk mixture to the seams, liberally smearing the mixture. Glass checked the boats as they dried in the March sun. A stiff, dry wind helped the process along. He was pleased with the work.

They left the next morning, Glass in one boat with their supplies, Red and Chapman in the other. It took a few miles to get the feel for their clumsy craft, pushing with cottonwood poles along the banks of the Platte, but the boats were sturdy.

A week had passed since the blizzard, a long time to sit in one place. But Fort Atkinson was a straight shot now, five hundred miles down the Platte. They would more than make up the time on the boats, floating all the way. *Twenty-five miles a day?* They could be there in three weeks if the weather held.

Fitzgerald must have passed through Fort Atkinson, thought Glass.

Glass pictured him, sauntering into the fort with the Anstadt. What lies had he invented to explain his presence? One thing was certain: Fitzgerald would not go unnoticed. Not many white men coming down the Missouri in winter. Glass pictured Fitzgerald's fishhook scar. Man like that makes an impression. With the confidence of a relentless predator, Glass knew that his quarry lay somewhere before him, nearer and nearer with each passing hour. Glass would find Fitzgerald, because he would never rest until he did.

Glass planted his long pole against the bottom of the Platte and pushed.

TWENTY-FIVE

MARCH 28, 1824

THE PLATTE CARRIED GLASS and his companions steadily downstream. For two days the river flowed due east along the buckskin foothills of low mountains. On the third day the river took a sharp turn south. A snowcapped peak rose above the others like a head on broad shoulders. For a while it seemed they were headed straight toward the peak, until the Platte veered again, settling finally on a southeastern course.

They made good time. Occasional headwinds slowed their progress, but more common was a stiff western breeze at their tail. Their supply of buffalo jerky eliminated the need to hunt. When they camped, the upside-down bullboats made good shelter. It took an hour every morning to recaulk the bullboats' seams with the supply they'd carried with them, but otherwise they could spend almost every daylight hour on the water, drifting toward Fort Atkinson with minimal exertion. Glass was grateful to let the river do their work.

It was the morning of the fifth day on the boats. Glass was spreading caulk when Red came tumbling back into camp. "There's an Indian over the rise! A brave on a horse!"

"Did he see you?"

Red shook his head vigorously. "Don't think so. There's a creek—looked like he was checking a trap line."

"You make out the tribe?" asked Glass.

"Looked like a Ree."

"Shit!" said Chapman. "What're Rees doing on the Platte?"

Glass questioned the reliability of Red's report. He doubted Arikara would wander this far from the Missouri. More likely Red had seen a Cheyenne or a Pawnee. "Let's go take a look." For Red's benefit he added, "Nobody shoots unless I do."

They moved forward on hands and knees as they approached the crest of the butte, their rifles in the crooks of their arms. The snow had long since melted, so they picked their way through clumps of sage and dry stalks of buffalo grass.

From the top of the hill they saw the rider, or rather his back, as he rode down the Platte at a distance of a half mile. They could barely make out the horse, a piebald. There was no way to know his tribe, only that Indians were close.

"Now what do we do?" asked Red. "He ain't alone. And you know they must be camped on the river."

Glass shot an irritated glance at Red, who had an uncanny knack for spotting problems and an utter inability for crafting solutions. That said, he was probably right. The few creeks they'd passed had been small. Any Indians in the area would hug tight to the Platte, directly in their path. *But what choice do we have?*

"Not much we can do," said Glass. "We'll put someone up on the bank to scout when we hit an open stretch."

Red started to mutter something and Glass cut him off. "I can pole my own boat. You men are free to go where you want—but I intend to float down this river." He turned and walked back toward the bullboats. Chapman and Red took a long look at the fading rider, then turned to follow Glass.

After two more good days in the boats, Glass guessed they had covered a hundred and fifty miles. It was nearly dusk when they approached a tricky bend in the Platte. Glass thought about stopping for the night, waiting to navigate the stretch in better light, but there was no good spot to put ashore.

Bookend hills forced the river to narrow, which deepened the water and sped the current. On the north bank, a cottonwood had fallen partway across the river, trapping a wild tangle of debris behind it. Glass's boat led the other by ten yards. The current carried him straight toward the downed tree. He sunk his pole to steer around. *No bottom.*

The current accelerated, and the protruding branches of the cottonwood appeared suddenly like spears. One good poke and the bullboat would sink. Glass raised himself on one knee and braced the other foot against the boat's ribbing. He lifted his pole and searched for a place to plant it. He saw a flat surface on the trunk and thrust his pole forward. The pole caught. Glass used all his strength to heave the clumsy craft against the current. He heard the rush of water against the boat as the current lifted its backside, pivoting the craft around the tree.

Glass faced backward now, giving him a direct view of Red and Chapman. Both braced for impact, rocking the boat precariously. When Red raised his pole he nearly bashed Chapman in the face. "Watch out, you idiot!" Chapman pushed his pole against the cottonwood as the current pressed hard from behind. Red finally extricated his pole and planted it loosely on the debris.

Both men heaved against the river, then ducked low as the current pushed them through the top of the half-submerged tree. Red's shirt caught a branch, bending it sharply back. The shirt ripped and the branch whipped backward, catching Chapman squarely in the eye. He cried out at the stinging pain, dropping his pole as he pressed his hands to his face.

Glass continued to stare backward as the current pushed both boats around the hill and toward the southern bank. Chapman stood on his knees in the bottom of their bullboat, facedown with his palm still pressed to his eye. Red looked downstream, past Glass and his boat. Glass watched as a terrified look captured Red's face. Red dropped his pole, desperately reaching for his rifle. Glass spun around.

Two dozen teepees stood on the south bank of the Platte, less than fifty yards in front of them. A handful of children played near the water. They spotted the bullboats and erupted in screams. Glass watched as two braves by a campfire jumped to their feet. Red had been right, he realized too late. *Arikara!* The current drove both boats directly toward the camp. Glass heard a shot as he watched the men in the camp grab weapons and rush toward the high bank along the river. Glass gave a final push with his pole and grabbed his gun.

Red fired a shot and an Indian tumbled down the bank. "What's happening?" yelled Chapman, struggling to see through his one clear eye.

Red started to say something when he felt a burning sensation in his belly. He looked down and saw blood oozing from a hole in his shirt. "Oh shit, Chapman, I'm shot!" He rose up in panic, ripping at his shirt to inspect the wound. Two more shots hit simultaneously, pitching him backward. His legs hooked the gunwale as he fell, tipping the rim of the bullboat into the rushing flow of the river. Water spilled across the gunwale and the boat flipped.

Half blind, Chapman found himself suddenly underwater. He felt the jarring chill of the river. For an instant, the wild rush seemed to slow, and Chapman struggled to process the lethal events surrounding him. Through his good eye he saw Red's body floating downstream, his blood leaching into the river like black ink. He heard the watery echo of legs crashing toward him from the river's edge. *They're coming for me!* He desperately needed to breathe, yet he knew with terrible certainty what waited on the surface.

Finally he could stand it no more. His head broke the surface and he gasped to fill his lungs. He would never draw another breath. His eyes had not yet cleared, so Chapman never saw the swinging ax.

Glass leveled his rifle on the nearest Arikara and fired. He watched in horror as several Arikara waded into the river, hacking at Chapman when his head broke the surface. Red's body floated forlornly downstream. Glass reached for Pig's rifle as he heard a wild cry. An enormous Indian hurled a spear from the shoreline. Glass ducked instinctively. The spear cleanly penetrated the side of the boat, burying its tip in the ribbing on the opposite side. Glass raised above the gunwale and fired, killing the big Indian on the shore.

He saw a flash of motion and looked up on the bank. Three Arikara stood in a deadly gauntlet, barely twenty yards away. *They can't miss.* He threw himself backward into the Platte as their trio of shots exploded.

For an instant he tried to hold on to the rifle. Just as quickly he let go.

He dismissed the idea of trying to make his escape by swimming downstream. He was already numb from the icy water. Besides, the Arikara would find their mounts in a few minutes—maybe they already had. A racing horse would easily outpace the meandering Platte. His only chance was to stay submerged as long as possible and get to the opposite bank. Put the river between him and them—then hope to find cover. He kicked furiously and used both arms to propel himself.

The channel ran deep in the middle of the river, deeper than a man's head. A sudden streak cut the water in front of him and Glass realized it was an arrow. Bullets pierced the water too, like mini torpedoes, searching for him. *They can see me!* Glass struggled to go deeper below the surface, but already his chest constricted for lack of breath. *What's on the opposite bank?* He hadn't even managed to look before chaos erupted. *Must breathe!* He pushed himself toward the surface.

His head cleared the water and he heard the quick staccato of shots.

He grimaced as he drew a deep breath, expecting the crash of a ball against his skull. Musket balls and arrows splashed around him—but none hit. He scanned the north bank before diving back below the surface. What he saw gave him hope. The river ran for forty yards or so along a sandbar. No cover there; if he climbed out they would shoot him down. At the end of the sandbar, though, the water joined with a low, grassy bank. It was his only chance.

Glass dug deep and pulled hard against the water, the current aiding his stroke. He thought he could just make out the end of the sandbar through the murky water. *Thirty yards.* The musket balls and arrows stabbed at the water. *Twenty yards.* He veered toward the bank as his lungs screamed for air. *Ten yards.* His feet hit the rocks of the bottom but he stayed submerged, his desperation to breathe still less than his fear of the Arikara guns. When the water became too shallow to remain submerged, he stood up, sucking for air as he dove for the tall grass on the bank. He felt a sharp sting in the back of his leg and ignored it, scrambling into a thick stand of willows.

From the temporary cover of the willows he looked back. Four riders coaxed their horses down the steep bank across the river. A half dozen Indians stood at the water's edge, pointing toward the willows. Something caught his eye farther upstream. Two Arikara were dragging Chapman's body up the bank. Glass turned to flee, sharp pain shooting up his leg. He looked down to find an arrow protruding from his calf. It had not hit a bone. He reached down, wincing as he ripped the arrow backward in a single, swift motion. He threw it aside and crawled deeper into the willows.

Glass's first lucky turn came in the form of an independent-minded filly, the first of the four horses to hit the water of the Platte. Aggressive quirting goaded her into the shallows, but the animal balked when the bottom disappeared and she was forced to swim. She whinnied and thrashed her head, ignoring the hard rein as she turned stubbornly back to shore. The other three horses had their own reservations about cold water and were happy to follow the filly's lead. The balking animals bumped into each other, churning the Platte and dumping two of their riders into the river.

By the time the riders regained control and whipped their mounts back into the river, precious seconds had passed.

Glass crashed through the willows, emerging suddenly at a sandy embankment. He scrambled to the top and looked down at a narrow back channel. Shaded from the sun during most of the day, the still water of the channel lay frozen, a thin dusting of snow on its icy surface. Across the channel, another steep embankment led to a thick mass of willows and trees. *There.*

Glass slid down the slope and leapt onto the frozen surface of the channel. The thin layer of snow gave way to the ice beneath. His moccasins gained no traction and he flipped backward, landing flat on his back. For an instant he lay stunned, staring up at the fading light of the evening sky. He rolled to his side, shaking his head to clear it. He heard the whinny of a horse and pushed himself to his feet. Gingerly this time, he picked his way across the narrow channel and clambered up the opposite bank. He heard the crash of horses behind him as he scrambled into the brush.

The four Arikara riders crested the embankment, peering down. Even in the dim light, the tracks on the surface of the channel were clear. The lead rider kicked his pony. The pony hit the ice and fared no better than Glass. Worse, in fact, as the animal's flat hooves found nothing to grip. Its four legs flailed spastically as it crashed to its side, crushing its rider's leg in the process. The rider cried out in pain. Heeding the clear lesson, the three other horsemen quickly dismounted, continuing their pursuit on foot.

Glass's trail faded quickly in the thick brush across the back channel.

It would have been obvious in daylight. In his desperate flight, Glass paid no heed to the branches he broke or even the footprints trailing behind him. But now there remained no more than a faint glow of the day. The shadows themselves had disappeared, dissolving into uniform darkness.

Glass heard the scream of the downed rider behind him and stopped.

They're on the ice. He guessed there was fifty yards of brush between them. In the growing darkness, he realized, the peril was not being seen, but being heard. A large cottonwood loomed beside him. He reached for a low branch and pulled himself up.

The tree's main branches formed a broad crotch at a height of about eight feet. Glass hunkered low, struggling to quiet his heaving chest. He reached down to his belt, relieved to touch the pommel of his knife, still secure in its scabbard. There, too, was the *sac au feu*. Inside were his flint and steel. Though his rifle lay on the bottom of the Platte, his powder horn still hung round his neck. At least starting fires would pose no problems. The thought of fire made him suddenly aware of his sopping clothing and the bone-deep chill from the river. His body began to shiver uncontrollably and he fought to keep still.

A twig snapped. Glass peered into the clearing beneath him. A lanky warrior stood in the brush. His eyes scanned the clearing, searching the ground for sign of his quarry. He gripped a long trading musket and wore a hatchet on his belt. Glass held his breath as the Arikara stepped into the clearing. The warrior held his gun ready as he walked slowly toward the cottonwood. Even in the darkness, Glass could see clearly the white gleam of an elk-tooth necklace around his neck, the shiny brass of twin bracelets on his wrist. *God, don't let him look up.* His heart hammered with such force that it seemed his chest could not contain its beating.

The Indian reached the base of the cottonwood and stopped. His head was no more than ten feet below Glass. The brave studied the ground again, then the surrounding brush. Glass's first instinct was to hold perfectly still, hope that the warrior would pass. But as he stared down he began to calculate the odds of another course— killing the Indian and taking his gun. Glass reached slowly for his knife. He felt its reassuring grip and began to slide it slowly from its sheath.

Glass focused on the Indian's throat. A swift cut across the jugular would not only kill him, but also prevent him from crying out. With excruciating slowness he raised his body, tensing for the pounce.

Glass heard an urgent whisper from the edge of the clearing. He looked up to see a second warrior step out of the brush, a stout lance in his hand. Glass froze. He had moved from the relative concealment of the tree's crotch, poising himself to leap. From where he was now perched, only darkness concealed him from the two warriors hunting him.

The Indian below him turned, shaking his head and pointing to the ground, then motioning toward the thick brush. He whispered something in response. The Indian with the lance walked up to the cottonwood. Time seemed suspended as Glass struggled to maintain his composure. *Hold tight.* Finally the Indians settled on a course, and each disappeared into a separate gap in the brush.

Glass didn't move from the cottonwood for more than two hours. He listened to the off-and-on sounds of his searchers as he plotted his next move. After an hour one of the Arikara cut back through the clearing, apparently on his way toward the river.

When Glass finally climbed down his joints felt like they had frozen in place. His foot had fallen asleep, and it took several minutes before he could walk normally.

He would survive the night, though Glass knew that the Arikara would return at dawn. He also knew that the brush would not conceal him or his tracks in the glaring light of day. He picked his way through the dark tangle, careful to stay parallel with the Platte. Clouds blocked the light of the moon, though they also kept the temperature above freezing. He could not shake the chill of his wet clothing, but at least the constant motion kept his blood pumping hard.

After three hours he reached a small spring creek. It was perfect. He waded into the water, careful to leave a few telltale tracks pointing up the stream—away from the Platte. He waded more than a hundred yards up the creek until he found the right terrain, a rocky shoreline that would conceal his tracks. He picked a path out of the water and across the rocks, working his way toward a grove of stumpy trees.

They were hawthorns, whose thorny branches made them favorites of nesting birds. Glass stopped, reaching for his knife. He cut a small, ragged patch from his red cotton shirt and stuck the cloth on one of the thorns. *They won't miss that.* He turned then, picking his way back across the rocks to the creek, careful not to leave a trace. He waded to the middle of the creek and began to work his way back down.

The little creek meandered lazily across the plain before joining with the Platte. Glass tripped repeatedly on the slippery rocks of the dark creek bed. The dousings kept him wet and he tried not to think about the cold. He had no sensation in his feet by the time he reached the Platte. He stood shivering in the knee-deep water, dreading what he had to do next.

He peered across the river, trying to make out the contour of the opposite bank. There were willows and a few cottonwoods. *Don't make any tracks crawling out.* He waded into the water, his breaths coming shorter and shorter as the water rose up to his waist. Darkness concealed a shelf beneath the water. Glass stepped off and found himself suddenly submerged to his neck. Gasping at the shock of the icy water on his chest, he swam hard for the opposite bank. When he could stand again he still stayed in the river, walking along the shoreline until he found a good spot to get out—a rocky jetty leading into willows.

Glass worked his way carefully through the willows and the cotton-woods behind them, mindful of every step. He hoped that the Arikara would fall for his ruse up the spring creek—they certainly wouldn't expect him to come back across the Platte. Still, he left nothing to chance. Glass was defenseless if they picked up his trail, so he did everything in his power not to leave one.

A faint glow lit the eastern sky when he emerged from the cotton-woods. In the predawn light he saw the dark profile of a large plateau, a mile or two away. The plateau ran parallel to the river as far as he could see. He could lose himself there, find a sheltered draw or cave to hide, build a fire—dry out and get warm. When things settled down he could return to the Platte, continue his trek toward Fort Atkinson.

Glass walked toward the looming plateau in the growing glow of the coming day. He thought about Chapman and Red and felt a sudden stab of guilt. He pushed it from his mind. *No time for that now.*

TWENTY-SIX

APRIL 14, 1824

LIEUTENANT JONATHON JACOBS RAISED HIS ARM and barked out an order. Behind him a column of twenty men and their mounts reined to a dusty halt. The lieutenant patted his horse's sweaty flank and reached for his canteen. He tried to affect nonchalance as he drew a long swig from the canteen. In truth, he hated any moment away from the relative safety of Fort Atkinson.

He particularly hated this moment, when the galloping return of his scout could herald a wide variety of misfortunes. The Pawnee and a renegade band of Arikara had been raiding up and down the Platte since the snow began melting. The lieutenant tried to check his imagination as he awaited the scout's report.

The scout, a grizzled plainsman named Higgins, waited until he was practically on top of the column before he reined his own mount. The fringe on his leather jacket bounced as the big buckskin slid to a sideways halt.

"There's a man walking this way—up over the ridgeline."

"You mean an Indian?"

"'Sume so, Lieutenant. Didn't get close enough to find out." Lieutenant Jacobs's first instinct was to send Higgins back out with the sergeant and two men. Reluctantly, he came to the conclusion that he should go himself.

As they neared the ridgeline they left one man to hold the horses while the rest of them crawled forward on their bellies. The wide valley of the Platte spread before them for a hundred miles. Half a mile away, a solitary figure picked his way down the near bank of the river. Lieutenant Jacobs pulled a small looking glass from the breast pocket of his tunic. He extended the brass instrument to its full length and peered through.

The magnified view bobbed up and down the riverbank as Jacobs steadied the scope. He found his target, holding on the buckskin-clad man. He couldn't make out the face—but he could see the bushy smudge of a beard.

"I'll be damned," said Lieutenant Jacobs with surprise. "It's a white man. What the hell is he doing out here?"

"He ain't one of ours," said Higgins. "All the deserters head straight for St. Louis."

Perhaps because the man appeared to be in no immediate danger, the lieutenant felt suddenly gripped by chivalry. "Let's go get him."

Major Robert Constable represented, albeit not by choice, the fourth generation of Constable men to pursue a career in the military. His great-grandfather fought the French and Indians as an officer of His Majesty's Twelfth Regiment of Foot. His grandfather stayed true to his family's vocation, if not to its king, fighting against the British as an officer of Washington's Continental Army.

Constable's father had poor luck when it came to military glory—too young for the Revolution and too old for the War of 1812. Given no opportunity to win distinction of his own, he felt the least he could do was to offer up his only son. Young Robert had yearned to pursue a career in the law and dreamed of wearing the robes of a judge. Robert's father refused to stain the family lineage with a pettifogger, and used a friendship with a senator to secure a spot for his son at West Point. So for twenty unremarkable years, Major Robert Constable inched his way up the military ladder. His wife had stopped trailing after him a decade earlier, and now resided in Boston (in close proximity to her lover, a well-known judge). When General Atkinson and Colonel Leavenworth returned east for the winter, Major Constable inherited temporary command of the fort.

Over what did he reign supreme? Three hundred infantrymen (equally divided between recent immigrants and recent convicts), a hundred cavalrymen (with, in an unfortunate bit of asymmetry, only fifty horses), and a dozen rusty cannons. Still, reign supreme he would, passing on the bitter brine of his career to the subjects of his tiny kingdom.

Major Constable was sitting behind a large desk flanked by an aide, when Lieutenant Jacobs presented the weather-beaten plainsman he had rescued. "We found him on the Platte, sir," reported Jacobs, breathlessly. "He survived an Arikara attack on the north fork."

Lieutenant Jacobs stood beaming in the bright light of his heroism, awaiting the certain accolades for his brave act. Major Constable barely looked at him before he said, "Dismissed."

"Dismissed, sir?"

"Dismissed."

Lieutenant Jacobs continued to stand there, somewhat dumbfounded at this brusque reception. Constable put his command more bluntly: "Go away." He held his hand in the air and whisked it, as if shooing a gnat. Turning to Glass, he asked, "Who are you?"

"Hugh Glass." His voice was as scarred as his face.

"And how is it that you find yourself wandering down the Platte River?"

"I'm a messenger for the Rocky Mountain Fur Company."

If the arrival of a badly scarred white man had not piqued the major's jaded interest, mention of the Rocky Mountain Fur Company did. Fort Atkinson's future, not to mention the major's ability to salvage his own career, depended on the commercial viability of the fur trade. What other significance could be found in a wasteland of uninhabitable deserts and impassable peaks?

"From Fort Union?"

"Fort Union's abandoned. Captain Henry moved to Lisa's old post on the Big Horn."

The major leaned forward in his chair. All winter he had dutifully filed dispatches to St. Louis. None contained anything more compelling than bleak reports about dysentery among his men, or the dwindling number of cavalrymen in possession of a horse. Now he had something! Rescue of a Rocky Mountain man! The abandonment of Fort Union! A new fort on the Big Horn!

"Tell the mess to send hot food for Mr. Glass."

For an hour, the major peppered Glass with questions about Fort Union, the new fort on the Big Horn, the commercial viability of their venture.

Glass carefully avoided a discussion of his own motivation for returning from the frontier. Finally, though, Glass asked a question of his own. "Did a man with a fishhook scar pass through here—coming down the Missouri?" Glass used his finger to trace a fishhook beginning at the corner of his mouth.

Major Constable searched Glass's face. Finally he said, "Pass through, no . . ."

Glass felt the sharp pang of disappointment.

"He stayed on," said Constable. "Chose enlistment over incarceration after a brawl in our local saloon."

He's here! Glass fought to steady himself, to erase any emotion from his face.

"I gather you know this man?"

"I know him."

"Is he a deserter from the Rocky Mountain Fur Company?"

"He's a deserter from many things. He's also a thief."

"Now, that's a very serious allegation." Constable felt the latent stirring of his judicial ambitions.

"Allegation? I'm not here to register a complaint, Major. I'm here to settle my account with the man who robbed me."

Constable inhaled deeply, his chin rising slowly with the breath. He exhaled loudly, then spoke as if patiently lecturing a child. "This is not the *wilderness,* Mr. Glass, and I would advise you to keep your tone respectful. I am a major in the United States Army and the commanding officer of this fort. I take your charges seriously. I will ensure that they are properly investigated. And, of course, you'll have an opportunity to present your evidence. . . ."

"My evidence! He's got my rifle!"

"Mr. Glass!" Constable's irritation was growing. "If Private Fitzgerald has stolen your property, I will punish him in accordance with military law."

"This isn't very complicated, Major." Glass could not keep the derision from his tone.

"Mr. Glass!" Constable spit out the words. His pointless career on a godforsaken outpost provided daily tests of his ability to rationalize. He would not tolerate disrespect for his authority. "This is the last time I'll warn you. It's *my* job to administer justice on this post!"

Major Constable turned to an aide. "Do you know the whereabouts of Private Fitzgerald?"

"He's with Company E, sir. They're out on wood detail, coming back tonight."

"Arrest him when he arrives at the fort. Search his quarters for the rifle. If he has it, seize it. Bring the private to the courtroom tomorrow morning at eight. Mr. Glass, I expect you to be present—and clean yourself up before you do so."

A jury-rigged mess hall served as Major Constable's courtroom. Several soldiers carried Constable's desk from his office, then set it up on a makeshift riser. The elevated seat allowed Constable to survey the proceedings from an appropriately judicious altitude. Lest there be any question about the official sanction of his courtroom, Constable flew two flags behind the desk.

If it lacked the splendor of a true courtroom, at least it was big. A hundred spectators could pack the room when the tables were removed. To ensure an appropriate audience, Major Constable usually canceled other duties for all but a few of the fort's inhabitants. With little competition in the way of entertainment, the major's official performances always played to a packed house. Interest in the current proceeding ran particularly high. Word of the scarred frontiersman and his wild accusations had spread quickly through the fort.

From a bench near the major's desk, Hugh Glass watched as the door of the mess hall burst open. "A-ten-SHUN!" The spectators rose to attention as Major Constable strode into the room. Constable was attended by a lieutenant named Neville K. Askitzen, dubbed "Lieutenant Ass-Kisser" by the enlisted men.

Constable paused to survey his audience before strolling regally to the front, Askitzen skittering behind him. Once seated, the major nodded to Askitzen, who gave an order permitting the spectators to sit.

"Bring forth the accused," ordered Major Constable. The doors opened again and Fitzgerald appeared in the doorway, his hands in shackles and a guard at either arm. The audience squirmed for a glimpse as the guards led Fitzgerald to the front, where a sort of holding pen had been constructed perpendicular and to the right of the major's desk. The pen placed him directly across from Glass, who sat to the major's left.

Glass's eyes bored into Fitzgerald like an auger in soft wood. Fitzgerald had cut his hair and shaved his beard. Navy blue wool replaced his buckskins. Glass felt revulsion at the sight of Fitzgerald, shrouded in the respectability that a uniform implied.

It seemed unreal, suddenly to be in his presence. He fought against the desire to rush at Fitzgerald, wrap his hands around the man's throat, choke the life from him. *I can't do that. Not here.* Their eyes met for a brief instant. Fitzgerald nodded—as if to politely acknowledge him!

Major Constable cleared his throat and said, "This martial court is hereby convened. Private Fitzgerald, it is your right to be confronted by your accuser, and to hear formally the charges brought against you. Lieutenant, read the charges."

Lieutenant Askitzen unfolded a piece of paper and read to the chamber in a stately voice: "We hear today the complaint of Mr. Hugh Glass, of the Rocky Mountain Fur Company, against Private John Fitzgerald, United States Army, Sixth Regiment, Company E. Mr. Glass alleges that Private Fitzgerald, while himself in the employ of the Rocky Mountain Fur Company, did steal from Mr. Glass a rifle, a knife, and other personal effects. If found guilty, Mr. Fitzgerald faces court-martial and imprisonment of ten years."

A murmur rippled through the crowd. Major Constable banged a gavel against the desk and the room fell silent. "Will the complainant approach the bench." Confused, Glass looked up at the major, who gave an exasperated look before motioning him toward the desk.

Lieutenant Askitzen stood there with a Bible. "Raise your right hand," he said to Glass. "Do you swear to tell the truth, so help you God?" Glass nodded and said yes in the weak timbre that he hated but could not change.

"Mr. Glass—you heard the reading of the charges?" asked Constable.

"Yes."

"And they are accurate?"

"Yes."

"Do you wish to make a statement?"

Glass hesitated. The formality of the proceeding had taken him completely by surprise. Certainly he had not expected a hundred spectators. He understood that Constable commanded the fort. But this was a matter between him and Fitzgerald—not a spectacle for the amusement of an arrogant officer and a hundred bored enlisted men.

"Mr. Glass—do you wish to address the court?"

"I told you yesterday what happened. Fitzgerald and a boy named Bridger were left to tend me after a grizzly attacked me on the Grand River. They abandoned me instead. I don't fault them for that. But they robbed me before they ran off. Took my rifle, my knife, even my flint and steel. They took from me the things I needed to have a chance on my own."

"Is this the rifle you claim is yours?" The major produced the Anstadt from behind his desk.

"That's my rifle."

"Can you identify it by any distinguishing marks?"

Glass felt his face grow flush at the challenge. *Why am I the one being questioned?* He took a deep breath. "The barrel is engraved with the name of the maker—J. Anstadt, Kutztown, Penn."

The major pulled a pair of spectacles from his pocket and examined the barrel. He read aloud, "J. Anstadt, Kutztown, Penn." Another murmur filled the room.

"Do you have anything further to say, Mr. Glass?" Glass shook his head no.

"You are dismissed."

Glass returned to his place across from Fitzgerald as the major continued. "Lieutenant Askitzen, swear in the defendant." Askitzen walked to Fitzgerald's pen. The shackles on Fitzgerald's hands clanked as he placed his hand on the Bible. His strong voice filled the mess hall as he solemnly stated the oath.

Major Constable rocked back in his chair. "Private Fitzgerald— you've heard the charges of Mr. Glass. How do you account for yourself?"

"Thank you for the opportunity to defend myself, Your Hon—I mean Major Constable." The major beamed at the slip as Fitzgerald continued. "You probably expect me to tell you that Hugh Glass is a liar—but I'm not going to do that, sir." Constable leaned forward, curious. Glass's eyes narrowed as he too wondered what Fitzgerald was up to.

"In fact, I know Hugh Glass to be a good man, respected by his peers in the Rocky Mountain Fur Company.

"I believe that Hugh Glass believes every word he said to be the God's honest truth. The problem, sir, is that he believes a whole bunch of things that never happened.

"Truth is, he'd been delirious for two days before we left him. Fever spiked up that last day, especially—death sweats, we thought. He moaned and cried out—we could tell he was hurting. I felt bad there wasn't more we could do."

"What *did* you do for him?"

"Well, I'm no doctor, sir, but I did my best. I made up a poultice for his throat and for his back. I made a broth to try and feed him. Course his throat was so bad he couldn't swallow or talk."

This was too much for Glass. In the firmest voice he could muster, he said, "Lying comes easy to you, Fitzgerald."

"Mr. Glass!" roared Constable, his face twisted suddenly into a stiff knot of indignation. "This is *my* proceeding. *I* will cross-examine the witnesses. And *you* will keep your mouth shut or I'll hold you in contempt!"

Constable let the weight of his pronouncement sink in before turning back to Fitzgerald. "Go on, Private."

"I don't blame him for not knowing, sir." Fitzgerald tossed Glass a pitiful glance. "He was out—or feverish—most of the time we tended him."

"Well, that's all well and good, but do you deny that you abandoned him? Robbed him?"

"Let me tell you what happened that morning, sir. We'd been camped for four days by a spring creek off the Grand. I left Bridger with Hugh and went down on the main river to hunt—been gone most of the morning. About a mile from camp I all but stepped on an Arikara war party." Another ripple of excitement passed through the spectators, most of them veterans of the dubious fight at the Arikara village.

"The Rees didn't see me at first, so I made my way back toward camp as quick as I could. They spotted me just about when I got to the creek. They came charging, while I went running up to our camp.

"When I got there, I told Bridger that the Rees were right behind me—told him to help me get the camp ready to make a stand. That's when Bridger told me that Glass was dead."

"You bastard!" Glass spat the words as he stood and moved toward Fitzgerald. Two soldiers with rifles and bayonets blocked his path.

"Mr. Glass!" yelled Constable, beating a gavel on the table. "You will hold your seat and hold your tongue or I will have you jailed!"

It took the major a moment to regain his composure. He paused to adjust the collar of his brass-buttoned jacket before returning to the interrogation of Fitzgerald. "Obviously Mr. Glass was not dead. Did you examine him?"

"I understand why Hugh's angry, sir. I shouldn't have taken Bridger's word. But when I looked at Glass that day he was pale as a ghost—not moving a twitch. We could hear the Rees coming up the creek. Bridger started yelling that we had to get out of there. I was sure Glass was dead—so we ran for cover."

"But not before taking his rifle."

"Bridger did that. He said it was stupid to leave a rifle and knife behind for the Rees. There wasn't time to argue about it."

"But you're the one with the rifle now."

"Yes, sir, I am. When we got back to Fort Union, Captain Henry didn't have the cash to pay us for staying back with Glass. Henry asked me to take the rifle as payment. Of course, Major, I'm glad for the chance to give it back to Hugh."

"What about his flint and steel?"

"We didn't take them, sir. I expect the Rees got that."

"Why wouldn't they have killed Mr. Glass—lifted his scalp in the usual manner?"

"I imagine they thought he was dead, same as we did. No offense to Hugh, but there wasn't much scalp left to lift. The bear carved him up so bad the Rees probably figured there wasn't no mutilating left to be done."

"You've been on this post for six weeks, Private. Why haven't you unburdened yourself of this story before today?"

Fitzgerald allowed a carefully calibrated pause, bit at his lip, and hung his head. Finally he raised his eyes and then his head. In a quiet voice he said, "Well, sir—I guess I was ashamed."

Glass stared in utter disbelief. Not so much at Fitzgerald, from whom no treachery arrived completely unexpected. But more so at the major, who had begun to nod along with Fitzgerald's story like a rat to the piper's tune. *He believes him!*

Fitzgerald continued. "I didn't know before yesterday that Hugh Glass was alive—but I did think that I'd abandoned a man without so much as a decent burial. Man deserves that, even on the front—"

Glass could bear it no longer. He reached beneath his capote for the pistol concealed at his belt. He pulled out the gun and fired. The ball strayed just wide of its mark, burying itself in Fitzgerald's shoulder. Glass heard Fitzgerald cry out and at the same time felt strong arms grabbing him from both sides. He struggled to break their grip. Pandemonium erupted in the courtroom. He heard Askitzen yell something, caught a flash of the major and his golden epaulettes. He felt a sharp pain at the back of his skull and all went black.

TWENTY-SEVEN

APRIL 28, 1824

GLASS AWOKE IN MUSTY DARKNESS with a throbbing head-ache. He lay facedown on a rough-hewn floor. He rolled slowly to his side, bumping against a wall. Above his head he saw light, streaming through a narrow slot in a heavy door. Fort Atkinson's guardhouse con-sisted of a large holding pen, for drunks and other common truants, and two wooden cells. From what Glass could hear, three or four men occupied the pen outside his cell.

The space seemed to shrink as he lay there, closing in like the sides of a casket. It reminded him suddenly of the dank hold of a ship, of the stifling life at sea that he had come to hate. Beads of sweat formed on his brow, and his breath came in short, sporadic spurts. He struggled to control himself, to replace the image of imprisonment with that of the open plain, a waving sea of grass, unbroken but for a mountain on a horizon far away.

He measured the passage of days by the daily routine of the guard-house: change of guard at dawn; delivery of bread and water around noon; change of guard at dusk; then night. Two weeks had passed when he heard the creak of the outside door opening and felt the suction of fresh air. "Stay back you stinking idiots or I'll smash your skulls," said a smoky voice that walked deliberately toward his cell. Glass heard the jangling of keys, then the play of a key in the lock. A bolt turned and his door swung open.

He squinted at the light. A sergeant with yellow chevrons and gray muttonchops stood in the doorway. "Major Constable issued an order. You can go. Actually, you have to go. Off the post by noon tomorrow or you'll be tried for stealing a pistol and for using it to poke a hole in Private Fitzgerald."

The light outside was blinding after two weeks in the dark cell. When someone said, "Bonjour, Monsieur Glass," it took Glass a minute to focus on the fat, bespeckled face of Kiowa Brazeau.

"What are you doing here, Kiowa?"

"On my way back from St. Louis with a keelboat of supplies."

"You spring me loose?"

"Yes. I'm on good terms with Major Constable. You, on the other hand, seem to have gotten yourself into a bit of trouble."

"Only trouble is that my pistol didn't shoot straight."

"As I understand it, it wasn't your pistol. This, though, I think belongs to you." Kiowa handed Glass a rifle as Glass finally focused enough to see.

The Anstadt. He gripped the gun at the wrist and the barrel, remembering the sturdy weight. He examined the trigger works, which were in need of fresh grease. Several new abrasions marred the dark stock, and Glass noticed a small bit of carving near the buttplate—"JF."

Anger flooded over him. "What happened to Fitzgerald?"

"Major Constable is returning him to his duties."

"No punishment?"

"He has to forfeit two months' pay."

"Two months' pay!"

"Well, he's also got a hole in his shoulder where there didn't used to be one—and you get your rifle back."

Kiowa stared at Glass, easily reading his face. "In case you're getting any ideas—I'd avoid using the Anstadt on the premises of this fort. Major Constable fancies his judicial responsibilities and he's eager to try you for attempted murder. He only relented because I convinced him you're a protégé of Monsieur Ashley."

They walked together across the parade ground. A flagpole stood there, its support ropes straining to hold firm against a stiff spring breeze. The flag itself snapped in the wind, its edges frayed by the constant beating.

Kiowa turned to Glass: "You're thinking stupid thoughts, my friend."

Glass stopped and looked directly at the Frenchman.

Kiowa said, "I'm sorry that you never had a proper rendezvous with Fitzgerald. But you should have figured out by now that things aren't always so tidy."

They stood there for a while, with no sound but the flapping of the flag.

"It's not that simple, Kiowa."

"Of course it's not simple. Who said it was simple? But you know what? Lots of loose ends don't ever get tied up. Play the hand you're dealt. Move on."

Kiowa pressed on. "Come with me to Fort Brazeau. If it works out, I'll bring you in as a partner."

Glass slowly shook his head. "That's a generous offer, Kiowa, but I don't think I could stay planted in one spot."

"So what then? What's your plan?"

"I have a message to deliver to Ashley in St. Louis. From there, I don't know yet." Glass paused a minute before adding, "And I still have business here."

Glass said nothing more. Kiowa too was silent for a long time. Finally he said quietly, *"Il n'est pire sourd que celui qui ne veut pas entendre.* Do you know what that means?"

Glass shook his head.

"It means *there are none so deaf as those that will not hear.* Why did you come to the frontier?" demanded Kiowa. "To track down a common thief? To revel in a moment's revenge? I thought there was more to you than that."

Still Glass said nothing. Finally Kiowa said, "If you want to die in the guardhouse, that's for you to decide." The Frenchman turned and walked across the parade ground. Glass hesitated a moment, then followed behind.

"Let's go drink whiskey," yelled Kiowa over his shoulder. "I want to hear about the Powder and the Platte."

Kiowa loaned Glass the money for a few supplies and a night's lodging at Fort Atkinson's equivalent of an inn—a row of pallets in the sutler's attic. Whiskey usually made Glass drowsy, but that night it did not. Nor did it clarify the jumble of thoughts in his head. He struggled to think clearly. What was the answer to Kiowa's question?

Glass took the Anstadt and walked outside into the crisp air of the parade ground. The night was perfectly clear with no moon, reserving the sky for a billion stars, piercing pinpricks of light. He climbed crude steps to the narrow palisade that circled the wall of the fort. The view from the top was commanding.

Glass looked behind him into the confines of the fort. Across the parade ground lay the barracks. *He's there.* How many hundreds of miles had he traversed to find Fitzgerald? And now his quarry lay sleeping, a handful of steps away. He felt the cold metal of the Anstadt in his hand. *How can I walk away now?*

He turned his back, looking across the ramparts of the fort toward the Missouri River.

Stars danced on the dark water, their reflection like a marker of the heavens against the earth. Glass searched the sky for his beacons. He found the sloping tails of Ursa Major and Ursa Minor, the steady comfort of the North Star. *Where's Orion? Where's the hunter with his vengeful sword?*

The brilliant sparkle of the great star Vega seemed suddenly to fight for Glass's attention. Next to Vega he picked out the Cygnus, the Swan.

Glass stared at Cygnus, and the more he stared, the more its perpendicular lines seemed clearly to form a cross. *The Northern Cross.* That was the common name for Cygnus, he remembered. It seemed more fitting.

He stood there on the high rampart for a long time that night, listening to the Missouri and staring at the stars. He wondered at the source of the waters, of the mighty Big Horns whose tops he had seen but never touched. He wondered at the stars and the heavens, comforted by their vastness against his own small place in the world. Finally he climbed down from the ramparts and went inside, quickly finding the sleep that had eluded him before.

TWENTY-EIGHT

MAY 7, 1824

JIM BRIDGER STARTED TO KNOCK on Captain Henry's door, then stopped. It had been seven days since anyone had seen the captain outside of his quarters. Seven days ago was when the Crow stole back the horses. Not even Murphy's successful return from a hunt could entice Henry from his seclusion.

Bridger took a deep breath and knocked. He heard a rustling sound from inside, then silence. "Captain?" More silence. Bridger paused again, then pushed open the door.

Henry sat hunched behind a desk made from two barrels and a plank.

A wool blanket draped his shoulders in a fashion that reminded Bridger of an old man huddled over the stove at a general store. The captain held a quill in one hand and a piece of paper in the other. Bridger glanced at the paper. Long columns of numbers crowded the page from left to right, top to bottom. Blotches of ink spotted the text, as if his quill had encountered frequent obstacles and stopped, spilling itself like blood onto the page. Wadded paper lay strewn across the desk and the floor.

Bridger waited for the captain to say something, or at least to look up.

For a long time, he didn't do either. Finally the captain raised his head. He looked like he hadn't slept for days, his bloodshot eyes peering out above sagging gray bags. Bridger wondered if it was true what some of the men were saying, that Captain Henry had gone over the edge.

"You know anything about numbers, Bridger?"

"No sir."

"Me neither. Not much, anyway. In fact, I keep hoping that I've just been too stupid to make all this add up." The captain stared back down at the paper. "Trouble is, I keep doing it over and over and it keeps coming out the same way. I think the problem's not my math—it's just that it doesn't come out the way I want."

"I don't know what you mean, Captain."

"What I mean is that we're belly-up. We're thirty thousand dollars in the hole. Without horses, we can't keep enough men in the field to get it back. And we got nothing left to trade for horses."

"Murphy just came in with two packs from the Big Horns."

The captain absorbed the news through the thick filter of his own past.

"That's nothing, Jim. Two packs of fur won't put us back on our feet. Twenty packs won't put us back on our feet."

The conversation was not moving in the direction Jim had hoped. It had taken two weeks for him to raise the gumption to come see the captain. Now the whole thing was off track. He fought the instinct to retreat. *No. Not this time.* "Murphy says you're sending some men over the mountains to look for Jed Smith."

The captain offered no confirmation, but Bridger plowed forward anyway. "I want you to send me with them."

Henry looked at the boy. The eyes staring back at him gleamed as hopeful as the dawn of a spring day. How long had it been since he felt even an ounce of that youthful optimism? *A long time—and good riddance.*

"I can save you some trouble, Jim. I've been over those mountains.

They're like the false front on a whorehouse. I know what you're looking for—and it's just not there."

Jim had no idea how to respond. He could not imagine why the captain was acting so strangely. Maybe he really had gone mad. Bridger didn't know about that, but what he did know, what he believed with unshakeable faith—was that Captain Henry was wrong.

They fell into another long period of silence. The feeling of discomfort grew, but Jim would not leave. Finally the captain looked at him and said, "It's your choice, Jim. I'll send you if you want to go."

Bridger walked out into the yard, squinting at the bright morning sunlight. He barely noticed the crisp air that nipped at his face, the vestige of a season about to pass. More snow would fall before winter at last gave way, but spring had fixed its grip on the plains.

Jim climbed a short ladder to the palisade. He perched his elbows on the top of the wall, gazing toward the Big Horn Mountains. With his eyes he traced again a deep canyon that seemed to penetrate the mountain's very core. *Did it?* He smiled at the infinite prospect of what might lay up the canyon, of what might lay on the mountaintops, of what might lay beyond.

He raised his eyes to a horizon carved from snowy mountain peaks, virgin white against the frigid blue sky. He could climb up there if he wanted. Climb up there and touch the horizon, jump across and find the next.

HISTORICAL NOTE

Readers may wonder about the historical accuracy of the events in this novel. The fur trade era contains a murky mixture of history and legend, and some legend no doubt has invaded the history of Hugh Glass. *The Revenant* is a work of fiction. That said, I endeavored to stay true to history in the main events of the story.

What is certainly true is that Hugh Glass was attacked by a grizzly bear while scouting for the Rocky Mountain Fur Company in the fall of 1823; that he was horribly mauled; that he was abandoned by his compatriots, including two men left to tend for him; and that he survived to launch an epic quest for revenge. The most comprehensive historical work on Glass was done by John Myers Myers in his entertaining biography *The Saga of Hugh Glass*. Myers makes a strong case for even some of the most remarkable aspects of Glass's life, including his imprisonment by the pirate Jean Lafitte and, later, by the Pawnee Indians.

There is some division among historians as to whether Jim Bridger was one of the two men left to care for Glass, though most historians believe that he was. (The historian Cecil Alter, in a 1925 biography of Bridger, makes a passionate contrary case.) There is considerable evidence that Glass confronted and then forgave Bridger at the fort on the Big Horn.

I took literary and historical liberties in a couple of places that I wish to note. There is persuasive evidence that Glass did finally catch up with Fitzgerald at Fort Atkinson, finding his betrayer in the uniform of the U.S. Army. However, accounts of the encounter are cursory. There is no evidence of a formal proceeding such as I portrayed. The character of Major Constable is wholly fictional, as is the incident in which Glass shoots Fitzgerald in the shoulder. There is also evidence that Hugh Glass had separated from the party of Antoine Langevin prior to the Arikara attack on the voyageurs. (Toussaint Charbonneau does appear to have been with Langevin, and to have survived the attack, although the circumstances are not clear.) The characters of Professeur, Dominique Cattoire, and La Vierge Cattoire are wholly fictional.

Fort Talbot and its inhabitants are invented. Otherwise, the geographic reference points are as accurate as I could make them. A spring 1824 attack against Glass and his companions by the Arikara Indians did take place, reportedly at the confluence of the North Platte River and the (later named) Laramie River. Eleven years later, Fort William—the predecessor of Fort Laramie—would be established at that site.

Readers interested in the fur trade era would enjoy historical treatments including Hiram Chittenden's classic *The American Fur Trade of the Far West* and Robert M. Utley's more recent work *A Life Wild and Perilous.*

In the years following the events portrayed in this novel, many of the central characters went on to continued adventure, tragedy, and glory. The following are notable:

Captain Andrew Henry: In the summer of 1824, Henry and a group of his men rendezvoused with Jed Smith's troop in what is now Wyoming. Though not enough to cover the company's debts, Henry had collected a significant number of furs. Smith stayed in the field, with Henry responsible for returning to St. Louis with their harvest. Though modest at best, Ashley believed the quantity of furs justified an immediate return to the field. He secured funding for another expedition, which left St. Louis under Henry's command on October 21, 1824. For reasons not recorded by history, Henry appears to have retreated from the frontier not long after.

Had Henry held his stake in the Rocky Mountain Fur Company for another year, he—like the other principals in the syndicate—might have retired a wealthy man. But once again, Henry demonstrated his peculiar propensity for bad luck. He sold his share in the company for a modest sum. Even this could have provided a comfortable life, but Henry took up the surety business. When several of his debtors defaulted, he lost everything. Andrew Henry died penniless in 1832.

William H. Ashley: It is remarkable that two partners in the same enterprise could ride it to such different conclusions. Though faced with mounting debts, Ashley remained steadfast in the belief that a fortune could be made in furs. After losing a bid for the governorship of Missouri in 1824, Ashley led a party of trappers down the south fork of the Platte. He became the first white man to attempt a navigation of the Green River, an effort that nearly ended in disaster near the mouth of what is today called the Ashley River.

With few furs to show for his adventure, Ashley and his men met up with a dispirited group of trappers from the Hudson Bay Company. Through a mysterious transaction, Ashley came into possession of a hundred packs of beaver. Some allege the Americans plundered the HBC's cache. More credible reports say Ashley did nothing more spurious than strike a hard bargain. In any event, Ashley sold the furs in St. Louis in the fall of 1825 for more than $200,000—securing a fortune for life.

At the rendezvous of 1826, Ashley sold his share of the Rocky Mountain Fur Company to Jedediah Smith, David Jackson, and William Sublette. Having created the rendezvous system, launched the careers of several legends of the fur trade era, and secured his own place in history as a successful fur baron, Ashley retired from the trade.

In 1831, the people of Missouri elected Ashley to replace Congressman Spencer Pottis (Pottis had died in a duel). Ashley twice won re-election, retiring from politics in 1837. William H. Ashley died in 1838.

Jim Bridger: In the fall of 1824, Jim Bridger crossed the Rockies and became the first white man to touch the waters of the Great Salt Lake. By 1830, Bridger had become a partner in the Rocky Mountain Fur Company, then rode the fur trade era to its crash in the 1840s. As the fur trade ebbed, Bridger caught the next wave of westward expansion. In 1838, he built a fort in what is now Wyoming. "Fort Bridger" became an important trading post on the Oregon Trail, later serving as a military post and Pony Express station. In the 1850s and 1860s, Bridger served often as a guide for settlers, exploration parties, and the U.S. Army.

Jim Bridger died on July 17, 1878, near Westport, Missouri. For his lifetime of accomplishment as a trapper, explorer, and guide, Bridger is often referred to as the "King of the Mountain Men." Today mountains, streams, and towns throughout the West bear his name.

John Fitzgerald: Little is known about John Fitzgerald. He did exist, and is generally regarded as one of the two men who abandoned Hugh Glass. He is also believed to have deserted the Rocky Mountain Fur Company, and then to have enlisted in the U.S. Army at Fort Atkinson. I have fictionalized other parts of his life.

Hugh Glass: From Fort Atkinson, Glass appears to have traveled downriver to St. Louis, delivering Henry's message to Ashley. In St. Louis, Glass met a party of traders bound for Santa Fe. He joined them, and spent a year trapping on the Helo River. By around 1825, Glass was in Taos, a center of the southwestern fur trade.

The arid streams of the Southwest played out quickly, and Glass again turned north. He trapped his way up the Colorado, the Green, and the Snake, eventually finding himself on the headwaters of the Missouri River. In 1828, the so-called free trappers elected Glass to represent their interests in negotiations to break the monopoly of the Rocky Mountain Fur Company. After trapping as far west as the

Columbia River, Glass turned most of his attention to the eastern face of the Rockies.

Glass spent the winter of 1833 at an outpost called "Fort Cass," near Henry's old fort at the confluence of the Yellowstone and Big Horn rivers. On a February morning, Glass and two companions were crossing the frozen Yellowstone at the outset of a trapping foray. They were ambushed by thirty Arikara warriors and killed.

ACKNOWLEDGMENTS

Many of my friends and family (and a couple of kind strangers) made the generous gift of their time, reading early drafts of this book and improving it through their critique and encouragement. Thanks to Sean Darragh, Liz and John Feldman, Timothy and Lori Otto Punke, Peter Scher, Kim Tilley, Brent and Cheryl Garrett, Marilyn and Butch Punke, Randy and Julie Miller, Kelly MacManus, Marc Glick, Bill and Mary Strong, Mickey Kantor, Andre Solomita, Ev Ehrlich, Jen Kaplan, Mildred Hoecker, Monte Silk, Carol and Ted Kinney, Ian Davis, David Kurapka, David Marchick, Jay Ziegler, Aubrey Moss, Mike Bridge, Nancy Goodman, Jennifer Egan, Amy and Mike McManamen, Linda Stillman, and Jacqueline Cundiff.

Thanks to a group of outstanding teachers from Torrington, Wyoming: Ethel James, Betty Sportsman, Edie Smith, Rodger Clark, Craig Sodaro, Randy Adams, and Bob Latta. If you ever wonder whether teachers make a difference, please know that you did for me.

Particular thanks to the fantastic Tina Bennett at William Morris Endeavor. While I take all responsibility for its shortcomings, Tina helped make this book better and then worked to make it a film. Thanks to Tina's talented assistant, Svetlana Katz, who (among other things) gave this book a name. I am grateful for early editing advice from Philip Turner. Stephen Morrison at Picador, with assistance from P. J. Horoszko, helped *The Revenant* return to life.

In 2002, Keith Redmon saw film potential in *The Revenant* and has worked steadfastly ever since to make a movie happen, along with his Anonymous Content colleagues Steve Golin and David Kanter.

Most important, special thanks to my family. Thank you, Sophie, for helping me experiment with deadfall traps. Thank you, Bo, for your uncanny imitation of a grizzly. And thank you, Traci, for your steadfast support and patient attention through a hundred labored readings.